THE UNIVERSITY OF
WINCHESTER

SUNY series in Global Politics
James N. Rosenau, editor

PRIVATE AUTHORITY AND INTERNATIONAL AFFAIRS

Edited by

A. CLAIRE CUTLER,
VIRGINIA HAUFLER,
and TONY PORTER

State University
of New York
Press

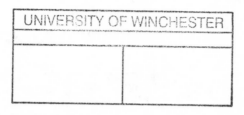
Published by
State University of New York Press, Albany

© 1999 State University of New York

Production by Susan Geraghty
Marketing by Dana Yanulavich

Printed in the United States of America

For information, address State University of New York
Press, State University Plaza, Albany, N.Y., 12246

Library of Congress Cataloging-in-Publication Data

Private authority and international affairs / A. Claire Cutler,
    Virginia Haufler, and Tony Porter.
        p.   cm. — (SUNY series in global politics)
    Includes bibliographical references and index.
    ISBN 0-7914-4119-9 (alk. paper). — ISBN 0-7914-4120-2 (pbk. :
alk. paper)
        1. International business enterprises. 2. International trade.
    3. International cooperation. 4. International economic relations.
    I. Cutler, A. Claire. II. Haufler, Virginia, 1957–
    III. Porter, Tony, 1953–   . IV. Series.
    HD2755.5.P752 1999
    338.8′8—dc21   98-20843
                                                                CIP

10 9 8 7 6 5 4 3 2 1

CONTENTS

LIST OF
TABLES AND FIGURES

PREFACE

The purpose of this volume is to bring to international relations scholarship an understanding of the changing role of business in contemporary world affairs. The premise with which we began this project was that firms do not simply compete in world markets, they also cooperate among themselves in ways that have political ramifications. In this project, we sought to explore the variety of ways in which businesses cooperate internationally to pursue both economic and political goals. We were particularly concerned to determine the degree to which the institutions created by the private sector operated autonomously or in coordination with governments and intergovernmental organizations. Our hope was to contribute to larger debates within the field of international relations by applying current perspectives on cooperation, norms, and regimes to the activities of the private sector, explicitly rejecting the state-centeredness of much research and theorizing.

Our contributors approach this subject from a variety of perspectives, but all aim to explain different aspects of interfirm cooperation: its structure, character, and placement within the political and economic system. The focus is global in most of the cases, rather than domestic or comparative. The outcome, as represented in this volume, provides an initial cut at understanding the significance of corporate power in the *global* system, as opposed to the interstate system. In a world in which major corporations determine so many of the most significant outcomes, such as decisions about investment and employment, we need to have a better grasp of the political significance of their global activities. Private authority is a form of "governance without government" at the international level, and we bring together empirical cases to explore its operation and effect.

But this subject is not just of interest to scholars of international relations. It goes straight to the heart of current concerns about the effects of globalization on the capacity of states to pursue their national interests. Private authority is unaccountable and perhaps uncontrollable without concerted international cooperation among states, backed by effective institutions. The great power wielded by international business has been perceived by many as a threat to democratic institutions and to the quality of life of the mass of people, and may lead to political mobilization to restrain this private exercise of authority. As we move into the next millennium, concern about the growing impact of business on the fate of individuals and societies is unlikely to subside.

This project began when Tony Porter and Virginia Haufler each realized they had finally found someone else developing a research project around the concept of a private international regime. Together with Claire Cutler, whose work on private international trade law was closely related, we organized a panel on this topic at the International Studies Association meeting in Chicago in 1995. The response to our panel was so gratifying, particularly the enthusiasm of Susan Strange and the critical but interesting comments of our panel chair Stephen Krasner, that we decided to pursue this topic further. In the fall of 1995 we submitted successful proposals to the International Studies Association (ISA) for a workshop, and to the Social Sciences and Humanities Research Council of Canada (SSHRCC) for a follow-on conference. The workshop, held prior to the International Studies Association meeting in San Diego in 1996, produced an exhausting and exhilarating exchange among the participants. We started with a focus on private international regimes and, finding that too narrow and state-centric, quickly expanded to consider interfirm cooperation more generally, private international law, and private authority. The following August we organized a conference at the beautiful campus of the University of Victoria (B.C.), bringing together most of the original workshop participants along with a number of other commentators. Susan Strange and Anne-Marie Slaughter each addressed the conference, and our discussants Mark Zacher, Andrew Moravcsik, and Sol Picciotto graciously—and sometimes ferociously—pushed us to develop a useful framework for understanding and explaining interfirm cooperation and the emergence of private authority.

This book project followed naturally from the work we did at the workshop and conference. We thank the ISA and SSHRCC for providing us with the financial support that gave us the opportunity to work with such a stimulating group of people. We all learned a tremendous amount from each other, and enjoyed our arguments together. The editors want to thank all our contributors for their hard work and enthusiasm. In addition, we would like to especially thank our series editor, James Rosenau, and the reviewers of the manuscript.

Virginia Haufler would like to thank her colleagues at the University of Maryland for their support and encouragement, along with the financial support of the Department of Government and Politics. She also credits the members of the Washington International Theory Seminar (WITS) with providing critical comments that helped improve and clarify our initial framework paper for the workshop and conference.

Claire Cutler would like to thank the president of the University of Victoria, Dr. David Strong, for his enthusiastic and early support, both moral and financial, for the Victoria conference. She also thanks friends and colleagues at the British Columbia International Relations Seminar, held at the University of British Columbia, for their useful comments on earlier drafts of the framework paper. Tony Porter would like to thank Bill Coleman for his suggestions. Finally, all three of us wish to express our appreciation of the benefits we gained from own collaboration on this project: we have had our intellectual horizons broadened by our discussions and in the process have become valued friends.

PART 1

Introduction

CHAPTER 1

Private Authority and International Affairs

A. Claire Cutler, Virginia Haufler, and Tony Porter

Are corporations truly "ruling the world" today?[1] President Clinton has declared that the U.S. government would keep its hands off the Internet, and encouraged other governments to do the same, leaving it to the private sector to develop rules to govern their own behavior. Elsewhere, a number of corporations have agreed to abide by environmental management standards voluntarily under the auspices of the International Standards Organization (ISO), an international organization dominated by private sector interests. In still another area, a group of American clothing manufacturers has developed policies that commit the participants to uphold a set of labor standards for themselves and all their subcontractors around the world. In all these cases and in many others the framework of governance for international economic transactions increasingly is created and maintained by the private sector and not by state or interstate organizations.

International commerce operates most effectively when it is undertaken under the umbrella of a system of rules that govern the behavior of the participants. We typically think of these rules as being formulated, monitored, and enforced by governments. In international affairs, this leads us to consider the question of how to get governments to cooperate in establishing rules for global governance in the absence of central government. But governments have not always been willing to cooperate, and sometimes have not even been interested in extending their domestic rule-making capacity to the international realm. In response, a significant degree of global order is provided by individual firms that agree to cooperate, either formally or informally, in establishing an international framework for their economic activity. Many areas of the world economy today operate under the strictures of "private authority." This book explores the phenomenon of international private authority, theoretically, historically, and empirically, asking: Why do firms cooperate across borders, how does such cooperation function, and in what ways does it acquire the mantle of authority?

In an era when the authority of the state appears to be challenged in so many ways, the existence of alternative sources of authority takes on great significance, especially when that authority is wielded internationally by profit-seeking entities.[2] The contributors to this volume examine different industries and issues in which the private sector took the lead in establishing norms, rules, and institutions that guide the behavior of the participants and affect the opportunities available to others. This approach emphasizes the fact that the traditional focus on state authority and sovereignty that dominates theoretical and practical discussions of international affairs is inadequate for explaining the full contours of the contemporary global economy. However, we do not argue this phenomenon is entirely new; for instance, merchants of a century ago and more played a large role in governance. Our contributors do, however, point to the unique characteristics of current private governance activities. More importantly, they bring to the fore the increased contemporary significance of an upward trend in the management of global affairs by economic actors. Finally, the authors question the value and meaning of privately wielded authority, particularly when it is taken to the international level. Given the rapid globalization of the world economy, the modern state may be unable to cope with the demand for global order, but it is not clear that market-oriented sources of authority are the most desirable alternative.

One of the key arguments we make is that international cooperation by firms in the areas of rule-making, standards-setting, and organization of industrial sectors is not simply a temporary, limited, or illegitimate phenomenon. In many of the cases discussed in this volume, the cooperation among firms is either given legitimacy by governments or legitimacy is acquired through the special expertise or historical role of the private sector participants. In other words, we do not believe we can simply discuss interfirm cooperation without linking it to the acquisition of authority. As states voluntarily abandon some of the functions that we traditionally associate with public authorities due to the force of liberal ideology, globalization, or the lack of state capacity to manage current issues, those functions that are needed for smoothly operating markets may be given to or taken up by firms. In addition, in areas where technology is complex or information plays a significant role, the private sector is sometimes viewed by participants as more capable than governments in designing appropriate rules and procedures. We see then through this process the emergence of private authority.

The concept of private authority is a difficult one to define. We elaborate the concept further in the concluding chapter, but here we introduce a fairly simple approach. First, authority exists when an individual or organization has decision-making power over a particular issue area and is regarded as exercising that power legitimately. Second, we stipulate that such authority does not necessarily have to be associated with government institutions. This volume focuses on international cooperation among firms, and we argue that the institutions established by their activities can become authoritative because of the perceived expertise of the participants; historical practice that renders such exercise of authority acceptable and appropriate; or because of an explicit or implicit grant of power by states. We can think of authority as consisting of two elements: the analytical element of how authority is structured, how it operates, and how it is recognized and distinguished from other forms of influence; and the more normative aspects of how authority is justified, who or what gives legitimacy, and why the authority of someone is accepted as such.[3] The former parallels the structural emphasis of many of the contributors to this volume, as they focus on institutions, regimes, and alliances that solidify the cooperation of firms across national boundaries. The latter normative discussion is brought up primarily in the final sections of the book, particularly in the conclusion.

In this chapter, we first will discuss the phenomenon of cooperation among market competitors and the forms this cooperation takes. Such cooperation ranges from loose and informal consensus to highly institutionalized agreements and associations. Then we will present the issues that arise when grappling with the concept of *private* authority, given that our understanding of authority typically revolves around its public, or governmental, nature. Finally, we briefly sketch the arguments and evidence given in each chapter, linking the contributions to the overall themes of the volume.

COOPERATION AMONG MARKET COMPETITORS

One of the key dimensions of the world economy today is the rise of the global corporation. It is widely recognized that the number of transnational corporations (TNCs) has grown dramatically in recent years.[4] The economic integration brought about through transnational production has also grown in scale, scope, and intensity. Firms are increasingly able to coordinate production on a global scale, creating much more complex relations than possible with arm's-length trade. Liberalization of markets has expanded the role of TNCs in areas such as telecommunications and financial services, which had previously remained relatively immune to globalization. A major area of TNC growth has been providing services to other TNCs for the coordination and management of these complicated global relations.

Although the literature on this globalization has been expanding rapidly, surprisingly little attention has been paid by political science scholars to the growth in various forms of cooperation among competing firms.[5] The impact of corporate actors on the world economy is widely acknowledged, and there is a sophisticated literature on the phenomenon of the multinational corporate form.[6] The field of industrial organization is a well-developed subfield of economics that pays attention to the dynamics of corporate competition, market structure, and business organization.[7] However, there is relatively little in the mainstream international relations field, despite the fact that the resources wielded by modern firms give them tremendous power and influence over the shape of international economic relations.[8] In the popular press, the modern firm is often vilified as too powerful, unaccountable, and amoral.[9]

Most analysis in international relations downplays the role of corporate actors in shaping the world political economy, taking the traditional state-centric perspective. There is little theorizing about cooperation among firms or about their efforts to develop private international institutions. If corporate interests are examined more closely, they typically are simply "added in" to models of domestic politics without attempting to examine the unique roles they play in ordering the global political economy above or beyond the domestic context.[10] Most of the current approaches to studying the politics of business focus on the factors that drive investment decisions, or examine the interests and influence of particular sectors in domestic politics, or the ways in which the modern corporation is restructuring world production.

The existence and effects of international cooperation among firms is an important element of the international political economy for a number of reasons. First, many of these firms control huge resources in terms of financial capital, technology, employment, and natural resources. Second, they deploy these resources in response to both the competitive *and cooperative* elements of their relations with other firms. Third, the norms, practices, and rules they establish among themselves also affect the opportunities available to the rest of society. Fourth, and most importantly as we argue here, such cooperation among private sector actors can become authoritative or government-like, even in the international sphere, thus challenging our notions of the character of political authority itself.

What exactly do we mean by "cooperation"? Robert Keohane, in discussing cooperation among states, defines cooperation as requiring active adjustment of behavior to reach mutual goals, thus distinguishing between harmony and cooperation.[11] The evidence of cooperation is in the adjustment process, which is typically demonstrated in the negotiation of treaties and agreements, and the establishment of formal organizations. However, such treaties, agreements, and organizations do not exhaust the range of cooperative behaviors possible. G. B. Richardson, an economist, argues that the essence of cooperation is the acceptance by participants of some degree of obligation and some assurance concerning their future conduct.[12] This broader definition focuses attention away from mutual goals and toward commitments, however informal, concerning behavior in the future. It suggests that cooperation involves both mutuality of interests or goals and an obligatory element. Indeed, as we shall see, it is the element of obligation that extends cooperation into the future and gives it the mantle of authority.

Why cooperate? After all, these are firms that are supposed to compete ruthlessly in the marketplace to attain the highest profits possible. And yet, there is a long history of cooperation, particularly in the form of cartels. The economic literature has identified a number of factors that are associated with the formation of cartels.[13] According to economists, cartels form where there is a high concentration of production, high barriers to entry, a small set of "fringe" producers that are large enough to affect the market but too small to be part of the cartel, a product for which there are no substitutes, and barriers to the ability to compete on nonprice factors while maintaining uncompetitively high prices.[14] Under these circumstances, firms perceive it to be in their interest to cooperate in order to reap superprofits and are able to create and maintain a cartel to do so. Thus, the structure of the market situation explains cooperation. However, as Debora Spar points out, these structural factors do not explain the process by which different firms come to cooperate to form a cartel, a process in which internal politics plays a big role.

We would argue that these structural factors, while important, cannot tell us enough about the wide variety of cooperative institutions that exist among firms. A cartel is an arrangement that is relatively limited; producer-members simply seek to limit the effects of the market by managing output and prices in a manner that maximizes profits. However, as the contributors to this volume point out, the cooperation we see among firms may be for a range of purposes, both political and economic. The markets in which this cooperation takes place may not in fact meet any of the structural conditions that are associated with cartels. This makes it difficult to develop a single framework for explaining interfirm cooperation, although such structural factors do indeed explain some of this behavior. We would add the following as facilitators of private cooperation: the existence of complex knowledge/technology; learning processes from repeated interactions with each other and with the market; functionalist demand for order and rules; and political opportunities.

The role of specialized knowledge and technical information in a complex, knowledge-based economy in which the technology itself changes rapidly and in unpredictable ways may lead to cooperation among firms in research and development, as discussed in the contribution by Mytelka and Delapierre on knowledge-based strategic partnerships. In addition, firms also may need to provide regularity and order in such a turbulent market and do so through their efforts to work together to develop standards for the field, as seen in the chapters by Haufler and Sinclair on norms and standards. The establishment of norms and practices within an industry can be viewed as a cooperative enterprise. This is particularly true historically within leading sectors—emerging industries in which the technology is new and the market uncertain, as laid out in the chapter by Porter.

Learning processes also provide an avenue by which cooperation emerges informally. The leaders of firms interact with each other outside of the market, in a social setting. They read the same management books, are often educated at the same universities, they face a similar economic and political environment, and often react in similar ways. On specific issues confronting their industry, they all may go through a process of learning about how to cope with new challenges. Repeated interactions over time build up common expectations about appropriate behavior. In essence, they may form a loose "epistemic community," although not one based on scientists and scientific knowledge as in the original use of this term.[15]

Markets cannot operate effectively or efficiently without some form of order or "rules of the road." Much of the institutionalist literature explains the creation of institutions as a response to the demand for a framework within which economic and social activity occurs, providing decreased transactions costs, information about behavior, and a degree of certainty about the future.[16] In emerging sectors of the economy, governments may be unable to provide such rules due to the technical complexity or rapidity of change in these areas, as pointed out by Spar's chapter on the Internet and Salter's chapter on standards-setting. Thus, governments may either ignore or delay regulating any new issues or conflicts that arise in that area, or may officially delegate such rule-making to the private sector. Given the demand for some form of regulation, the private sector itself may establish the means to regulate itself, as seen in a historical context in Cutler's chapter on maritime transport. This dynamic of course cannot be separated from the special knowledge and expertise of the private sector. Again, as in the case of learning processes, the firms may be viewed as members of an epistemic community, one that is closely integrated with the production of authority.[17]

Firms do not always cooperate simply to adjust their own mutual behavior. Some of the obligations they incur among themselves have to do with political and social goods. Firms may cooperate in lobbying domestic governments or providing public goods, as seen in the Burke chapter, or may engage in international interest group activities, as seen in Sell's contribution on the intellectual property rights negotiations. Political cooperation may be a function of the domestic political system, as in corporatist systems of interest representation. In such cases, the governing structure delegates power to particular representative groups and in fact may actually help organize the cooperation necessary to form those groups. At the international level we do not see a parallel with domestic corporatism, but we do see a number of cases where some decision-making power has been delegated by interstate organizations to nongovernmental organizations.[18]

It may be useful here briefly to describe the varieties of cooperative arrangements among firms. This list of six categories is not exhaustive, and the categories themselves are not exclusive—many elements may exist in one set of relationships. These are loosely ordered from the least to the most institutionalized. It is important to note, however, that while interfirm cooperation may move in a linear fashion from low to high degrees of institutionalization, we are not suggesting the necessity of such linear movement. Nor are we suggesting that there is a necessary relationship between degree of institutionalization and the strength of cooperative arrangements. However, as will be discussed in the next section, we believe these cooperative arrangements are significant to the degree they represent the deployment of private authority in international affairs.

Informal Industry Norms and Practices

Many informal avenues of cooperation exist, revealed in the common norms and knowledge held by business leaders. These norms may evolve into customary law among the participants. Indeed, much of international commercial law is customary in origin.[19] This type of cooperation verges on what Keohane and others consider "harmony"—no mutual adjustment by participants is needed since independent behavior leads to the mutually desired outcome. However, the attainment of such harmony about goals and the means to those goals requires a great deal of interaction and effort; it is not automatic. This is particularly true given that firms are not unitary actors, but complex organizations with multiple goals and interests.[20] Business practices and norms established by custom have an evolutionary quality to them and thus often appear to be spontaneous developments; however, this appearance obscures their nature as purposeful actions that over time acquire legitimacy.[21]

There are recognized norms of business behavior that guide the conduct of business in a particular industry and that we would argue are a form of cooperation, though of the loosest kind. They often evolve from a learning process in which the value of a particular norm is spread, contagion-like, throughout the rest of the industry. Some might argue these norms are not really cooperation, since they do not require face-to-face negotiation nor do they seem to demonstrate the "mutual" side of mutual adjustment. Instead, they appear to be similar responses to environmental conditions. We argue, however, that informal industry practices constitute a form of cooperation because they do reflect a common approach to problems, even in issue areas for which there are multiple solutions. They are a "focal point," to use that terminology, around which behavior converges.[22] And increasingly, the behavior under question involves businesses located in different states, under different political and legal systems and different cultures. One example of these industry practices is the tacit but well-recognized norm in the Eurobond market that emerged in the 1960s restricting issuers to blue chip companies or governments. Another would be the more elaborate conventional relations between the leading securities firms and others in bond syndicates. Other norms, like the terms of trade governing maritime transport, reflect industry practices that evolved into customary law throughout a long period of time.

Coordination Services Firms

These are firms whose primary function is the coordination of other firms. Examples include multinational law, insurance, and management consultancy firms, debt-rating agencies, stock exchanges, and financial clearinghouses. These firms may set the standards of behavior for other firms, enforcing a certain code of conduct. For instance, insurers insist that business customers behave in particular ways in order to obtain coverage, and will not pay losses to those firms that violate their standards. Distinguishing between these coordination services firms and firms more generally can be difficult and involves disputable interpretation. We label these as a form of cooperation because the function of these firms requires them to work closely and cooperatively with their customers, and because their activities often promote recognized parallel practices among otherwise disconnected firms. Unlike other types of cooperation among firms, the cooperation here is across sectoral lines and not within one industry. Note, however, the operation of these coordination services firms depends to a large degree upon commonly developed norms and practices that are usually produced in business associations (a form of cooperation discussed below). These coordination services firms only recently began to operate on a global basis, as the transnationalization of production reached a level at which it was profitable for, say, an accounting firm to go abroad to conduct business.

Production Alliances, Subcontractor Relationships, and Complementary Activities

Here we note three types of production alliances: strategic partnerships, joint ventures, and networks.[23] Such alliances involve agreements between two or more firms based in different countries that normally compete, but that decide to cooperate in joint production of tangible or intangible goods or services. Typically, their cooperation in a particular market to produce a particular product or service is matched by continuing intense competition in other areas. While the formality of such agreements can vary, they are all entered into with explicit intent and involve specific contractual obligations that are limited to the firms involved. The member firms do not seek directly to modify the conduct of other nonparticipating market actors by their agreements, although there are often unintended effects on the market as a whole. A particular type of strategic alliance or joint venture may well be imitated and thereby spread beyond the original participants, but this effect would then be best treated as an industry practice for the purposes of this typology.

Networks exist when there are extensive and complex subcontractor relationships among numerous firms. These networks are increasingly common and have expanded on a global basis. Often, the firm itself is disaggregated to such a high degree that it is simply a name attached to a large number of subcontractors. For instance, there is no Nike corporation in the traditional sense; Nike, Inc. consists of the brand name, which is given to products from subcontracted facilities around the world.

In many fields of production today, the activities of one firm are dependent on the activities of others. The different phases of the production process, which may be located in different firms, are "complementary" and require the firms to coordinate their activities. Their plans must be matched in order to assure the smooth and efficient operation of each.[24] Thus, their relationships are characterized by a high degree of cooperation that benefits all participants directly.

Cartels

These are formal or informal organizations between three or more producers to coordinate their output and prices. As already discussed above, the explicit goal of a cartel is to restrict competition among the participants in order to limit the effects of the market and maximize profits.[25] It may be difficult in practice to distinguish between cartels and production alliances, especially when this involves license sharing, since both organizations structure the market. This is not simply an academic question but is a matter of intense debate in the practice of antitrust law. Despite these difficulties, the distinction remains relevant in theory and in law, especially given that production alliances today are widely accepted as legitimate forms of business organizations while cartels are not. Cartel behavior certainly is not a new phenomenon, but it is important to note it as one of the categories of interfirm cooperation.

Business Associations

Firms within a sector often cooperate on issues of concern to them through forming a business or trade association, and many of these today span national borders. There are two main types of business association. The first is what we call the self-regulatory organization. These legally constituted organizations develop and enforce binding obligations on their members and often for the industry as a whole. They often are professional organizations, and they formalize the norms and practices of the profession or industry. They constitute an important form of self-regulation, in which the members agree to meet set standards, subject themselves to monitoring by the association, and even allow themselves to be punished for violations. For professionals, the association provides a "seal of approval" for their behavior that is vital for success when reputation is particularly important.

The second type of business association is what we call the representative organization. It too establishes standards and norms for the industry as a whole, and increasingly does so across borders. However, a more significant function for such organizations is to operate in the political system. In corporatist systems, they often have a formal position within the political structure. In other systems, they represent their members to the politicians on issues of importance to the industry. They also may play a quasi-formal role as advisors to government, particularly on technical issues. In the past, these organizations operated primarily on the domestic level, with the exception of the International Chamber of Commerce. Internationally, such political representation has just begun to emerge and gain attention as formerly closed international negotiations are opening up to nongovernmental organizations.

Today many negotiations explicitly provide a seat at the table to a variety of representative organizations, including business associations. We can expect to see business lobbying at the international level increase in the coming years.

These two types of business association are not mutually exclusive. Many such organizations perform both self-regulation and political representation, though they may weigh the two activities in different ways. In any case, business associations of all types are one of the most visible signs of interfirm cooperation. The point we would like to stress here is that their membership and activities can be international in scope; they are not limited to a national base.

Private Regimes

A private regime is an integrated complex of formal and informal institutions that is a source of governance for an economic issue area as a whole. Private regimes differ from the previous five types of arrangements by the pervasiveness and breadth of their activities, and they may incorporate the other types of organization within their scope.

Early efforts to develop and formalize the concept of an international regime in the international relations literature culminated in the now classic volume edited by Krasner that presented a consensus definition: an international regime consists of "principles, norms, rules and decision making procedures around which actor expectations converge in a given issue area."[26] The concept of international regime has been used as an analytic framework by political scientists, legal theorists, and business scholars and thus appeals to those with a variety of interests.[27] It has been used for some time in international law to capture the ordering effects of formal and informal agreements on state action. It closely resembles the notion of a "social institution" as developed by sociologists such as Talcott Parsons to explain the reproduction of social regularities over time.[28] The concept clearly includes decentralized and informal social institutions within its scope, although the influence of these is often said to be mediated by state power. In addition to its focus on cooperation, regime theory gives us leverage on understanding the relationship between formal and informal aspects of institutionalized behavior. Unfortunately, most regime theory to date has assumed that states are the main—even only—participants in regimes. This is ironic given the influence in regime theory of Coasian economics, which emphasizes the ability of private actors to solve market failures by devising agreements independent of government.[29] Even the more liberal variants of regime analysis place more emphasis on the sovereign state than on important nonstate actors.

To date, the literature on regimes has remained stubbornly state-centric. For instance, in a recent review of the literature, the authors explicitly limit themselves to studying state behavior alone.[30] However, the definition itself, and its utility in explaining certain forms of cooperation, does not require the relevant actors to be states.[31] Issue areas can be organized and institutionalized as private regimes or as mixed public/private ones, where the private actors can be either firms or nongovernmental organizations. Private international regimes are created by negotiation and interaction among firms within a particular industry sector or issue area, and generally incorporate a number of business associations, both national and international. They formulate rules and procedures for dealing with conflicts among the participants, and between the participants and their customers. Often, they create "soft law," in the form of voluntary and formally nonbinding agreements, to govern their activities.[32] The interfirm cooperation represented in international regimes operates on multiple levels in complex ways, and often involves extensive interaction and cooperation with the state. Indeed, one of the important analytical goals in studying private international regimes is to understand the degree to which the private actors in a regime are independent of the public ones.

In ordering the above types of cooperation by the degree of their institutionalization we are implicitly suggesting that hierarchical integration in particular industries may be an important source of private authority. For instance, informal industry practices may be produced by coordination services firms but then be codified as industry standards in trade associations. These standards in turn may be adopted and enforced by self-regulatory organizations. Such integration could be regarded as a measure of institutionalization itself. Moreover, the relationship between types of institutions most likely will vary across industries. As noted before, we are not suggesting that every industry over time will progress linearly from lower to higher degrees of institutionalization. Instead, we need to identify variations in the coordinating arrangements that develop and to investigate the factors that cause such variations.

We argue here that private cooperation in international affairs is an important ordering element that forces us to consider the significant role of nonstate actors. In doing so, we do not disagree with the critics of liberal pluralism, particularly its idealist variants, who point to the excessive optimism of assuming that states would be superseded by international or supranational organizations as new international actors proliferated. The older formal institutionalism in international relations, which had focused primarily on codified international law, has been supplanted by a functional institutionalism that incorporates an attentiveness to the roles of power and anarchy in explaining world affairs. Realism, which traditionally ignored or downplayed international cooperation, has been challenged by the evident significance of coordinated activity among competitive sovereign states and has sought to integrate this into its models. Critical approaches have begun to emphasize the role of both states and ideology in reproducing capitalism, thereby bringing to the fore the importance of material, ideational, and institutional factors.[33] These trends across divergent theoretical approaches reflect a common interest in the role of both formal *and* informal institutions, including both state behavior *and* norms, in reproducing regularized practices at the international level. We extend these trends here into the realm of business.

In doing so, we take advantage of the increasing interdisciplinary linkages found in international relations theory today and consider the degree of institutionalization as an important element in our discussion of interfirm cooperation and private authority. This is in tune with the new institutional economics, with its focus on transactions costs, intrafirm hierarchies and principal-agent issues.[34] We also incorporate some elements of the renewed recognition of the importance of social institutions in constituting political identities and establishing the range of acceptable actions for both states and firms,[35] and highlight the importance of analyzing practices in addition to behavior and hidden structures.[36]

The initiation and strengthening of interfirm cooperation, which often goes beyond temporary, ad hoc arrangements to take on more enduring institutionalized characteristics, provides the participating firms with further resources for influencing their environment. This is occurring in the context of an expansion in the range of social and political activities organized by nongovernmental actors in general. The enhanced global influence of private actors corresponds with current developments at the domestic level. The large-scale privatization of state holdings, the delegation of regulation to industry associations, and the increased reliance on market forces in general characterize domestic developments in many states—and increasingly is creeping into the international sphere. We argue that it is particularly important to acknowledge the degree to which this represents a private source for authority within international society.

NONSTATE ACTORS AND AUTHORITY

Interfirm cooperation is significant for international relations because, as we argue here, so much of it leads to the emergence of private authority over transnational affairs. Private actors are increasingly engaged in authoritative decision-making that was previously the prerogative of sovereign states. The International Federation of Stock Exchanges, a private organization, produces rules for securities markets that mirror those produced by the International Organization of Securities Commissions, an intergovernmental organization.[37] Private arbitration services are producing trade decisions that are increasingly like those produced by intergovernmental panels or domestic courts.[38] The pronouncements of debt-rating agencies have an unprecedented influence over fiscal policy[39] and are increasingly relied upon in international bank regulation.[40]

Private firms and industry associations displayed an unprecedented prominence in the Uruguay Round of trade negotiations,[41] the conclusion of the North American Free Trade Agreement, and negotiations over a variety of issues within the European Union. They were highly visible in the negotiations leading up to the United Nations Conference on the Environment and Development in Rio De Janeiro, and have become integrated into decision-making processes with regard to the Montreal Protocol on Ozone abatement. Even in national security issue areas we see the participation of firms in lobbying, decision-making, and implementation in the Chemical Weapons Treaty. Major firms often now have official positions both within the domestic political structure, such as through industry advisory panels, and also within the international institutions where negotiations take place.

These developments lead us to question the nature of the boundaries between public and private authority, both domestically and globally.[42] Indeed, they suggest that we need to reconsider our notions of authority and governance more generally. Despite increased recognition of the constraints imposed by globalized markets and transnational actors, the viewpoint of most observers remains stubbornly state-centric when considering questions of global governance and regulation. The degree to which private arrangements can substitute for the regulatory functions usually associated with states (or even interstate organizations) is often not recognized.

As noted, the existing regimes literature has generally underestimated the role of private actors. At the same time, the regimes approach has certain features that are useful in understanding the above changes but that are absent from alternative approaches. For instance, the new institutional economics and the business literature on strategic alliances generally tend to underestimate the importance of the authoritative and legitimate rule-making provided by the state and therefore may neglect the degree to which inter- and intrafirm arrangements interact with this rule-making. The corporatist literature on "private interest government"[43] addresses the interpenetration of public and private actors, but only at the domestic level. Gramscian approaches highlight the power of private actors but many are focused on macro-level analysis rather than the sector or issue-specific level at which many key decisions are made.[44] The emerging literature on global civil society tends to implicitly underestimate the qualitative difference between the power and influence of corporations and other nongovernmental organizations (NGOs).

Can private authority be reconciled, theoretically, with the state-centric approaches that dominate the discipline of international relations? How does private authority affect the distribution of power and wealth among all actors in international affairs? What is the impact of private international authority on the relationship within states between governments and societies? Does private authority weaken or enhance democratic institutions and processes? At the global level, does private authority affect the participation of states and other nonstate actors in the development of global norms and institutions? Does the level of development of a state affect its ability to influence private regulatory norms and arrangements? To answer these questions, scholars must directly address many difficult empirical, theoretical, and normative problems. None of the answers to these questions are self-evident.

The concept of "private authority" is not easily derived from most theorizing about political authority. This is largely because political theorists tend to define the concept in ways that automatically imply the instrumentality of a state or government.[45] Moreover, controversy over the meaning of authority "is invariably cast in the form of a dispute over the relation between the notions of authority, power, and legitimacy. . . . The very question of what politics is and what the field and scope of political study consists in."[46] This suggests that at root the question of authority is an ontological one going to the very definition of politics and political activity one fixes upon. Ruggie tells us that politics is about "rule," which at least since the emergence of the Westphalian system, has come to be associated with rule by a government or state.[47] Susan Strange observes that the state has been said to "colonize" the study of international relations.[48] Indeed, the very definition of the field as "international relations" reflects a preoccupation with territorially specific and state-bounded notions of authority that focus upon the state as the essential actor and unit-of-analysis.[49] In contrast, definitions of the field in terms of global relations do not necessarily invoke a state-centric ontology, but are potentially consistent with a variety of nonstate actors and activities.[50]

The problem is to define authority in a way that goes beyond identification of the essential actors and examines more directly the fundamental meaning of the term. This is confused by the various meanings and interpretations given to the terms "public" and "private." We associate political authority automatically with the public realm of the state. In contrast, we regard as nonpolitical or apolitical the private realm of individual and market activity. However, this does not mean that the private sphere is about "privatized or apolitical judgment"; rather, it is about "nonauthoritative judgment" in the sense that it is "not entitled to prescribe behavior."[51] According to liberal and democratic theory, only the public sphere is empowered and entitled to prescribe behavior for others, for only public authorities are accountable through political institutions. The private sphere cannot be regarded within liberal and democratic theory as functioning authoritatively for society because it lacks accountability. However, this does not mean that the private sphere cannot, in fact, function authoritatively. Indeed, private actors might not function democratically at all and yet exercise considerable "authority" over their peers. Authority in this sense can take the meaning of being regarded by one's peers as "an authority"—as an expert, a scholar, or a specialist.[52] It can also take the meaning of being "in authority" as a spokesperson, a political leader, or a commander, but this meaning begins to merge with public definitions of authority. Private authority can thus evoke a sense of legitimacy and achieve a high degree of acceptance through recognition by others of specific knowledge, expertise, and representational skills. Moreover, to the extent that such authority extends beyond the members of a private group, association, industry, or sector to influence society more generally through a delegation of authority from governments or through privatization and deregulation, we see private authority as beginning to merge into the public realm.

Notions of authority derive largely from theorizing about domestic political authority, where the tendency to associate authority with the existence of a public realm, occupied by the state, is almost irresistible. After all, political authority by definition cannot be "private," it must be public; therefore, it is difficult to situate or locate authority among private actors. This is even further complicated when we attempt to theorize about private authority "outside" the state, in the international realm. In the international system, there is no central government and we face "the problem of order in the absence of an orderer."[53] The public sphere, which we can identify at the domestic level, is barely perceptible in the international realm, as evidenced in the perennial search for reasons to account for the binding nature of public international law. The binding nature of private international arrangements is even more obscure and problematic.[54] In order to understand private *international* authority, we must move away from associating activities that are public and authoritative with the state. Further, we must differentiate between government and governance, which allows us analytically to consider the existence of *private* international authority as a form or instance of governance.

One of the goals of this volume is to draw on case studies of sectors or issue-areas to generate insights into the analytical foundations of global authority. How is it possible to identify private international authority empirically? First, those subject to the rules and decisions being made by private sector actors must accept them as legitimate, as the representations of experts and those "in authority." Second, there should exist a high degree of compliance with the rules and decisions. Third, the private sector actors must be empowered either explicitly *or implicitly* by governments and international organizations with the right to make decisions for others. For the contributors, this challenge involves conceptualizing the relationships between private actors, global institutions, and state capabilities. To what extent can corporate actors prevail upon global institutions and national governments for support and resources to advance their agendas? Are the relationships reciprocal in that states and international organizations also are able to advance their interests through the agency of corporate actors? To what degree must the analyst consider the "agent-structure problem" and the mutually constitutive nature of these relations?[55] Relatedly, is it necessary to distinguish the relationship between private authority and states from that between private authority and societies? Finally, have different historical periods configured these relationships differently?[56] These are some of the analytical concerns that are central to the study of private global authority.

THE IMPORTANCE OF HISTORY: TRENDS IN PRIVATE AND PUBLIC AUTHORITY

In this section we turn briefly to the historical dimension of the issues we have been addressing. Our interest in this is driven in part by a sense that something is changing: that private authority is becoming more evident as states experience more difficulty in coping with globalization. It would be a mistake, however, to overemphasize novelty in world politics; there are echoes of the present in the prominent international role of organized private actors of the Middle Ages[57] or the intense cartelization of the interwar period.[58] A historical perspective thereby strengthens our ability to assess and explain the significance of private authority today. History has always had a powerful normative dimension in theorizing as well, whether acknowledged or not. Teleological arguments that buttress beliefs that things *must* or *cannot* change have fallen out of fashion, but history softly urges us to ask not just where we are headed but also whether it is in the "right" direction. This is an inescapably normative question.

While the number of interesting historical questions that could be asked about private global authority is limitless, here we focus on only a few that are reflected in the chapter contributions. One of the key historical questions we need to research more fully is the degree to which the private authority we see today is generated by cyclical or recurrent features of the global political economy. We see this most clearly in the contribution by Porter. At the same time, we need to analyze the degree to which current activity is qualitatively or quantitatively different, involving long-range secular trends. Are things irreversibly changing, or are we simply entering another historical cycle? The institutionalization of global governance appears to be on an upward trend that even the most enthusiastic proponents of cyclical theories[59] must acknowledge. Some theorists have suggested that growing reflexivity—an institutional or individual actor's capacity to monitor and creatively alter her conduct—is a defining and continuing characteristic of modernity.[60] The expansion of markets, democracy, and electronic information exchange also are candidates for irreversibility. This suggests there is a secular transformation underway that buttresses the authority of private sector actors.

While each of these trends is likely to be strongly related to changes in private global authority over time, the exact features of this relationship are not at all clear. For instance, is the growth of private authority an expression of democracy—a growth in global civil society—or is it the consolidation of an untrammeled domination of capital over our increasingly globalized daily lives? Such questions intersect with long-standing philosophical debates that are central to our understanding and practice of democracy: Is democracy enhanced by expanding or restricting the range of decisions that are regarded as "properly" private as opposed to public? Here we can do no more than draw attention to a few reasons to consider such historical questions in ongoing research. First, we need to determine who decides what is "properly" public or private, which is an intensely political issue that has only been addressed at any length by feminist scholarship. Second, we need to understand past and present political struggles because they may be a significant determinant of how and where each society divides up the public and private spheres. Third, such research can further the reflexive process of reproducing, perhaps differently, the private/public frontier.

CASE STUDIES IN PRIVATE COOPERATION AND AUTHORITY

We have organized the chapters that follow in accordance with three of the main themes discussed above: interfirm cooperative arrangements and self-regulation; interfirm cooperation and its effects on those outside the cooperative arrangements; and the historical dimension of inter-firm cooperation. In the concluding chapter we return to the concept of private authority in international affairs and explore its meaning and significance in more detail, reflecting on the case studies.

The part on interfirm organizing begins with an analysis by Debora Spar of the creation of rules to regulate the anarchy of the Internet. She argues that in the absence of government regulation the firms that provide access and content for the Internet have created the beginnings of a private regime that governs the activities of Internet participants. Here, the structure she sees is that of a regime, and the causes for cooperation lie in a functionalist demand for ordering. Government has taken a hands-off attitude, either explicitly or implicitly sanctioning the privately organized regime and thus awarding it a degree of authority. Next, Webb analyzes private international regimes in the international minerals industry, focusing on efforts to establish norms of behavior that facilitate private oligopolistic market management. He pays particular attention to public efforts, through mixed public-private institutions such as study groups, to facilitate private market management by transnational mining firms. Standards setting is a crucial element in the functioning of a complex economy, and Salter's chapter analyzes the important private sector role in creating the standards that govern much market activity. Her approach draws upon the regime framework to analyze the creation of private and public standards for industrial production. Finally, Mytelka and Delapierre argue that knowledge based industries respond both to their structural market conditions and the character of state intervention or state weakness. Such industries tend to create cooperative relationships that Mytelka and Delapierre call knowledge-based oligopolies, a loose form of strategic alliance. The participants seek through these relationships to manage their competitive environment. Instead of addressing the concept of authority directly, these authors leave the implication that when governments cannot manage competitiveness issues, major corporations will do so instead.

In the next part, we group selections that have in common a focus on the effects of interfirm cooperation on nonparticipants; in other words, against whom is private authority exercised? Sinclair argues that bond-rating agencies have developed strong standards for the financial industry as a whole, affecting the decisions and options available to those they rate. The rest of the financial community accepts the role played by the ratings agencies, awarding them the authority to judge their behavior. Sinclair's chapter, unlike most of the others in this volume, draws upon recent scholarship in Gramscian international relations theory to frame his argument. In her chapter, Sell looks at the cooperation among a small group of corporations in developing international intellectual property rights legislation. These firms lobbied internationally to have their preferences incorporated into a binding interstate treaty. This chapter provides us with insight into the relationship between pubic and private authority, as the participants chose to pursue a strategy of gaining public sanction for their privately developed agreement. Haufler examines two cases in the insurance industry that compare efforts to develop norms in common, one successful and one less so. The insurance industry is an important intermediary in economic transactions and their underwriting norms can affect the ability of customers to do business and can also affect policy outcomes. Burke's piece contributes a detailed examination of what happens when the private sector becomes a provider of public goods, and the degree to which they are acknowledged as authoritative entities. In this case, she looks at the international oil industry in Ecuador, and the effects of its activities on the indigenous population.

The next part of this volume addresses the evolution of public and private international authority. Porter analyzes the ways in which leading sectors in the economy of a hegemonic state evolve from private ordering to public ordering in their behavior. The degree of cooperation among firms varies over time, and this leads to different degrees of public and private intervention. In her contribution, Cutler, like Porter, emphasizes the importance of historical developments, though going back much further in time. Through an examination of maritime law, she shows how private authority was a vital element of the medieval economy. These two contributions are particularly important in pointing out the historical context of private authority. There appears to have been a historical trend in which private authority was displaced by state authority throughout the late nineteenth and early twentieth centuries. The cases presented in this volume indicate this trend is being reversed with the current expansion of private authority.

In our final chapter, we come back to the topic of private authority. What is important to understand about interfirm cooperation is not just that it exists, but that in many cases it has taken on the mantle of authority. The public at large has come to accept that certain private sector actors not only rule particular issues, but that they should do so. This perspective forces us to rethink our notions of authority itself. Further, it leaves us with a dilemma: If states are decreasingly performing their traditional authoritative functions—if the private sector is indeed expanding its authority over many areas of economic life—what does this mean for our public life? What happens to democracy and accountability, and how will this private authority affect the distribution of power and resources in the world? How will it affect world politics in general? These are some of the larger issues raised by the concept and practice of private international authority.

NOTES

1. David C. Korten, *When Corporations Rule the World* (London: Earthscan, 1997).
2. One attempt at thinking about authority outside the state in international relations was James Rosenau and Otto Czempiel, eds., *Governance without Government: Order and Change in World Politics* (Cambridge: Cambridge University Press, 1992); see also James Rosenau, *Along the Domestic-Foreign Frontier: Exploring Governance in a Turbulent World* (Cambridge: Cambridge University Press, 1997). For a recent survey of the modern state, see *The World Development Report 1997: The State in a Changing World* (Oxford: Oxford University Press, 1997). An excellent examination of corporate activity in the modern economy is J. Rogers Hollingsworth and Robert Boyer, eds., *Contemporary Capitalism: The Embeddedness of Institutions* (Cambridge: Cambridge University Press, 1997).
3. These two elements of authority are taken from Stephen Lukes, "Perspectives on Authority," in Joseph Raz, *Authority* (Oxford: Basil Blackwell, 1990), pp. 203–17 and are further developed in the concluding chapter.
4. United Nations Conference on Trade and Investment, *World Investment Report 1994: Transnational Corporations, Employment and the Workplace* (New York and Geneva: United Nations, 1994). In this discussion, we use the term "transnational corporations (TNCs)" to refer to corporations with foreign assets. We do not distinguish here between TNCs and "multinational corporations (MNCs)"; technically, the two are distinguished by the fact that the entire production process is globalized in a TNC, with separate parts of the process contributing to the final output, while in a MNC the production process is complete within each national base.
5. Studies of the phenomenon of globalization have proliferated in recent years. See, for instance, James Mittleman, ed., *Globalization: Critical Reflections*, IPE Yearbook vol. 9 (Boulder and London: Lynne Rienner, 1996); Paul Hirst and Grahame Thompson, *Globalization in Question* (Cambridge: Polity Press, 1996); Malcolm Waters, *Globalization* (London and New York: Routledge, 1995); Kevin R. Cox, ed., *Spaces of Globalization: Reasserting the Power of the Local* (New York: Guilford, 1997); Suzanne Berger and Ronald Dore, ed., *National Diversity and Global Capitalism* (Ithaca: Cornell University Press, 1996); James Rosenau, *Turbulence in World Politics* (Princeton: Princeton University Press, 1990).
6. The literature on the nature of the firm is too vast to cover here, but see Alfred Chandler, *The Visible Hand* (Cambridge: Harvard University Press, 1977); Oliver E. Williamson, *Markets and Hierarchies: Analysis and Antitrust Implications* (New York: The Free Press, 1975) and *The Economic Institutions of Capitalism: Firms, Markets and Relational Contracting* (New York: The Free Press, 1985); Louis Putterman and Randall S. Kroszner, eds., *The Economic Nature of the Firm*, 2nd ed. (Cambridge: Cambridge University Press, 1996); Gary Miller, *Managerial Dilemmas: The Political Economy of Hierarchy* (Cambridge: Cambridge University Press, 1992).
7. For instance, see Jean Tirole, *The Theory of Industrial Organization* (Cambridge: MIT Press, 1990); Richard Schmalensee and Robert Willig, eds.,

Handbook of Industrial Organization (Amsterdam: Elsevier Press, 1989); F. M. Scherer, *Industrial Market Structure and Economic Performance*, 2nd ed. (Chicago: Rand McNally, 1980).

8. There are a few in political science and business schools who wish to stimulate a more vigorous research program integrating political science and business studies. See, most prominently, David Vogel, *Kindred Strangers: The Uneasy Relationship between Politics and Business in America* (Princeton: Princeton University Press, 1996) and John Dunning, *The Globalization of Business* (London: Routledge, 1993). This is not to say that there is no research being done on the politics of business activity—quite the contrary, there is a lot of interesting work in this area, but business politics still plays a relatively minor role in mainstream international relations research programs at present. In the 1970s, the work on transnational relations and on dependency theory focused strongly on transnational corporations, but that has since faded. For some recent exceptions, see John Stopford and Susan Strange, *Rival States, Rival Firms* (Cambridge: Cambridge University Press, 1991); Lorraine Eden and Evan H. Potter, eds., *Multinationals in the Global Political Economy*, (New York: St. Martin's Press, 1993); Susan Strange, *Retreat of the State* (Cambridge: Cambridge University Press, 1997); Craig N. Murphy, *International Organization and Industrial Change* (Oxford: Oxford University Press, 1994); and the interdisciplinary volume edited by J. Rogers Hollingsworth and Robert Boyer, *Contemporary Capitalism.*

9. See, for instance, the classic by Richard Barnet and Ronald Muller, *Global Reach* (New York: Simon & Schuster, 1974); and, more recently, William Greider, *One World, Ready or Not* (New York: Simon & Schuster, 1997) and David Korten, *When Corporations Rule the World.*

10. See, for instance, the collection edited by Thomas Risse-Kappen, *Bringing Transnational Relations Back In* (Cambridge: Cambridge University Press, 1996). For an approach that attempts to create a new paradigm for understanding international diplomacy as a game among both firms and states, see John Stopford and Susan Strange, *Rival States, Rival Firms.*

11. Robert Keohane, *After Hegemony* (Princeton: Princeton University Press, 1984).

12. G. B. Richardson, "The Organization of Industry," in Louis Putterman and Randall S. Kroszner, eds., *The Economic Nature of the Firm: A Reader* (Cambridge: Cambridge University Press, 1996), p. 138.

13. For an excellent overview of the economics of multinational corporate behavior, see Richard E. Caves, *Multinational Enterprise and Economic Analysis*, 2nd ed. (Cambridge: Cambridge University Press, 1996).

14. Debora Spar, *The Cooperative Edge: The Internal Politics of International Cartels* (Ithaca: Cornell University Press, 1994), p. 4.

15. Peter Haas describes an epistemic community as a group of scientists, technicians, and specialized policymakers who have a similar understanding about causality in an issue area. See Haas, *Saving the Mediterranean* (New York: Columbia University Press, 1990); see also Peter Haas, "Protecting the Baltic and North Seas," in Haas, Robert O. Keohane, and Marc A. Levy, eds., *Institutions for the Earth: Sources of Effective International Environmental Protection* (Cambridge: MIT Press, 1993), pp. 133–82.

16. This varied literature is too extensive to summarize here, but see, for instance, Douglass North, *Institutions, Institutional Change, and Economic Performance* (Cambridge: Cambridge University Press, 1990); Robert Keohane, *International Institutions and State Power* (Boulder, Colo.: Westview Press, 1989); Karol Soltan, Virginia Haufler, and Eric Uslaner, eds., *Institutions and Social Order* (Ann Arbor: University of Michigan Press, 1998).

17. Peter Haas analyzes the influence of an epistemic community on goverment policymaking, while we would like to emphasize here that a business-oriented epistemic community may at times be so closely involved in authoritative decision-making itself that it is difficult to disentangle the private and public sector actors. See Haas, *Saving the Mediterranean* (New York: Columbia University Press, 1990).

18. Our emphasis here has been on the growth of private authority relative to public authority but, as we note in our concluding chapter, this shift is not necessarily inexorable or unilinear. There are numerous examples of states, historically, having expanded public authority at the expense of private authority (the chapters by Cutler and Porter provide examples) and even today, for instance, there are initiatives in the European Union to demand more accountability from the private sector (a point made by Lynn Mytelka in commenting on this chapter).

19. This is discussed in detail in the chapter by Cutler, this volume.

20. Echoes of the polar positions in the realist-liberal debate are paralleled by disagreements over the appropriate model for the firm—unitary or disaggregated. Do firms simply operate as unitary rational actors in interfirm cooperative arrangements, or does their joint activity begin to produce a relatively autonomous institution that can modify the interests and identities of its constituent units?

21. Customary international law appears to have a natural or spontaneous quality because it evolves over a long period of time. However, two tests of whether a norm has attained the status of a binding rule of law direct us to purposeful activities and positive acts of will. To establish that a norm has attained the status of law it must meet an empirical test of whether the norm is generally observed by states, and a normative test of whether states believe they are under an obligation to observe that norm. See generally, *Akehurst's Modern Introduction to International Law*, 7th ed., revised by Peter Malansszuk (London and New York: Routledge, 1997), chapter 3. For an example of the almost irresistible tendency to regard customary law as natural and spontaneous in origin, see Bruce Benson, "The Spontaneous Evolution of Commercial Law," *Southern Economic Journal* 55 (1988–89): 644–61.

22. On the concept of a focal point, see Judith Goldstein and Robert Keohane, *Ideas and Institutions* (Ithaca: Cornell University Press, 1993).

23. Lynn Mytelka, *Strategic Partnerships: States, Firms and International Competition* (London: Pinter, 1991).

24. G. B. Richardson, "The Organization of the Firm," in Louis Putterman and Randall S. Kroszner, eds., *The Economic Nature of the Firm: A Reader* (Cambridge: Cambridge University Press, 1996), p. 140.

25. See Debora Spar, *The Cooperative Edge*, p. 37.

26. Stephen Krasner, ed., *International Regimes* (Ithaca: Cornell University Press, 1982), p. 2. A few of the notable precursors to Krasner's volume are John Gerard Ruggie and Ernst Haas, co-editors of the special issue of *International Organization* on "International Organization: International Responses to Technology," 29.3 (Summer 1975); and Robert Keohane and Joseph Nye, *Power and Interdependence* (Boston and Toronto: Little, Brown, 1997). The literature on regimes is now quite large; see, among others, Volker Rittberger, ed., *States and International Regimes* (Oxford: Clarendon Press, 1993); Mark. W. Zacher with Brent Sutton, *Governing Global Networks: International Regimes for Transportation and Communications* (Cambridge: Cambridge University Press, 1996); and, for a business-oriented perspective, Lee Preston and Duane Windsor, *The Rules of the Game in the Global Economy: Policy Regimes for International Business* (Boston, Dordrecht, London: Kluwer Academic Publishers, 1992).

27. Lee Preston and Duane Windsor, *The Rules of the Game*; Anne-Marie Slaughter, "International Law in a World of Liberal States," *European Journal of International Law* 6 (1995): 503–38.

28. On the distinction between organizations, regimes, and social institutions, see Oran Young, *International Cooperation: Building Regimes for Natural Resources and the Environment* (Ithaca: Cornell University Press, 1989), chapter 2.

29. Ronald Coase, *The Firm, the Market and the Law* (Chicago: University of Chicago Press, 1990); Robert Keohane, *After Hegemony* (Princeton: Princeton University Press, 1984).

30. Andreas Hasenclever, Peter Mayer, and Volker Rittberger, "Interests, Power, Knowledge: The Study of International Regimes," *Mershon International Studies Review* 40.2 (October 1996): 177–228.

31. On private regimes, see Tony Porter, *States, Markets and Regimes in Global Finance* (New York: St. Martin's Press, 1993); Virginia Haufler, "Crossing the Boundary between Public and Private," in Volker Rittberger, ed., *Regime Theory and International Relations* (Oxford: Clarendon Press, 1993); Virginia Haufler, *Dangerous Commerce* (Ithaca: Cornell University Press, 1997); A. Claire Cutler, "Canada and the Private International Trade Law Regime," in A. Claire Cutler and Mark W. Zacher, eds., *Canadian Foreign Policy and International Economic Regimes* (Vancouver: University of British Columbia Press, 1992).

32. See Cutler, this volume, for a discussion of hard law and soft law.

33. Robert W. Cox, *Production, Power and World Order* (New York: Columbia University Press, 1987); Stephen Gill, ed., *Gramsci, Historical Materialism and International Relations* (Cambridge: Cambridge University Press, 1993).

34. The new institutional economics approach to analyzing markets and hierarchies is most closely associated with Ronald Coase. *The Firm, the Market and the Law*; Oliver Williamson, *Markets and Hierarchies* and *The Economic Institutions of Capitalism*; and Douglass North, *Structure and Change in Economic History* (New York: Norton, 1981) and *Institutions, Institutional Change, and Economic Performance*. See also Amir Barnea, Robert A. Haugen, and Lemma W. Senbet, *Agency Problems and Financial Contracting* (London:

Prentice Hall, 1985); Karol Soltan, Virginia Haufler, and Eric Uslaner, eds., *Institutions and Social Order* (Ann Arbor: University of Michigan Press, 1998).

35. See, among other sociological institutionalists, James G. March and Johan P. Olsen, "The New Institutionalism: Organizational Factors in Political Life," *American Political Science Review* 78.3 (September 1984): 734–49 and *Rediscovering Institutions: The Organizational Basis of Politics* (New York: Free Press, 1989); David E. Apter, *Rethinking Development: Modernization, Dependency Theory, and Postmodern Politics* (Newbury Park, Calif.: Sage, 1987); Peter B. Evans, Dietrich Rueschemeyer, and Theda Skocpol, eds., *Bringing the State Back In* (Cambridge: Cambridge University Press, 1985); and George M. Thomas, John W. Mare, Francisco O. Ramirez, and John Boli, eds., *Institutional Structure: Constituting State, Society, and the Individual* (Newbury Park, Calif.: Sage, 1987). For a perspective on sociology from an international relations scholar, see Martha Finnemore, *National Interests in International Society* (Ithaca: Cornell University Press, 1996).

36. Anthony Giddens, *The Constitution of Society* (Cambridge: Polity Press, 1984).

37. Porter, *States, Markets and Regimes in Global Finance* and his chapter in this volume.

38. A. Claire Cutler, "Global Capitalism and Liberal Myths: Dispute Settlement in Private International Trade Relations," *Millennium: Journal of International Studies* 24.3 (1995): 377–97 and her chapter in this volume.

39. Timothy Sinclair, chapter in this volume.

40. Porter, *States, Markets and Regimes in Global Finance.*

41. Susan Sell, chapter in this volume.

42. A. Claire Cutler, "Artifice, Ideology and Paradox: The Public/Private Distinction in International Law," *Review of International Political Economy* 4.2 (1997): 261–85.

43. Wolfgang Streeck and Philippe C. Schmitter, eds., *Private Interest Government: Beyond Market and State* (London: Sage, 1985).

44. But see Mark Rupert, *Producing Hegemony: The Politics of Mass Production and American Global Power* (Cambridge: Cambridge University Press, 1995)

45. For two very good volumes that explore many of the problems discussed here see Joseph Raz, ed., *Authority* (Oxford: Basil Blackwell, 1990) and Bruce Lincoln, *Authority: Construction and Corrosion* (Chicago: University of Chicago Press, 1991).

46. R. B. Friedman, "On the Concept of Authority in Political Philosophy," in Joseph Raz, ed., *Authority* (Oxford: Basil Blackwell, 1990), p. 56.

47. "Territoriality and Beyond: Problematizing Modernity in International Relations," *International Organization* 47.1 (1993): 151.

48. "Political Economy and International Relations," in Ken Booth and Steve Smith, eds., *International Relations Theory Today* (University Park, Pa.: Pennsylvania State University Press, 1995), p. 169.

49. John Agnew, "The Territorial Trap: The Geographical Assumptions of International Relations Theory," *Review of International Political Economy* 1 (1994): 5.

50. Justin Rosenberg, *Empire of Civil Society: A Critique of Realist Theory of International Relations* (London: Verso, 1994); Cox, *Production, Power and World Order.*

51. Friedman, "On the Concept of Authority in Political Philosophy," p. 79.

52. Ibid.

53. Richard Ashley, "Untying the Sovereign State: A Double Reading of the Anarchy Problematic," *Millennium: Journal of International Studies* 17.2 (1988): 229.

54. See Cutler, "Artifice, Ideology and Paradox," for the problematic status of private international law.

55. Alexander Wendt, "Anarchy Is What States Make of It: The Social Construction of Power," *International Organization* 46.2 (1992): 391–425; Wendt, "The Agent-Structure Problem in International Relations Theory," *International Organization* 41 (1987): 335–70; Alexander Wendt and Raymond Duvall, "Institutions and International Order," in Czempiel and Rosenau, eds., *Global Changes and Theoretical Challenges.*

56. Cox, *Production, Power and World Order*; Cutler, "Global Capitalism and Liberal Myths"; Rosenberg, *Empire of Civil Society.*

57. Cutler, "Global Capitalism and Liberal Myths."

58. Porter, *States, Markets and Regimes in Global Finance.*

59. Joshua Goldstein, *Long Cycles: Prosperity and War in the Modern Age* (New Haven and London: Yale University Press, 1988); Christian Suter, *Debt Cycles in the World-Economy: Foreign Loans, Financial Crises, and Debt Settlements, 1820–1990* (Boulder, Colo.: Westview, 1992).

60. Ulrich Beck, Anthony Giddens, and Scott Lash, *Reflexive Modernization: Politics, Tradition and Aesthetics in the Modern Social Order* (Stanford: Stanford University Press, 1994).

PART 2

Ruling Themselves: Interfirm Organizing in the Global Arena

CHAPTER 2

Lost in (Cyber)space: The Private Rules of Online Commerce

Debora L. Spar

Cyberspace is a funny place. It is a sea of instant information, an advertisers' mecca, a global dating service, and a site of unprecedented business development. It spans geographical space yet exists nowhere, really, in the visible, physical world. Since it burst into public consciousness in the early 1990s, it has been a virtually endless source of fascination, debate, and frustration. It is also a realm governed by private authority.

That private networks should flourish in cyberspace is a shock to some observers and an affront to many. The Internet, after all, was created by the state—designed and supported by the U.S. Department of Defense and National Science Foundation (NSF). It grew at the hands of scientists and researchers, and spawned a community fiercely committed to public discourse and openly opposed to any commercial trespass. With such a short and idiosyncratic history, the Internet might reasonably be expected to be the province of either governments or the general public. And yet, increasingly, it is neither. While governments strain at the margins to rule the Net, and even as vast regions remain rambunctiously personal and uncontrolled, private firms and networks—complete with rules, norms, standards, and expectations—are rapidly expanding their sway.

How did this happen and what does it mean? This chapter proposes a number of related hypotheses. It begins with a basic assumption that, in cyberspace as elsewhere, rules matter. They set the boundaries of permissible behavior, clarify the terms of interaction, and provide some sense of security and predictability. Rules are especially important, the chapter suggests, for business. For despite an occasional sense of operating in unchartered or unordered territories, business in fact operates primarily where rules apply. In particular, business depends on three critical sets of rules: rules of property, rules of exchange, and rules of enforcement. These rules provide the bedrock for commercial activity; without them, business of any sort becomes a far riskier and more uncertain venture.

Yet in cyberspace there are few rules—or at least few of the kinds of rules that national governments customarily create and enforce. The legal status of electronic property rights remains ambiguous, as do the legal and practical issues surrounding online exchange. Enforcement authority is limited on the Internet, and there are few agencies with either the power or predisposition to punish those who violate the norms of online conduct. Theoretically, this state of affairs puts both firms and their would-be customers in a subtle but significant quandary. Without any firmly established rules, they can either risk doing business in a lawless and unregulated realm, or they can attempt to construct some basic rules of the game. If they choose the latter—and this chapter suggests they already have—then they face a subsequent choice: either to let governments assume their normal rule-making powers or, instead, to design and enforce the rules of cyberspace themselves. Once again, this chapter suggests that the latter choice has already been made. Fundamentally, I argue, governments cannot set the rules of cyberspace. That is because cyberspace, unlike governments, slips seamlessly and nearly unavoidably across national boundaries. The only way for governments to rule cyberspace is through coordinated international agreement—an ambitious and highly unlikely prospect, especially when many nations still cannot agree on basic standards for intellectual property protection.[1] With governments pushed effectively to the sidelines, firms will have to write and enforce their own rules, creating private networks to facilitate and protect electronic commerce.

Already, this movement is well underway. Governments are backing away from the regulation of cyberspace and the private sector is moving in. As this trend continues, private entities will extend and embed their reach, carving out chunks of cyberspace where their own "rules, norms, and standards" apply. In the process, these private entities will tilt the delicate balance between business and government closer to the side of business. They will also make cyberspace a quieter place, more orderly and predictable than it currently is, but less raucous, less accessible, and possibly less democratic than many "Netizens" would like to see. That is the dual impact of private authority.

The discussion below is divided into six sections. The first provides a brief history of the Internet, describing its evolution from a defense system to a research community and then to a public and commercial forum. The second section discusses the general importance of rules in cyberspace; the third through fifth describe the specific importance of rules of property rights, rules of exchange, and rules of enforcement. The chapter concludes by examining the probable shape and impact of the Internet's private authorities.

FROM SCIENCE TO SALES:
THE COMMERCIAL EVOLUTION OF THE INTERNET

The Internet got its start in the late 1960s as a communications infrastructure called ARPANET, run by the Department of Defense and its Advanced Research Project Agency (ARPA). Consisting of a series of links joining together discrete computer networks, the ARPANET was an experiment in "internetworking," designed to give university research scientists an opportunity to create a solid "network of networks" to facilitate the exchange of scientific and military information. Taking advantage of recent developments in computer technology, and trying also to make the system impervious to nuclear attacks or natural disasters, the ARPANET developers structured the system in a highly decentralized manner. Information flowed from one computer network to another through a variety of media (telephone wires, fiber-optic links, satellites) and through a variety of physical sites.

Over time, this decentralized network of networks became known as the Internet. Following the model of the national telephone system, and even employing many of its connections, the Internet's pathways remained out of sight and mind to its users. No one needed to know how messages moved from one place to another, only that they got there securely. Unlike the telephone system, the logical structure of the Internet allowed any single user to broadcast a message simultaneously to numerous sites on the network. This possibility reflected the Internet's scientific purpose: to enable a small elite of researchers to share critical information among themselves.

For roughly twenty years, this community quietly flourished online. Expanding rapidly from just four host computers in 1969 to nearly two thousand by 1985, the Internet became a common mode of communication between university researchers, government scientists, and outside computer engineers. As small discussions enlarged to incorporate new entrants, electronic bulletin boards were formed, and, for the first time, people began to "meet" in cyberspace. Still, the culture of the Internet remained akin to that of a small and like-minded community. The users were overwhelmingly computer-literate, highly educated, and scientifically minded. Many were hackers, and insisted that commerce had no place in their slowly expanding community. This mindset was reinforced by the NSF, which assumed responsibility for the Internet during the course of the 1980s and explicitly prohibited any users from engaging in commercial or other nonresearch purposes.[2]

By the late 1980s, however, this policy had effectively disappeared. Aware of the growing commercial interest in the Net, as well as its own budgetary limits, the NSF began slowly to privatize the Internet. Initially, private firms just provided infrastructural services to the Net's established user base. Then in 1989, commercial service providers emerged, offering Internet access to a wide new range of private and commercial customers. In 1990, the Internet was officially opened to commercial ventures. As a result of this privatization, the Net was transformed. In the early 1980s the Internet community had consisted only of about twenty-five linked scientific and academic networks. By 1995, when the last piece of the NSF backbone was retired in favor of higher-speed, privately owned backbones, the Net had grown to include over 44,000 networks extending between 160 countries and including 26,000 registered commercial entities.[3] Extending far beyond academia and the Defense Department, roughly 62 million people had direct access to the Internet by the spring of 1997, and that number was doubling every year.[4]

More than just an increase in numbers, the entrance of the newcomers—or "newbies"—meant a fundamental change in the culture of the Internet and the community it had spawned. Arriving online primarily through commercial services such as Prodigy or America Online, these new users understandably had little interest in the research questions that had bound previous users together. The newbies were also largely unfamiliar with much of the Internet's specific protocols or with the systems that sat at its foundation. Cyberspace for the newbies was simply an adventure—an opportunity to meet people, gain information, and perhaps recreate some sense of small-town intimacy and immediacy. But many newcomers also came to cyberspace for profit, to explore the potential of a vast new realm and stake a claim in a technology that promised to revolutionize the very nature of transactions. As a result, the Internet's relatively new business district—the ".com domain"— quickly swelled to become the largest sector of the Net, and the transformation of commerce seemed well underway.

From a historical perspective, this transformation to online exchange is even more profound than many current analysts have noted. Historically, the evolution of commerce has depended on and coincided with the development of institutions to secure the means and rules of exchange. Because transacting is inherently risky and costly, institutions and relationships have emerged over time to mediate these risks and costs and thus allow for exchange to proceed. The history of these relationships and institutions marks the history of commercial evolution. It begins with primitive exchanges (three pigs for a cow) that rest almost everywhere on personal familiarity and are therefore limited to the scope of a trader's immediate circle of contacts. Driving the need for familiarity is the risk inherent in the transaction: if the cow dies the following morning, the unfortunate purchaser wants some recourse to the seller and the best means for assuring, that is, to know precisely, who he is and where he lives. Security comes also from the knowledge that the traders will transact again, thereby reducing the likelihood that either will succumb to the temptation to cheat the other.[5] For interaction to progress beyond the limited bounds of familiarity, the traders (and their society) must develop the institutions that allow them to replace their personal ties with more formal and impersonal ones. As societies develop these formal ties, commerce expands beyond the community and economic growth ensues. The nature of these ties—things like private property, contract law, a common currency, and a means of enforcement—is to reduce the cost of transactions and ensure their security in the absence of a long-term personal relationship. Thus there are laws and courts and police to turn to if the cow dies. As transactions become more complicated, so too must the rules evolve, reducing the risks and costs that remain inherent in exchange.

What the Internet does, particularly for intangible goods such as financial services, is to reduce commerce to its most basic component: the transaction. The technological promise of the Net is that it makes transactions free and instantaneous. At the click of a mouse, it allows potential customers to download software, buy a magazine article, or borrow thousands of dollars. By pushing commerce closer and closer to the bare-bones level of the transaction, the Internet potentially allows buyers and sellers of information to remove many of the intermediate steps that have historically encumbered their exchange—the software distributors, book binders, tellers, and checkbooks. By removing these steps, the Internet promises to increase efficiencies and lower costs.

In the process, however, the Internet also removes many of the rules and institutions that have developed over time to support modern commerce. Rules that work in the tangible sphere—rules such as private property, contract law, and local enforcement—just may not translate easily into cyberspace. They almost certainly will not translate if transactions in cyberspace are anonymous and ephemeral, and if they move freely across national boundaries. Yet this is precisely the radical commercial promise of the Internet: to make individual transactions anonymous, immediate, international, and inexpensive.

For this promise to be met, the Internet must develop new rules and norms of commercial interaction. And the most likely creators of these rules are the firms that stand to benefit most directly from their creation.

THE RULES OF EXCHANGE

Once upon a time, the Internet did have rules. In its earliest days, the Net was very much a community of like-minded individuals who developed clear codes of conduct and working norms of behavior. The rules were rarely written or even explicit, but they did not have to be, since they were widely observed by all those traveling on the Net. Just as early automobile drivers developed the rules of the road, so too did the early Internet users develop their own norms of behavior. They created symbols to express emotions such as joy [:-)] and sorrow [:-(]. They created rules, such as Don't-change-the-subject and Read-the-FAQ-file, and they even created a language of sorts, with expressions such as "FAQ" [frequently asked questions], "flame" [to subject someone to extremely harsh criticism], and "spam" [flooding mailboxes with unsolicited mail].

Despite its outward image as the untamed realm of hackers, therefore, the early Net was actually a rule-bound orderly community. The strength of its rules was powerfully demonstrated in 1994, when a now-infamous pair of Arizona lawyers posted an advertisement for their services on hundreds of electronic bulletin boards, bombarding many uninterested users with multiple copies. Seeing the advertisement as a violation of the Net's then-existing norm against private commerce and "junk-mail," thousands of users "flamed" the lawyers' office with a torrent of hate mail and cyber-threats. With this spontaneous response they demonstrated not only the power of online norms but also the ability of the Internet community to monitor and enforce these norms, punishing violations with online's closest approximation of force.

Since the lawyers' venture, however, online community has changed to include a much more diverse population and a host of explicitly commercial enterprises. Under these circumstances, the old rules no longer make sense.[6]

Accordingly, the rules of the Internet are now rapidly evolving, pulled and prodded by the often-conflicting interests of business entities, governmental agencies, and traditional Net users. In general, governments have tended, initially at least, to approach the Internet as if it were any other realm of public activity: they presume some authority to control certain kinds of speech, or to prohibit the sale of restricted goods, or to stem the flow of information deemed damaging to the state.[7] At the same time, traditional users have clamored to maintain the old rules of interaction: to keep cyberspace a realm of open communication and universal access, removed from any form of governmental intervention. The business community, by contrast, has been relatively quiet, with managers avoiding public debate as they concentrate on the more immediate tasks of staking a claim in cyberspace. Yet merely by staking and securing their position, firms have already changed the Internet's rules. In particular, just by concentrating on their commercial requirements, firms have begun to establish, on their own and from the ground up, three distinct sets of rules: rules of property, rules of currency, and rules of enforcement. Together, these rules and their makers constitute a powerful, if still emerging, source of private authority and private international governance.

PROPERTY RIGHTS

All economic systems are based fundamentally on a shared understanding of property rights. Developed over decades or even centuries, these rights clarify the basis of ownership and exchange. They provide a consistent way of defining who owns what, and how these possessions can be transferred from one owner to another. Without well-accepted rules of property, most commercial exchange either would not occur, or would be exceedingly costly. Property rights reduce the costs of exchange by clarifying ownership and providing some means for punishing those who violate it. They define not only possession but also theft.

In modern market economies, property rights also provide the incentives that drive innovation and growth. If property is communal or property rights ill-defined, no one in the community has much incentive to produce anything more than he or she can consume. What creates the incentive, and thus what drives technological and economic progress, is a system that clearly defines private property and enables the owner of this property to appropriate it for his or her own benefit.[8] Without the ability to appropriate the returns from one's property, few people in any community are likely to invest in specialization, or technological advance, or even a hard day's work. To generate these types of investments, communities and economies create and preserve rules of private property.[9] And as economies evolve, they must ensure that their property rights evolve as well.[10]

This connection between property rights and commerce applies with full force to the Internet. For even if electronic commerce fundamentally transforms the nature of business, it does not eliminate business's basic need for an infrastructure that clarifies ownership and allows owners to reap the economic rewards of their possessions. On the Internet, however, there is only a limited system of online property rights, and a more commonly accepted notion that "what is yours is mine."[11] This norm of sharing was eminently reasonable in the early days of the Net, when its purpose lay in facilitating communication among researchers. It is much less reasonable as a norm for commercial activity. In fact, it simply will not work, since few entrepreneurs have a long-term interest in sharing the profits from their product. They may want to advertise their product on the Net, they may even want to sell it directly on the Net, but they also want to make money from it—to appropriate the returns of ownership and recoup the costs of investment and innovation. So long as all information on the Net is treated as common property, this cannot be done.

To understand the extent of the problem, consider three industries poised on the Internet's cutting edge: software, publishing, and financial services.[12] In each of these the product being sold is essentially information. The producers earn their profits from the sale of intangible goods—text and ideas. On the Internet, these goods can be disseminated and reproduced at extremely low costs. This presumably gives the author of the text or the originator of the ideas new ways of distributing their work. It also potentially denies them the proceeds from this work. Once information is transmitted into the vast and anonymous realm of cyberspace, it can be endlessly copied and altered—for free, and without detection. That is why the Internet is such an exciting development for people who want to access information. That is also why it creates problems for firms in the business of selling information. Few firms that create property want to leave this property untended and unprotected in an accessible public space. Yet this is precisely the situation that faces information-based firms as they consider the move toward electronic commerce.

There is, of course, a fairly obvious way to solve such problems of property rights. If the problem is the absence of law, then the solution may rest—and historically has often rested—with the creation of law by a central government.[13] In cyberspace, that law would come, most probably, from an extension of existing copyright law. Since copyright law deals already with intangible products such as ideas and expressions, and since it provides for the commercialization of intellectual property, its extension into cyberspace would seem to make a great deal of sense. By guaranteeing the owners of intellectual property that their information and ideas remained "theirs" online, copyright law should allow information-based firms to move more confidently onto the Internet.

Accordingly, lawmakers in Washington and elsewhere have recently been tinkering with the statutes of copyright law. In September 1995, a working group convened under the auspices of the White House Infrastructure Task Force recommended changes in the language of the 1976 copyright law to include transmission explicitly as a form of distribution. The working group also endorsed a "fair use" provision that would limit any noncommercial use of intellectual property that damages the legal owner of the property.

Shortly after the recommendations were published, Congress began considering bipartisan legislation to protect digital intellectual property, while the U.S. delegation to the World Intellectual Property Organization (WIPO) sought to incorporate the proposals into the organization's own, updated, treaty on copyright protection. By the end of 1996, however, both efforts had failed. The proposed bills did not get beyond congressional subcommittees in the House of Representatives or the Senate, and WIPO member states rejected U.S. efforts to dominate the treaties under consideration. In the domestic area, critics argued that the White House working group's proposals would establish a publishers' monopoly over the free flow of information, completely undermine consumers' "fair use" rights, and eliminate an individual's right to read or browse digital works.[14] Moreover, private sector actors and certain industry associations suggested that it was too early in the evolution of the Internet to impose "top–down" solutions and that their own "bottom–up" proposals would offer better consumer protection.

Similar concerns bolstered opposition arguments in the WIPO negotiations. Developing countries in Africa and Asia joined a broad coalition of private sector information technology firms, arguing that the rapidly evolving world of cyberspace was not ready for a restrictive set of intellectual property rights laws. Or as one African delegate put it, "We are not familiar with digital technologies. . . . So we don't want to do anything that might threaten our ability to benefit from new technology—particularly when we're not sure what the real impact of those changes will be."[15] In the end, at both the international and domestic levels, the efforts of the Clinton administration resulted in little more than a broad recognition that intellectual property rights protection would remain a central, yet contentious, issue. No public governance mechanisms were established.

Meanwhile, as the U.S. and other governments have struggled to deal with the ramifications of intellectual property in the digital environment, private firms have started to move directly into the rule-making business. Although firms clearly can not write the rules of intellectual property, they can establish rule-bound areas of the Internet, "virtual communities" where the rules are already upheld and enforced. In these areas, firms perform the functions that governments, for a variety of reasons, are not yet capable of providing. For a fee, or on a contractual basis, they can protect the rights of online property. Just as medieval merchants developed the customs and practices that eventually became commercial law in Europe, so have private firms and entrepreneurs begun to create the rules of their own commercial game.

IBM, for instance, recently launched an ambitious infoMarket Rights Management project, which uses a series of advanced technologies (digital watermarks, hardware systems, digital containers) to give copyright holders effective control over the dissemination of their works. While some of the technologies remain still in the testing stage, IBM has convinced a number of other leading software and hardware companies to coordinate their efforts and create interoperable standards to ensure the protection of digital intellectual property rights.[16] Other firms, like Infringatek, offer investigative services to find and punish online violations of intellectual property rights; and several organizations, such as the Business Software Alliance, the Software Publishers' Association, and the Copyright Clearance Center, have floated their own efforts to license and monitor the use of intellectual property in cyberspace.[17] While most of these initiatives were born in the United States, their collaborative efforts span national borders. While most work with at least the implicit approval of national governments, they are clearly private organizations, generating private sources of authority. And they seem likely, before long, to develop effective means for creating and even policing intellectual property rights.

MEANS OF EXCHANGE

Insofar as firms create the online rules of property, they are acting not out of a direct interest in the rules themselves, but rather from a defensive, almost instinctual, interest in preserving their property. Their concern lies, not with a general construction of property rights per se, but rather with the specific cases of their own property and their own means of financial preservation. By contrast, the second area of online rules—the rules and means of exchange—is explicitly about the rules themselves, and already it is compelling firms to venture directly into the business of making rules and creating institutions.

In most economic systems, the means of exchange is money—currency of one form or another that is widely accepted as payment for transactions. Though the form of the currency has evolved over time—from shells to gold to coin, cash, and checks—the rules and processes surrounding currency have remained largely the same. Typically currency is issued by a central government that retains a monopoly over its creation. The government deems the currency valid for all transactions and often, though not always, backs the currency with fractional reserves of gold, precious metals, or other countries' currencies. Even when the currency is not directly backed by a tangible asset, the government's management of its supply creates a value based on confidence (that the government will always accept it as a store of value) and scarcity (that there is never quite enough to go around).

In contrast to the rules of property, which must change to meet the demands of electronic commerce, these existing rules of money could probably function quite well as a means of conducting electronic exchange. There is nothing intrinsic about electronic commerce that forces the existing means of exchange to change, no technical obstacles to routing and recording even nontraditional transactions through this well-established route, no new demand for financial oversight or regulation. Instead, the means of exchange are changing because of the vast financial opportunities that this change appears to present.

The source of this opportunity lies again with the instantaneous and nonphysical nature of electronic transactions. If electronic purchases become commonplace, they are likely to include such minute transactions, dubbed "micropurchases," as buying an article from the *Atlantic Monthly* or browsing through three minutes of the *New York Times*. The cost of processing these services through the traditional route would overwhelm the price of the service itself; for small online entrepreneurs, this cost could even doom the business from the start. If payment for an exchange can be made electronically and instantly, however, then the cost of transacting can be reduced dramatically, allowing commerce to flourish online. As an added benefit, electronic exchange could function essentially like cash, allowing both buyer and seller to maintain their anonymity. Neither anonymity nor speed are critical to exchange, of course, and electronic commerce might well succeed even if transactions remained slow and personal and cumbersome. But because the real attraction of the Internet lies in its capacity to reduce these costs of transaction, firms and entrepreneurs are currently scrambling to create the electronic means of exchange that would allow electronic commerce to reach its fastest, cheapest, and most anonymous potential.

Technologically, the creation of electronic money rests with the issuance of an anonymous electronic note. An institution—a bank or other service provider—sells electronic money to its customers, coding the e-cash onto a wallet-sized card or transmitting it directly to another online merchant. It debits the amount of the e-money, plus a small transaction fee, from the customer's old-fashioned account. Critical to the process are three aspects: (1) that the electronic transfers remain anonymous; (2) that they remain secure; and (3) that the transaction fees remain minimal. In the past, similar requirements were met by agencies of a central government. Governments printed the currency, allowed it to circulate anonymously, punished those who stole or copied it, and covered their expenses through taxes. On the Internet, however, there is no central authority to establish the means of exchange. There is also little interest on the part of national governments, since e-cash raises a host of troubling questions for governments and their law enforcement agencies. How, for instance, will e-cash expand the possibilities of tax evasion and money laundering? And how will governments be able to track the assets of individuals or the trading balances of states? If e-cash proliferates, it is likely to allow many aspects of economic activity to escape the scrutiny of government agencies. And thus government agencies have little incentive to play any role in its creation.

For private firms, by contrast, the incentives are vast. First, there is the simple cost-cutting potential of electronic payment. Many firms, and particularly banks, have a considerable interest in cutting the costs of intermediate transactions and moving directly to electronic payment systems. Several institutions, such as Citibank and Wells Fargo, already employ proprietary software systems that allow customers to do their banking online. As banks and other financial systems increasingly compete on the basis of transactions, rather than relations, these payment systems will become critical to their success.

The real prize, though, will come from pushing electronic payment out of proprietary networks and into the broader reaches of cyberspace. Eventually, the value of e-cash, like the value of any currency, will be determined by the market's demand for it. To increase demand, the currency must be widely accepted. In the past, governments ensured this acceptance simply by proclaiming their currency "legal tender." In the future, the game will be inherently more competitive. Firms that establish the most accessible and secure means of exchange will capture the market of all those seeking to conduct electronic transactions beyond their internal border. And success in this game will breed further success, since the acceptability of a currency increases its attractiveness to other users.

Not surprisingly, then, the race to develop the means of electronic exchange has already become one of the most spirited competitions in cyberspace. To a large extent, it is a race of technology: winning will entail the refinement of encryption algorithms and the development of secure "electronic wallets." The race, however, is also about rules and norms, since technology alone cannot support a full-fledged system of electronic exchange. If payment systems are ever to proliferate along the Internet, they will require some trusted entity to oversee and regulate their use. The problem is not the widely publicized threat of credit card theft. Rather, it is the confidence with which any major financial institution can ever hope to approach the Internet. Even with major leaps in encryption technology, few institutions are liable to feel sufficiently comfortable with even the most secure electronic payment system to entrust it with millions or billions of dollars worth of transactions. Performing these transactions in their own internal networks is a far cry from allowing them to occur across the blatantly public spaces of the Internet. If these firms are ever to move onto the broader reaches of the Net, they will need some means of recourse. They will need, at a minimum, to know that some identifiable and credible entity is backing the value of their money and preventing widespread fraud and abuse. Historically, these tasks have fallen to governments. On the Internet, by contrast, private firms have already begun to perform the equivalent functions. And to perform these functions fully, they have also had to bundle their means of exchange with a third and linked set of rules: rules of security and enforcement.

SECURITY AND ENFORCEMENT

Before any e-cash changes hands, and indeed before any real financial transactions occur online, the parties to the exchange must have confidence that their transaction is secure. They must know (1) that the buyer or seller is really who they claim to be (authentication); (2) that the information being exchanged is not stolen en route or altered (message integrity); and (3) that the payment being offered is real. Without this security, exchange once again will falter.

Ensuring the security of property and transactions is an age-old problem, one that has historically been solved by the central and coercive powers of the state. With the advent of modern mail delivery, for instance, most governments issued strict regulations against mail fraud and tampering and enforced these regulations by making the delivery of mail a state monopoly. Similarly, most national telephone systems remained under the control of the state, or at least in the hands of a few regulated monopoly carriers. While these monopolies clearly created commercial problems of their own, they effectively controlled the security problem, especially when combined with prohibitions against private interventions (tampering or interception) and allowances for government oversight (wiretapping those suspected of criminal activity). In most of the developed world, consumers generally feel confident about the security of information transmitted by either mail or phone.

On the Internet, by contrast, there is no such security. Instead, as information travels through the complex network of networks, it passes through many different computers and sorters, creating many possible points and paths of interception. Although laws like the Electronic Communications Privacy Act of 1986 specifically forbid eavesdropping on electronic transmissions, such laws are extraordinarily difficult to enforce: no policing agency controls the multiple points of access. This basic lack of control should theoretically pose a major impediment to the growth of electronic commerce.[18] A second security problem, that of information integrity, is also particularly sensitive. Once information is put online, the creators of this information can do little to ensure that it will not be electronically altered. Thus, hospitals worry about patient records being changed and authors and publishers are concerned that their views might be misrepresented. Moreover, just as nature of the Internet makes it difficult to detect the theft of information, it also makes it virtually impossible to trace alterations or tampering, especially since anyone can operate online under a false name—recall the famous New Yorker cartoon, where a dog sitting at the keyboard turns to his canine companion and remarks, "On the Internet, nobody knows you're a dog." As the Internet grows, problems of security seem destined to mount: in 1990, the federally funded Computer Emergency Response Team (CERT) reported 130 break-ins on the Internet. That number grew to 1,300 in 1993 and 2,300 in 1994.[19]

Usually break-ins, like tampering, fraud, and theft, are considered the purview of government agencies: if someone breaks into your house or taps your phone line, you call the police. On the Internet, though, governments have not yet defined precisely what constitutes crime, nor have they established the institutions to trace or apprehend the criminals. Despite several attempts to ban online pornography, for instance, Congress has not yet found any effective means for enforcing these bans, or even for detecting violations. The most ambitious bill to emerge so far, the ill-fated Communications Decency Act of 1996 (CDA), was roundly criticized, not only as unconstitutional, but as utterly unenforceable.[20] As one observer wrote, "Enforcing a local smut ordinance on the unbounded Internet . . . is akin to ordering dandelions to quit floating their spore. How do you control a decentralized network of more than 50,000 interconnected networks? How do you censor information when it flows down infinite paths among 30 million computers?"[21] In June of 1997, the Supreme Court struck down the CDA, and explicitly rejected any future efforts to impose broadcast-style content regulation on the Net.[22] Meanwhile U.S. courts, which are just beginning to wrestle with the definition of online service, have rendered completely contradictory decisions about the responsibilities of servers, and thus about the types of activity for which they can even be held accountable.[23] Elsewhere, national governments continue to debate the extent and feasibility of their own policy options. Only China and Singapore have actively tried to control those bits of cyberspace that waft across their borders—and many observers are skeptical about these countries' long-term ability to fully monitor and enforce their laws, even if they effectively barricade their national systems against the mass of Internet communication.

The most spectacular government failure to date, however, has been the Clipper chip. Clipper is a computer chip that uses a high-level security algorithm from the National Security Agency (NSA) to encrypt digital data. The original NSA proposal, endorsed by the White House in February 1994, was to embed a Clipper chip in all telephones and computers used in the United States. Because the government would keep a decryption key under its own control, it could eavesdrop as appropriate on all electronic transmissions.

Although the White House pledged that the Clipper key could only be used with a warrant, making it just a high-tech version of standard wiretapping, the Internet community resoundingly denounced the proposal. Civil libertarians and old-time hackers lobbied vehemently against what they saw as an unconstitutional invasion of privacy and ban of free speech. Along with Whitfield Dixie, the inventor of public key cryptography, they argued (along similar lines as the National Rifle Association) that government limits on privacy would serve only to aid real criminals. Or as one cryptographer noted, "If privacy is outlawed, only outlaws will have privacy."[24]

Under a barrage of criticism, the White House eventually retreated, conceding that more public debate would be necessary before bringing Clipper to a congressional vote. Reportedly, the NSA continues to work on encryption systems with limited backdoor access,[25] and the Clinton administration has reintroduced legislation to develop a "key management infrastructure for public key-based encryption."[26] But Clipper, for the moment, is gone. And the administration's most recent bill, the Electronic Data Security Act of 1997, is considered by most industry and policy analysts as, effectively, "dead on arrival."[27]

Meanwhile, private firms and consortia have been rushing to create their own enforcement mechanisms. The first and most obvious commercial opportunity lies with the technologies of electronic security. Theoretically, cutting-edge technologies such as encryption and firewalls can solve security problems by fully protecting online transmissions. Encryption scrambles electronic signals and verifies access to communications with mathematically coded "digital signatures." Firewalls establish physical filters between networks. Neither technology has yet been completely perfected. Yet most industry insiders believe that they soon will be powerful enough to guarantee transaction security.[28] And the firms that reach perfection first are likely to generate a windfall of enthusiasm and profits. Currently, the leader in digital-security software is RSA Data Security. An early pioneer in the field of encryption, RSA has already licensed its encryption algorithms to major Net players such as IBM, Netscape, and Open Market. Many other companies, though, such as Verisign and Microsoft, have also joined the race.

Simultaneously, there is another commercial race underway in cyberspace, a race less obvious in some respects but ultimately more important. The development of secure technologies is absolutely critical to the expansion of Internet activity. But it is not sufficient. In order to truly facilitate the expansion of electronic commerce, even the most sophisticated technologies will have to be embedded in broader, secure networks. They will have to be distributed over a wide enough space to ensure that their standards become the norm—or at least sufficiently prevalent so that two parties to a transaction can reasonably expect to communicate with one another and employ similar means of interaction.[29] By definition, security (and exchange) cannot operate in a vacuum. On the vast and twisted pathways of the Internet, individual security precautions have only a limited value. Value lies, instead, in a wider network of users. Within the boundaries of the network, participants can reap the benefits of a shared standard, and of the more all-encompassing security it brings. Thus, to a considerable extent, the race to create online security mechanisms has been, and is likely to remain, a cooperative effort. By joining forces and establishing common protocols, all participants to the protocol are likely to benefit.

Consider, for example, the recently created Secure Electronic Transaction (SET) protocol, a joint effort by Visa and Mastercard to develop a structure that will enable bankcard transactions to be conducted easily and securely across the Internet. Like IBM with its intellectual property rights management, and RSA with its encryption protocols, Visa and Mastercard also clearly recognize the value of scale and standards, both of which are boosted by interfirm cooperation. Accordingly, the two credit card giants have assiduously tried to bring other industry players into their shared protocol: GTE, IBM, Netscape, Terisa, and Verisign, among others, have all joined the project and provided advice and assistance.[30] In the process, they have increased the value of the standard to each of the firms involved. They have also created a powerful instance of private cooperation and governance: the standard they set becomes a rule, and the means for creating security without the direct intervention of the state.

CONCLUSIONS

The vision described in this chapter is not necessarily a popular one. It irks, simultaneously, both those who advocate a free and unregulated Internet and those who would like governments to assume a greater role in cyberspace. It puts private firms smack on the edge of the new frontier, armed with the equipment to develop, colonize, and perhaps exploit the territories they discover. Why should cyberspace, this bold, exciting, and inherently international new space, lend itself to this sort of development? Why should we find private authorities and private modes of governance cropping up along the Internet?

The answer is because, as regime theorists and institutional economists have long argued, rules matter. Rules define the terms of interaction, and fix the stability and predictability that permit interaction to occur. Without rules, or norms, or standards, there can be only anarchy.

On the Internet, some degree of anarchy is acceptable, even desirable. In fact, many users came to cyberspace precisely because of its anarchy: its anonymous, uncensored, secretive lack of rules. Yet as the Internet becomes increasingly a mass media, anarchy can no longer suffice. Some users will still want chaos. But others would no doubt prefer to exchange the adventure of cyberspace for a more regulated and predictable environment.

If this environment could be physically confined within national borders, governments might easily seize the regulatory initiative, ruling the Internet in line with their own legislative traditions and perceived national interests. If international organizations were nimbler and more powerful, they might be able to set transnational laws for cyberspace, preventing violations from sneaking in through renegade countries. Or if governments could agree, quickly, on cross-border rules and standards they might be able to preempt private efforts. But none of these conditions applies. International organizations lack the power to police cyberspace; national governments lack the authority; and the slow pace of interstate agreement is no match for the rapid-fire rate of technological change. If rules are to emerge along the Internet, private entities will have to create them.

These private entities need not be just commercial firms. University consortia and library groups, for example, have long coordinated their Internet usage, developing sophisticated protocols and standards of behavior. So have industry associations such as the Electronic Frontier Foundation and the Business Software Alliance, as well as looser groupings such as the Cyberspace Law Institute, and the influential Internet Engineering Task Force.[31] Even systems operators ("sysops"), individual users who assume responsibility for managing bulletin boards, are in effect a source of private governance. They are making rules, implementing them, and enforcing them. This is considerably more than most national governments can yet do in cyberspace.

In the abstract, these private, electronic authorities are neither good nor bad; like hegemonies, they can be benevolent as well as despotic. They can be exclusive and inaccessible, or open to all comers. They can provide their services for free, extending a largesse that comes only with size, or they can use their heft to control information and extort rents. At this point in their evolution, it is simply too early to tell.

What is evident, though, is that private entities will play an ever-increasing role in the development and management of electronic interaction. They will set the rules and standards for discourse, intermediate transactions, and serve as checkpoints for buyers and sellers. They will control, not the Internet of course, but their own growing corners of commerce and communication. They will assume quasi-governmental functions in many instances, regulating activity in their particular spheres through a combination of formal and informal rules, administrative and technical means.

What gets lost in this vision of private governance, however, are governments. Even if private authorities turn out to be wholly benevolent in cyberspace, even if they are inclusive and fair and reasonably priced, they are still undeniably private. And any extension of their power signals a corresponding decrease in the regulatory and legislative reach of national governments. This may be a perfectly acceptable departure, a reasoned response to the exigencies of cyberspace. The recent chairman of the U.S. Federal Communications Commission, Reed Hundt, for example, made explicit his desire not to propose any rules for the Information Highway, preferring to let market forces determine by themselves the rules of the road. His sentiments were subsequently reflected in the Clinton administration's rather remarkable "Framework for Global Electronic Commerce," a policy paper issued in the summer of 1997 that explicitly recognized, and endorsed, market-driven standards and private sector efforts to develop the rules of Internet commerce. Given the government's natural limits in cyberspace, such a hands-off policy is almost certainly a wise one. But it does represent a significant departure, not just for theorists of international relations, but also for policymakers and those who bear the brunt of their decisions. We do not know much yet about either cyberspace or private authorities. But in cyberspace, as elsewhere, one truth is likely to apply: power lies with those who make the rules.

NOTES

I would like to thank Elizabeth Stein, Lane LaMure, and Paul Barese for valuable research assistance on earlier drafts of this paper. Support for the research was generously provided by the Division of Research, Harvard Business School. An earlier and more commercially focused version of this paper, co-authored with Jeffrey J. Bussgang, appeared in the *Harvard Business Review*, May–June 1996.

1. Recent disputes between the United States and China are among the most public displays of this disagreement. See for instance, "China-U.S. Intellectual Property Rights," *East Asian Executive Reports* 18.4 (April 15, 1996): 4. See also the Sell chapter in this volume.

2. The NSF's acceptable-use policy statement read in part: "NSFNET Backbone Services are provided to support open-research and education in and among U.S. research and instructional institutions, plus research arms of for-profit firms when engaged in open scholarly communication and research. *Use for other purposes is not acceptable.*" Cited in Michael-Sullivan Trainor, *Detour: The Truth about the Information Superhighway* (San Mateo: IDG Books, 1995), p. 175. Emphasis added.

3. *Time*, Special Issue: "Welcome to Cyberspace," Spring 1995, p. 9; Sullivan-Trainor, "Detour," p. 175.

4. pvs2000.com/pvscontent/istats.htm May 1997

5. This can be represented more formally as the familiar observation that cooperation is more easily achieved when interaction is iterated over time.

6. This evolution from one set of rules to another is similar to that described in the Porter chapter in this volume.

7. In general, states have focused on rules that touch upon areas deemed closest to their own national interest. Thus, Vietnam and Saudi Arabia each permit only a single government-controlled gateway for Internet service; Germany has blocked sites that violate national obscenity laws; and the United States has repeatedly attempted to block the export of powerful encryption technologies. See Karen Sorenson, "Silencing the Net: The Threat to Freedom of Expression," *Human Rights Watch*, http://itn.rdg.ac.uk/misc/mailing_lists/rre00000112.htm; and Steward A. Baker and Michael D. Hintze, "United States Government Policy on Encryption Technology," *Computer and Telecommunications Law Review*, June 1997, 109–112.

8. Marxists, of course, would insist that the communal state represents the natural and desirable condition of economic organization. With a handful of exceptions, though, it is exceedingly difficult in the 1990s to find evidence of the long-term viability of an economic system based on communal rights.

9. The argument of this section draws extensively on the work and writings of Douglass C. North. See in particular, North, *Structure and Change in Economic History* (New York: W.W. Norton, 1981); and North and Robert P. Thomas, *The Rise of the Western World: A New Economic History* (Cambridge: Cambridge University Press, 1973). See also William H. Riker and Itai Sened, "A Political Theory of the Origins of Property Rights: Airport Slots," *American Journal of Political Science* 35 (November 1991): 951–69.

10. In this context, it is interesting to note that at every major junction in the evolution of capitalism, the transformation of commerce has coincided with and been facilitated by a change in the structure of property rights and the incentives they create. Hunters and gatherers became farmers once they developed the means to protect "their" lands; feudal lords turned to commerce once they were allowed to own and bequeath property; and oceanic exploration flourished once the kings of Europe offered bounties for discovery and cleared the seas of pirates. Where property rights fail to develop, economic growth stagnates, as is

the case in the less-developed world. Insufficient property rights can also explain the demise of Soviet-style commerce, where property rights were clear (all in the hands of "the people"), but did not establish the incentives necessary to fuel economic growth. What allowed the system to grow, by contrast, was a rigid structure of state-controlled disincentives (coercion). Once the coercive apparatus declined, so too did any substantial economic activity.

11. Anne Wells Branscomb, *Who Owns Information?* (New York: Basic Books, 1994), p. 6.

12. On financial services in particular, see the Sinclair chapter in this volume.

13. See Douglass C. North, *Institutions, Institutional Change, and Economic Performance* (Cambridge: Cambridge University Press, 1990); Riker and Sened, "Origins of Property Rights." For an examination of various other means for governing property rights, see John L. Campbell, J. Rogers Hollingsworth, and Leon N. Lindberg, *Governance of the American Economy* (Cambridge: Cambridge University Press, 1991).

14. To browse a document, a computer must make a temporary copy in its random access memory. By defining an unlicensed, temporary digital reproduction as a copyright infringement, the U.S. working group's report technically banned browsing. See Pamela Samuelson, "The Copyright Grab," *Wired*, January 1996, 134–91; and Samuelson, "Big Media Bite Back," *Wired*, March 1997, 61–184.

15. Quoted in John Browning, "Africa 1, Hollywood 0," *Wired*, March 1997, 186.

16. See Richard J. Linn Jr., "Using Technology to Manage Intellectual Property," in Brian Kahin and Kate Arms, eds., *Proceedings: Forum on Technology-Based Intellectual Property Management* (Annapolis, Md.: Interactive Media Association, 1996); and Mark Stefik, "Trusted Systems," *Scientific American*, March 1997.

17. See Linn, "Using Technology," p. 9.

18. See for instance "Internet Security," *Internet World*, February 1995, p. 32.

19. *Technology Review*, April 1995, p. 33.

20. The act, which was approved by the Senate in June 1995, outlawed the use of "telecommunications facilities" to transmit any obscene information or image, or any indecent information or image to a person under 18.

21. Joshua Quitter, "Vice Raid on the Net," *Time*, April 3, 1995.

22. See Mike Godwin, "Free Speech 1, Censorship 0," *Wired*, September 1997, p. 94.

23. In two recent high-profile decisions, one court held that servers are publishers and therefore responsible for the content they deliver, while the other ruled that servers are merely passive conduits for information and thus retain no liability or responsibility. See Constance Johnson, "Courts Struggle with Definition of Cyberspace," *Wall Street Journal*, July 27, 1995, p. B1.

24. Philip R. Zimmermann, *PGP(tm) [Pretty Good Privacy] User's Guide*, Volume 1: Essential Topics, Revised October 11, 1994, available at web.mit.edu/network/pgp.html. Zimmermann, the author of PGP, an encryp-

tion program which is distributed as freeware, has been prominent in the campaign to which this paragraph refers.

25. See for instance, "It's Alive: Clipper's Still Kicking," *Internet World*," February 1995, p. 62.

26. Baker and Hintze, "Policy in Encryption Technology," p. 112.

27. Ibid.

28. See David Klein, "How Far Away Is Real Web Commerce?" *Interactive Age*, March 13, 1995, p. 14; and "Beyond the Firewall," *Internet World*, February 1995, p. 48.

29. See Kevin Kelly, "New Rules for the New Economy," *Wired*, September 1997, pp. 140–97.

30. Linn, "Using Technology," p. 12.

31. For more on the IETF, see Walter S. Baer, "Will the Global Information Infrastructure Need Transnational (or Any) Governance?" in Brian Kahin and Ernest J. Wilson III, eds., *National Information Infrastructure Initiatives* (Cambridge: MIT Press, 1997), p. 542.

CHAPTER 3

Private and Public Management of International Mineral Markets

Michael C. Webb

International political economy typically makes a sharp distinction between public and private actors and their functions. Studies of international cooperation and regimes generally focus on relations among governments alone. If private actors such as transnational corporations (TNCs) are seen at all, it is usually as merely a source of influence on government policies and intergovernmental agreements. Concepts such as "regulation" and "management" typically are applied only to the actions of governments and intergovernmental regimes.

This chapter argues that the conventional association of "management" and "regulation" with public actors—governments—is inadequate. Intergovernmental regimes are not the only social institutions capable of managing and regulating international commerce. Nongovernmental actors—especially TNCs—are also capable of collaborating transnationally to achieve goals typically associated with governments. This chapter shows that collective self-rule by TNCs can be an important influence on economic outcomes and the distribution of gains from international commerce. I focus on the wide range of private, public, and mixed public-private mechanisms that have been developed by mineral-producing firms, metal traders, and governments of producing and consuming countries to avoid atomistic competition in international mineral markets. I show that private, public, and mixed mechanisms can all be used to achieve similar purposes, especially market stabilization and price support. This is clearly so in cases such as aluminum, where the collapse of private management (in the form of tacit oligopolistic collusion) led directly to intergovernmental market management to stabilize the market and recreate conditions favorable to private market management. This example and others also show, however, that there are important limits to self-management by private actors, especially when interfirm cooperation must extend across national, ideological, and developmental boundaries to be effective.

As emphasized in the introduction to this volume, the importance of private self-management means that the focus in the literature solely on inter*governmental* cooperation and conflict often misses important social institutions that influence market outcomes. It may also lead to misunderstanding the sources of intergovernmental cooperation, by neglecting its relationship to transnational cooperation among private actors. The concept of regime needs to be broadened to include social institutions created by nongovernment actors that generate transnational norms and rules that guide behavior by private actors. If one defines regimes as "sets of implicit or explicit principles, norms, rules and decision-making procedures around which actors' expectations converge in a given issue area,"[1] it is clear that such expectations may be shared among nonstate actors and between nonstate and state actors, as well as among state actors alone. Market actors may be regulated by interstate regimes, but as this chapter shows, there may also be collective self-rule by market actors alone. Except in the case of illegal cartels, this collective self-rule typically operates with the tacit acceptance of states, but there may also be explicit state support for mechanisms of private self-management.

While public and private forms of market management can sometimes serve as substitutes for each other, some fundamental differences are apparent in the area of international mineral markets. Intergovernmental market management draws on the legitimate authority that national governments have to develop rules for private actors in the marketplace, and on the legal enforcement mechanisms at governments' disposal. Private management lacks such a formal basis for authority and legitimacy. Private international mineral regimes and collaborative public-private initiatives like study groups exercise influence on market behavior primarily by means of tacit understandings among producers—that is, by means of intersubjective norms. As Friedrich Kratochwil and John Ruggie have argued, *convergent expectations*—rather than any particular institutional structure—provide the constitutive basis of regimes."[2] Thus, the fact that private self-management by TNCs usually lacks a formal institutional framework (except in the case of private self-management backed by mixed private-public institutions like study groups) does not invalidate the description of such cooperation as a regime, so long as the convergent expecations have a discernable impact on actor behavior. Furthermore, as the fragility of intergovernmental regimes in the area of commodity market management suggests, formal institutions are not necessarily more influential. Informal shared norms may well be more resilient in the face of changing market conditions than formal interstate regimes precisely because of their greater flexibility."[3] On the other hand, antitrust laws generally prevent private actors from negotiating formal market-management agreements, and the difficulty of negotiating specific obligations has undermined purely private cooperation in some cases (in some of these, states have stepped in to provide legitimacy for more formal private agreements, e.g., regarding aluminum).

The key norm that underlies collective self-management of markets by mineral TNCs is the idea that competition for market share should be restrained in order to support prices and profits. Recent public-private institutions such as study groups appear to be designed to promote such norms, and the involvement of governments provides the norms with a stronger basis in legitimate public authority. Regime theory helps to illuminate the main functions of these bodies. They collect, analyze, and disseminate information about market trends that can alter the behavior of individual producers. Many participants hope that improved information will discourage overproduction and the development of excess capacity. These bodies also help to socialize new market entrants into the behavioral norm of self-restraint in the pursuit of market share. This is especially important with the growth of state-owned mining firms in developing countries since the 1970s (a trend that is being reversed) and, since 1990, the growth of exports from producers in the former Soviet Union, who often are subject neither to a profit constraint nor to constraints from central planners.

Of course, often underlying this socialization process are implicit or explicit threats of loss of access to major markets in the United States or the European Union. If producers in question do not conform to oligopolistic norms of self-restraint, they face the threat of antidumping and countervailing-duty trade sanctions in importing, producing countries. Private producing firms have no legitimate authority to discipline other producers who violate these norms. It is also difficult for private firms to impose "market discipline" on state-owned producers because the profit constraint facing private producers limits their ability to prevail in price wars with producers that have access to state subsidies. But governments retain the prerogative to enforce those norms if domestic firms suffer when the norms are violated.

Thus, while governments may delegate managerial authority to private transnational actors by default (as I argue in the conclusions), in the cases considered in this chapter private regimes lack the authority and power to enforce their own norms. They must rely instead on developing shared understandings of self-interest that encourage all producers to behave as responsible oligopolists. The key mechanism here is learning processes from repeated interactions in international markets (see the introductory chapter to this volume); advice from leading firms, recognized market authorities, and study groups encourage firms that do not practice self-restraint to learn the lesson that they (and their competitors) will be better off if they act in accordance with the norm of oligopolistic self-restraint. But the status of market "authorities" is always tenuous. As discussed in the introductory chapter, empirical criteria for the identification of private authority include: (1) that those subject to private actors' rules must accept them as legitimate; (2) there should be a high degree of compliance; and (3) private sector authorities must be explicitly or implicitly empowered by governments with the right to make decisions (see p. 18). In this chapter, we will see that while these conditions have held for extended periods in a number of mineral markets, more often they have not. Interestingly, the third condition—implicit or explicit delegation of authority by governments—has often held in part, in the sense that western governments have tolerated and encouraged collective market management by private mining TNCs, although nonwestern governments have often disgreed. Thus, this chapter is as much about attempts to establish private authority as it is about the exercise of that authority (though note that private regimes, in the sense of clear shared expectations that shape actor behavior, can exist in the absence of clearly recognizable authority relations).

I should also note the relationship between these private regimes and the broader political and ideological environment in which they operate. The private and public-private regimes examined in this paper also help to spread western liberal norms about what is appropriately within the scope of the public sphere and what is private. The norms just discussed are in sharp contrast to the norms that developing countries sought to promote in the 1970s, which would have subordinated market competition among private producers to intergovernmental agreements based on equity considerations as well as market pressures. The socialization dynamic identified earlier rejects the international equity norms that developing countries had promoted in the 1970s in favor of a norm of responsible (i.e., oligopolistically self-restrained) private firms acting solely under a profit constraint. The increasing emphasis on private self-management of markets therefore both reflects the neoliberal shift in dominant transnational ideologies in the 1980s and 1990s, and further reinforces that shift.

This chapter makes these arguments through an examination of attempts to manage international markets for six minerals and metals: bauxite and aluminum, copper, lead and zinc, and nickel. These are among the most important nonferrous, nonenergy minerals in international trade. I examine private, public, and mixed private-public efforts to manage international markets for these minerals and metals in three historical periods, each characterized by a different pattern; the 1950s and 1960s, the 1970s, and the 1980s and 1990s. Before looking at these case studies, I examine alternative mechanisms for managing markets.

ALTERNATIVE MECHANISMS FOR MANAGING MARKETS

The most important problems in international mineral markets addressed through international market management are price instability and low prices. Price instability imposes costly burdens of adjustment on producers and consumers, and on both governments and firms. While all producers dislike sharp downward movements in prices, many also dislike sharp upward movements that encourage consumers to search for substitutes and stimulate excess investment in new production, thereby increasing supply and depressing prices in the long run. While consumers generally prefer lower prices, many also recognize that sharp declines can be harmful if they lead to underinvestment in production and thereby threaten security of supply in the long term. Consumers' interest in low prices is also tempered by the generally low contribution that raw-material input prices make to the total price of finished goods. Thus, "for political leaders in advanced importing states, the basic objective of raw materials policy is to avoid the unexpected, not to maximize economic welfare through perfect competition."[4] These considerations mean that there is a public interest in market stabilization that goes beyond the private interests of specific producing and consuming firms.

Of course, public and private interests in stabilization do not eliminate differences over appropriate levels around which to stabilize prices. Even here, however, differences between producers and consumers are not necessarily that great, assuming that both types of actors have a long-term interest in the market. Forward-looking producers seek prices that are above competitive market levels, but not so high as to attract new entry or encourage consumers to switch to substitutes. Oligopoly theory thus suggests that oligopolistic industries will set prices at levels above competitive market prices, but below monopoly prices. Similarly, consumers are often tolerant of prices above the competitive level if these are stable, since consumers' interest in price stability is strong enough to discourage the pursuit of purely competitive price levels. Indeed, the historical record suggests that differences between producers and consumers often are not as significant an obstacle to price stabilization as are differences among producers, whose costs of production and time horizons vary significantly.

North-South polemics have often posed the issue of market management in either-or terms; either free markets, or markets managed by governments on behalf of Southern countries. Stabilization efforts are typically associated with government intervention. But both in theory and in practice, stabilization also can be pursued by private actors, individually or in conjunction with other private actors, or by private actors collaborating with governments. Furthermore, I will argue, management efforts often resemble international regimes, even when their "members" are private corporations rather than states—that is, they can constitute private regimes, even though the strength of those private regimes varies (as does that of interstate regimes). In such cases, private arrangements can be a substitute for the regulatory functions usually associated with the state (see the introductory chapter to this volume). In the following discussion of possible managerial forms, I will emphasize the prescriptions and proscriptions for actor behavior embodied in the regime. These may take the forms of formal rules or informal "social institutions around which expectations converge in international issue areas."[5] I will begin by distinguishing between "public" forms of market management (i.e., those involving governments) and "private" forms of management (i.e., those involving private actors), and then will consider mixed public-private forms of collaboration to manage mineral markets.

Public Forms of Market Management

Most discussions of international mineral regimes have focused on the possibilities for producer cartels and producer-consumer international commodity agreements (ICAs). A cartel attempts to stabilize or support prices by reaching agreement among producers to limit production or exports or both, or by collectively financing the purchase of stocks to keep them off the market. An ICA may use the same mechanisms, but attempts to stabilize prices at a level acceptable to the governments of producing and consuming countries. Intergovernmental market management in either form is difficult to implement. Producers face serious international and internal problems in reaching and implementing agreements to serve their collective interests in higher prices.[6] ICAs also face some nearly insurmountable obstacles, including the same differences among producers that impede cartels and the additional difficulty of reaching agreement on a price level acceptable to consumers as well as producers.[7] The formal character of some intergovernmental cartels and ICAs may create the appearance of a strong regime, but formal agreements often face severe difficulty adapting to changing market conditions.[8]

Market management by governments could also take the form of regulation of international commodity exchanges. Rather than attempting to directly affect market prices, governments could regulate the trading of commodities among individual buyers and sellers. This approach to market stabilization has been attractive to those Northern governments that disdain direct intervention yet recognize that to be efficient, markets must operate within an appropriate legal framework. Most of the minerals considered in this study are traded on the London Metal Exchange (LME). Government regulation might include measures to enhance market transparency and prevent insider price manipulation. Alternatively, governments might seek to manage markets in a fashion overtly intended to serve public interests other than market efficiency, as with United Nations Conference on Trade and Development (UNCTAD) proposals for developing country representation on the governing board of the LME.[9]

Market management efforts by governments do have an advantage over purely private management efforts in the area of enforceability. Governments have the right to make and enforce rules for private actors within their jurisdiction, including rules agreed through intergovernmental negotiation (thought enforcement is not always effective). In the case of an intergovernmental cartel or ICA, participating governments are expected to ensure that domestic producers and exporters do not exceed their production or export quotas, and in some cases to restrict imports from nonparticipating countries. Private actors lack these legal rights and powers.

Private Forms of Market Management

Prices can also be stabilized and supported, and commodity exchanges regulated, by the actions of agents involved in the production, consumption, and trade of particular minerals. While the focus here is on private actors, in the sense of nongovernmental actors pursuing their private interests (rather than the public interests governments are expected to pursue), some of these actors may be state owned.

Cartels. Private producers might try to raise and stabilize prices by forming a cartel. While this was common in the first half of this century (see Tony Porter's chapter in this volume), a formal cartel is unlikely today because it would be illegal in many leading countries.[10]

Tacit oligopolistic collusion. A much more important form of transnational market management, in both theory and practice, is what industrial organization economists call tacit oligopolistic collusion. This occurs when oligopolistic firms recognize their shared interest in keeping prices above the competitive level, and are able to work out methods to avoid price-cutting without formal agreements. The pricing problem facing oligopolists can be modeled as a Prisoners' Dilemma, which is also the game theory model most commonly used to understand international cooperation among states. Oligopolists will each be better off if they cooperate with each other to avoid cutting prices to the competitive level, but each faces incentives to defect from the cooperative outcome by cutting prices and expanding sales at the expense of their cooperating competitors. If producers respond rationally to these incentives, they will forfeit the opportunity to achieve higher profits and prices will settle at the competitive level. Producers thus have incentives to try to achieve the cooperative outcome even though antitrust laws prohibit them from relying on formal agreements among themselves. The concept of tacit oligopolistic collusion includes the variety of techniques that producers can use to avoid the competitive market outcome.[11]

Whether or not producers will be able tacitly to collude in maintaining prices above competitive levels depends on three types of factors: structural market conditions, agents' internal characteristics, and social institutions. The international mineral industries discussed in this paper generally exhibit structural market conditions that facilitate the emergence of tacit oligopolistic collusion. In most cases, a small number of producers account for the bulk of sales, and significant barriers to entry keep others from entering to benefit from high prices. Important factors here include the very large scale of competitive mining operations and the high capital intensity of the industry. This chapter does not examine market structures in great detail, but instead starts with the presumption that most of the mineral industries considered in this chapter meet the structural conditions for oligopoly. The second factor, agents' internal characteristics, is crucial to their ability to meet their tacit or explicit commitments to their collaborators and their ability to punish defectors.[12] I do not investigate this variable in detail, though I do note the importance of certain internal factors (especially the severity of the profit constraint, which depends on access to government subsidies) and that certain internal characteristics (especially whether the producer is privately owned or state-owned) are crucial for the emergence of the intersubjective understandings upon which tacit collusion depends.

This chapter focuses on the third type of factor, namely social institutions that influence the likelihood of tacit cooperation among firms in structurally oligopolistic industries. For tacit oligopolistic collusion to emerge, producers must develop convergent expectations (or shared expectations) about each others' behavior. Before firms will be willing to cooperate rather than defect, they must have confidence that others will not defect from those cooperative arrangements to take advantage of them. Trust is therefore crucial. What appears a first glance to be purely tacit collusion, with individual firms acting atomistically and rationally in their individual long-run self-interest, is in fact completely dependent on shared intersubjective understandings. In the absence of trust, firms that tried to keep prices above the competitive level would expose themselves to enormous risks.

Three kinds of social institutions can be important in the establishment and maintenance of tacit oligopolistic collusion. One is mechanisms for making information about prices and market trends rapidly and widely available. As oligopoly theory emphasizes (consistent with international regime theory), timely information is essential for deterring secret price cutting by firms (potential defectors) that might want to benefit from others' efforts to keep prices high[13] and for discouraging overinvestment in production, a key source of downward pressure on primary commodity prices. A second is shared behavioral norms. Collusion works best among large, privately owned firms that share clear understandings of the long-run interests of their firms and the industry. These norms of responsible producer behavior can be clearly discerned in statements by industry leaders, and focus on self-restraint in pricing and in capacity expansion. Responsible oligopolists are slow to cut prices when when demand is weak (and instead accumulate inventory or cut production), just as they avoid inflating prices when markets are tight to avoid attracting new entrants or losing consumers to substitute products.

A more specific shared behavioral norm is price leadership in producer pricing systems. In an industry with few sellers and a large number of buyers, producers may be able to maintain listed prices for their products that generally apply to all buyers. Producer prices in an oligopolistic industry can be stable if producers maintain large inventories to accommodate short-term fluctuations in demand, and if different producers avoid the temptation to undercut each other's posted prices to gain larger sales. Price leadership is a tacit coordination system "under which list price changes are normally announced by a specific firm accepted as the leader by others, who follow the leader's initiatives."[14] The price leader sends "clear signals that indicate the way toward the profit-maximizing price in good times and serve as a rallying point in depressed times." Price leadership—a social institution—thus enables oligopolistic firms to solve the key problem of coordinating their behavior without explicit (and therefore illegal) agreement.[15] Effective price leadership systems are a clear manifestation of private authority. They meet the three criteria set out in the introductory chapter of this volume; follower firms accept the legitimacy of the price leader's decisions, compliance can be high, and such systems often are tacitly accepted by government authorities.

A third kind of social institution that may facilitate the maintenance of tacit oligopolistic collusion is expert knowledge. Pronouncements on market conditions by recognized experts can provide a focal point for tacit collusion. Such market authorities may be private (e.g., widely recognized analysts with private firms) or they may be partly public (e.g., international organizations like study groups). Producers that ignore the pronouncements of acknowledged market authorities can expect to come under severe criticism from others.

Domestically, attention on institutions suspected of facilitating tacit oligopolistic collusion has focused on trade associations. Their role in disseminating price information that discourages price cutting is widely recognized, as is the possibility for persuading disruptive producers to fall into line.[16] Equivalent purely private associations at the international level are less common in the minerals industry, though some do exist (e.g., the International Primary Aluminum Institute). As we shall see below, these functions have more commonly been performed by mixed public-private institutions.

Tacit oligopolistic collusion may appear to be a relatively weak social institution in contrast to intergovernmental cartels or ICAs. It is weak in the conventional sense of strict rules that constrain behavior, but its lack of formalization may enhance its effectiveness. Formal agreements among governments or private producers are notoriously unable to cope with the underlying volatility of demand, supply, and price of minerals, and often break down when it proves impossible to renegotiate price and output levels in response to changing market conditions. Tacit oligopolistic collusion is much less rigid, which makes it appear weaker in the short run but also makes it more resilient in the long run.

Mineral exchanges and futures markets. When minerals are traded on an international exchange like the London Metal Exchange (LME), individual producers and consumers can stabilize their own revenues or costs by hedging—that is, by buying and selling futures and options—even if cash prices are volatile. Hedging on futures markets is often advocated by opponents of direct government intervention, including many western economists and governments, as a strategy for dealing with price instability. However, it is a costly strategy and is risky, requiring a high degree of technical sophistication to use effectively.[17]

Supporters argue that markets like the LME are efficient (because they react instantly to information) and that speculation can be stabilizing (as it must be if all speculators are to consistently earn profits). However, such an outcome depends on the mechanisms that exist to regulate and supervise the market. Regulation and supervision are needed to ensure that traders do not use insider information and powerful market positions to manipulate prices. Regulation could be public, if government agencies play an active role in setting rules for traders and in overseeing their activities. Alternatively, such a market could be largely self-regulating, as is the case with the LME. The LME is a private company run by traders, who set rules for themselves under very broad oversight from the British government. The importance of the LME means that we need to examine the private rules and norms that regulate trading on the Exchange to fully understand the roles of private self-management in the area of minerals pricing, although these will be explored only briefly in the present chapter.

Enforcement of private mechanisms for managing markets. Private mechanisms for managing international mineral markets generally lack enforcement mechanisms as effective as those available to governments. In the case of violation of cartel agreements or price undercutting in violation of tacit oligopolistic collusion, firms may try to punish defectors by launching a price war. Price wars are of limited utility in international mineral trade. They punish those who wage them, and are generally won by those that can sustain losses the longest. In a purely privately owned industry, this would be low-cost producers with strong financial positions. But in international mineral markets, many producers (privately owned as well as state-owned) can draw on government subsidies to avoid being forced to close or cut production. In such a situation, a price war might be ineffective at best and suicidal at worst.

Enforcement of the norms and rules of the self-regulating private LME comes in part through the legal rights that are delegated to it by the British state. For example, the LME has the legal right to demand the payment of margins on future and option contracts, and to appropriate funds from those who fail to meet margin calls. More generally, traders that violate the norms and rules of a privately managed international mineral market like the LME can be banned from trading on it. In earlier years, informal market regulation was facilitated by the fact that most traders were British or had strong connections to Britain.[18] But in recent years more and more trading firms are becoming foreign-owned, and in general the volume of transnational trading is increasing in parallel with the massive increase in the overall volume of trading. Growth in the volume of trading and the expansion of transnational trading have made regulation of mineral and metal trading much more difficult.

Mixed Public-Private Regulation

While the preceding sections made a distinction between public and private forms of market management, in practice it would be difficult to find arrangements that had no private or no public involvement. For example, the cartels studied by Deborah Spar involved both states and private firms,[19] and the weak public international commodity regime discussed earlier was heavily influenced by private firms that produced, traded, and consumed the commodities in question. The form of mixed public-private regime that I focus on in this chapter is public support for the kinds of private international regimes described in the preceding section. Private actors have often called on governments for support to reestablish private oligopolistic self-management (though they do not use these terms), especially when faced with competition from nonwestern, government-owned producers. As noted above, private actors alone have limited powers of enforcement and therefore call on governments to use their powers to persuade noncooperating producers to adhere to these norms. In the cases considered in this chapter, the most important mechanism of enforcement has been control over market access. Private producing firms based in major western importing countries (the United States and the European Union) have called on governments to limit market access for producers based in developing or transitional economies whose exports are disturbing international markets.

Governments often have been willing to provide this support, and to encourage the establishment of mixed public-private institutions (and sometimes purely private institutions) intended to support private market stabilization, even tacit oligopolistic collusion. An important model for these mixed institutions is the so-called study group, in which governments of producing and consuming countries are the formal members but whose meetings provide a forum for contacts among private industry representatives. The involvement of governments helps to legitimize these forums and to shelter private firms participating in them from antitrust actions. Even consuming country governments may be willing to join study groups because consumers are more interested in stabilizing prices and supply than in minimizing prices. Also, many consuming country governments want to support import-competing domestic producers and nationally based mining companies with overseas operations.

Regime theory helps to illuminate the main functions of these bodies. They collect, analyze, and disseminate information about market trends that can alter the behavior of individual producers. Many participants hope that improved information will discourage overproduction and the development of excess capacity. Study groups ostensibly avoid explicit agreements on prices, market shares, and production levels, but they can help generate informal understandings on such issues. Study groups also produce authoritative assessments of market conditions that may encourage self-restraint in pricing and output decisions. They also help to socialize new market entrants into the self-restraining behavioral norms that make tacit oligopolistic collusion possible. This is especially important with the growth of state-owned mining firms in developing countries since the 1960s (a trend that is being reversed) and, since 1990, the growth of exports from Russia and China, whose producers often are subject to neither a profit constraint nor constraints from central planners.

Of course, often underlying this socialization process are implicit or explicit threats of loss of access to major markets in the United States or the European Union. If producers in question do not conform to oligopolistic norms of self-restraint, they face the threat of antidumping and countervailing-duty trade sanctions in importing, producing countries. Private producing firms have no legitimate authority to discipline other producers who violate these norms, and privately owned producing firms are severely limited in their ability to engage in price wars with state-owned firms, which usually cannot be driven out of business. But governments retain the prerogative to enforce those norms if domestic firms suffer when the norms are violated.

PRIVATE MANAGEMENT OF MINERAL MARKETS IN THE 1950s AND 1960s

Most international mineral markets in this period were dominated by a small number of large, vertically integrated transnational mining and metal processing firms based in Western Europe, North America, and Japan. Many had established mining operations in developing countries during the colonial period to supply their metal processing facilities in western industrialized countries. Others had established mines in mineral-rich Northern countries like Canada and Australia. Transnational mining operations had often been developed with the active encouragement of Northern governments, concerned about security of mineral supply during the intense early stages of the Cold War. In Japan, which was completely dependent on imports for most minerals, smelters had financed the establishment of mines abroad in return for long-term supply contracts. Compared to subsequent periods, most mineral prices were relatively stable and remunerative, supported by strong demand in the booming western economies and Japan, and by tacit oligopolistic collusion.

International market management during these years was primarily private. The intergovernmental regime was weak, as the key norms defined in the charter of the proposed International Trade Organization (never ratified) allowed for the possibility of international stabilization efforts only in cases of severely unstable international markets, and there was little interest among any governments in international commodity agreements for minerals (tin was the only exception).[20] Many international mineral markets were subject to tacit self-management in the form of private international regimes. Shared norms of oligopolistic self-restraint in output and pricing among the private western TNCs that dominated most of these markets helped to stabilize prices for consumers, in some cases even when the mineral was also traded on the LME. Producer pricing systems and price leadership were common. Western governments tolerated tacit oligopolistic collusion and in one case—lead and zinc—provided support for mainly private market management in the form of a study group that later became a model for other minerals. Private self-management of mineral markets in this period was generally multilateral (involving TNCs from a number of western countries that controlled much production in developing countries) and loosely institutionalized, though there were occasional more explicit arrangements.

Aluminum and Bauxite

Private self-management of markets was clearest in the case of aluminum and bauxite. Six firms based in developed countries accounted for the vast bulk of aluminum production and owned or controlled most world bauxite production, often through joint ventures involving two or more of the six (bauxite is the raw material in aluminum production).[21] These interconnections eroded the possibility of competition among bauxite consumers and strengthened their oligopsony. Most bauxite production was traded within vertically integrated aluminum firms, with prices being determined as an internal transfer price. Management of international trade in bauxite (and alumina, an intermediate product) by aluminium companies produced stable prices in the 1950s and '60s, though at lower levels than producing-country governments desired.[22]

Tacit oligopolistic collusion was strongly evident in markets for aluminum. Leading producers recognized their interdependence and maintained effective producer price systems and stable prices.[23] Producers kept prices above competitive levels, though low enough to maintain the attractiveness of aluminum in relation to substitute products.[24] Periods of weak demand for aluminum were met by inventory accumulations rather than price cuts or cuts in production;[25] as noted earlier, stockpiling surplus output is a risky strategy for producers in the absence of strong shared expectations that other producers will pursue this strategy rather than cut prices. When this was insufficient to support producer prices at their prerecession level, regional groups of producers cooperated more actively. This included a "'gentleman's agreement' to purchase aluminum from Eastern Europe, a cooperative arrangement by European producers to finance stockpiling, and a similar agreement between US producers to buy surpluses from the US government stockpile."[26] "There is plenty of evidence that [OECD] governments are not only aware of oligopolistic behavior in the market, but that these governments positively support these activities and cooperation between firms, which are seen as a guarantee of stable prices, adequate investment flows, and minimal disturbance to the economies of the industrialized countries."[27] Private authority was clearly evident in the price leadership system, shared norms and trust were highly influential, and governments lent tacit support, though the threat of antitrust prosecution in the United States should prices rise too high showed the limits of that support.

Copper

Private market management by transnational copper producers was less successful than in the case of aluminum, but was still influential. World copper production was dominated by a small number of North American and European firms that owned most copper production in developing countries. Particularly in North America, producers were able to stabilize and support prices by means of a producer price system based on price leadership. Outside North America, prices were more heavily influenced by trading on the LME and were therefore more volatile. Nevertheless, between 1961 and 1964 the major transnational firms cooperated to maintain a fixed price for copper on the LME, and then when prices rose in the face of strong demand, they kept their prices below LME levels and rationed supplies to traditional consumers. This collective self-management system broke down in mid-1966 when the Chilean and Zambian governments forced the mining companies operating in their countries to increase prices to the LME level.[28]

These cases are clear examples of tacit oligopolistic collusion. Price coordination by producers outside North America relied on a shared understanding of the problems of the industry and a high degree of trust among the firms involved. Price support operations and then rationing supplies to keep prices below LME levels both made sense only for firms that could trust their competitors not to take advantage of their self-restraint. Markets were being managed privately, and in a fashion that served both the private interests of TNC producers and the public interests of consuming countries.

Lead and Zinc

Private self-management was also apparent in lead and zinc markets during the 1950s and 1960s, though it evolved into a form of collaborative private-public management.[29] Most lead and zinc is produced by a small number of privately owned mining companies working ore deposits located in developed countries. Stable oligopoly allowed producer pricing systems based on price leadership to emerge for the North American markets for lead and zinc and for the international market for zinc, though both metals also were traded on the LME. Private self-management came under pressure in the late 1950s from weak prices and import restrictions introduced by the United States. Producers then sought public support for market stabilization, and governments agreed in 1959 to establish the International Lead and Zinc Study Group (ILZSG).[30] Its assessment of trends in the industry and provision of accurate information on the balance of world supply and demand has "enabled the world lead and zinc industry to plan effectively with regard to market trends"[31] and usually to avoid the overexpansion of capacity that often leads to depressed primary commodity prices. The expert character of the ILZSG's pronouncements lend them considerable authority and they are widely reported and discussed in the international business press. The group also facilitates consultations among governments and private industry on market problems and may make suggestions and recommendations for addressing market problems to member governments.[32] ILZSG meetings apply "moral suasion" to producers or governments whose actions threaten to upset the market. Emphasis is put on the idea that "we've all got to do some cutting" when the market is characterized by high inventories and surplus production. On occasion, recommendations about production levels are made during meetings of the group, and these are then implemented on a voluntary, independent basis by the group members. The group's meetings also provide an opportunity for producing firms to meet without fear of violating national antitrust laws. The private industry is well represented at ILZSG annual meetings, with private industry advisors often outnumbering government officials. According to Canadian government officials, private meetings among industry representatives occur and are condoned by officials as they are believed to help keep things running smoothly in the international industry.[33]

The ILZSG is therefore an early example of intergovernmental support for primarily private self-management of markets by producing firms. The success of this flexible, informal mechanism linking mainly western privately owned firms meant that there has been little interest in more formal mechanisms.[34]

Nickel

Nickel in the 1950s and 1960s provides an unusual example of unilateral private market management. During this period the international nickel market was completely dominated by Inco, a private firm mining rich deposits in Canada. Inco set the world price for nickel in accordance with its long-term interests, which included avoiding high prices at times of peak demand by rationing the supply of nickel to its customers. Similarly, when demand fell below the amount Inco wanted to supply at the posted price, Inco built up huge stockpiles to avoid reducing its price or production levels. Unilateral private market management produced steadily increasing real prices, but also a gradual erosion of Inco's market position to other producers willing to undercut its prices. Governmental actions tended to limit rather than facilitate private market management in this case. The constant threat of antitrust investigation in the United States encouraged Inco to adopt a restrained pricing policy and to avoid aggressive tactics against its much smaller competitors.[35]

The 1950s and 1960s, then, were a period of extensive private self-management of international mineral markets by transnational mining firms operating with the tacit consent of western governments (and the explicit support, in the case of the ILZSG). This private self-management was loosely institutionalized and flexible, yet based on strong shared norms of oligopolistic self-restraint. The dominance of western mining companies was central to this pattern, and was also a key source of discontent among the governments of producing countries outside the western world.

THE CHALLENGE FROM
DEVELOPING COUNTRIES IN THE 1970s

International mineral markets began to change in the late 1960s, as newly independent and assertive developing-country governments nationalized western-owned mines and set up state-owned mining operations in an effort to gain a greater share of the returns from mineral production and export. State-owned producers tended to pursue a broader set of social goals—including employment, regional development, and the maximization of export earnings—than private producers, whose preeminent focus was on profit maximization and who generally left social spending up to governments. State-owned producers also often had better access to state subsidies than western-owned private producers, at least before the debt crisis took hold in the early 1980s. While higher costs eventually undermined the competitive position of many developing-country producers later in the 1980s and in the 1990s, during the 1970s and early 1980s it appeared that state-owned producers were less responsive to market forces than privately owned producers. In particular, state-owned producers often appeared to be slower to cut production when prices fell, and this tended to make international markets less stable and to push prices down.

Private self-management of international markets by transnational firms broke down in most mineral industries during the 1970s and early 1980s. Inspired by OPEC's success in oil, the governments of developing-country producers of bauxite and copper established intergovernmental arrangements intended to raise prices. Simultaneously, the Group of 77 (G77) and the UNCTAD Secretariat, inspired by dependency theory and the growing assertiveness and political unity of the Third World, proposed a radical revision of the intergovernmental commodity trade regime. They proposed the establishment of producer-consumer international commodity agreements to stabilize commodity prices around an upward trend indexed to the prices of manufactured goods. The norms promoted by the G77 and the UNCTAD Secretariat were based on principles of international equity rather than market efficiency, and were radically at odds with those promoted by leading western governments since the late 1940s.[36]

Aluminum and Bauxite

Developing-country producers of bauxite joined in the general Third World effort to alter international mineral market management in the 1970s, though they tended to favor collaboration with private firms more than Third World producers of other commodities. A number of countries nationalized portions of their bauxite mines, though most permitted TNCs to retain some equity stakes. In 1974–75, eleven developing countries and Australia (the largest producing country) created the International Bauxite Association (IBA). Jamaica then led a loosely coordinated effort by some developing country producers to raise taxes on production and exports, and to persuade the aluminum companies to set higher internal transfer prices for bauxite.[37] This effort achieved some success in part because their oligopoly permitted aluminum firms to pass on the higher costs to consumers, and many saw profits rise over the next few years.[38] This is an unusual example of public-private collaboration initiated by developing-country governments. The aluminum firms retained the upper hand and by the time the IBA began recommending minimum prices for bauxite in 1978, the most militant IBA members were becoming more conciliatory in response to their falling shares of TNC investment and bauxite production. Consequently, the IBA's recommendations had little impact.[39]

The ability of the major aluminum producers to manage the international market was eroding in the late 1970s due to changes in the structure of the industry, but remained stronger than in most other metal markets. A number of new, independent producers were established in developing countries, and this led to an increase in arm's-length international trade, in contrast to the traditional importance of intrafirm trade within vertically integrated aluminum TNCs. Prices became more volatile (though producer pricing systems did not entirely break down) and aluminum began trading on the LME (despite the hostility of the major producing firms) in October 1978.[40] But the oligopolistic practice of accumulating inventory when demand was soft helped to support prices through the 1975 recession and profits remained strong for most of the 1970s.[41] In Europe, firms continued to collaborate to buy surplus aluminum from Eastern Europe when it appeared on the market to support West European prices (a practice begun in 1963) until the European Commission announced an antitrust investigation in 1975.[42] This evidence of continued informal collaboration showed that the major firms continued to have some trust in each other and in their shared understandings, but private management of the international aluminum market was slowly eroding.

Copper

Copper experienced one of the sharpest swings away from private market management during the late 1960s and the 1970s. Producer pricing systems collapsed in the face of growing assertiveness on the part of governments in developing producing countries, many of which nationalized copper mines and insisted on maximizing short-term prices. These governments sought to further increase their influence over international markets by collaborating with each other, and created CIPEC (the French-language acronym for the Council of Copper Exporting Countries) in 1967. In 1974–75, inspired by OPEC's success, CIPEC members agreed to cut production by 15 percent to support prices, although most did not implement the agreed-upon cutbacks.[43]

This failure again shows that formal intergovernmental agreements are not necessarily more effective than informal private shared understandings. The failure of CIPEC led many of its members to favor collaboration among producing and consuming governments under the auspices of UNCTAD's Integrated Programme for Commodities (IPC). Extremely contentious negotiations in 1976–79 failed to produce any agreement. The UNCTAD Secretariat pushed hard for an agreement, given the importance of copper trade for many developing countries and the unsuitability of most other primary commodities for the strongest regulatory instruments proposed in the Secretariat's IPC. The idea of an ICA for copper was rejected by most developed country governments and by privately owned Northern mining firms. Both groups were particularly opposed to the suggestion that producers based in developed countries should sacrifice market share (for example, by accepting disproportionate shares of any production cuts needed to stabilize prices) in order to make room for developing-country producers. The equity norms promoted by developing countries clashed sharply with the efficiency norms and norms of oligopolistic self-restraint favored by Northern governments and firms. Divisions among developing producing countries were also apparent, with Chile opposed to any agreement that might constrain the growth of its state-owned mines.[44]

Thus, the late 1960s witnessed the breakdown of private transnational management of international copper markets, and the failure of a major attempt to create an intergovernmental mechanism for managing the market. The absence of private and public management made the copper market extremely volatile.

Lead and Zinc

International markets for lead and zinc continued to be managed relatively effectively by private mining firms, with the assistance of consultations and information sharing in the ILZSG. Producer pricing systems for lead and zinc did not break down, nor did the dominance of large private mining firms. As developing countries and state-owned firms were not very important in lead and zinc production, there was little interest in formal intergovernmental collaboration.[45] The ILZSG continued to facilitate private market management by encouraging firms to limit production to support prices when markets were weak. For example, at a meeting in July 1978, producers that had exercised restraint in production were praised, and many delegations "hoped that the pressure of recognition would encourage other countries to exercise restraint and speed up the return to orderly markets."[46]

Nickel

Nickel in the 1970s provides a striking example of the substitutability of private and public market management. The unilateral private market management practiced by Inco in the 1950s and 1960s broke down in the 1970s, and the governments of the main developed producing countries—Canada and Australia—sought intergovernmental collaboration to restore nickel market stability. Nickel production by government-owned firms in developing countries had grown rapidly in the 1960s, and these producers faced strong economic and political pressure to maintain production and exports even when demand weakened. These changes produced the first real price war for nickel in 1976–77. Inco and Falconbridge (another Canadian nickel producer) initially responded to depressed demand by accumulating inventory, as they had in the past, but rival firms refused to cooperate and instead maintained production. In 1977 the two Canadian producers were forced to cut production and lay off workers, putting pressure on the Canadian government to assist the industry.[47]

The Canadian government responded by seeking some form of public market management that could recreate the favorable market conditions that Inco had privately created in the past. The prime minister suggested that the government might try to form an international nickel cartel or a compromise arrangement between producing and consuming countries. Both options were quickly renounced by Inco (which was concerned about the reaction from antitrust officials in the United States) and by Canadian officials.[48] Instead, Ottawa supported an Australian proposal for an international nickel study group (INSG) modeled on the ILZSG. The INSG was not created until the 1980s, so further discussion of it will be deferred until later. Nevertheless, it is important to note why the idea gained support in Canada and Australia. Both governments sought a form of market management that avoided the rigidity and political controversy associated with an ICA or cartel, yet that would help to stabilize the industry. It was hoped that better information on consumption trends and consultations would help to convince developing-country producers to be more responsive to market forces, and in particular to cut production when markets were weak and exercise restraint when expanding production capacity.[49] In this way (though officials did not describe it in these terms), an INSG could help to socialize newer producers into the oligopolistic behavioral norms that generate stability in markets characterized by tacit oligopolistic collusion. It is ironic that these two governments had strongly opposed Third World proposals for intergovernmental market management that threatened private management of markets for other minerals, yet favored a form of intergovernmental action to replace collapsed private market management for nickel (both governments also participated in the infamous uranium cartel of the 1970s).

The strength and character of international mineral market management was therefore changing dramatically in the 1970s on all three dimensions. Private management was eroding and various producer governments (in the North as well as the South) were attempting to replace it with public management, though the latter was rarely very effective (e.g., the IBA, CIPEC, and the INSG proposal). Multilateral private arrangements were, in many cases, being replaced by unilateral efforts. Attempts were made in some minerals to negotiate formal agreements and rules to guide individual producers (e.g., CIPEC and the IBA), but these generally were less effective than the informal understandings that had characterized earlier tacit oligopolistic collusion. In this confused context, only those markets that retained elements of prior private market management—aluminum and lead and zinc—survived the period without major instability and depressed prices.

DEPRESSED MARKETS AND PUBLIC-PRIVATE COLLABORATION IN THE 1980s AND 1990s

Recent years have witnessed further dramatic changes in international mineral industries. Prices were severely depressed during the recession of the early 1980s and did not recover until late in the decade. Weak markets forced many high-cost mines to close and triggered drastic cost-cutting at others. The trend toward mine nationalizations in developing-countries was at first halted and later reversed. The Third World debt crisis restricted developing-country governments' access to the private international capital needed to finance nationalizations and new mine investments, and made many desperate for the investment funds and access to Northern markets that transnational mining companies could bring. Disillusionment with the effects of nationalization (in many cases, corrupt and ineffective management led to declining output and reduced returns to producing countries) and pressure from Northern governments and international financial institutions also caused developing-country governments to reassess their strategies. By the early 1990s, some of the state-owned mines developed in the 1970s were being privatized, sometimes by selling shares in them to transnational mining companies. In other cases, mineral deposits were being developed as joint ventures between transnational mining firms and state agencies. This form of investment retained for the state some of the greater control that had previously been sought through full ownership, and provided private mining firms with better political insurance against expropriation.[50]

A declining role for direct state intervention was also apparent in the growth of private trading and hedging on international mineral exchanges, particularly the LME. The LME survived the collapse of the International Tin Agreement in 1985 despite enormous losses for some of its traders, and trading grew extremely rapidly in the late 1980s and 1990s. LME prices became increasingly important for the global industry, as the erosion of oligopoly that had begun in the 1960s and 1970s forced producers of such minerals as aluminum, nickel, and zinc to abandon producer prices. Advocates saw the higher volume of trading as increasing liquidity and therefore the opportunities for producers and consumers to use hedging strategies to cope with instability, but others believed that increasing speculative activity was making instability worse.

In terms of international market management, the period also saw a thorough retreat from the ambitions for intergovernmental regimes characteristic of the preceding period. UNCTAD failed to create any new ICAs for minerals, and the Third World largely abandoned the effort to restructure international commodity markets and intergovernmental regime norms.[51] Producer government associations formed in the 1970s declined, symbolized by the termination of the International Bauxite Agreement in 1994 (ironically, the same year that western aluminum producers reached a tacit agreement with their Russian competitors to cut production and restore aluminum prices). Northern governments, and many Southern governments, lost all interest in formal intergovernmental market management after the messy collapse of the International Tin Agreement in 1985. Coordinated private international market management was also weak for much of this period. Producers decided individually how to respond to depressed market conditions, whether by cutting costs and production or by seeking government subsidies and protection from foreign competitors.

But as state ownership receded and proposals for intergovernmental regulation faded, renewed efforts were made to reestablish private international market management. These efforts generally were supported by western governments, and often took the form of producer-consumer study groups. As discussed earlier, a major focus of these various efforts was to persuade nonwestern, nonprivate producers to follow oligopolistic norms of behavior in their production and pricing decisions. On occasion, tacit and explicit agreements on production and market shares were reached to try to support prices. New efforts along these lines were apparent in such minerals as aluminium, copper, and nickel, in addition to the continued activity of the study group for lead and zinc. The resurgence of transnational mining firms and the spread of public-private collaboration ought to have improved the prospects for market management, thereby bringing greater stability to international mineral markets, but in the 1990s instability was driven by exports from the postcommunist transitional economies and by trading on the LME. The increased role of the LME generated increased private and governmental interest in the regulation of private market activity, although the norms and rules shaping trading activity continued to be mainly private. Because of the growing importance of the LME and its private norms and rules for self-management, the discussion of management of markets for individual minerals in this section will be followed by a brief discussion of the LME.

Aluminum and Bauxite

Bauxite and aluminum provide some excellent examples of the decline of direct intergovernmental market management and public support for the restoration of private market management. Intergovernmental collaboration in the IBA gradually eroded and the organization was disbanded in 1994.[52] It had continued to recommend minimum prices for bauxite but these were very low and had little impact.[53] Some producers tried to generate interest in producer-consumer collaboration under UNCTAD auspices, but consuming governments and aluminum firms were uninterested, as were certain bauxite producers more interested in increasing market shares and maintaining good relations with the aluminum TNCs.[54] Paradoxically, the end for the IBA came at a time of very low prices. In the words of a Jamaican industry representative, "Given the state of the market and the problems facing bauxite producers, now is the time they should be getting closer together to defend their common interests."[55] The failure of attempts to negotiate intergovernmental market management left bauxite production and trade under the continued dominance of private aluminum producers, although bauxite producing governments had improved their ability individually to negotiate more favorable agreements with the aluminum firms as compared with the pre-IBA period.

In aluminum, private management of the international market collapsed in the 1980s, and the dire conditions facing private aluminum producers, once large-scale exports from Russia began in the early 1990s, triggered intergovernmental efforts to restore private oligopolistic market management. The major aluminum firms lost the ability to set producer prices as production from new smelters in developing countries came on stream in the 1970s. Aluminum began to be traded on international metal exchanges, first the LME in 1978 and then the New York Commodity Exchange (COMEX) in 1983; as noted earlier, this happened despite strong opposition from the major producers. Mutual restraint among the majors broke down completely in 1983–84, when ALCAN aggressively cut prices to maintain output while others cut output in a vain attempt to replicate the tacit collusion that had reduced supplies and supported prices in the past.[56] Aluminum prices became very sensitive to speculative pressures as banks and investment funds from outside the metals industry became more active.[57] Opportunities arose for traders to manipulate the market. Market "squeezes," as they are called by traders, apparently have been engineered by some of the large trading firms, whereby traders buy up as much of the physical supplies available on the cash market to create an artificial shortage and drive prices up. Clever traders with strong financial backing can benefit from both the price increase and the inevitable decline.[58] The aluminum firms have been very critical of this market manipulation and price volatility, in part because they believe that some potential consumers avoid the metal because of its price volatility,[59] but they have been unable to do much about it (see below on LME regulation).

Market management also has to deal with long-term trends in price levels and market conditions. Exports from Russia increased in the early 1990s in the wake of the collapse of central planning and the disintegration of the Soviet Union. Russian producers turned to western markets as demand from the shrinking Soviet defense industry disappeared. They were willing to sell at very low prices because of artificially low energy costs, corruption, and a desire to maximize hard currency earnings. European and American aluminum firms initially lobbied for intergovernmental collaboration to encourage Russian producers "to adjust their sales and pricing policy to the market economy rules and mechanism"—that is, to adopt the self-restraining norms of western producers.[60]

But in the absence of reciprocal self-restraint by Russian producers, European and American producers began to lobby for import restrictions, and the European Union imposed import quotas in August 1993.[61] In the face of these threats, the Russian government met with western industry and government representatives in a series of meetings in the fall of 1993 and winter of 1993–94. The result, in January 1994, was a Memorandum of Understanding (MOU) among the Russian, Australian, Norwegian, Canadian, and American governments and the European Commission, the purpose of which was to coordinate management of the international aluminum market without causing American firms to run afoul of U.S. antitrust laws. The essential problem was to recreate the kind of shared understandings that had once facilitated tacit oligopolistic collusion, since antitrust legislation would not permit western producers to commit themselves to specific targets. In the words of one delegate to the meetings, "The problem is that, unless some kind of trust can be built up between the producers, everyone wants to see others make the first cuts. . . . We hope we now have a formula to generate that trust, one that will produce the worldwide cuts necessary to bring the market back into balance."[62]

The key provisions of the agreement reached at the end of January 1994 included a commitment by Russia to cut output by 500,000 tons over the next six months. No targets were identified for specific western producers, but there was a clear understanding that western producers would cut their production by 1.0 to 1.5 million tons.[63] As a well-placed insider put it, "Having taken the precaution of involving their governments in these talks, the producers were able to implement the smelter closures they agreed were necessary without immediately being arraigned for operating a cartel."[64] The other crucial component of the MOU was a package of measures to stabilize the industry in the longer run. Russia agreed to provide information about its industry to the International Primary Aluminum Institute (IPAI), the private international trade association for the aluminum industry, and eventually to have its aluminum producers join the IPAI.[65] The implications of this are significant; western governments were using their powers (primarily the threat of trade restrictions) to persuade another government to force its producers to join a private industry association whose main function was to supply information and analysis needed to facilitate private market management.

In fact, Russian output and exports did not decline by anywhere near 500,000 tons, if at all.[66] As the director of one of Russia's largest aluminum firms put it, "we're a private company now and we decide what to do."[67] Clearly he had not yet absorbed western norms favoring private market management! Nevertheless, speculation by investment funds and banks drove prices up faster than producers expected or desired, and oversupply later declined as western world production fell.[68] The MOU had clearly facilitated tacit oligopolistic collusion among western producers and begun the process of integrating the Russian aluminum industry into the private market management system that had characterized the aluminum industry for much of the period since World War II. Government action—the threat of loss of access to the European and American markets—was needed to get the process of restoring private market management underway. But aluminum firms and governments were not yet willing or able to tame growing speculation on the mineral exchanges, and aluminum prices have remained volatile and subject to manipulation on the LME.

Copper

Most copper producers around the world suffered badly during the recession of the early 1980s. Demand for copper stagnated, and real prices fell to their lowest levels since the 1930s. North American copper companies put much of the blame for falling prices on government-controlled producers in developing countries that had maintained or increased production despite weak demand.[69] This was particularly galling to American copper producers whose Chilean mines had been nationalized with modest compensation in the late 1960s, and who were now being driven out of business by the industry they had once controlled. American copper producers demanded protection, alleging that exports from Chile were subsidized. The Reagan administration rejected import restrictions and encouraged the search for other ways to help the industry.[70] Support grew in Congress for the establishment of an international commission modeled on the ILZSG to review conditions in the industry and consider action that individual countries might take to improve market conditions. Unstated was the hope that this commission would provide a forum in which foreign producers could be persuaded to voluntarily limit their exports to the United States. The Reagan administration pursued the idea vigorously. Formal preparatory meetings were held in 1986–87. Many participants were unenthusiastic. Chile and other developing countries feared that they would come under pressure to limit their exports. Despite these and other reservations, continued American diplomatic efforts produced agreement on terms of reference for the proposed ICSG in 1989, and by 1992 enough countries had joined for the group to begin to function.[71]

While it is too early to tell what impact the ICSG has had on the prospects for tacit oligopolistic collusion, there are indications that collaboration among major producers is increasing, replacing the confrontational politics of the late 1960s and 1970s with relations that more closely resemble the transnational private market management of the 1950s and 1960s. Some state-owned producers have been privatized and there are growing links among state-owned and private-western producers in mining, refining, and marketing. Officials of Codelco, the leading Chilean state-owned producer, argue that the industry "has evolved towards an increase in mutual trust, commitment, interaction and collaboration among the major companies, without impairing their individual strategies to increase competitiveness."[72] American diplomacy and threats of protectionism clearly helped to encourage Chilean producers' greater willingness to cooperate with other copper producers in managing the international industry,[73] another example of public support for the restoration of private market management.

Despite these developments, copper markets have experienced severe instability due to the vagaries of private market regulation at the LME. Copper trading on the LME has been plagued by attempts by trading firms and speculators to manipulate copper prices, generating costly instability for copper producers and consumers and for the wider economy. Copper, along with aluminum, has been particularly attractive to fund managers, private investors, and speculative metal traders because it is a large and liquid market.[74] Copper trading on the LME between 1990 and 1996 was subject to repeated "technical squeezes" by traders seeking to drive the cash price (the price for copper for immediate delivery) up by buying up available copper, storing it in LME warehouses, and refusing to sell it on the cash market when prices climbed. As a result, prices were artificially inflated for much of this period (though periods of squeezed markets were punctuated by sharp declines when traders reversed their strategy). Producers and consumers were very critical of the LME for inflating and destabilizing copper prices.[75] The role in these market manipulations played by Sumitomo Corporation and its chief copper trader, Yasuo Hamanaka, was widely known among copper traders and to LME executives since at least 1991. But the LME did little before 1996, arguing that it lacked the power to discipline Sumitomo because it was not a member of the exchange. However, it could have disciplined traders acting on Sumitomo's behalf, and it could have improved market transparency (the secrecy of the LME facilitates price manipulation). Its failure to act is undoubted linked to the fact that speculative activity generated such large fees and profits for the mineral traders who run the LME. The British government failed to step in because of its preference for self-regulation by financial markets, and because such market manipulation did not immediately threaten the interests of investors using the LME for financial reasons (as opposed to actual producers and consumers). When the LME and the British government finally did act in May 1996, demanding that Sumitomo halt Hamanaka's activities, the price of copper collapsed.

As in the case of aluminum and other minerals, the case of copper therefore suggests that the restoration of conditions for private oligopolistic market management in the 1990s—with government support—has not yet stabilized markets and prices because of the growth of speculative trading on the privately regulated LME (see below for a more detailed discussion of private market management by the LME).

Lead and Zinc

Private market management continued to be important in international lead and zinc markets in the 1980s and early 1990s, assisted by discussions among governments and firms in the ILZSG, but stability was severely impaired by the growth of loosely regulated speculative activity on the LME. The zinc industry was hurt by the recession of the early 1980s, but not as badly as most other mineral industries. When demand for zinc fell, producers did cut production enough to keep supply and demand in rough balance, and zinc prices fell by less than most other metals. Canadian officials credit the ILZSG with helping producers to exercise the self-discipline in production and pricing policies that mitigated the worst effects of the recession.[76] Zinc producers also colluded tacitly (or secretly) in a number of efforts to support zinc prices on the LME, the hope being that this would reduce pressure on them to cut their producer prices. Efforts to do so in 1986 failed and some producers suffered large losses.[77] But heavy intervention on the LME had the perverse (for producers) effect of further stimulating the growth of speculative trading, which led the LME to introduce (in 1988) a new contract for "special high grade zinc." This proved attractive to traders and in 1989 it replaced the European producer price as the basis for most internationally traded zinc.[78]

Producers then tried to influence the price for this LME contract. A notable effort occurred in summer 1992, when a group rumored to include six to eight of the largest zinc producers and a major trading firm engineered a technical squeeze using the options market that pushed the cash price far above the future price and to the highest level in two years, despite very large stocks in LME warehouses. This tacit collusion rested on clear shared understandings.[79] Otherwise, those producers attempting to raise the price would merely end up paying above-market prices for stocks dumped on the market by noncolluding producers. In contrast to copper, the LME acted decisively to end these technical squeezes. In 1989 and 1992 it imposed strict limits on backwardation (the extent to which the cash price could exceed the three-month futures price). In this case the LME had a private interest in maintaining orderly market conditions, as it wanted to maintain the credibility of its recently introduced "special high-grade zinc" contract.[80] European producers also tried to negotiate coordinated capacity reductions (with the European Union's approval) on at least three occasions in the 1980s and 1990s, but these plans never came to fruition because stronger firms hoped that their weaker competitors would be forced to shut down even without financial compensation from the remaining producers. This did not happen, and prices remained depressed.[81] The zinc market also continued to experience periodic market squeezes, particularly after the copper crisis in 1996 encouraged speculators to move from copper to other metals.

Thus, the oligopolistic zinc industry repeatedly tried to collaborate to influence prices on the LME and to redress the problem of oversupply, but with no real success. The ILZSG continued to try to facilitate collaborative market management in its consultations and analyses, though the willingness to discuss coordinated action varied. For example, the United States occasionally tried to discourage others from collaborating in response to weak market conditions.[82] The group's authoritative analyses of market conditions did continue to provide a focal point for tacit coordination—for example, in April 1994, a period of depressed prices following the failure of European collaboration to cut production capacity, the ILZSG forecast a continuing supply surplus "unless metal production is reduced from levels currently planned."[83] In a longer-term effort to stabilize the market, the ILZSG has made a concerted effort to bring producers from the former Soviet bloc and China into the group.[84] But overcapacity among traditional producers and the speculative gyrations of the LME have impeded private stabilization efforts, even when backed by governments.

Nickel

Nickel experienced the same depressed conditions in the early 1980s and LME-driven volatility in the late 1980s and early 1990s as other metals. Also as in these other cases, various governments tried to facilitate the restoration of private market management. Trading of nickel on the LME began in April 1979 and by 1982 the major producers were forced to abandon producer prices. Western firms and governments blamed state-owned producers in developing countries and the Soviet Union for failing to reduce output when demand was weak. Inco occasionally tried to play the role of oligopolistic leader by announcing production cuts that it hoped others would follow to reduce oversupply and raise prices, but few followed and Inco simply lost market share.[85] The LME's nickel market was plagued by the same kinds of price manipulation experienced by other LME-traded metals. In February 1988, a technical squeeze apparently engineered by European metal merchants drove the cash price of nickel up to $10 per pound, far above the range (two to four dollars) in which it generally traded. The LME intervened dramatically but briefly, halting trading and urging members to release nickel to the market. This failed to ease conditions, and the squeeze persisted through March. Prices then collapsed in January 1989 when the merchants that had been hoarding nickel to force the price up dumped it back on the market.[86] These gyrations triggered talks between major stainless steel producers (the main consumers of nickel) and some nickel producers to find an alternative basis for pricing nickel, and some signed long-term contracts at prices that eliminated the LME's peaks and troughs.[87] However, this attempt to privately manage international nickel trade had a minimal impact, and the LME continues to have a dominant impact on nickel pricing, despite ongoing evidence of market manipulation by traders.

As discussed in the preceding section, the idea for an International Nickel Study Group (INSG) modeled on the ILZSG was developed by the Canadian and Australian governments in the late 1970s as a response to depressed market conditions. Indifference among other governments meant that the INSG did not come into operation until 1990. While most of the major producers joined, the USSR agreed to participate only as an observer, as did the United States, and Britain declined to participate.[88] In the early 1990s, the INSG tried to manage the rapid growth of nickel exports from Russia and China. With Russia having observer status in the INSG, executives of its producer Norilsk met in closed sessions with the INSG, which apparently sought to persuade Norilsk to cut output and reduce the volume of unofficial (i.e., smuggled) exports of nickel.[89] Norilsk subsequently announced production cuts and stricter export controls, but exports from Russia actually increased in the following year.[90] Nevertheless, the INSG did persuade Russia and China to begin supplying better statistics about their production and exports, and sought to bring both countries into full INSG membership.[91] Their involvement was essential if private management of the international nickel industry was ever to be restored, though the lack of support from some leading western governments undoubtedly also weakens its ability to facilitate private self-management of the nickel market by producers.

Self-Regulation by the London Metal Exchange

The prospects for private management to stabilize all of these mineral markets were heavily influenced in the late 1980s and 1990s by the growth of speculative activity and market manipulation on the LME. As discussed earlier, commodity exchanges can be an efficient mechanism for setting prices and speculation can be stabilizing, but only if the market is regulated effectively. Given the growth of trading on the LME and its increasing importance for international minerals trade, it is important to examine how the LME is managed in order to fully understand patterns of international market management. The LME is a largely self-regulating market, and the character of its private self-management has an enormous impact on the private and public interests of economic agents and communities in the international mineral industry.

The LME sets its own trading rules under broad oversight from Britain's Securities and Investments Board (SIB). The current regulatory regime was created by the Financial Services Act (FSA) of 1986, which was intended to facilitate the use of markets like the LME by financial investors. This mean stricter regulation to protect investors from abuse by brokers and from the potential collapse of a broker.[92] However, the British government's concerns generally have not extended to regulating attempts to manipulate prices (so long as individual investors are protected) or to trying to prevent sharp short-term price fluctuations. Britain is neither a major producer nor a major consumer of internationally traded minerals, and the government therefore perceives the public interest that it needs to protect primarily in terms of enhancing the growth of its financial services industry. This leads to regulation designed to protect investors, but not to protect producers or consumers.

Other kinds of regulation are left up to the LME. The LME is a private company owned by its member firms and is a self-regulating exchange within the framework established by the 1986 FSA. Its trading rules are determined by a board of directors, most of which (eleven of sixteen in 1995) are elected from among member firms.[93] The board has given the LME powers that it can use to investigate and halt market manipulation by member firms. These include the right to demand information on traders' own positions and the positions of major clients, to impose limits on backwardation (when spot prices exceed future prices, often a sign of market manipulation), to fine member firms that try to manipulate prices, to halt trading temporarily, and even to halt trading and identify a price at which traders must settle their outstanding positions. This last right was challenged in the courts after the tin crisis of 1985, and the courts upheld the LME's right to take such dramatic action,[94] thereby providing public support and legitimacy for the actions of a private self-regulating body.

Nevertheless, the actual practice of self-regulation by the LME has tended to tolerate or even encourage attempts to manipulate prices by speculators and investors. A brief chronology of the LME's actions and inactions regarding attempts to manipulate copper prices in 1991–96 makes this clear. As noted earlier, Yasuo Hamanaka, a copper trader working for Sumitomo, began trying to push copper prices up by buying up copper stocks and keeping them off the market (in LME warehouses) in 1991, and rumors and knowledge of his activities were widespread among LME insiders at this time. Traders generally were reluctant to sound the alarm about activity that generated fees and speculative profits for themselves.[95] In fact, the LME operated in such a way as to punish those who called attention to market manipulation. When a trader working for Sumitomo reported improper activity by Hamanaka (who had asked for an invoice for $250 million in trades that had never taken place, ostensibly for "tax purposes") to the LME's chief executive, the latter merely sought private assurances from Sumitomo that the activity was satisfactory to it. The whistle-blowing trader, however, lost Sumitomo's business (which went to another firm that promised strict confidentiality) and was ostracized by other traders.[96] This episode shows that the market was being privately managed mainly in the private interests of traders themselves, rather than in the public interest of openness and propriety.

The LME's managers tolerated speculation in part by refusing to improve market transparency. Producers and consumers suffering from market manipulation on the LME demanded that it publicly identify the owners of stocks in LME warehouses. This would enable outsiders to see who was trying to manipulate the market and respond appropriately. The LME responded by requiring traders to report daily any large positions held by their clients to LME administrators.[97] But this information was not made public. The LME's managers preferred quiet, behind-the-scenes regulation. The LME operated much like a private club, and has jealously guarded information about trades. It is described as "one of the last gentlemen's clubs in the U.K.," albeit one in which 90 percent of the trading firms that constitute the club's members are foreign-owned and whose activities have global ramifications.[98] The LME did introduce modest restrictions on backwardation in the copper market on more than one occasion in 1992–93, but these measures were in force only briefly and did not fundamentally alter the situation.[99] Periodic technical squeezes and other market gyrations persisted until 1996, when Hamanaka lost his job as a result of measures finally taken by the LME. Copper prices then fell almost 30 percent.

For our purposes, a number of lessons can be drawn from this episode. First, copper trading was self-regulated by the LME, which generally tolerated questionable trading activity that inflated prices and increased their volatility for almost six years. Private management of this market primarily served the private interests of traders and speculators, at the expense of actual copper consumers and producers in the real economy. Second, public regulation has been impeded by governmental unwillingness to take responsibility and by intergovernmental competition. The British government preferred traditional loose regulation because it attracted financial services to London. The LME's success in rapidly increasing turnover since the mid-1980s and contributing an estimated £250 million to Britain's international trade in services (in 1995) encouraged British regulators to adopt a hands-off approach.[100] They disclaimed responsibility for Sumitomo's actions because Sumitomo was not a member of the LME or any other exchange regulated by the Securities and Investments Board. Japanese law supposedly prohibits Japanese firms from speculating in commodity markets, but various Japanese authorities claimed either that their agency was not responsible or that they lacked jurisdiction since Hamanaka's activities were in London.[101]

Markets for other metals traded on the LME have suffered from similar manipulation by traders, though not so badly. The LME has taken some steps to improve private self-regulation in the wake of the copper crisis and the increasing frequency of market squeezes and other distortions in the markets for other metals that trade on the LME. And investigation of the LME's self-regulatory practices by the SIB concluded in December 1996 that the LME's methods were fundamentally sound, though it did recommend some modest improvements (more outside directors on the board, somewhat greater transparency). The LME moved on these issues in the fall of 1997, in part because growing speculative activity and repeated market squeezes for other minerals since the spring 1996 copper crisis were beginning to undermine the LME's credibility. Speculation has become so large a problem that it threatens the private interests of LME traders, who will lose business if the mineral industry loses confidence in the LME. However, the very mobility of financial capital that has contributed so much to the growth of trading on the LME imposes severe constraints on the ability of the LME to make its self-regulation stricter, because those investors and speculators who are attracted to the LME by its loose regulation might well take their business elsewhere.

In summary, the 1980s and 1990s have witnessed sustained efforts by private mining firms and western governments to restore collective self-management of mineral markets that had broken down in the 1970s and early 1980s. The collapse of developing-country efforts to create collaborative intergovernmental mechanisms to manage markets, and the increased willingness of developing-country governments to cooperate with western TNCs, are both conducive to the restoration of private market management. Western governments have given their tacit support for this process through their participation in mixed private-public institutions such as the study groups for copper, lead and zinc, and nickel, and the aluminum MOU. But self-management appears to be unable to cope with two problems that have emerged in the 1990s. First, the expansion of exports from previously communist countries has destabilized markets and producers in these countries have rejected western behavioral norms of oligopolistic self-restraint. Second, private self-regulation by mineral traders at the LME has encouraged speculation and market manipulation, which serves the private interests of mineral traders at the expense of actual producers and consumers of minerals and metals.

CONCLUSIONS

This chapter has shown that private mining firms are constantly cooperating tacitly to manage international mineral markets or trying to establish private market management, often with the tacit or explicit support of western governments. In the 1950s and 1960s they were relatively successful, operating producer pricing systems (sometimes characterized by price leadership, a clear example of the exercise of private authority) for most of the minerals reviewed in this chapter. In the 1970s, private market management broke down in the face of challenges from developing countries, which believed that equity norms ought to play a much larger role compared to the market norms that guided western governments' approach to mineral market management, and which sought to maximize short-run returns from high mineral prices rather than taking the long-run view of western oligopolists. The clash between competing interests and norms meant that both private and public management of most mineral markets were weak during this period. In the 1980s and 1990s, after a period of severely depressed markets, the conditions for private market management began to be restored. Developing producing countries had failed in their attempts to create intergovernmental management based on their prefered norms and became more willing to cooperate with western private mining transnationals. Western governments created study groups for copper and nickel in support of industry efforts to reestablish norms of oligopolistic self-restraint. However, these changing conditions failed to replicate the success of similar efforts in the 1950s and 1960s because of the growth of speculative trading on the LME and exports from the former Soviet Union. Interestingly, private self-regulation of the LME tolerated attempts by traders to manipulate markets, and those attempts undermined private self-management by mining TNCs.

As this summary indicates, the direction of change over time in the strength of private self-management is different in the case of international mineral markets from the general trend identified in the concluding chapter to this volume. In that chapter, it is suggested that globalization and spread of liberal ideology in recent years have increased the scope for the exercise of private authority. The different trend apparent in the case of minerals appears to be due to a number of factors. First, the mineral industry has a long history of "globalization," and in the 1950s and 1960s it was as globally oriented as many other industries are only becoming today. Private TNCs dominated the production and trade of many minerals in that earlier period, and developed mechanisms of self-management to stabilize and support prices. Second, the recent collapse of the Soviet bloc (itself sometimes seen as a source of globalization) has brought new producers into the market who do not share western behavioral norms. Third, the globalization of financial markets—as manifested in the increase in trading of minerals and metals on the LME by financial investors—has undermined the efforts of the mining and metals industry to regulate itself (though private self-regulation of the LME has become more important to economic outcomes than ever before).

The varying success of private market management and the strength of private regimes can be explained by a variety of factors. In the introduction to this chapter, I identified three: market structure, internal characteristics of important actors, and social institutions. There have been few dramatic changes in market structures in these mainly oligopolistic industries, but those changes that have occurred have had a dramatic impact on private market management. Nickel's shift from near-monopoly to oligopoly ended Inco's ability to serve as a price leader, while the growth of smaller independent aluminum producers in the 1970s weakened tacit oligopolistic collusion among the major producers.

There have been more dramatic changes in the internal characteristics of key actors, and these have had a substantial impact on the prospects for private market management even when basic market structures have not changed significantly. Private market management broke down in a number of minerals in the late 1960s and 1970s because of the emergence of state-owned producers in developing countries that had very different interests and were guided by different ideologies than private western mining transnationals. As these producers changed again in the 1980s and 1990s to resemble private mining companies more closely, the prospects for collaborative market management improved. However, the internal characteristics of producers in the former Soviet Union, which became much more important exporters to the world market in the 1990s, were sharply different. These producers were guided by neither market imperatives nor central planning, and their actions were highly disruptive. A major focus of collective action by western producers of such minerals and metals as nickel and aluminum therefore was to persuade these firms to adopt the behavioral norms of western oligopolistic industries.

These changes in the internal character of important actors obviously had a crucial impact on the potential for informal social institutions to emerge to manage these markets. But the prospects for social institutions were also shaped by broader political and ideological dynamics. Politically, the role of governments in supporting or challenging private market management is obviously critical. Tacit western support for oligopolistic market management was important in the 1950s and 1960s, while the challenge from developing-country governments in the 1970s undermined market management by private firms. Western government support for study groups and the aluminum MOU were important factors in the recreation of conditions favorable to private market management in the late 1980s and 1990s. Just as this chapter has shown that it is a mistake to study intergovernmental regimes without paying attention to their relationships with private regimes, it is also apparent that in this area, private regimes do not emerge without the tacit or explicit support of governments.

Social institutions were also heavily influenced by the power of different states. This is shown most clearly in the relative success of western and Third World governments in creating regimes consistent with their ideologies and interests. The Third World failed entirely to create intergovernmental regimes (producer cartels or producer-consumer ICAs) organized around the norms favoring international equity that they preferred—specifically, that markets should be managed by governments to promote more stable and remunerative prices for developing-country commodity exports, which had been suffering from declining terms of trade.[102] For developing countries, however, the end of intergovernmental efforts to manage commodity markets has been accompanied by extremely low prices that have worsened their economic conditions and prospects.[103] Private market management may serve the public interests of western consuming countries and the private interests of mineral producing firms, but it has not advanced the public interests of developing producing countries.[104] I have tended in this chapter to associate the term "public" with community-wide interests, and "private" with the interests of specific market participants, but different communities have different collective interests, and the use of the term public can often obscure these differences.

Western norms favoring "free" markets clearly have been dominant throughout the period covered by this study. But as this study reveals, the constant rhetorical support for "free markets" in western countries is highly misleading. Some producing firms and some governments are almost always trying to collaborate to manage international markets and prevent them from approximating freely competitive atomistic markets. In the absence of tacit oligopolistic collusion, mineral markets are almost certainly less stable.[105] Consequently, western governments have usually tolerated, and often encouraged, the development of tacit oligopolistic collusion. In a sense, transnational groups of private metal producers have been delegated authority to manage international markets by default; governments do not wish—or are unable—to collaborate directly with each other to stabilize markets, yet have a powerful interest in seeing markets stabilized. Groups of private producers that hope to achieve this outcome are tolerated or encouraged. Western governmental support for private market management occasionally is more explicit, as in the study groups and the aluminum MOU. Without these kinds of public support, private management could not emerge.

Despite the shared preference for "free" markets, there are differences of ideology and interest among western governments regarding the management of mineral markets. Governments of continental European countries have been more supportive of market management than the United States, as evidenced by the European Union's consideration of collaborative arrangements among zinc producers and its imposition of import quotas for aluminum, and by the United States' occasional dissent from discussions of collaboration in the ILZSG. Nevertheless, even the United States has favored government support for mechanisms that facilitate private market management on a number of occasions, and it has been more successful in establishing such mechanisms than other western governments. This is clearest in the contrast between the relatively quick establishment of the study group for copper, of which the United States is a major producer, and the slow and tentative establishment of the study group for nickel, of which Canada and Australia are the main developed-country producers.

The importance of ideology in shaping prospects for private self-management is also apparent in the increasing role played by the LME in the international minerals industry. Western governments have moved sharply toward more open capital markets and have sought to develop financial industries as engines of growth in their own right rather than as the servant of industries that produce goods and other services. Britain took a lead in this direction, in part with the FSA of 1986, which sought to increase the attractiveness of the LME and other markets based in London to global investors. Other governments have moved in similar directions. The impact on international mineral markets has been dramatic. Massive increases in the volume of trading on the LME (up over 1,000 percent in the past ten years) have brought private benefits to the traders who run the LME (an interesting case of private authority in its own right) and to the City of London. But these have come at the expense of much worse price instability for actual producers, consumers, and the communities that depend on the minerals and metals industry.

As yet, there has been little interest—and no action—among the major western governments in public regulation to ameliorate these problems. Belief in the benefits of "free" markets is deeply ingrained and governments have difficulty even considering the need for public action to counter harmful effects of the exercise of private power in markets— witness not only the LME, but the much larger and more destabilizing foreign exchange markets, where no proposals for dampening excessive speculation have yet been seriously considered. But public regulation and private regulation are often substitutes for each other, and in the wake of the copper crisis and ongoing instability in markets for other minerals traded on the LME, one can imagine that governments may seek to reclaim some of the authority for regulating that market from the traders who have been delegated the responsibility for self-regulation. Similarly, one can imagine that if a group of private metal producers were to use the authority to manage their market effectively delegated to them by western governments to restrict supplies and inflate prices, that delegation would also be retracted, in the form of antitrust investigation. At present, however, the combination of LME-driven instability and the growth of exports from Russian producers guided by very different behavioral norms make such strong private self-management of mineral markets unlikely.

NOTES

1. Stephen D. Krasner, "Structural Causes and Regime Consequences: Regimes as Intervening Variables," in Krasner, ed., *International Regimes* (Ithaca: Cornell University Press, 1983), p. 2.

2. Friedrich Kratochwil and John Gerard Ruggie, "International Organization: A State of the Art on an Art of the State," *International Organization*, 40.4 (Autumn 1986): 764.

3. Deborah Spar makes a similar argument in the case of cartels; see Debora L. Spar, *The Cooperative Edge: The Internal Politics of International Cartels* (Ithaca: Cornell University Press, 1994).

4. Stephen Krasner, "The Quest for Stability: Structuring the International Commodities Markets," in Gerald and Lou Ann Garvey, eds., *International Resource Flows*, (Lexington, Mass.: Lexington Books, 1977), pp. 39–40.

5. Kratochwil and Ruggie, "International Organization," p. 764.

6. See especially Spar, *The Cooperative Edge.*

7. See Jock A. Finlayson and Mark W. Zacher, *Managing International Markets: Developing Countries and the Commodity Trade Regime*, (New York: Columbia University Press, 1988).

8. Spar, *The Cooperative Edge*, pp. 31–33.

9. Alfred Maizels, *Commodities in Crisis* (Oxford: Clarendon Press, 1992), p. 177. Regulation by developed-country governments also is intended to serve the government's interests, but is phrased in terms of enhancing market efficiency.

10. Though see Susan Strange, *The Retreat of the State: The Diffusion of Power in the World Economy* (Cambridge: Cambridge University Press, 1996), pp. 158–60.

11. The theory on which these arguments about tacit oligopolistic collusion are based is developed in Jean Tirole, *The Theory of Industrial Organization*, (Cambridge: MIT Press, 1988), chapters 5–6 and 8–9; and F. M. Scherer and David Ross, *Industrial Market Structure and Economic Performance*, 3rd ed. (Boston: Houghton Mifflin, 1990), chapters 6–8.

12. Spar, *The Cooperative Edge.*

13. Scherer and Ross, *Industrial Market Structure and Economic Performance*, pp. 245, 308–10.

14. Ibid., p. 248.

15. Ibid., pp. 261 (quote), 248–49.

16. Ibid., pp. 235–36, 313.

17. For a representative advocacy of hedging on commodity exchanges, see Eduardo Borensztein et al., *The Behavior of Non-Oil Commodity Prices*, Occasional Paper 112 (Washington, D.C.: International Monetary Fund, August 1994), pp. 15, 21–22.

18. This is detailed in Robert Gibson-Jarvie, *The London Metal Exchange: A Commodity Market*, 3rd ed. (Cambridge, England: Woodhead-Faulkner, 1988).

19. Such as the diamond cartel, involving DeBeers and the Soviet government; Spar, *The Cooperative Edge*.

20. Finlayson and Zacher, *Managing International Markets*.

21. Scherer and Ross, *Industrial Market Structure and Economic Performance*, pp. 271, 314.

22. Finlayson and Zacher, *Managing International Markets*, pp. 206–8.

23. Marian Radetzki, *A Guide to Primary Commodities in the World Economy* (Oxford: Basil Blackwell, 1990), p. 76.

24. Scherer and Ross, *Industrial Market Structure and Economic Performance*, p. 356.

25. Ibid., p. 272.

26. David E. Hojman, "The IBA and Cartel Problems: Prices, Policy Objectives, and Elasticities," *Resources Policy*, December 1980, pp. 290–91.

27. Ibid., p. 290.

28. Michael C. Webb with Mark W. Zacher, *Canada and International Mineral Markets: Dependence, Instability, and Foreign Policy* (Kingston, Ont.: Centre for Resource Studies, 1988), pp. 17–19; Gibson-Jarvie, *The London Metal Exchange*, pp. 144–45; Rudolf Wolff and Co., *Wolff's Guide to the London Metal Exchange*, 5th ed. (Surrey, England: Metal Bulletin Books, 1995), pp. 165–67.

29. Because lead and zinc are often co-produced and zinc is the more valuable of the two, private market management tends to focus on zinc, and lead markets tend to be less stable.

30. Webb, *Canada and International Mineral Markets*, p. 59.

31. Canada, Department of Energy, Mines, and Resources, *The International Minerals Scene* 1.1 (July 1978): 8.

32. International Lead and Zinc Study Group Document LZ/13, September 13, 1960, p. 1.

33. Webb, *Canada and International Mineral Markets*, pp. 59–61, based in part on interviews with Canadian government officials and industry spokesmen, 1983.

34. On the latter point, see United Nations Document TD/B/4, February 1965.

35. Webb, *Canada and International Mineral Markets*, pp. 68–69.

36. Finlayson and Zacher, *Managing International Markets*; see also Stephen D. Krasner, *Structural Conflict: The Third World against Global Liberalism* (Berkeley: University of California Press, 1985).

37. Finlayson and Zacher, *Managing International Markets*, pp. 209–10; Radetzki, *A Guide to Primary Commodities*, pp. 117–18; Hojman, "The IBA and Cartel Problems," pp. 292–93.

38. On the importance of the low share of bauxite costs in total aluminum production costs, see Finlayson and Zacher, *Managing International Markets*, p. 210; on increased profits, see Steven Kendall Holloway, *The Aluminum Multinationals and the Bauxite Cartel* (Basingstoke, England: Macmillan, 1988).

39. Finlayson and Zacher, *Managing International Markets*, p. 211; Radetzki, *A Guide to Primary Commodities*, pp. 117–18. Jamaica's revenues from bauxite remained far higher even after the loss of market share than before the 1974 measures; Holloway, *The Aluminum Multinationals and the Bauxite Cartel*, p. 83.

40. Shernaz Choksi, "Aluminum Price Behavior: A Decade on the LME," *Resources Policy*, March 1991, pp. 13–14. On aluminum firms' hostility to the LME, see Gibson-Jarvie, *The London Metal Exchange*, pp. 200–201; one producer threatened to halt LME trading by buying up all the stock offered for sale on the LME, but the threat was never carried out (and perhaps could not have been).

41. Scherer and Ross, *Industrial Market Structure and Economic Performance*, pp. 272, 309–10; Holloway, *The Aluminum Multinationals and the Bauxite Cartel*.

42. Holloway, *The Aluminium Multinationals and the Bauxite Cartel*, p. 35.

43. Karen A. Mingst, "Cooperation or Illusion: An Examination of the Intergovernmental Council of Copper Exporting Countries," *International Organization* 30.2 (Spring 1976): 263–87; Finlayson and Zacher, *Managing International Markets*, pp. 192–93, 196.

44. For descriptions of the UNCTAD copper negotiations, see Finlayson and Zacher, *Managing International Markets*, pp. 192–96, and, from a Canadian perspective, Webb, *Canada and International Mineral Markets*, pp. 23–32.

45. Webb, *Canada and International Mineral Markets*, p. 62.

46. Canada, Department of Energy, Mines, and Resources, *The International Minerals Scene* 1.2 (September 1978): 5; *The International Minerals Scene* 2.1 (January 1979): 4.

47. Webb, *Canada and International Mineral Markets*, pp. 71–72; Robert D. Cairns, "A Reconsideration of Ontario Nickel Policy," *Canadian Public Policy* 7.4 (Autumn 1981): 527–28, 530.

48. *Globe and Mail*, October 25, 1977, pp. B2, B16; Webb, *Canada and International Mineral Markets*, pp. 72–73.

49. Webb, *Canada and International Mineral Markets*, pp. 73–76.

50. Marian Radetzki, "The Decline and Rise of the Multinational Corporation in the Metal Mineral Industry," *Resources Policy*, March 1992, pp. 2–8.

51. Christopher L. Gilbert, "International Commodity Agreements: An Obituary Notice," *World Development* 24.1 (1996): 1–19.

52. *Financial Times*, December 12, 1991, p. 28, and November 4, 1994, p. 27.

53. *Financial Times*, November 17, 1987, p. 34, and August 8, 1990, p. 24.

54. Holloway, *The Aluminum Multinationals and the Bauxite Cartel*, p. 81; Finlayson and Zacher, *Managing International Markets*, pp. 211–13; *Financial Times*, December 3, 1993, p. 26.

55. *Financial Times*, February 17, 1994, p. 28.

56. Holloway, *The Aluminum Multinationals and the Bauxite Cartel*, pp. 79–80.

57. Rudolf Wolff and Co., *Wolff's Guide to the LME*, chapter 5; *Financial Times*, March 3, 1987, p. 32; October 21, 1987, p. 38.

58. Such a market squeeze, apparently engineered by a Swiss trading firm, occurred in mid-1990; *Financial Times*, November 23, 1990, p. 32.

59. *Financial Times*, November 23, 1990, 32; October 27, 1987, p. 38.

60. The quote is from the President of the European Aluminum Association; *Financial Times*, February 11, 1993, p. 30. For similar statements from the American industry, see *Financial Times*, August 12, 1993, p. 22.

61. *Financial Times*, August 20, 1993, p. 22, and December 23, 1993, p. 20.

62. Quoted in *Financial Times*, January 25, 1994, p. 32.

63. *Financial Times*, February 1, 1994, p. 32. On individual announcements, see *Financial Times*, January 14, 1994, p. 30; February 4, 1994, p. 28; February 25, 1994, p. 36; on their impact on western world output, see *Financial Times*, April 21, 1994, p. 42; September 13, 1994, p. 36.

64. Rudolf Wolff and Co., *Wolff's Guide to the LME*, pp. 111–12.

65. *Financial Times*, February 1, 1994, p. 32.

66. *Financial Times*, July 22, 1994, p. 26; March 7, 1995, p. 31.

67. Valentin Gavrichkin, of the Volgograd aluminum plant, quoted in *Globe and Mail*, February 3, 1994, p. B9.

68. *Financial Times*, October 25, 1994, p. 32; December 30, 1994, p.23; *Globe and Mail*, Decmber 20, 1994, p. B9.

69. Webb, *Canada and International Mineral Markets*, pp. 32–34; Finlayson and Zacher, *Managing International Markets*, p. 196.

70. *Mining Journal*, August 17, 1984, p. 107; September 7, 1984, pp. 161–62; *Globe and Mail*, June 21, 1984, p. B12; August 31, 1984, p. B4.

71. Webb, *Canada and International Mineral Markets*, pp. 35–38; *Canadian Minerals Yearbook*, various issues.

72. Isabel Marshall et al., "The Competitive Strategy of Codelco and Other Leading Copper Producers: Changes during the Last Decades," *Resources Policy*, June 1993, p. 96.

73. See Marshall et al., "The Competitive Strategy of Codelco and Other Leading Copper Producers," p. 93, on the U.S. threat.

74. *Financial Times*, 21 October 1987, p. 38; July 30, 1991, p. 24.

75. See, for example, *Financial Times*, December 4, 1991, p. 34; 9 October 1990, p. 34.

76. Webb, *Canada and International Mineral Markets*, p. 66.

77. *Financial Times*, February 3, 1987, p. 32.

78. *Financial Times*, December 22, 1989, p. 24.

79. *Financial Times*, July 23, 1992, p. 30.

80. *Financial Times*, December 22, 1989, p. 24, and June 16, 1992, p. 32.

81. *Financial Times*, September 17, 1987, p. 38; June 22, 1993, p. 34; February 11, 1994, p. 30; July 1, 1994, p. 32.

82. See reports of meeting in Canada, Dept. of Energy, Mines, and Resources, "Thirtieth Session of the International Lead and Zinc Study Group, October 17–24, 1985," mimeograph, p. 12.

83. *Financial Times*, April 28, 1994, p. 36.

84. "Chinese Lead-Zinc Comes into Focus," *Metal Bulletin*, online edition, June 13, 1996.

85. *Financial Times*, October 9, 1992, p. 30; November 5, 1992, p. 32.

86. *Financial Times*, January 10, 1989, p. 28.

87. *Financial Times*, November 10, 1994, p. 36.

88. *Mining Journal*, November 8, 1985, p. 356; Energy, Mines and Resources Canada, *Canadian Minerals Yearbook 1990: Review and Outlook* (Ottawa: Minister of Supply and Services Canada, 1991), p. 44:4.

89. *Financial Times*, October 14, 1992, p. 32.

90. *Financial Times*, November 18, 1993, p. 34; February 8, 1994, p. 32.

91. *Financial Times*, April 26, 1994, p. 34.

92. Rudolf Wolff and Co., *Wolff's Guide to the London Metal Exchange*; Robert Gibson-Jarvie, *The London Metal Exchange*.

93. Rudolf Wolff and Co., *Wolff's Guide to the London Metal Exchange*, p. 53.

94. Ibid., p. 52.

95. *Globe and Mail*, June 19, 1996, pp. B1, B7.

96. "Why Mr. Copper Chose British Provincial Team," *Financial Times*, online edition, July 5, 1996; *Globe and Mail*, June 20, 1996, p. B8, and June 25, 1996, p. B10.

97. *Financial Times*, July 30, 1991, p. 24; October 6, 1993, p. 32.

98. *Globe and Mail*, June 19, 1996, pp. B1, B7; Gibson-Jarvie, *The London Metal Exchange*, describes these informal clublike procedures in some detail.

99. Normally the future price should be higher than the cash price, to reflect the costs of storage and financing. During market squeezes, the cash price rises as the trader tries to buy up available stocks, while the future price continues to reflect perceptions of the fundamental supply-demand balance. Traders call this cash premium "backwardation." On events in 1992 and 1993, see *Financial Times*, April 22, 1993, p. 36; July 30, 1993, p. 34; August 3, 1993, p. 22; September 9, 1993, p. 36; October 14, 1993, p. 34; June 28, 1996, p. 10; *Globe and Mail*, June 20, 1996, p. B8.

100. *Globe and Mail*, June 19, 1996, pp. B1, B7.

101. "Lack of Single Watchdog Helped Conceal Losses," and "Sumitomo Shares Fall 16.5%," June 18, 1996; "Sumitomo to Probe Cartel Allegation," June 29, 1996; "Sumitomo Refuses UK Access to Copper Files," July 17, 1996, all in *Financial Times*, online edition.

102. Finlayson and Zacher, *Managing International Markets*, pp. 19–20.

103. Maizels, *Commodities in Crisis*. The problem is worse for developing countries that are dependent on agricultural commodity exports than for those dependent upon mineral exports.

104. Although nationalization was not a panacea; corrupt and inefficient management of nationalized mineral producers in some developing countries made conditions worse than they had been under private transnational management; Radetzki, "The Decline and Rise of the Multinational Corporation in the Metal Mineral Industry," p. 5.

105. Margaret E. Slade, "The Two Pricing Systems for Non-Ferrous Metals," *Resources Policy*, September 1989, which compares price fluctuations under producer pricing and the LME.

CHAPTER 4

The Standards Regime for Communication and Information Technologies

Liora Salter

In every discipline, some words have life histories. Introduced initially for their powerful, often metaphoric, effect, these words become center-pieces of disciplinary debates. The debates focus on definitions and on the capacity of particular concepts to generate empirical studies. In the worst-case scenario, definitional battles become more important than the situations or issues that the words are intended to describe. In such cases, words lose their connection with definitions or research, and become instead proxies for debates about worldviews, ideologies, or competing conceptual frameworks. To possess these words, in the sense of offering *the* authoritative definitions of them, becomes the point of the exercise. After a short time, any word performing mainly as essen-tially contested concept loses its capacity to convey any meaning at all. It is dropped from the vocabulary of a discipline as being too imprecise or contested, and is replaced by a new concept. The cycle begins again.

It seems to an outsider that, within the discipline of international relations,[1] *regime* is a candidate for such a life history.[2] Were this to occur, it would be a pity. The reason why *regime* was so attractive ini-tially was because it dealt with situations that otherwise seemed to have no name or any salience in debates about politics.[3] *Regime* has had a jagged history as a concept in the discipline of international relations since it was introduced by Krasner more than a decade ago, however.[4] Recently, *regime* seems to be central to a debate about international interstate relations. For an outsider to the discipline, the significance of regimes lies elsewhere. In my definition, a modification of Krasner's ear-lier one, *regime* refers to any social space (larger than the household, but not necessarily international in scope) with inherently fuzzy boundaries and an ill-defined common bond, which nonetheless is characterized by specific institutions and practices and is governed by established rules and conventions shaping behavior and expectations.

To focus on regimes thus is to ask questions such as: What roles do the various participants play in constructing and reconstructing the regime over time? Who are the participants: state actors, private actors, or some hybrid of the two? To what extent does the regime hold together? Does cooperation sustain the regime, or is cooperation transitory, perhaps even illusory? Perhaps instead, conflict binds the participants together, causing them to act as if they were subject to formal rules. How does any semblance of a common bond emerge in the absence of a visible and coherent organizational form? Where is the regime centered—internationally, locally, or some combination of the two?

With new provisions added to Krasner's original definition, regimes can easily be distinguished from states, firms, and organizations.[5] States, firms, and organizations all operate within established boundaries. Each of these has a demonstrable common bond, formally established and evidenced in territorial boundaries, constitutions, bylaws, or whatever. To be sure, there is often contestation about both the boundaries and common bond of particular states or organizations, but these are in the nature of challenges to official declarations. A regime is characterized by the absence of official declarations.

In Krasner's original definition, and in the modified version of it offered here, the phenomenon of rule-governed behavior in the absence of formal rules is not necessarily connected to relations among states. Nor is the authority of a regime necessarily derived from state authority. In fact, in a regime, there is often no formal constitution, few if any legal rules pertaining to the regime as a whole, and few widely accepted notions of where the regime begins or ends.[6] Nonetheless, those who operate within a regime act as if such constitutions, legal rules, and accepted notions were visible to all. Herein lies the elegance of Krasner's original formulation. It is easy to see how, in theory at least, international interstate relations might have the quality of regimes, as his colleagues have since argued, but regimes and interstate relations are not always, or often, coterminous.

In the case study that follows, I will speak about the standards regime. The case deals with standards for communications and information technologies, and it fits easily within the modified definition of *regime* offered above. This regime is comprised of organizations, firms, and nation-states, but is coincident with none of them. The regime is, as this chapter will demonstrate, highly dependent upon nation-states, but not coincident with relations between states either. If there is a common bond, it lies in a vague commitment on the part of its participants to standardization. Finally, there is no such thing as formal membership, or even formal membership criteria in the standards regime. Yet the standards regime is characterized by a diverse array of institutions and institutional arrangements easily recognizable as such. It is governed by many established practices and rules. In short, the standards regimes meets all the criteria of the definition of regime presented here: ill-defined boundaries and common bond, combined with established institutions, recognized rules, and working practices.

What is especially interesting about every instance of a standards regime is how impossible it is for analysts to draw neat boundaries around it. Although its participants include formally constituted states, firms, and organizations, the regime as a whole has no officially recognized or recognizable organizational form. Participants inside the standards regime often refer to "the standards environment" or "the standards community." Hawkins speaks of the "standards milieu."[7] In other contexts, I have spoken somewhat metaphorically about the standards regime in terms of "micro-climates" and also, more prosaically, as involving "spheres of influence and interest."[8] Participants in the standards regime accept all these descriptions as accurate. The fuzziness of the standards regime seems to be inherent, but everyone recognizes the regime's existence. *Regime* is as good a word as any—as *environment*, *community*, or *milieu*—to capture the presence of form in the absence of formal organization in the sphere of political and economic relations.

There seems to be another, quite different tendency in the international relations literature: to match regimes to particular sectors, as if, for example, the automotive or security sectors each generated its own regime.[9] The standards regime to be discussed here is also specific to one sector, yet my research has demonstrated conclusively that standards regimes connected to very different sectors (producing different kinds of standards) have much more in common with each other than one would expect.[10] Occupational health and safety, environmental, and the new communications technology standards are all generated in a remarkably similar manner. Standards organizations everywhere have many of the same kind of organizational participants.[11] Counterintuitive as this finding may be, their practices, rules, norms, and conventions are similar, as are relationships among their participants.

THE PLAN OF THE CHAPTER

The chapter begins with a short primer about standards. This is simply to clear away misconceptions about standard setting. The chapter then provides brief descriptions of the standards regime a decade ago and today, to identify the implications of the changes now underway. In this connection, the chapter concentrates on two issues: the interplay of local, national, and international decision-making and the interplay of public and private sectors within the regime as a whole. The chapter concludes by returning to the broader issues raised by private governance.

An argument will be made that the standards regime has always been characterized best as "co-management."[12] Even today, it involves a symbiotic relationship between public and private sectors. This relationship has changed in some important respects over the last ten years, however. While standard setting has always involved both public and private participants, expectations have now shifted from public to the private venues. Even though many of the same public and private organizations are involved, the result of changing venues is that the orientation of the regime has changed, especially concerning the issues commanding attention within it.

A second argument will be made concerning the epicenter of the standards regime. Given that the chapter concentrates mainly on the new communications and information technologies, one would expect that this epicenter would have shifted from local and national venues to global ones. This sector is often cited as the exemplar of globalization. It is true that politics or public policy deliberations at a national level are no longer seen to be relevant in communication and information industries.[13] Standard setting also is now also presumed to be international in scope. At the same time, behind the international profile of the standards regime lies another reality. National allegiances have not diminished in importance. The local venue is no less important than the global one within the regime. Here too, the regime is a hybrid of elements, with no single direction of change apparent.

To the extent that the regime is now global, it is global in the limited sense of involving only the technically expert highly industrialized market leaders, Japan, the United States, and Europe.[14] Global and international are not synonyms, even in this, the most globalized of sectors. Instead "global" tends to mean increasing influence of particular national players that now concentrate their actions in a world stage even while they pay heed to their own national priorities.

THE CASE STUDY

Because the standards regime—the standards environment or community, to use its own terminology—is so little known or understood, a description is necessary first.

Standards

Standards reflect decisions about the acceptable design, capacities, or byproducts of products, industrial processes, or technological systems. There are standards for electric kettles, for quality management, for pollution, and for telephone networks. Indeed, there are standards for virtually every aspect of every industrial activity in the western world. Some of these standards are made into regulations. Their enforcement occurs—more or less adequately—through government agencies. The vast majority of standards reflect either agreements based on contracts between private parties[15] or, alternatively, voluntary agreements with no apparent means of enforcement at all.[16] Notwithstanding the role of governments in regulating some standards, standards seem to reflect a classic case of a private governance regime, and of a regime increasingly global in its scope and influence.

The standards most commonly in view concern pollution, labor, pesticides, and health. At first glance, these standards are different from others, say for quality management or telephone systems. They are designed in the first instance to protect health, safety, or the environment. The differences are partly illusory.[17] Safety standards also deal with the products and byproducts of industrial activity. Even pollution abatement standards have important economic consequences, factored initially into production and marketing decisions. Safety and environmental standards are also used extensively as instruments of trade politics. For example, any international pesticide standard will not even be discussed, let alone adopted, unless it is considered to be important for trade. Moreover, although these some of these standards become regulations (and in a few cases, may even be developed by governments), government involvement in their implementation, and enforcement is a complicated issue, and much less extensive than it appears. The overwhelming influence of industry in the making, implementation, and enforcement of standards designed to protect human health, safety, and the environment is openly acknowledged within the standard-setting regime.

This chapter deals primarily with another type of standards, standards for the new communication, and information technologies. These standards reflect technical decisions, made by engineers, about the design, quality, connectability, and compatibility of different communication systems. Like health and safety standards, the communication and information technology standards are explicitly tied to issues of trade. Like them also, the active engagement of industry in the generation and implementation of standards is taken for granted. Further, some of these standards also become government regulations, which are then unevenly enforced. Finally, like health and safety standards, technical standards have important social implications.[18] These concern cultural and national sovereignty and North-South relations. In other words, while this chapter deals with one type of standards only, technical standards, the analysis of the standards regime discussed here has considerable applicability to other standards regimes, including those for health, safety, and the environment.

It goes without saying that the standards regime is oriented to producing standards. These standards are simply indicators. They take the form of numbers or complex technical documents. The existence of standards indicates that negotiation has occurred about the acceptable design or performance characteristics of an industrial product, process, or byproduct of these. This negotiation always includes industry, even when governments are heavily involved. Participants in these negotiations always take economic, social, and political considerations into account as well as technical efficiencies or human health and safety. Most interesting about standards regime are the questions that the negotiations raise: Who was involved, which interests were brought to the table, was compromise actually achieved and, if so, what is its import? These questions pertain only incidentally to the actual standards. They deal with how the regime operates.

The Significance of Standards

Standards are important. Noble calls them "the sine qua non of capitalist prosperity."[19] Standards reduce the inherent chaos of industrial capitalism. They provide some stability within a set of agreed-upon boundaries.[20] Health, environment, and safety standards help industry deal with the risks of its activities. They off-load at least some of the risks of production on standard-setting bodies, insurance companies, and governments. Their existence permits firms to continue with activities that otherwise might attract lawsuits or public controversy.

Communication and information technology standards set limits on uncertainty about new technologies by reflecting agreements about how they will be developed and operated. They determine the technical pathways of development, much in the same way that roads determine where new housing and industry will be located. In doing so, they solidify North-South differences internationally. They "hardwire" existing differences between participators and nonparticipators in shaping the "new economy."[21] They make change to these relationships harder, if not impossible. Indeed, if ever there was a possibility for indigenous economic development or for smaller nation-states to exert significant control over the powerful forces represented by the new information technologies, it is undermined by widespread agreement upon technical standards developed by multinationals with other agendas in mind.[22]

Having just suggested that standards are important, it is necessary to raise arguments to the contrary. In fact, relatively few standards exist, compared to the theoretical need for them. For example, it is quite common to see products built to different, and often incompatible, specifications (i.e., nonstandardized products) all competing in the market. Anyone who has ever used a computer knows how rarely the putative need for total interconnectivity actually governs the availability of technologies. Often, as well, the formal standards process is bypassed (even, as it turns out, by its own participants) by firms seeking to establish their own technical specifications as dominant in the market. Despite the value that standards have in the mass-production process, and in fending off lawsuits and maintaining insurability, the fact is that some firms (all firms some of the time, actually) choose to assume the risks of not having standards or of not abiding by standards. They choose to produce products that fail to measure up to the standards, and they delay the introduction of new standards. The benefits of doing things cheaply or quickly, without bothering about conformance, often outweighs the risks of having no standards or ignoring them.

Everyone in the standards regime recognizes these contradictory attitudes toward standards. They know it costs vast sums to develop a standard. Standards are slow to develop. Standards are often not completely satisfactory. Standards often contain too many optional elements to be useful. These factors all encourage firms to disregard standards or to downplay their importance. Firms disregard standards, even while they continue to pay huge sums to participate in standardization. Something is occurring in the standards regime to account for this. More on this point momentarily.

State Involvement in the Standards Regime

Later, the issue of state involvement in the standards regime will also be taken up in some detail. For now, a few facts are important. Governments are heavily involved in so-called public interest (health, safety, etc.) and in radio spectrum standards. Yet governments rarely, if ever, are responsible for the original decisions upon which these regulations are based.[23] Standards and regulations are not synonyms, although they are often thought to be so, especially in the United States. Most standards, including regulatory standards, originate as voluntary standards.

In occupational health and safety, for example, a little-known private organization, the American Conference of Government Industrial Hygienists (ACGIH), provides the foundation documents upon which the great majority of government regulatory standards are based. ACGIH sets voluntary standards. OSHA, the Occupational Safety and Health Administration of the U.S. government, originally adopted ACGIH standards in 1968, and has revised relatively few of them since. ACGIH standards are also adopted in Canadian provinces, and by countries throughout the world. Only a few of them are revised. Moreover, ACGIH standards are the basis for many environmental standards.

In fact, the relationships between governments and industry, and between regulatory and voluntary standards, are complex. Governments are often involved in industry standards organizations in one way or another. They are participants in, or supporters of the voluntary standards process. They officially recognize voluntary standards. The private organization just mentioned, ACGIH, is made up of *governmental* hygienists and of participants from the military, as well as insurance company officials, academics, and industry. So, while the data for ACGIH comes from industry exclusively, and the resulting standards are guidelines mainly for industry, ACGIH cannot be said to be exclusively private in orientation. Yet it is officially a private sector organization. The relationship between ACGIH and government regulation is typical. Its equivalent can be found in the standards regimes associated with almost every domain of economic activity.

Governments can treat industry-originated standards in several different ways. As just discussed, any voluntary standard can be "referenced" and thus used (perhaps with some modification) as a government regulation. Alternatively, such standards can be adopted by government, but used only as guidelines. ACGIH publishes its standards in a little booklet that it sells worldwide. Inside the cover is a warning to all users (including national or local regulatory bodies) that the information (i.e., the ACGIH standards) is being made available only for the guidance of anyone who might wish to use it. Reader discretion is advised. Yet government officials routinely refer to the ACGIH booklet as if it were a product of their own efforts. In doing so, they sanction the guidelines published therein without formally adopting them as regulations.

Governments do also participate directly in standardization. Pesticide standards are developed internationally by a governmental agency under the auspices of the United Nations, for example. And the International Telecommunications Union (ITU) is also an intergovernmental body, again related to the United Nations, although predating it. Radio frequency standards are promulgated by national governmental bodies, negotiated internationally by an intergovernmental organization. OSHA, in the United States, is a government agency responsible for occupational health and safety standards only. Environmental agencies routinely set environmental standards within national jurisdictions.

Although each of these organizations appears to be governmental in nature, the result can hardly be said to be purely governmental. As noted, industry not only supplies all the data for consideration in every case, but sets the agenda for when standards will, or will not, be developed. Industry members sit on the government committees that actually generate the standards. Industry officials contribute directly and indirectly to policymaking. In short, even while the private standards organizations are rarely exclusively private, so too governmental standards are thoroughly interpenetrated by industry priorities. The situation is not a matter of capture. It is simply the way the standards regime operates, and is expected to operate, by all its participants.

It is worth emphasizing that the standards regime also includes public bodies that are not governmental. That is, it includes nonprofit groups that have a public mandate and that conduct their deliberations in a public manner. ACGIH is an example of a private organization having a public mandate. It conducts its deliberations in a public forum, according to agreed upon rules designed to protect the public interest. Nongovernmental standards-development organizations are normally accredited by yet other nongovernmental organizations whose mandate it is to oversee standards development. The accreditation ensure that the public mandate and process is being complied with.

Standards Development versus Standards Enforcement

The general presumption is that the standards, having been developed at great cost, will actually be used. Nothing requires this in most cases. ITU standards are actually called "recommendations." It is not uncommon to find the seemingly anomalous situation of firms or countries voting to adopt a standard that they themselves do not implement. This is as true for the private or nongovernmental standards organizations as it is for governmental or intergovernmental ones. Thus, the distinction between standards and regulations noted above is important. Regulations have the force of law. Standards do not have the force of law unless or until they are promulgated as regulations.

Standards can also be developed on a contractual basis. In this case, firms contribute as participants to the development of a standard by an accredited standards organization. The standards organization then is in a position to enter contracts with all firms. Later, for a fee, firms receive the right to use the standard or to represent their products (or themselves) as being in accordance with the standard or as being "certified." Contracted standards are not regulatory, but they have the force of law, and can be enforced through the courts.

"Market" Standards versus Formal Standards

Thus far, all of the discussion has been about formal standards. Sometimes formal standards are called de jure standards. It has been emphasized here that formal or de jure standards can be developed inside or outside government, with more or less governmental participation. It has also been noted that nongovernmental standards (even standards set by industry organizations) can be recognized as formal standards, through accreditation or contracts, for example. Formal standards are simply standards established by a standards development organization, or by an industry association that operates, from time to time, as a standards development organization. Or they can be standards developed (or adopted) by government as either guidelines or regulations. Formal standards are those recognized officially.

In the standards regime, formal standards are distinguished from market and de facto standards. De facto refers to the all but complete acceptance of a standard by competitors in the market. This occurs as a result of the market clout of a single company. "Windows" is an example of a de facto standard created through the dominance of a single firm, Microsoft. Not everyone relies upon "Windows," of course, but its dominance in the market is so complete that all firms must pay heed to it, even if they produce technology conforming to different standards themselves. *Market standards* reflect convergence within the market upon an agreed upon product or technical specification. Many firms are involved. In the case of floppy disks, for example, a market standard exists. Any firm can manufacture floppy disks, but all do so now according to the same standard.

Many participants in the standards regime say that, traditionally, the formal standards organizations have only standardized what were, in fact, already market standards. It is true that formal standards organizations traditionally have recognized market standards, but this is changing. They now even deal with standards for technologies not yet commercialized.

Traditionally, standards organizations have been reluctant to deal with de facto standards, however this is because standards organizations base their decisions upon achieving compromise among competitors in the market. Such decisions would have no credibility if only one producer/vendor were involved. Furthermore, because standardization depends upon a firm submitting something (a product, technology, etc.) to be standardized, the formal standards organizations would have nothing to standardize if only one producer/vendor were involved. Firms that have established de facto standards have no need of the recognition that formal standardization bestows. They have no desire to negotiate with other firms in order to achieve it. This last aspect of the standards regime is changing. Formal standards achieved widespread acceptance.

In the standards regime, another distinction is commonly made: between proprietary and nonproprietary standards. It will help to make sense of this distinction if it is understood that, in general, standards are considered to be public goods. That is, nonproprietary standards developed by competing companies are widely disseminated for use by others. Proprietary standards (or the technologies and products based on them) belong to particular firms, which restrict their use in order to generate profit. Proprietary standards are invested with a legal intellectual property rights.

Traditionally, formal standards organizations have been reluctant to deal with proprietary issues, for obvious reasons. Viewing the standards as public goods worked well when only a few of the most basic elements of products or industrial processes were being standardized. Today, however, complex technologies are being standardized. As a result, standards organizations are thus forced to come to terms with proprietary issues connected to their standardization efforts. The meaning of "public goods" is at issue. Defining it—that is, coming to terms with proprietary issues—has been exceedingly difficult for the formal standards organizations.

The proprietary issue is complicated by something almost ironic in nature. Formal standards organizations themselves rely upon the sale of their standards. That is, their standards are published, then copyrighted and sold. Most formal standards organizations jealously guard proprietary rights in connection with the standards they publish. They jealously guard these proprietary rights, even as they promote these same standards as being public goods.

The Operation of the Formal Standards Organizations

The formal standards organizations are normally organized in levels.[24] Each organization hosts a high-level policymaking meeting, which makes decisions governing the organization as a whole. Below this level is usually a technical assembly. Below this are technical committees or subcommittees. At the lowest level are working groups. The policymaking level attracts many participants, and is formally responsible for approving standards. The working groups actually make decisions, which they offer up as recommendations for later approval. A working group might involve only a handful of people, mainly from industry.

Participants continually refer to standardization as operating from the "bottom up." "Bottom–up" means that the actual work of the typical standards organization is supposed to be done at the lowest level, and is supposed to be supported entirely by contributions from whomever chooses to attend meetings at this low level. The higher-level meetings are supposed only to review and approve that which has been developed and recommended from below.

The hierarchy is more of an illusion than fact, however. The whole process is based on negotiations. The working groups focus on technical issues, to be sure, but their contributions are not disinterested. These originate in firms promoting their own particular solutions to technical problems. These same firms are represented at every other level in the typical standards organization. Negotiations continue throughout, not just concerning recommendations from the working groups, but also concerning which technical issues should be addressed at all. In other words, there is much more integration between the lowest and highest levels of standards organizations than is recognized on their organizational charts. Negotiations at the bottom are not very different, in fact, from negotiations at the top.

In recent years, the policy level—the top level of the typical standards organization—has become more important, however. Each organization now seeks to position itself to have influence on government policies and the market.[25] Standards organizations have become competitors with each other. Of course, this competition concerns the actual standards being produced. It also concerns the influence each organization will have on national and intergovernmental policymaking. Indeed, one will often hear grumbling from the participants in the lowest levels, the technical working groups, about the increasing gap between what the working groups do (set standards), and how the organization is being run from above (promoting policy and lobbying).

Voluntarism and Consensus in Standardization

Firm participation in standard setting operates on a voluntary basis . An ongoing commitment to standards participation is implied when firms contribute often to developing particular standards. This commitment cannot be counted upon. Firms can send participants to one meeting, and not to the next. Contributions (written submissions in support of a standard) are also voluntary. Any firm can decide not to make a contribution, and still attend the meetings.

The voluntary nature of industry participation in standardization is what gives firms control over the regime. Because developing standards is dependent upon data from industry, control is exercised by firms deciding whether, when, and how to participate. Without their participation, nothing moves forward. Thus firms need not declare themselves for or against a standard. They can signal their intentions simply by deciding whether to attend meetings and whether to make contributions to the deliberations.

In many organizations, standards are set by consensus. Consensus does not mean that all participants agree upon the standard, however. It means, rather, that all participants agree not to raise objections about the decision. Thus a standard can be adopted as a consensus standard even if it fails to accord with the interests of key participants. This happens when a participant[26] determines that the standard (or absence of a standard) does not impinge seriously and negatively upon its interests. It occurs if there is a trade-off involved. It occurs if a participant decides that its market strategies will be furthered regardless of the decision on a standard. It also occurs whenever a participant agrees to adopt a standard that it has no intention of using later. In short, consensus implies negotiation, but consensus does not necessarily reflect compromise. Consensus operates as a complicated way of signaling or masking participants' interests and intentions.

Consensus has another meaning in the standards regime. Strictly speaking, it refers to procedural requirements for developing and approving formal (accredited) standards. A consensus standard, it is said, should reflect a balance of interests—often among major producers, major users, labor, and government. In fact, this balancing of interests may be a good deal more informal (and unreliable) than such requirements suggest. In meetings of the formal standards organizations, "consensus" will be declared if there are no sustained or vehement objections from the floor. In this context, consensus means only that voting is not done.

Summary

New technologies impose high up-front costs. Litigation for product deficiencies does also. The chaotic state of markets today has created a situation of extreme risk for investors and developers of the new technologies. This is as true in the health sector as it is for the new communication technologies. Standards naturally reflect a strategy to reduce this risk. Standards represent agreements about the rules of the game, about the parameters of the new products and systems to be developed, about acceptable levels of impingement or harm, and about the points of interconnection among products and systems. Standards help protect firms and governments against law suits, and they are the bedrock of insurability. Some new technologies must be standardized in order to be marketable at all. The push toward developing and adopting standards is unmistakable.

Yet, ironically, standardization is incredibly difficult to achieve, especially given the market turbulence and fierce competition among firms.[27] Seldom are companies willing to relinquish the information necessary to produce a standard. Seldom are they willing to negotiate with others about the technologies at the front edge of their own competitive strategies. Further, the costs of achieving any specific standard (participation in meetings, developing contributions for discussion) are far higher than can be justified within a sound business strategy. Many participants also accept the economists' logic that standards impede free markets and innovation.

Standards are thus an embodiment of a paradox. The oft-criticized formal standards organizations, and all their myriad of committees, continue to exist and command significant resources from their participants. New industry forums spring up weekly and these too develop something like standards. Yet the production of actual standards remains very slow. The need for standardization is far greater than the actual standards being produced.

THE CONTRADICTORY CHARACTER
OF THE STANDARDS REGIME

One cannot understand the standards regime properly without appreciating this paradox. There are two points worthy of more discussion. First, it is easy to see how the standards regime has been transformed from a mainly public regime to a private regime in the space of a decade. Yet neither was the former regime actually public, nor is the new one properly described as a private regime. Second, especially in the field of new communications and information technologies, it is simply presumed that globalization is propelling all developments. Yet accompanying this globalization is an increased salience of local and national initiatives. To explain these contradictions, it will be helpful to compare the standards regime a decade ago with the situation today.

Public and Private Elements

A decade ago, there were three main approaches to standard setting in telecommunications (and few formal standards being developed at all for the information technologies). The first approach, in evidence everywhere but North America, involved state-owned telephone companies, operating largely according to government policy dictates. Their standards took the form of technical specifications. These were developed within the telephone companies, and only as required. On occasion, officials from various state-owned telephone companies would meet together to discuss the standards necessary for their quite different systems to interconnect. The second approach was North American. It involved large privately owned telephone companies whose monopoly status resulted in some form of state regulation of prices and service availability. Yet, even here, standards were largely developed in-house, and were coordinated among telephone companies on a need-to-deal basis. The third approach complemented the other two, at least in theory. The ITU provided a forum (one among several), where discussions about interconnection could take place (and negotiations could occur about apportioning the radio spectrum). Standards were developed almost exclusively at the national level, however. They were brought forward as "positions" to the international forum, where consensus could sometimes be achieved to designate them as official standards for everyone.

It would be easy to see this early stage of standard setting as primarily public in orientation. The presence of state-owned companies and regulation suggests as much. Standardization, to the extent that it occurred, was a matter of public policy. Regulators were everywhere in evidence. Many of these regulators were not independent, but operated directly under the authority of government departments. To the extent that coordination was required, a United Nations agency (the ITU) did it. The counterargument is equally persuasive, however. Even as the standards regime was mainly public in orientation, so too, it was always driven by industry. The state-owned companies may have set their own standards internally, but they did so in preparation for their own (and government) procurement, which was for purchase of equipment and services from industry. This meant that negotiation had to occur to bring the government procurement specifications into line with industry priorities. As well, even though the private telephone companies in the United States and Canada were regulated by government agencies, they operated largely according to their own dictates. Finally, even though the ITU officially relegated its industry "members" to a second-class status, practically speaking, the national contributions were first generated within industry, reviewed, and agreed upon in national committees where industry had representation, and then forwarded as "the national positions" to the international organization. Perhaps most significant in determining the relative influence of public and private participants is the fact that the greatest proportion of technical decision-making occurred independently of the standards regime just described. Neither the newly important information technologies, nor the cable and equipment manufacturers, fell within the ambit of standard setting as just described.

In short, in the old era, standard setting appeared to be very much a public or governmental activity. This was so even though industry participated actively in standards development, and even though the governmental standards organizations set only a very few of the standards being used in the communication sector.

Today, most (but not all, especially if one includes the developing world) of the state-owned telephone companies have been privatized. Slowly, probably inexorably, competition is being introduced. Traditional regulation is being dismantled or enfeebled. Where regulation persists, agencies are independent of government departments. The ITU has also been dramatically reformed so that its industry participants have their status upgraded to match their real importance.[28] Another long-standing international standards organization, the International Organization for Standardization (ISO), has also now become prominent in the communications and information technology sector.[29] It is a nongovernmental organization. Delegates to a recent European conference only echoed their colleagues at meetings everywhere by speaking about standards as essentially part of a sound business strategy. Everyone now agrees that standardization should be industry-led. In the new world of standards, industry reigns supreme and virtually everyone agrees that this is as it should be.

The new standards regime is no less complicated than the old, however, and it bears more resemblance to past practice than its participants openly acknowledge. Many of the formal standards organizations are still either intergovernmental or organized on the basis of national delegations. In each country, national committees, comprised of industry and governmental participants, still meet, often under the auspices of a government department (in government meeting rooms, in fact). These committees prepare national positions, taking care to ensure that industry's voice is adequately represented of course, but representing these positions as if they involved a national public interest. Foreign ministries are often involved, because standards have such important implications for trade. Furthermore, government officials remain very active participants in many of the private standards organizations,[30] especially because governments are major users of the standards and technologies. The ITU and, indirectly, even some of the private sector organizations, are still supported by governments.

Government involvement in standard setting is most evident in the European case where standardization has come to the attention of the Brussels bureaucrats, and where financial support is still being provided for developing specific standards. But even outside Europe, it is not uncommon to find standards written into government procurement policies. Standardization is considered to be an important plank of an industrial strategy. Its attraction is that it is an industrial (governmental) strategy compatible with privatization and liberalization. Early standards adoption by national standards bodies is viewed as a legitimate means for governments seeking to gain competitive advantage for nationally based industries. Finally, many consortia developing the new technologies and their applications are heavily supported by governments, even though they are also said to be industry led. These consortia generate many standards. In short, even in a world where the private sector now reigns supreme, the public sector is well represented.

What has changed, dramatically, are expectations of the standards regime. The prevailing view is now that standards are developed exclusively in support of industry (and thus only when and where industry needs them). The role of governments is understood today only to be a facilitator. Guidelines for public officials participating in standardization reflected this constricted notion of the public interest. Routinely, such officials now stress that their task is only to support and strengthen the hand of industry. They participate in order to ensure that the governments' needs, as major users of the technologies, are not overlooked. It is widely recognized that the formal standards organizations will develop only a small portion of the standards needed, that industry and the market will look after the rest. It is widely believed that formal organizations should represent mainly only the final stage in the standards process, the official approval and dissemination stage.

Looking at the past and present together, it is evident that the standards regime is, and has always been, a hybrid regime, involving public and private elements acting in both concert and competition with each other. But something has changed significantly today. In the past, the regime appeared to be public in nature, even as it was populated in almost equal measure by public and private elements. Today the regime appears to be exclusively private in orientation, even while it is partly supported, directly and indirectly, by government participation. Of course, standard setting is not now, nor perhaps has it ever actually been, fully public or an intergovernmental activity exclusively. And although governments remain crucial participants in the regime today, public no longer constitutes its defining feature. Indeed, the standards regime is now widely conceived of as a purely private governance regime (an alternative to state-based regulation) notwithstanding the major role still played by governments within it.

National, Regional, and Global Politics

Just as formal standards organizations are organized hierarchically, so too it is generally presumed that international standards should be preeminent and that national and regional organizations should feed the international system. There is supposed to be a hierarchy of standardization, in other words, with the international standards at the top, and local or national standards at the bottom. Yet, traditionally, national standards operated as nontariff barriers to trade. As such, they are integral national trade strategies. Firms promote national standards, much though they may suggest otherwise at international meetings. Their reasons are simple. Having a more stringent standard at home impedes imports from other countries that cannot easily meet the standards. Having stringent standards also increases the costs of production, which privileges the larger companies while imposing considerable constraints on firms that cannot afford to keep up. The question is how much has this situation changed?

Only a decade ago, it was relatively easy to sort out activities within the standards regime as either national, local (firm or sector based), or international. The primary decisions were taken at the local level. These were reflected in positions negotiated at the national level. National decisions were later represented in the international organizations. On the face of it, the situation has now changed radically. Today, the standards regime is understood to be inherently and necessarily international in orientation. Virtually everyone involved argues that adherence to international standards is essential. Yet, as was the case in dealing with the public versus private nature of the standards regime, the situation is much more complicated than it appears.

The case for the internationalization of the standards regime does seem compelling. Not only does everyone involved believe that both the technologies and the standards must now be global, but actions have been taken to reorganize the relationships among the organizations to give prominence to international bodies.[31] Every action is said to be in support of international standards.

In Europe, the drift toward an international orientation can be seen most clearly, inasmuch as the national standards bodies within Europe are rapidly having their roles reduced, becoming mainly only the dissemination and implementation arm of the European and international organizations. Earlier European attempts to create uniquely European standards have mainly been discarded, and Europe's so-called fortress walls are crumbling in the favor of global priorities in the standards regime. It is now commonly said that having a "European standard" should only be a fall-back position, and that European standards should be pursued only where international standards have not yet emerged or where there are distinctly different needs to be served. The intellectual property policies of the European standards organization, which might have imposed barriers to the integration of European standards into global priorities, have been replaced—after much rancorous debate—with policies more friendly to global capital.

In Europe as well as elsewhere, all eyes are being directed to something called the global information infrastructure (GII). It is presumed that this GII will consist of an internationally encompassing network of networks made compatible through agreed-upon international standards. All standards organizations are being directed, in turn, to focus their efforts on providing the necessary standards for the GII. The GII initiatives are propelled by intergovernmental bodies such as the G7 and the Organization for Economic Cooperation and Development (OECD). Their high-level strategy groups seek to involve, for the first time, very senior industry management, not governments, in setting priorities for standards organizations. Senior management priorities are almost invariably global in orientation, because the senior management in question is drawn from multinational companies.[32]

Finally, as an illustration of the drift toward an international orientation, it is useful to note again the new development in the standards regime, the growing importance of industry consortia and forums dealing with standards-related issues. These are organized without reference to national allegiance. Or rather, they often invite participation from anyone worldwide, and they are often problem- as opposed to nationally or regionally specific. Because they often deal with a single technology, they have no obvious reason to promote national contributions or even to recognize the nationalities of their participants. These consortia and forums represent industry initiatives. Multinational companies play the central roles in developing and furthering their objectives. Seeking global influence for their own technologies or solutions to technical problems, firms use forums to recruit support from smaller companies and to disseminate information about their preferred technical options.

If the standards regime were indeed as international in orientation as it seems from this description, it would be hard to account for much of what is still occurring, which is decidedly not international in orientation. "Going global" does not reflect a diminished role for those with local or national allegiances.[33] In fact, many of the working rules of the old standards regime remain largely intact. This is so for several reasons.

First, recall that a standard cannot even be considered initially unless and until there are contributions to initiate it. Thus, whatever occurs at the international level is often only a reflection of what is produced and submitted at a local or national level first. Taken together, national formal standards organizations (especially in Europe, the United States, and Japan), individual firms (which still often profess national allegiance), and industry organizations (which are often national or at most regional in nature) all remain the bedrock of the standards regime. Indeed, as noted previously, an argument can be made that the international standards organizations now reflect only the last stage of the standards process. They are important mainly for the legitimacy they bestow upon standards developed nationally or locally.

Second, it is relatively easy for any informed observer to identify the "home base" of each of the new consortia or forums. For example, participants will speak about how "the Australians don't want to" despite the fact that no national position has been taken in a forum meeting. Or they will speak about how a particular technology being promoted through one forum represents an attempt to dislodge "the dominance of the European standard" in the same field. In theory, anyone can attend and contribute to the new forums, but in practice, each forum represents a sphere of influence for the interests of its major participants, most of whom can be readily identified as having national allegiance.

Third, in the old ITU, all decisions (including standards) had to be approved at the highest level, the policy level. Participation at this level was restricted to national delegates, and these national delegates came from developing countries as well as highly industrialized ones. To be sure, the reality was that the intergovernmental organizations were seldom swayed by delegates from developing countries on important issues. That said, delegates from the developing countries often had enough clout at this high level to change the general orientation of the proceedings, or to delay, or otherwise complicate, matters that otherwise would have gone according to the agenda of the industrialized countries exclusively.

As noted earlier, a few years ago, the ITU was reformed. It was made possible for standards to be developed more quickly, and thus not to be dependent upon approval on high-level policy meetings (held only every four years). A separate Developmental Bureau was set up to support the interests of the developing countries. The effect of the reforms has been effectively separate the technical work done in the Standards Bureaus and approved at lower levels, from the commitment of the ITU to developing countries. Developing countries are involved either at the highest level or in the Development Bureau. The Development Bureau serves mainly as an educational arm of the ITU, more oriented to dissemination and acceptance of standards by developing countries than to shaping policies affecting standardization.

Fourth, the GII remains, for now, mainly rhetoric not reality. Meanwhile national and regional initiatives (Canada's Information Highway, for example) are well underway to develop national information infrastructures. These are likely to have more impact than global efforts. Pilot projects are being funded by national governments to develop and promote particular technologies seen as conferring national advantage.

Finally, national and regional organizations are still producing standards different from those proposed at the international level. For example, in Canada, manufacturers are regularly faced with a choice between using North American and international standards. Given the closer industry linkages in the North American context, the North American Free Trade Agreement, the Canadian manufacturers' propensity is to choose the North American alternative. This is true, even though Canada has traditionally been one of the strongest supporters of the international standards organizations.

In short, the standards regime is a hybrid regime in another sense than described above. It is still very local or national, even while it is global in orientation. Even as it becomes more commonplace to speak of global developments, it is also easier to identify the national or local allegiances of those involved. Even though some national organizations have been eclipsed, others have been strengthened, and new ones have emerged that are demonstrably powerful within the standards regime.[34] At any moment in time, and with respect to any particular decision about a standard, it is exceptionally difficult to locate the epicenter of action, the degree to which any standard is national, local, or global in origin.

But here too, expectations have changed. The old regime used the term "international" to refer to the importance of standards for everyone throughout the world. Included was a notion that developing countries had a role to play in some of the formal standards organizations, especially in the intergovernmental ones. Today, the more commonly used term is "global." "Global" refers to the key participants from the industrialized world. It also refers to advanced technologies, developed by experts located only in the most industrialized countries. When participants in the standards regime speak of "international" standards now, they are speaking not of standards development (which is now presumed to be "global") but of standards dissemination (which remains "international.")

In short, the profile of the standards regime was formerly national, but the old regime combined elements of local, national, and international activity. Today, as just noted, the profile of the regime is global. "International" has now a much more restricted meaning. Local and national initiatives also remain very important. Even while national initiatives are still being pushed, the regime is said to be necessarily and inevitably as global as the technologies it deals with.

ANALYSIS OF THE CASE STUDY

It has been suggested here that the standards regime is, and always has been a hybrid regime. This is reflected in relationships between public and private sectors and relationships between local or national initiatives and global ones. Significant changes have occurred in the past decade, but they cannot be accurately described only as globalization. Nor can they be described as the withdrawal of governments from domains they previously controlled. The regime involves a continual rebalancing of a complex mix of forces.

Collaboration in the Standards Regime

The standards regime also presents an interesting view of collaboration. Given all that has been said in this chapter thus far, it would be foolish to conclude that substantive collaboration takes place within it. The regime is purposefully anarchic, and its participants act as if they had total freedom to operate as they see fit. Negotiation is always present, but real compromise is elusive. It is more commonplace for firms to delay standards than for firms to agree on standards that compromise their interests. Yet the standards regime is designed to promote collaboration among competitors. It will help to understand what their collaboration means if the spotlight is taken off the standards themselves, and placed upon the regime as a whole. While the standards are seldom the product of true collaboration or compromise, the regime is properly understood as collaborative.

The regime is collaborative in two senses. First, by bringing all major firms and governments to meetings, the regime affords its participants opportunities for information gathering and market surveillance. All participants watch the flow of contributions. They note who participates in each meeting. They pay close attention to who is elected to various committees. Information also circulates in the informal discussions accompanying the meetings. This information concerns not only emerging new technologies, but also pending government policies, restructured regulatory regimes, emerging intellectual property regimes, potential or new strategic and other alliances.

Second, the standards regime brings erstwhile competitors into close contact with each other. It provides scope for mutual appraisal. A standards committee is thus a proxy for market competition. Yet participation in standards committee lacks the risks and constraints associated with actual markets. The fact that the regime is supported by voluntarism and consensus ensures that firms' longer-term interests need not necessarily be jeopardized. Yet, because of this collaboration with others, firms can keep markets in flux longer than they might otherwise be, perhaps long enough to change the odds of their own eventual success.

In short, collaboration has little connection with compromise. It is independent of the actual decisions on standards. It refers instead to the willingness of firms and governments to be involved in the standardization. The regime could not exist without its participants' commitment to work together. Collaboration is connected to the process, not necessarily to its products.

The Stability of the Regime

The standards regime has some formally constituted organizations operating with codified rules, but no one set of rules pertains to the regime as a whole. Yet the standards regime is governed by a set of quite stable expectations. These expectations concern: the working practices of standardization, the ways that formal and informal relations will be played out, the ground rules for firm involvement, expectations of the proper role for governments, the ground rules for firms' interactions with each other, and ground rules for how decisions should be made.

All participants govern themselves according to the ground rules, informal though they are. In fact, effective participation in the regime requires knowledge of, and adherence to these rules. Participants from developing countries are unlikely to understand the ground rules, and often lack resources to adhere to them. Thus they are disenfranchised within the regime, even while they constitute members in some of the formal standards organizations.

Participants in the regime have no question about whether a standards regime exists. They know the regime extends beyond any one organization and is under the control of no national state or intergovernmental agency. As noted earlier, they call it "standards community" and they speak about the "standards environment." They move easily from one organization meeting to the next, participating in formal standards bodies and industry trade associations alike, and also pursuing de facto standardization in the market. That different formal rules exist in each venue seems to be of no consequence. The real participants handle the differences with ease.

Membership in the regime is thus hard to pin down. Despite the fact that these participants are players in fiercely competitive markets, they regularly seek out opportunities to interact through the regime and to pursue strategies through it. That the regime appears so anarchic provides an excellent cover. The formal standards organizations have rules governing membership, as do some of the industry organizations. High membership fees also restrict membership. Furthermore, to be an effective participant, participants must also attend many conferences and seminars, each also imposing high registration fees. It would seem, then, that the rules governing formal membership are apparent to all. But recall that standardization is a "bottom–up" activity. Formal membership is very different from participation. Participation is entirely dependent upon the individual participants' own strategies. Participation, not formal rules, determines real membership in the regime.

The same firms appear on the meeting attendance lists. The same firms are members of all the major standards organizations. These firms are also likely to be dominant in the market, and thus capable of establishing de facto or market standards. In short, notwithstanding any criteria for formal membership in specific organizations, it is very easy to see who the real members of the regime are.

PUBLIC/PRIVATE GOVERNANCE AND AUTHORITY: THE STANDARDS CASE

The case study of standards was presented here because it sheds light on several concepts of interest in this volume, and because it demonstrates some aspects of changes now unfolding in the international arena.

Regime

Perhaps this case study's most useful contribution is drawing attention to the concept of regime. Never was there a better example than the standards regime of how order might be created in the absence of a single, identifiable orderer. The standards regime is one with inherently fuzzy boundaries that nonetheless is governed by established ground rules and established working practices. As noted, it is anarchic even while participants recognize the regime as being reasonably stable. It comprises many long-standing organizations, but the regime is larger in scope than any one or two of them. The regime involves national governments, but is broader in scope than either governmental or intergovernmental relations. An ill-defined common bond unites its participants. They know who they are, and they speak openly about the character of their regime. This common bond is hard to pin down. It is made up of vague commitments to standardization and willingness to collaborate through standardization, but it also includes presumptions about sound public policy. The regime persists despite the fact that some of its participants come and go, and that fundamental restructuring of the main organizations is frequently done. The regime persists despite the fact that expectations about the character of the regime are changing.

Governance

The point has been made here that standards are often ignored, and that the compromises that seem to support the regime are often only illusory. Why, then, link the standards regime to governance? There are two answers to this question. First, it would be mistaken to put aside the perception that the participants themselves have of the regime. They believe their standards are influential in creating interconnectivity. They believe that they are creating an information infrastructure that does link all countries into the global economy. They believe that this infrastructure should, and will, "govern" relationships among firms and countries. They are not at all surprised when the regime fails to achieve its goals. Notwithstanding its obvious limitations, they believe that they are creating a system of governance for the development of new technologies and products. Participants in this regime have few illusions about any form of governance. They are cynical about national governments and intergovernmental regimes too.

Second, even if it were true that the standards regime were not, in itself, a governance regime, it is so closely intertwined with other governance regimes that it deserves the same label. As noted, the formal standards organizations are now very much oriented to policymaking. The regime constitutes a venue for lobbying for particular public policies and its participants use their status in the regime to support their lobbying efforts elsewhere. Participants see the standards regime is one of the more important venues for negotiating new working rules for governance of the globalized economy.

The Public/Private Distinction

The standards case suggests caution be exercised in defining any regime by reference to distinctions between public and private authority. As stressed here, the standards regime is a hybrid regime. Furthermore, public authority within the regime is itself quite complicated. It is certainly not limited to governmental authority, but arises in conjunction with publicly mandated nongovernmental organizations and, sometimes, it is even attached to products whose origins are in the private sector.

The variable that seems to define something as being public in the standards regime is the process by which decisions are made. Standardization is usually considered to be public if a consensus process is used, if notice is given before decisions are made, if comments are solicited from all interested parties, and if the final product is available for public use (i.e., is a public good). Even here, however, the situation is not very clear-cut, as should now be evident. Not all government standards are developed thus, yet these too are public. Even market standards can be considered public goods.

Rather than seeking to designate regimes as public or private, this case study suggests attention be paid to the continual interplay of public and private elements in any regime. Attention should be paid especially to different notions of *public* that abound within regimes.

Authority

Authority is the most difficult concept to come to terms with in the analysis of the standards regime. This is because, as noted above, this is a regime that is ordered in the absence of a single orderer.

Some things about authority can be said with ease, however. In this regime, authority is not synonymous with government authority. It is associated with adherence to procedural rules, but is present even where such rules are not. In fact, authority attends to the products of the regime. Standards bear the imprint of the formal organizations that publish them, and are considered to be authoritative on this basis. But authority extends even to market and de facto standards.

Standards derive their authority from the fact that they appear to reflect a consensus. This consensus is more a matter of perception than reality. Once adopted, however, standards take on a life of their own. They are seen to be the best possible technical choices.

In this case study, then, authority is best understood as a sociological and psychological phenomenon. It is most closely allied with expectations. Authority exists regardless of how these expectations come to be. As soon as it is given to understanding that a standard exists, it is seen to be legitimate and it operates as a coercive force in the marketplace.

Calling something a standard designates it as inherently legitimate. But are standards really coercive? After all, standardization is voluntary; participation is voluntary and adherence to standards is also voluntary. To view the situation solely thus is mistaken. To the extent that standards (any kind of standards) are accepted in the market, they become coercive for all firms and their customers. To produce technologies that do not conform is to incur great risk. Customers follow market leaders; market leaders set standards. Customers are afraid of "orphaned" products or technologies; standardization is insurance against "orphans." Customers demand compatibility; standards are about compatibility. Thus, even voluntary standards are coercive in a sociological, if not a formal sense.

The main significance of the authority lies mainly outside the highly industrialized world, however. In the industrialized world, as noted earlier, firms often ignore formal standards, even formal standards they themselves have approved. Developing countries seldom have this luxury. They have no choice but to accept and be guided by standards if they want to participate in an increasingly global economy. Formal standards are simple the rules of the game, the price of entry.

Of course, formal standards (including ones developed in UN agencies) also reflect the priorities of their expert developers. These undoubtedly reflect the interests of the multinational firms that sponsor standards development. That such priorities might not fully accord with the needs of developing countries goes without saying. Or that standards adoption by developing countries might preclude other kinds of technical solutions, including those developed indigenously, can also be taken for granted.

New Developments in Governance

The case study of standards has also been useful in identifying the nature of many changes now underway worldwide. In the standards case, as elsewhere, it is easy to see the drift from public to private governance, and from the local and national levels to the global one. The case study provides a useful caution here too.

What seems to have changed are the profile of the regime and expectations concerning it. The public profile of standard setting has been eclipsed, but the public presence has not disappeared. Furthermore, the local or national levels seem now to be subordinate to the global one, but decisions taken at the local or national levels remain very powerful.

Changing the profile of a regime is not inconsequential. If a regime is presumed to be private in nature, its public participants are disadvantaged. This is very apparent in the standards regime where governments now speak of themselves as being solely facilitators of standardization, and where developing countries are virtually excluded from the important venues for decision-making. If a regime is presumed to be global in scope, the national allegiances of those who operate globally within it are masked, even while national governments are forced to take a back seat in decision-making.

NOTES

1. For the purposes of the discussion here, international relations will be considered a discipline. It has a specialized language, a recognized community of scholars, and an identifiable literature characterized by debates specific to the community. For an extended discussion of disciplines and interdisciplinarity, see Liora Salter and Alison Hearn, *Outside the Lines: Issues and Problems in Interdisciplinary Research* (Montreal/Kingston: McGill-Queen's University Press, 1996).

2. Several articles in this collection provide an overview of the concept of regimes in the international relations literature in particular. See also, Tony

Porter, *States, Markets and Regimes in Global Finance* (New York: St Martin's Press, 1993), pp. 11–26.

3. The observation that some important issues and situations have no salience in political debates or academic writing is hardly a new one. The comment here owes a debt to feminist studies.

4. Regimes are "principles, norms, rules and decision making procedures around which actor expectations converge in a given issue area." See Stephen D. Krasner, ed., *International Regimes* (Ithaca and London: Cornell University Press, 1983), p. 1.

5. Haas et. al. refer to regimes as "rule structures that do not necessarily have organizations attached." See Peter M. Haas, Robert O. Keohane, and Marc A. Levy, *Institutions for the Earth* (Cambridge: MIT Press, 1993).

6. This is what Ruggie refers to as an unbounded territory, when he is attempting to describe nonterritorial global economic regions, where distinctions between what is internal and external are "exceedingly problematic." See John Gerard Ruggie, "Territoriality and Beyond: Problematizing Modernity in International Relations," in *International Organization* 47.1 (Winter 1993): 172–73.

7. Richard Hawkins, "Standards for Communication Technologies: Negotiating Institutional Biases in Network Design," in Robin Mansell and Roger Silverstone, *Communication by Design* (Oxford/New York: Oxford University Press, 1996), p. 180.

8. This is discussed at length in Liora Salter, *The Mandates and Workplans of Seven Designated Canadian Standards Organizations* (Ottawa: Department of Communication [now Industry Canada], 1992).

9. See, for example, Peter F. and Edward Long, "Testing Theories of Regime Change: Hegemonic Decline or Surplus Capacity," in *International Organization* 37.2 (Spring 1993).

10. For a discussion of the standards regime as it is exists in occupational health and safety and in the environment, see Liora Salter, *Mandated Science: Science and Scientists in the Making of Standards* (Dordrecht/Boston: Kluwer, 1988).

11. Absent from the standards regime in communications and information technologies is any evidence of significant public participation, including participation of civic organizations or social movements. In the standards regime for environmental standards, however, the picture is somewhat different, because civic organizations (for example, Greenpeace) are very active. Yet it can be argued that relatively few environmental standards are responsive to the politics of environmental standard setting, the majority being derived by a complicated calculation extrapolated from occupational health and safety standards. In standard setting, it is useful to distinguish between the politics from which the demand for standards emerges, on one hand, and the practice of actually developing the standards, on the other. The former is more conducive to participation than the latter. For a discussion of environmental standard setting in Canada, including some case studies, see William Leiss and Christina Chociolko, *Risk and Responsibility* (Montreal/Kingston: McGill-Queen's University Press, 1994).

12. Liora Salter, "Capture or Co-Management: Democracy and Account-ability in Regulatory Agencies," in Gregory Albo, David Langille, and Leo Pan-itch, eds., *A Different Kind of State? Popular Power and Democratic Adminis-tration* (Toronto: Oxford University Press, 1993), pp. 87–100.

13. Liora Salter, "The Housework of Capitalism: Standardization in the Communications and Internation Technology Sectors," in *International Journal of Political Economy* 23.4 (Winter 1993): 105–33.

14. A distinction between international and global, taken up briefly later in this paper, may prove a useful way to capture the distinction between a regime that is inclusive with respect to its membership, and one that involves only technically expert and interested parties associated with political and economic power.

15. Many of the standards approved by the Canadian Standards Associa-tion (CSA) and by Underwriters Laboratory (USA), and the International Orga-nization for Standardization (ISO) take the form of contracts. For further infor-mation on CSA, see Miriam Cu-Uy-Gam, "Telecom Standards Planned," *Computing Canada* 9.17 (August 1983); John E. Kean, "The Role of the Cana-dian Standards Association," in *ASTM Standardization News* 22 (January 1994): 28–33. For further information on Underwriters Laboratory (UL), see Larry Caldwell, "How to Get a UL/CSA/ETL Licence to Print Your Own Labels," *Wire Journal International* 27 (February 1994) and August Schaefer, "The Evolution of Safety Testing and Quality Assessment at UL" *ASTM Stan-dardization News* 23 (June 1995): 38–43. The ISO 9000 series are contract-based standards.

16. In this connection, it is important to distinguish between setting and adopting of standards, on one hand, and their implementation or enforcement, on the other. Standards may be developed and adopted as voluntary or as mandatory standards, but both kinds of standards may not be implemented or enforced. It should not be assumed that voluntary standards lack implementa-tion or enforcement, or that mandatory ones are always subject to provisions for enforcement.

17. For a detailed analysis of these standards, see Salter, *Mandated Science*.

18. For a discussion of the interplay of social and technological issues, see B. P. Bloomfield And T. Vurdubakis, "Boundary Disputes: Negotiating the Boundary between the Technical and the Social in the Development of IT Sys-tems," *Information Technology and People* 7.1 (1994): 9–24.

19. David F. Noble, *America by Design: Science, Technology and the Rise of Corporate Capitalism* (New York: Knopf, 1979), p. 70.

20. In this sense, voluntary standards are very much like regulations, even though they are not mandatory. They derive their influence from the engagement of interested parties in their creation, from the ongoing involvement of such par-ties in the assessment of specific cases and enforcement, and from the perception that they are enacted in the public interest. Although the view of regulation offered here is well established in the literature. It is developed more fully in Liora Salter, "Capture or Co-Management: Democracy and Accountability in Regulatory Agencies," in Gregory Albo, David Langille, and Leo Panitch, eds., *A Different Kind of State? Popular Power and Democratic Administration* (Toronto: Oxford University Press, 1993), pp. 87–100.

21. The new economy is used here nontechnically to refer loosely to all of the changes now occurring, especially in production and distribution processes, which are derived from the emerging communications and information technologies.

22. In this connection, it is useful to note that, whatever the final outcome of the political and economic negotiations of the new Europe and of NAFTA, technical harmonization (regarding standards) across these regions will have been accomplished in a very few years. For further discussion, see Liora Salter, "Have We Reached the Information Age Yet?" in *International Journal of Political Economy* 23–24.1 (Winter 1994): 3–26.

23. In most cases, governments do not do the testing, and are thus dependent upon industry—which wants a standard to be approved—to produce the data. In a few cases, however (building materials in Canada, for example), government laboratories have been used for testing and associated laboratory work. Government laboratories are used where the number of producers in the sector is high and each producer is relatively small. Governments are now withdrawing from doing testing, however, and they are closing laboratories, preferring to contract out for testing services to accredited laboratories operated within the private sector.

24. For fuller description, see Salter, "Housework."

25. In some senses, the standards organizations are themselves competitors, because they deal with overlapping issues and some of the same technologies. Furthermore, even if it were the case that duplication was to be eliminated, it will still be true that these organizations compete about which organization should be responsible for the standard development initially. Each organization has carved out a sphere of technical work that is its own, but the technological systems being dealt with do not lend themselves to easy to compartmentalization, such as distinctions between wire and wireless or computing and telecommunications technologies. The new technologies are, in fact, distinguished by their blend of technological means of accomplishing similar goals.

26. Both firms and governments participate in standards organizations, often on the same delegation. Whether governments speak for all, or alternatively, whether a private sector organization is delegated to do so, is mainly inconsequential. "Positions" are negotiated beforehand. Thus it is necessary to speak of both firms or countries as participants, and as making strategic choices, both separately and together.

27. For further discussion, see Richard Hawkins, "Standards for Communication Technologies: Negotiating Institutional Biases in Network Design," in Robin Mansell and Roger Silverstone, eds., *Communication by Design* (Oxford: Oxford University Press, 1996).

28. Reform of ITU is ongoing, but because of the split between the political and technical levels of the organization (represented respectively by its Plenipotentiary and its Standards Bureaus) and because of the ITU's complicated decision-making rules, changes are slow to occur. For discussion of the changes now in process, see Mansell and Silverstone, *Communication by Design*.

29. ISO is a long-standing standards organization, but in partnership with the International Electrotechnical Commission (IEC) it set up a joint committee

to deal with communications and information technologies only about a decade ago. In theory, there should be little overlap between the JTC 1 (Joint Technical Committee) and the work of ITU, inasmuch as JTC 1 deals with information technologies and computing mainly. In practice there is considerable overlap and, some would say, rivalry.

30. For example, governments are officially members in ETSI (European Telecommunications Standards Institute), provide financial support to some of the delegations to ISO committees, indirectly underwrite some of the costs of participating in seminars and conferences associated with standards organizations, and sit as user members in private sector organizations and forums.

31. The Global Standards Collaboration represents an informal organization of six formal standards bodies (national, regional, and international) that holds regular meetings, among other things, to sort out issues involving how information flows from one organization to the next, "recognizing the pre-eminence of the ITU."

32. See membership lists of the various strategic and user committees set up by each of these organizations, for example, OECD, *ICT Standardization in the New Global Context*, DST1/ICCP(95)2.

33. The term national allegiance is used expressly to avoid discussion about the degree to which multinational firms are nationally owned or controlled.

34. United States Committee T 1 is an example of a national (private sector) organization with increasing strength and profile.

CHAPTER 5

Strategic Partnerships, Knowledge-Based Networked Oligopolies, and the State

Lynn K. Mytelka and Michel Delapierre

Since the beginnings of the industrial revolution "(s)tate intervention, which had freed trade from the confines of the privileged town, was now called to deal with two closely connected dangers which the town had successfully met, namely, monopoly and competition."[1] While monopoly has been fairly easy to regulate, other market structures that affect competition have proved more difficult to identify, giving rise to a persistant tension between firms and states with regard to the rules of competition. This tension increased toward the end of the last quarter of the nineteenth century when the mass production model came into its own and larger firms attempted to exploit fully the scale economies of new technologies. Maximizing throughput and operating at full capacity, however, brought with it a vulnerability to fluctuations in demand[2] and to variations in the price and supply of inputs. In their attempt to smooth out variations in price and throughput, strategies such as vertical integration, trust-building, patent pooling, and a variety of market-sharing arrangements were pursued by these firms. Modern industrial capitalism thus came to be characterized by oligopolistic market competition in which size figured as an important barrier to the entry of potential competitors.

Some attempts were made, particularly in the United States with the passage of the Sherman Anti-Trust Act in 1890, to regulate oligopolistic market behavior, notably when it constituted a restraint on interstate commerce or acted to monopolize trade. Following the crash of 1929, however, governments became more tolerant of such behavior and cartels proliferated in Germany and the United States while cartel-like structures became powerful in Japan.[3] After the Second World War, the United States lobbied forcefully within emerging international organizations to develop rules and regulations governing combinations and conspiracies in restraint of trade and engineered the break-up of cartels in the defeated Axis powers. Efforts to achieve an international agreement on restrictive business practices, however, were not as successful. In the OECD, for example, attempts at cooperation in the area of restrictive business practices began in 1967 but led only to the adoption in 1976 of a set of voluntary 'Guidelines for Multinational Enterprises' in which firms are urged to refrain from participating in cartels and engaging in abuses of market power such as predatory pricing and anticompetitive mergers and acquisition. Similarly negotiations within the UN Conference on Trade and Development (UNCTAD) led, in 1980, to the adoption of a nonbinding "Set of Multilaterally Agreed Equitable Principles and Rules for the Control of Restrictive Business Practices."[4] Exceptions to such agreements were, however, the norm. Thus, in the 1970s when the problem of excess capacity leading to noncompetitiveness and predatory pricing in the steel, synthetic fiber, and other industries emerged, governments sanctioned "crisis" cartels in Europe and Japan to bring about an orderly reduction in capacity.

During the 1980s yet another rationale for collaboration among firms emerged as a result of the growing knowledge-intensity of production. Product life cycles across a wide range of industries began to shorten and firms were obliged to spend increasing amounts on R&D and other intangible investments.[5] To amortize these costs, companies required wider markets, particularly when the home market was saturated and foreign markets were dominated by public monopolies.[6] In their drive to penetrate overseas markets, home states were enlisted in a project to open markets and deregulate. Deregulation involved not only the elimination of public monopolies through privatization but also the ability of firms to shape the terms on which competition within newly deregulated markets would take place. These included a relaxation of antitrust regulations prohibiting collaboration in research and development. A 1984 regulation adopted by the European Community, for example, exempted R&D collaboration from a number of restrictive practices. In the same year, the United States enacted the National Cooperative Research Act to encourage joint R&D. While initially these regulations were designed with a mercantilist objective in mind, by the end of the decade, reciprocity had became the leitmotif of bilateral relationships and market opening and deregulation policies were made the cornerstone of international negotiations,[7] thus assuring their broader legitimacy and further stimulating the globalization of competition.

Rising R&D costs and the need for wider sales networks resulting from the new competitive pressures, gave impetus to a wave of mergers and acquisitions (M&As) aimed at consolidating positions at home and accessing markets abroad. The value of cross-border M&As reached $229 billion in 1995, twice the 1988 level.[8] While mergers and acquisitions created critical mass, they also added to the inertia of the firm and this conflicts with the need for flexibility to which the rapid pace of innovation, and the heightened uncertainty resulting from both the erosion of frontiers between industries and discontinuities in what were previously incremental technological trajectories[9] were giving rise. Strategic partnerships[10] in R&D, production, and marketing were one solution to these contradictory pressures. Indeed, participation in these networks has since become an essential component in the ability of firms to access technology and markets.[11]

The globalization of knowledge-based competition exacerbated the problem of uncertainty still further by making earlier strategies of vertical integration and cartelization less effective in reducing the uncertainties, risks, and costs association with investments in scale and knowledge production. Strategic partnerships alone could not substitute for the kind of stability that traditional oligopolies represented. They did, however, come to constitute the basis for a new form of global oligopoly that we have called a knowledge-based networked oligopoly.

The second section of the chapter characterizes this new form of oligopoly, differentiates it from traditional oligopolies, and analyzes the conditions under which it emerges. In so doing it builds upon a long tradition of research on oligopolistic market behavior[12] and more recent work on Schumpeterian dynamics.[13] The third section provides evidence for the emergence of knowledge-based networked oligopolies in the information technology and health care industries. The concluding section argues that private regulation through knowledge-based networked oligopolies is substituting for both the market and public regulation in shaping the global division of labor and it suggests that there is a growing need for states, singly or in concert, to pay greater attention to the consequences of such behavior.

TRADITIONAL OLIGOPOLIES AND THE EMERGENCE OF KNOWLEDGE-BASED NETWORKED OLIGOPOLIES

The formation of traditional oligopolies is based on three relatively static pillars: (1) the ability to identify a small number of competitors, mainly other domestic firms, among whom mutual interdependence and forebearance are practiced, (2) the set of products or the industry within which oligopolistic competition takes place, and (3) the technological trajectory that these products will follow.[14] The globalization of knowledge-based competition, however, has made it increasingly more difficult to identify potential rivals, as the rapid growth in market share of Japanese automobile producers in the U.S. market during the 1970s, of Japanese semiconductor manufacturers in the 1980s, and of Korean producers of Dynamic Random Access Memories (DRAMs) in the 1990s illustrate.[15]

Even more difficult to predict in this period of technological discontinuity, are one's competitors when these may emerge from other "industries" through a combination of hitherto unrelated generic technologies as has taken place in what are currently known as the biotechnology and multimedia industries. Indeed what constitutes an industry is itself uncertain since horizontal segments can emerge within any existing industry and become a potential platform for the configuration of new industrial sectors. The reconfiguration of the "computer" industry is a case in point. At its origin, all computer manufacturers were wholly integrated companies that produced their own hardware, proprietary operating systems (software), and semiconductors. IBM was the dominant actor in the new industry worldwide. When Digital Equipment Corporation (DEC) sold its first minicomputer without software bundled in, their "naked-mini" broke with this tradition. Initially the naked-mini was designed for engineers who would write their own software. But the possibility now existed for software producers to emerge. This first horizontal segment that cuts across all products in the computer industry, is now dominated by Microsoft. Another horizontal segment to emerge and to form the basis for a distinct industrial sector was semiconductors, with, once again, a single firm, Intel at the top of the global industry.

Horizontal segments with some degree of exclusivity can emerge within any industry and just as they emerge, they can also disappear. Which segments are critical for one's own industry, moreover, is not always clear. Yet firms require some degree of predictability in planning investments and in developing new products. There is thus a need for some measure of agreement on what constitutes an industry and what the rules of competition are within it. It is in this context that knowledge-based networked oligopolies have a strategic role to play.

The new oligopolies share three principal characteristics:

1. They are knowledge-based, that is, involve collaboration in the generation of, use of, or control over the evolution of new knowledge. As a result, the new knowledge-based oligopolies are dynamic, seeking to organize, manage, and monitor change as opposed to rigidifying the status quo.

2. They are composed of networks of firms rather than of individual companies. Alliances thus form the basic structure and building-blocks of the global oligopoly.

3. In terms of their organization, the new oligopolies can form within or across industry segments and sometimes do both at the same time. They are moving and reshaping themselves much as an amoeba would, stretching out its "foot" to include new actors when the assets they bring to the network are complementary and eliminating others whose resources are no longer critical.

Table 5.1 draws a systematic comparison between earlier forms of oligopolisation and the new knowledge-based networked oligopolies in using the electrical and information technology industries.

Knowledge-based networked oligopolies, we believe, emerge within industries in which the three pillars upon which traditional oligopolies can be constituted—rivals, industries, technologies—are themselves undergoing radical change. We find evidence of these oligoplies in the information technology and biopharmaceutical industries where technological ruptures and globalization of competition are pronounced. These are also industries in which international strategic partnering activity has grown rapidly.

Data from the MERIT-CATI data base, for example, show that the number of interfirm technology collaboration agreements in biotechnology, information technology, and new materials rose from an annual average of 63 per year in the 1975–79 period, to 300 per year in 1980–84, and reached 536 per year in the 1986–89 period.[16] Strategic partnerships in these three "core technologies" fell off sharply toward the end of the 1980s, reaching a low of 280 in 1991 but rose again to 430 in 1993.[17] In biopharmaceuticals, the number of strategic partnerships had increased by 34 percent in 1993 over the year 1989.[18] In contrast to the intensive pattern of strategic partnering observed in the information technology and biopharmaceutical industries and despite its growing internationalization, the food industry remains a traditional oligopoly. Firms are large and vertically integrated and the industry is highly concentrated within food categories. Neither biotechnology nor other technological ruptures have as yet revolutionized its technological base and the industry configuration is still stable with no new horizontal segments to form the base for market power within a new industrial structure.[19]

KNOWLEDGE-BASED NETWORKED OLIGOPOLIES
IN THE "INFORMATION TECHNOLOGY"
AND "BIOTECHNOLOGY" INDUSTRIES

As traditional oligopolies come under pressure, one might expect that contestability would open markets further to competition. Instead,

TABLE 5.1
A Comparison of the Principal Characteristics of a Traditional and a Knowledge-Based Networked Oligopoly: The Electrical and the Information Technology Industries

	Traditional Oligopolies	Knowledge-Based Networked Oligopolies
Foundation	Size	Knowledge
Basis of Competition	Costs and market shares nationally and globally	Continuous innovation at the global level, although more traditional oligopolistic rivalry may exist within segments of the industry and in national markets that are relatively closed
Basis of Regulation	The ability to manage the *stocks* of competences as embodied in patents that are pooled and allocated in function of position held by the firms within the oligopoly	The ability to manage the *flow* of knowledge through the use of knowledge-producing and sharing alliances in research and development, production, and marketing
Means of Regulation	Negotiated arrangements including cross-licensing among leaders of the "technology cartel," patent pooling through joint ventures, allocation of markets geographically. Patent pooling allows the leaders to oblige licencees to acquire whole packages of patents thus creating a cost-barrier to entry, enables them to select which firms can become licencees, to impose restrictive clauses on the use of such licenses, and ensure that such firms do not seek recourse through the legal system to obtain better conditions for the use of these patents, thereby reducing the likelihood that licensing will create future rivals. The welfare consequences are felt immediately in the form of higher prices.	Informal and formal arrangements are concluded through which research is undertaken jointly, thus creating reasearch barriers to entry, orchestrating the pattern of diversification in the industry, and shaping the direction of R&D, which in turn influences the standards for new products, the timing of their commercialization, and the price at which they will be offered on the market. R&D alliances among competitiors, for example, potentially lock out rivals, while R&D alliances with users lock in potentially large clients monopolizing downstream or upstream markets as effectively as vertical integration has done in the past. Through technological lock-in, moreover, the welfare consequences, in terms of future opportunities and constraints on technological change, are potentially enormous.

knowledge-based networked industrial structures, by setting industry standards, rules, and competitive practices, enable participating firms to control the evolution of technology, reduce the shocks of radical change, and maintain their position within these shifting hierarchies. While new opportunities for entry do appear as a result of technological ruptures, high R&D barriers to entry often limit the possibility for catching up to large vertically integrated firms with deep financial pockets. This has characterized the most recent phase in the transformation of both the information technology and biopharmaceutical industries. Through a combination of mergers and acquisitions and strategic partnerships, established firms in the electronics industry have overtaken rivals and through standard-setting barred the passage of newcomers, while large pharmaceutical firms have made strategic use of alliances to catch up in biotechnology and transform the nature of their industry. In a world of uncertainty, as we shall see below, managing discontinuities has thus become part of the firm's strategic capability.

Information Technology

The evolution of the information technology industry is replete with illustrations of the way in which knowledge-based networks are engaging in new forms of oligopolistic competition that set industry standards, orient technological trajectories, alter the very shape of industries, and play an increasingly important role the allocation of R&D and production activities around the world. In the past, when products became obsolete, divisions could be closed down and entire firms replaced by newcomers. The data processing industry provides several examples of this. Vacuum tube manufacturers, for example, were replaced by firms that manufactured transistors and most of the latter failed to make the transition to the newer semiconductors when these gained ground. This process of change was often led by a front-runner.

Under current competitive conditions, however, it is rare for a firm, like IBM, to be able to establish itself in a durable fashion at the top of an industry hierarchy from whence it can orient and define the technological trajectory of its industry. The continuous entry of newcomers, with new solutions, applications, or products, engenders a perennial process of reclassification at the top of industry hierarchies and leads to a struggle among the cluster of firms at the top as they seek to maintain their place within the group of front-runners. Creating new, more flexible barriers to entry by latecomers has thus become a critical means for firms at the top to reduce the costs of staying ahead, window on the myriad of technological advances that someday might challenge their primacy, and hedge against the uncertainties and unpredictabilities inherent in knowledge-based, globalized competition. It is in this context that knowledge-based networked oligopolies are replacing the role that was previously assumed by a stable leader and coming to serve as the basis for a new form of regulation within the semiconductor, information and communication technology, and multimedia segments of what was formerly the data-processing industry. By cutting across market segments, the new knowledge-based networks are continuously redefining industrial boundaries, thus creating new discontinuities that make entry for newcomers more difficult.

Until the early 1980s, the data-processing industry was characterized by large vertically integrated firms that, using their own hardware (main-frame computers), proprietary operating systems (software), and semiconductors. IBM, Burroughs, NCR, Digital Equipment (DEC), and Fujitsu were typical. Their systems were noncompatible. IBM was the dominant actor in the new industry worldwide and as late as 1985 held 32.2 percent of the data-processing market.[20]

As noted above, Digital Equipment Corporation undermined IBM's dominance by producing its minicomputer without software, allowing new software producers to emerge. Lotus, Borland and Microsoft became major players on this first horizontal segment to emerge in what was then the computer industry. Microprocessors were a second horizontal segment to form the basis for a distinct industrial sector. Firms such as Intel, Motorola, Texas Instruments, and NEC were leaders in the merchant segment of this industry. With the exception of Apple, which followed the earlier practice of integrated production, the advent of the personal computer created a major forward-linking market for software and semiconductor firms, most of which now purchased components for the new PCs from these suppliers and worked closely within them in a two-way collaborative development process.

The use of standardized components reduced the barriers to entry based on proprietary technology, which had been the bulwark of computer firms against their potential rivals. Instead of strengthening IBM's hold over the PC market, the very success of its PCs thus spawned a host of clone manufacturers who could buy components from the same sources. In 1981 IBM itself signed an agreement with Intel for the supply of microprocessors. This further strengthened the front-runners in each of the horizontal segments, enabling them to consolidate their position of power vis-à-vis their customers. Soon Intel and Microsoft became giants in their own right and challengers to the hegemony of IBM.[21] Although IBM's share of the market fell to 17.4 percent in 1995, it, along with Fujitsu, Hewlett Packard, NEC, and Hitachi, occupies one of the top five places in the data-processing industry. Figure 5.1 illustrates, however, that the formerly integrated core companies of the

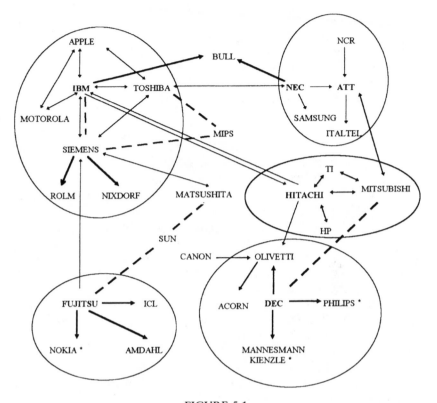

FIGURE 5.1
Evolution of the Main Nodes in the
Data Processing Networked Oligopoly: 1989–1997

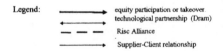

Note: *Data-processing activities

information and communications industries—IBM, AT&T, DEC, and Fujitsu—have been obliged to form alliances with other computer firms that they would have eschewed in the past and to collaborate on the development of key components. The IBM-Motorola-Apple alliance, for example, has led to the development of a RISC microprocessor, the Power-PC, which directly competes with Intel's Pentium chip.[22]

Since the one megabit DRAM, each new generation of DRAMs has involved principal players in rival alliances that collectively constitute a global DRAM oligopoly. Development of 256 megabit DRAMs is currently underway in three alliances; a network of four firms including IBM, Siemens, Toshiba, and Motorola, an alliance between Hitachi and Texas Instruments, and a three-way partnership involving NEC, AT&T, and a newcomer, Samsung. To further strengthen their position in the evolving information technologies industry, these firms are absorbing the data-processing activities of former rivals. Fujitsu's takeover of ICL and Nokia's data-processing business, Siemen's takeover of Nixdorf and AT&T's of NCR are cases in point. Alliances between the four principal nodes then cement the oligopoly on a global scale while allowing the flexibility for new, but subordinate members, to be drawn in as technology and patterns of competition change. Moreover, the relationship between the nodes is more complex and flexible than earlier vertical integration strategies had been. Hitachi, for instance, supplies computers to DEC but printers to DEC's rival IBM, which in turn provides notebooks to Hitachi, which the latter sells under its own brandname. Firms that are cut off from these networks now face high barriers to entry as the technological frontier continues to advance.

The development of HDTV and its relationship to the creation of a multimedia industry provides another illustration of the emergence of knowledge-based networked oligopolies.[23] By the 1980s the United States had largely abandoned the manufacture of television sets. Only Zenith electronics was still nationally owned. Japanese firms were in the forefront with Philips and Thomson holding a strong position in Europe and a toehold in the U.S. market. This was the conjuncture within which several major Japanese electronics firms, such as NEC and Hitachi, with the strong backing of the Ministry of Post, Telegraph and Telephone[24] launched the first stage of their development of high resolution television—the analog-based Hi-Vision. Neither Hi-Vision nor its eventual digital successor would be downward compatible. By the end of 1993 nearly $3 billion had been invested in this project. A few years after their Japanese rivals, a European consortium composed of Philips, Thomson, Bosch, and Thorn Emi began a similar two-stage process with the adoption of the D2 MAC standard, whose advantage was its downward compatibility. Working within the EUREKA 95 project, an analog version of an HDTV system was developed. The combined budget of the European and the various national programs supporting HDTV totaled $1 billion as of February 1993.[25] In choosing to work first with analog technology these consortia built upon what they knew best and each sought to minimize risks through strong state support both financial and in terms of TV programming. The Japanese and European standards were mutually incompatible and both required global markets and worldwide acceptance of their standard. To that end, they each sought to capture the U.S. market.

Catalyzed, in part, by the U.S. government, which had come to recognize the wide scope of application for such technology in the telecommunications and computer industries, American firms embarked on the development of their own HDTV technology. Since it was clear that the future was digital by the time General Instrument, AT&T, Zenith, and MIT started their consortium, an opportunity for the Americans to leapfrog Japanese and European firms presented itself. By abandoning the two-stage process, moreover, the rules of the game were changed, making possible the reentry of American firms into a new global oligopoly centered on what they would later call the information superhighway.

The U.S. firms, however, would not have the field entirely to themselves, for unlike their Japanese competitors, European firms, over the 1980s, had learned to window on alternative technologies. In parallel with the analog-based Eureka consortium, Europe's top television manufacturers formed a strategic alliance with U.S. partners to develop the new digital technology. Among those associated with Philips and Thomson in the U.S.-E.U. consortium were NBC and Compression Laboratories. When the U.S. government called for technical trials, the all-U.S. team thus found itself confronting an equally digitalized U.S.-European team.

Clearly the digital techniques were superior to the Japanese and the earlier D2–MAC European analog technologies and both were eliminated once the United States decided to adopt a digital standard. To establish that standard, joint development work was to be undertaken by the all-U.S. and the U.S.-E.U. consortia. Shortly thereafter the D2 MAC standard was abandoned in Europe and a new Eureka Consortia in Advanced Digital Television Technologies was put in place.[26] Facing the inevitable, the Japanese government, despite the harsh reaction from industry, shut down its domestic Hi-Vision program.[27] A cluster of firms tied together by the development of common technical specifications was thus put into a position from which they could shape the direction of technological change in an emerging sector. Gone were the days when a single dominant firm could, through its own R&D efforts, set the rules for an industry.

Nor can the shape of a knowledge-based networked oligopoly today be taken as a permanent structure, as the HDTV story illustrates. By the mid-1990s, the consortia that had set the standard for HDTV was itself under siege as new linkages brought together firms from the information technology industry, IBM, Apple, and Microsoft, with content providers Time Warner, Disney, Sony Music, cable operators such as Tele-Communications Inc., and major broadcasting networks, CBC, BSkyB, and others. Strategic partnering activity was once again critical as rival networks of firms, cutting across these hitherto distinct industries began to form and to compete in establishing new standards and changing existing rules of competition as they moved to create a new multimedia industry.

Biopharmaceuticals and the Emergence of a "Health Care Industry"

Like information technology, biotechnology is highly knowledge-intensive. On average, $240 million is required to bring a new drug to market. Also like information technology, biotechnology has wide applicability across many industries. However, in contrast to information technology, these applications markets are still quite distinct and different kinds of biotechnology processes and products are taken up by seed companies, new materials firms, the chemical and the pharmaceutical industries. Within the latter, moreover, traditional oligopolies had developed within therapeutic categories and these have remained strong although there is evidence that the new gene sequencing and genetic engineering techniques will enable large networked firms to cross over from one therapeutic category to another. What is most remarkable about the transformation of the pharmaceutical industry into a bio-pharmaceutical industry, however, and what differentiates it from the data-processing industry, is the speed with which the large pharmaceutical firms captured and managed this process.

A number of factors account for the role of large pharmaceutical firms in the ongoing transformation of this industry. The relationship of these large pharmaceutical firms to the smaller dedicated biotechnology firms (DBFs), who pioneered these new techniques, and the relationship of the large pharmaceutical firms to each other are critical elements here. Unlike the star performers in the semiconductor industry, the newer DBFs were initially too small and specialized to become dominant players on this new potentially important horizontal market segment. Their ability to grow and strengthen an independent biopharmaceutical segment, moreover, was limited by the long period of research and clinical testing that was required before biotechnology products began to reach the market. The knowledge and experience of the larger pharmaceutical firms in clinical testing and certification by the Food and Drug Administration and the substantial financial resources they could apply to these activities as well as to research, put them at a clear advantage when compared to the smaller DBFs. Genentech and Chiron, two of the top biotechnology firms in the emerging biopharmaceutical industry are not Intel and Motorola, as we shall see below. Indeed, with the notable exception of Amgen, few of the major dedicated biotechnology firms have survived as independent players into the 1990s.

During the decade following the discovery of rDNA techniques, large pharmaceutical firms entered into a period of intense competition. Firms have appeared and disappeared in rapid succession among the top ten. From 1982 to 1989 Bristol-Myers, for example, moved from 10th to 2nd place after its acquisition of Squibb, Glaxo moved from 19th to 3rd place, Bayer dropped from 2nd place to 6th, Ciba-Geigy from 5th to 8th, and Pfizer from 6th to 11th. Between 1989 and 1992, however, this process started to slow down as only two of the top ten firms changed: American Home Products dropped from the list and Hoffman–La Roche moved from 16th to 9th. Amongst the top five, Ciba-Geigy replaced SmithKline Beecham in fifth place.[28] Although calculated differently, the Fortune 500 shows the same degree of stability at the top between 1990 and 1995, with all of the top ten firms simply jockeying for position among themselves.

Advancing within the top ten during the 1990s has largely taken place through a process of concentration with two spectacular in-country mergers and acquisitions that strengthen core firms in the global knowledge-based networked oligopoly. In the United Kingdom, Glaxo acquired Wellcome PLC in 1995 propelling the former into first place and and in Switzerland, the merger of Sandoz and Ciba-Geigy in 1996 moving the Novartis, as they will now be called, into second place worldwide.[29]

Within the pharmaceutical industry, evidence is accumulating that, alongside these mergers and acquisitions, a networked, knowledge-based biopharmaceutical oligopoly is emerging. Over the 1980s biotechnology inputs came to play an increasingly important role in the pharmaceutical industry, especially in diagnostics.[30] By the end of that decade, the top ten pharmaceutical firms, had begun to solidify their position in biotechnology through a rash of acquisitions and alliances. This was made easier by the financial difficulties of small dedicated biotechnology firms who faced not only high costs for research but for product development, clinical testing, and marketing.[31] Genentech, the second largest dedicated biotechnology firm by sales, and Syntex, another innovative biotechnology firm, were both acquired by Hoffmann–La Roche. Chiron, the fourth largest DBF, acquired Cetus in 1991 but was itself taken over by Ciba-Geigy and later merged into Novartis. Glaxo-Welcome acquired Affymax; Rhone-Poulenc-Rorer acquired Institut Merieux, Connaught Bio Sciences, and 37 percent of Applied Immune Sciences. American Home Products took over the Genetics Institute, American Cyanamid acquired Immunex in 1992 and was itself taken over by American Home Products in 1994, and Hoechst acquired Mario-Merrell-Dow and the U.S. diagnostics firm Syva in 1995. Only Amgen, the top independent DBF, was able to solidify its position in biopharmaceuticals through the acquisition of Synergen.

When not acquiring DBFs outright, the top twenty pharmaceutical firms were engaging in strategic partnerships. In the newer areas of the emerging 'health care industry' diagnostics, therapeutics, and drug delivery, strategic partnering activity developed rapidly in the 1990s. Total biotechnology alliances of the top twenty pharmaceutical firms increased from about 150 in the 1988–90 period to over 350 in the 1994–96 period.[32]

Some of these partnerships link large pharmaceuticals to each other in traditional oligopolistic fashion—through cross-licensing, distribution, and marketing agreements. Most of these partnerships, however, link a large pharmaceutical company to a network of smaller dedicated biotechnology firms whose research is increasingly financed by the larger pharmaceutical firm and whose results are licensed on an exclusive basis to that company (outlicense). SmithKline Beecham,[33] for example, claims to have more than 140 such partnerships worldwide, including its links to university research institutes.[34] Glaxo has more than ten strategic partnerships with American DBFs and fifty with universities in the United States alone.[35] Research on new gene therapies to deal with retroviruses and cancer, is exclusively done by Rhone-Poulenc Rorer (RPR),through Gencell, its network of sixteen American DBFs in which RPR holds a minority interest.[36] Through these alliances, pharmaceutical firms, once exclusively rooted in chemical processes, are now quite at home in biotechnology.

Competition among the large pharmaceutical firms, moreover, is increasingly based on these knowledge-based networks. Thus Merck (U.S.) is collaborating with Celltech (U.K.) in the development of an asthma drug that Celltech invented, as well as with Astra (Sweden), a member of the traditional oligopoly in asthma drugs head by Glaxo, itself allied with the small American biotechnology firm ICOs in the development of a rival asthma drug. Strategic partnerships, as this example illustrates, can be used to reinforce the traditional oligopolies within therapeutic categories. In the $23 billion market for antibiotics, traditional oligopolists are forming partnerships with gene-sequencing firms. By identifying the genetic structure of bacteria, researchers can work on treatments that attack genes essential for its survival. Pfizer has worked closely with Microcide and Incyte on such products. Building networks of alliance partners is yet another strategy currently being employed by the more aggressive of the large pharmaceutical firms. As gene therapies develop, biopharmaceutical firms are beginning to establish closer links to medical delivery systems—managed health care units and clinics.

In sum, alliance formation has intensified and this emerges most clearly if we take a dynamic perspective. Thus, in the early 1980s, few of the big pharmaceutical companies had formed R&D partnerships. For top-ranking firms such as Hoechst, Bayer, and Hoffman–La Roche alliances were marginal. A few companies, Ciba-Geigy and Eli Lilly, for example, had a small number of alliances with U.S. DBFs and only Sandoz had formed R&D partnerships with smaller pharmaceutical firms.[37] In the mid-1980s several large pharmaceutical companies became involved in technology partnerships but principally the linkages between them were in marketing. Their R&D ties were primarily to the small dedicated biotechnology firms, while their earlier links to universities began to decline. By the mid-1990s, all of the largest pharmaceutical companies were involved in technology partnerships and much of the competition in the growing diagnostic market, in vaccines, and in therapeutics was based on knowledge-based networks that linked large pharmaceutical firms to a host of small DBFs.

Equally important for the reconfiguration of this industry and the emergence of a networked knowledge-based oligopoly within it, is the way in which biotechnology is serving to break down the walls between therapeutic categories and build links across new horizontal segments within the emerging industry. The rules of the game in clinical diagnostics, for example, have been changing along these lines,[38] as has the role of human genetics and gene therapies.[39] Core biopharmaceutical firms such as Bayer, Johnson & Johnson, SmithKline Beecham, and Hoechst have diagnostic divisions, while SmithKline Beecham and Hoffmann–La Roche have recently concluded alliances with companies that specialize in gene sequencing. To the extent that these trends in concentration and alliance formation continue, there is a danger that alliances, which have created new opportunities for small and medium-sized enterprises, will be transformed into new barriers to entry as the biopharmaceutical industry evolves and large pharmaceutical firms become major actors in health care delivery.

POLICIES AND PRACTICES: A NEW CONTRADICTION

The 1970s and 1980s marked the passage from an era in which technological change was mainly incremental and time was available to amortize heavy tangible and intangible investments, to one in which competition is based on an accelerated pace of technological change that involves a shifting combination of generic technologies and the systematic commercialization of technological competencies over as wide a range of applications as possible or what elsewhere has been called a "technology bunching" strategy. As firms extend their competencies to new domains,[40] traditional patterns of vertical integration within the firm that linked markets, products, and technology in linear fashion are undermined, industry hierarchies are destabilized, and static, product-based oligopolies are weakened. The uncertainty this and related phenomena generated gave impetus to the formation of strategic alliances.

Through networked, knowledge-based alliances, clusters of key players are now building new barriers to entry and laying the basis for global oligopolies within the shifting boundaries of traditional industries as they merge into those of the future. In so doing they have become critical actors in the allocation of R&D and production facilities around the world. By exercising major influence over the location of activities worldwide, knowledge-based networked oligopolies have implications for employment, trade, and international prices. Through international specialization within the network, dominant information technology and pharmaceutical firms are able to take advantage of economies of scale and scope in research, development, and (in biopharmaceuticals) clinical testing, to reduce their costs and the risks associated with research and to increase their efficiency relative to individual firms that are not part of networks. Networked firms thus create more formidable obstacles to new entry in a market whose boundaries are themselves undergoing a continuous process of change.

Dynamic knowledge-based networks have also become critical actors in shaping technological trajectories and are thus in a position to privilege certain lines of inquiry over others. This, too, has important consequences for global welfare, particularly as private gain outweighs public welfare considerations in the choice of illnesses upon which to work. The lack of attention to tropical diseases and to treatments that would be affordable in the developing world lends credence to this proposition.

Knowledge-based networked oligopolies, moreover, can become the vehicles for a number of restrictive business practices that are harder to detect than when such practices are undertaken by a single firm or a cartel of individual firms. To fix prices, competing alliances in the new "health care industry" would not need to enter into formal cooperative agreements regarding the price and sales conditions applying to drugs, if through alliances they controlled downstream delivery systems. Small DFBs can no longer aspire to becoming competitors or through licenses multiply the number of potential competitors, if their results are directly appropriated by alliance partners.

At the heart of the analysis of noncartel anticompetitive practices is an assessment of the extent to which a firm exercises market power by virtue of its dominant position within a market. But identifying that market and those rivals when they are networks and assessing the market power of these networks lies beyond traditional methodologies employed by competition authorities around the world. While merger control is gaining increasing attention at national, regional, and international levels[41] and despite the negative static (allocative and price implications) and dynamic (technological) welfare effects that these oligopolistic practices are likely to generate, governments have taken few actions to strengthen national or international rules and regulations governing such behavior. Indeed, as Goodman and Pauly observed with regard to the role of deregulation and market opening in the stimulation of speculative capital flows, states seem bent on further liberalization.[42] Thus the World Investment Report 1997 concludes:

> In view of the mix of procompetitive and anti-competitive elements that might be involved in these agreements . . . some jurisdictions (which otherwise have a strict approach to competition-law enforcement) have tended, during the past decade and a half, to narrow the range of activities that constitute violations of their competition laws in this context. . . . Therefore, an increasing number of agreements and business practices are examined by courts under the "rule-of-reason" standard of interpretation. And given the potentially positive economic implications that especially R&D alliances have, an increasing number of authorities appear to exempt them from competition regulation.[43]

The attempt within the OECD to negotiate a multilateral agreement on investment (MAI) reinforces this impression. Overwhelmingly driven by market-opening goals, the bulk of the provisions under negotiation focused on making the legal environment the most hospitable possible for foreign private investors. These articles, therefore, dealt primarily with the rights of establishment and the freedom to pursue activities within the host market on a basis no less favorable than that accorded by the state to national investors.[44] The text barely touched upon issues such as restrictive business practices, the heading under which public regulation of private market-shaping behavior would normally figure.

This brief exploration of trends in oligopoly formation, however, is not meant to demonize strategic partnering activity, which remains a potentially important means for small and medium-sized firms in knowledge-intensive industries to remain at the technological frontier and to grow. Rather, it suggests that there is a need to monitor such activity more systematically, to develop the tools with which to assess the impact of partnering activity as it continues to develop in the future, and to undertake the kind of research that will be required to better inform future policymaking with respect to strategic partnering activity. This is particularly true since, in large part, the emergence of these new forms of oligopoly is a result of the interaction between deregulation and market-opening policies of states on the one hand and the new competitive practices of large, global firms, on the other. International cooperation will clearly also be needed.

NOTES

1. Karl Polanyi, *The Great Transformation* (Boston: Beacon Press, 1944), p. 66.

2. A review of the work of the "regulation" school on the relationship between technological change, production, and demand can be found in Robert Boyer, "Technical Change and the Theory of Regulation," in G. Dosi et al., eds., *Technical Change and Economic Performance* (Cambridge: Cambridge University Press, 1988), pp. 67–94. An excellent discussion of the new institutional mechanisms developed in the United States to ensure the profitability of investment in mass-production equipment through the stabilization of markets is found in chapters 3 and 4 of Michael Piore and Charles Sabel, *The Second Industrial Divide: Possibilities for Prosperity* (New York: Basic Books, 1984).

3. The electrical cartel discussed by Newfarmer, the chemical cartel by Freeman, and later the petrochemical and shipping cartels were among the best known. Richard Newfarmer, *Transnational Conglomerates and the Economics of Dependent Development: A Case Study of the International Electrical Oligopoly and Brazil's Electrical Industry* (Greenwich, Conn.: Jai Press, 1980); Christopher Freeman, *The Economics of Industrial Innovation* (Harmondsworth, England: Penguin, 1974). See also W. Lazonick and M. O'Sullivan, "Organization, Finance and International Competition," *Industrial and Corporate Change* 5.1 (1996): 1–50, and the contribution by Tony Porter in this volume.

4. The UNCTAD set does provide for consultation procedures as a conflict avoidance mechanisms, but given its nonbinding character, there is no tribunal to make judgments or enforce rulings. While GATT/WTO agreements have such binding institutional machinery, it applies only to practices that affect international trade. UNCTAD, *World Investment Report 1997*, Transnational Corporations, Market Structure and Competition Policy (Geneva: United Nations), p. 224.

5. This includes a wide variety of knowledge-based activities such as training, design, advertising, management routines, production organization, software development, and patents.

6. The telecommunications industry is a classic example, but many markets for consumer durables were saturated during the 1970s and rising unemployment and inflation coupled with slow overall growth led to a fragmentation of markets into a mosaic of niches during this period.

7. The GATT Uruguay round leading to the formation of the new World Trade Organization and negotiations between the European Union and the fifteen Eastern and Central European aspirants to membership are illustrative.

8. UNCTAD, *World Investment Report 1996*, Investment, Trade and International Policy Arrangements (Geneva: United Nations), p. 10.

9. Digitial switching in the communications industry, for example, is not an incremental extension of earlier electromechanical switching technology, nor could compact discs based on laser technology derive logically from earlier phonograph records.

10. Strategic partnerships are distinguised from more traditional forms of linkage between firms such as joint ventures, licensing, or subcontracting

arrangements by three main characteristics: (i) they are two-way relationships focused on joint knowledge production and sharing as opposed to a one-way transfer of technology, (ii) they tend to be contractual in nature and may involve little or no equity participation, and (iii) they are part of the longer-term planning activity of the firm rather than simply an opportunistic response to short-term financial gains. "Strategic partnerships are thus not about the statics of allocative choices but about the dynamics of innovation and competition." Lynn K. Mytelka, "Introduction," in L. K. Mytelka, ed., *Strategic Partnerships and the World Economy* (London: Pinter Publishers, 1991), p. 1.

11. These points are discussed more fully in Lynn K. Mytelka and Michel Delapierre, "The Alliance Strategies of European Firms and the Role of ESPRIT," *Journal of Common Market Studies* 26.2 (1987) and Mytelka, ed., *Strategic Partnerships and the World Economy.*

12. See E. H. Chamberlain, *The Theory of Monopolistic Competition* (Cambridge: Harvard University Press, 1933) and F. T. Knickerbocker, *Oligopolistic Reactions of Multinational Enterprise* (Cambridge: Harvard University Press, 1973).

13. R. Nelson and S. Winter, *An Evolutionary Theory of Economic Change* (Cambridge: Harvard University Press, 1982) and B.-A. Lundvall, "Innovation as an Interactive Process: From User-Producer Interaction to the National System of Innovation," in G. Dosi et al., *Technical Change*, pp. 349–69.

14. This discussion of traditional oligopolies was originally developed in Michel Delapierre and Lynn K. Mytelka, "Decomposition, Recomposition des Oligopoles," *Economie et Sociétés* 11/12 (1988): 57–83; Lynn K. Mytelka, "Dancing with Wolves: Global Oligopolies and Strategic Partnerhips," in J. Haagedoorn, ed., *Technical Change and the World Economy: Convergence and Divergence in Technological Strategies* (Aldershot, England: Elgar, 1994); and Michel Delapierre and Lynn K. Mytelka, "Blurring Boundaries: New Inter-Firm Relationships and the Emergence of Networked, Knowledge-Based Oligopolies," in M. Colombo, ed., *The Changing Boundaries of the Firms: Explaining Evolving Inter-firm Relations* (London: Routledge, 1998).

15. Over the seven-year period 1976–1982 the share of foreign firms in the U.S. automobile market rose from 18% to 30% (W. Adams and J. W. Brock, "Joint Ventures, Antitrust, and Transnational Cartelization," *Northwest Journal of International Law and Business* 1.3 (Winter 1991): 433–83, 458). Korean firms, Samsung, Goldstar and Hyundai, that held virtually no share of the world market for semiconductors in 1989, accounted for 8.9 percent of the world market in 1994 (Dataquest, Market statistics, 1992, 1995).

16. J. Hagedoorn and Schakenraad, *Leading Companies and the Structure of Strategic Alliances in Core Technologies* (Limburg: University of Limburg, MERIT [1990]), tables, 1, 2, and 3.

17. J. Hagedoorn, "Trends and Patterns in Strategic Technology Partnering since the Early Seventies," *Review of Industrial Organization* 11 (1996): 601–16.

18. R. Acharya, A. Arundel, and L. Orsenigo, "The Evolving Structure of the European Biotechnology Industry and Its Future Competitiveness," paper presented at a conference on Biotechnology in the European Union (Grenoble, December 7–8, 1995).

19. Changes in the organization of production within the automobile industry are leading to the emergence of new horizontal segments. See Lynn K. Mytelka and Michel Delapierre, "Industrial Dynamics, Knowledge-Based Networked Oligopolies and the Emergence of New Modes of Competition," paper presented to the DRUID Seminar, Copenhagen Business School and Aalborg University, Skagen, Denmark, June 1–3, 1997.

20. All rankings and calculations of market share are derived from the Fortune 500 listings for the years 1985 through 1995.

21. By 1992 Intel provided 33% of the world's microprocessors and 72% of the 32-bit high-performance chips (*Financial Times*, August 26, 1993).

22. The competition in RISC technology for workstations is another anti-Intel strategy putting into play four clusters around SUN, MIPs, IBM, and H-P. to develop RISC components. For details see Gomes-Casseres, 1994. B. Gomes-Casseres, "Group versus Group: How Alliance Networks Compete," *Harvard Business Review* 3.3 (July–August 1994): 62–66, 70, 72–74.

23. The following paragraphs draw heavily on Delapierre and Mytelka, "Blurring Boundaries."

24. *International Herald Tribune*, February 24, 1994.

25. *International Herald Tribune*, February 20–21, 1994.

26. *Les Echos*, June 17, 1994.

27. "Tokyo Admits It Backed Wrong Horse," *The Financial Times*, February 23, 1994.

28. Rankings for 1982 are from U.S., Department of Commerce, *A Competitive Assessment of the US Pharmaceutical Industry* (1984); for 1989, Sharp: 1991, p. 215; and for 1992, *Financial Times*, March 10, 1994. M. Sharp, S. Thomas, and P. Martin, "Transferts de techologie et Politique de l'Innovation. Le cas des Biotechnologies," in F. Schwald, ed., Les defis de la mondialisation: innovation et concurrence (Paris: Masson, 1994).

29. Pharmacia (Sweden) and Upjohn Inc. (USA) also merged in 1995.

30. On the technological convergence between biotechnology and pharmaceutical, see V. Griffith,. "Hand in Hand," *Financial Times*, September 6, 1994.

31. Clinical testing and marketing, moreover, were activities in which the large, integrated pharmaceutical companies had acquired considerable experience.

32. Mark Edwards, "How the Elephants Dance," *Signals*, online magazine of Recombinant Capital, http://www.recap.com.

33. SmithKline merged with Beecham in 1989 and bought Sterling laboratories from Eastman Kodak in 1994.

34. *Financial Times*, November 27, 1995.

35. *Financial Times*, November 27, 1995.

36. Rhône-Poulenc Rorer, *Rapport Annuel 1995*, and interview, Senior official RPR, May 6, 1996.

37. P. Barbanti, A. Gambardella, and L. Orsenigo, "The Evolution of the Forms of Collaboration in Biotechnologies." Paper presented at the conference on Les Accords de Cooperation pour la recherche et le Developpement en biotechnologie, Grenoble, 1992.

38. M. Rich, "Search for Early Symptoms," *Financial Times* 27, p. 11.

39. C. Cookson, "Transatlantic Courtships Warms Up," *Financial Times*, November 27, 1995, IV.

40. Sony, a manufacturer of consumer electronic goods, for example, moved into the computer industry. This move does not constitute a classic case of diversification or an opportunistic response to financial gain but an exploitation of existing technological competencies in other domains.

41. See examples of new rulings in the United States, the United Kingdom, and Germany in UNCTAD, *World Investment Report 1997*, chapter V.

42. J. B. Goodman and L. W. Pauly, "The Obsolescene of Capital Controls? Economic Management in an Age of Global Markets," *World Politics* 46 (October 1993): 50–82.

43. UNCTAD, *World Investment Report 1997*, p. 205. The report illustrates this with examples of exemptions of R&D aggrements in the European Union and hearings held by the U.S. Federal Trade Commission in 1996 on this point.

44. A. R. Parra, "The Scope of New Investment Laws and International Instruments," *Transnational Corporations* 4.3 (December 1995): 29.

PART 3

Ruling Others— The Effects of Private International Authority

CHAPTER 6

Bond-Rating Agencies and Coordination in the Global Political Economy

Timothy J. Sinclair

All too often, social scientists neglect important institutions and processes they consider technical because they find it hard to make the connections between these things and the social and political struggles they are accustomed to.[1] Rich rewards await those who do delve beyond the realm of the obvious to penetrate this forbidden zone. This chapter undertakes such a task. It considers the issue of private authority in the seemingly unlikely form of bond-rating agencies. This task is pursued by considering these agencies as examples of coordination services firms (CSFs), and by evaluating the impact of their activities on the global political economy (GPE).[2] The development of the GPE, in which production is intermeshed transnationally, generates increased demand for forms of economic coordination. Rating agencies are a particularly important study of coordination because the capital markets in which they operate are crucial for raising funds in the GPE.

What is a coordination services firm, and why should we view it as a form of private authority? In the introduction, the editors of this volume suggest that coordination services firms are those which set the standards for the behavior of other firms, enforcing a code of conduct on them individually and as a whole.[3] They also observe that it can be difficult to distinguish between these firms and firms more generally, but that coordination services firms play an important enough role to be singled out as private instances of power. This chapter will distinguish coordination services firms, and elaborate on the effects and significance of this role in the GPE, using the example of bond-rating agencies.

The chapter is organized in four parts. In the section that follows, trends in the financial markets and the basic purpose and characteristics of the agencies are discussed. The function of this section is to give the reader some understanding of this type of coordination services firm. This more factual element is followed by a conceptual part, in which the idea of rating coordination is analyzed. This section identifies the core elements of this ontology: the social forces involved and their relationship to coordination, the issue of epistemic authority, which is at the center of the capacity of rating agencies to act as coordination services firms, and the problem of coordination itself, in terms of the purposes we can attribute to it and the permutations it takes. This discussion is followed by a section that presents three arguments about different aspects of rating coordination: information coordination, risk coordination, and strategic coordination. In conclusion, the chapter provides some comment on prospects for coordination in the GPE.

CAPITAL MARKETS AND BOND RATING

Financial markets change and so do the problems they present to those interested in making use of them. Most of us are familiar with bank lending.[4] Banks act as financial intermediaries in that they bring together the suppliers and users of funds. They borrow money, in the form of deposits, and lend money at their own risk to borrowers. However, in recent years disintermediation has occurred on both sides of the balance sheet. Depositors have found more attractive things to do with their funds at the same time as borrowers have increasingly obtained funds from sources other than banks. Mutual funds, which sweep depositors' money directly into financial markets, now contain around $2 trillion in assets, not much less than the $2.7 trillion held in U.S. bank deposits.[5] In 1994, 28 percent of American households owned a mutual fund, up from 6 percent in 1980. However, the proportion of household assets held in bank deposits fell between 1980 to 1990, from 46 to 38 percent.[6] The shift on the borrowing side is just as marked. In 1970, commercial lending by banks made up 65 percent of the borrowing needs of corporate America. By 1992, the banks' share had fallen to 36 percent, with the balance made up of securities of various types.[7] The reasons for this development seem to lie in heightened competitive pressures in the GPE and the high overhead costs of individual bank intermediation.[8] However, the degree of disintermediation varies greatly, with the universal banking system in Germany least affected.[9]

Disintermediation is changing the role of banks. It creates an information problem for suppliers and users of funds. In a bank-intermediated environment a lender can to a great extent depend on the prudential behavior of the bank, which is regulated and required to maintain reserves. However, in a disintermediated financial environment the supplier of funds must make a judgment about the likelihood of repayment by the user or debtor. Given the high costs of gathering suitable information with which to make an assessment by individual investors it is not surprising that institutions have developed to provide centralized judgments on creditworthiness. There seems to be something like a consensus within financial economics that credit rating turns uncertainty about the future of enterprises and their financial liabilities into probable risk that can be priced in the market by investors. This is a more efficient solution to the information problem than banks provide because of the economies of specialization inherent in rating and the clearly disinterested nature of the analysis. Bank credit analysis is driven by the bank's status as a financial market player that credit rating agencies strongly distance themselves from.

The principal-agent metaphor can be used to identify the different parties in the rating process and to specify the lines of accountability between them.[10] The agencies themselves identify the investors in securities as their principals, defining themselves as agents. However, it is not clear that issuers of securities see the relationship this way. Perhaps their confusion is magnified by the fact that it is the issuers who pay for the ratings and not investors.

Rating agencies possess professional analytical capacities and ongoing knowledge of the affairs of vast numbers of issuers of debt securities. The disintermediation process has heightened the importance of their role because their analytical and local knowledge has increased absolutely, as they now rate more issues in more locations, and relatively, because comparable specialists—banks—are less active. The agencies claim to make judgments on the "future ability and willingness of an issuer to make timely payments of principal and interest on a security over the life of the instrument."[11] The more likely it is that "the borrower will repay both the principal and interest, in accordance with the time schedule in the borrowing agreement, the higher will be the rating assigned to the debt security."[12] The objective in the case of both major agencies is globally comparable ratings. New York remains the analytical core, where rating expertise is defined and reinforced. Ratings are determined on all manner of issuers: corporations, financial institutions, municipalities, and sovereign governments, in terms of long-term obligations such as bonds, or short-term obligations like commercial paper. The raters produce a letter symbol (and usually a rationale and commentary) reflecting a relative ranking on a scale from most to least creditworthy. The agencies are adamant that a debt rating is "not a recommendation to purchase, sell, or hold a security, inasmuch as it does not comment as to market price or suitability for a particular investor," because investors' risk/return trade-offs vary.[13] Increasingly, rating agencies rate the issuing company or government in addition to particular securities issues. Raters maintain surveillance over issuers and issues, and will warn investors when they consider that developments may lead to a revision to an existing rating in either an upward or downward direction.

The major bond-rating agencies had their beginnings in the early part of this century as a result of failed railroads and dubious land schemes in the United States.[14] Two major agencies dominate the market in ratings, listing around $3 trillion each.[15] A host of smaller agencies compete for market niches. The two major agencies are Moody's Investors Service (Moody's) and Standard & Poor's (S&P). Both are headquartered in New York. Moody's is owned by Dun and Bradstreet, the information concern, while S&P is a subsidiary of publishing company, McGraw-Hill. Both agencies have branches in the major centers of financial activity in North America, Europe, and Asia. Recent branch expansion has taken place in Asia and Latin America. Three American agencies dominate the second tier. These are Fitch Investors Service, Duff & Phelps, and Thomson Bankwatch (which some might argue is Canadian). Fitch is mainly in the business of municipal and corporate rating, while Chicago-based Duff & Phelps largely rates industrial corporations. Thomson evaluates financial institutions. IBCA, a London-based agency that has its roots in rating banks, has in recent years expanded its business into the corporate area. It now has offices in New York and Tokyo, as well as other locations in Europe. It recently merged with Euronotation of France, in what was rumored at the time to be the first step toward the creation of a "true European rating agency."[16] More recently, however, it has shown more interest in U.S. expansion.[17] In addition, there are a host of domestically focused agencies in a number of countries, including Japan, Italy, China, India, Malaysia, Indonesia, Thailand, France, Canada, Israel, Brazil, Mexico, Argentina, South Africa, and the Czech Republic.[18] Rumors have frequently circulated in the financial community about the creation of a German rating agency but these have not led to anything concrete.[19] The original American rating agencies, Moody's, S&P, and Fitch obtained income as information services. Faced with a continental economy and subsequently the disclosure requirements of the New Deal, the agencies developed to sift through large volumes of information and present it in an easily digested format to investors. Over time, this information-sorting function evolved into rating. In the late 1960s and early 1970s raters began to charge fees to bond issuers. Now, 75 percent of the income of these agencies is obtained from fees charged to issuers, as opposed to information sales.[20] In Canada, the Dominion Bond Rating Service gets more than 80 percent of its revenue from rating fees, while the Canadian Bond Rating Agency sources 50 percent of its revenue this way.[21] In the case of rating agencies in Japan and the Third World, financing typically comes from some combination of ownership consortia, which often include financial institutions and government. This is a cause of some disquiet in financial markets where these agencies are typically viewed as less independent than they should be.

Rating-agency judgments are not regulated. However, some process of "recognizing" the activities of the agencies by capital markets regulatory agencies is customary. This is especially significant in the United States given that this recognition has been written into laws that govern the prudential behavior of public pension funds in many states.[22] A central feature of the United States and other states' processes of governmental recognition is the regulators reliance on wide acceptance of a firm's rating output in the market as the best indicator of its right to be recognized. The agencies are resistant to periodic efforts to develop more invasive forms of regulation, and hold up this standard of use as the best test of their output. They also resist further incorporation of ratings in public policy. For example, in December 1994 the Securities and Exchange Commission (SEC) proposed mandating the disclosure of ratings in prospectuses. Standard & Poor's commented in their submission that the proposal "would transform the rating agency from an independent evaluator in the registration process [of securities] to a participant in that process."[23] In the end, the SEC took no further action.

SOCIAL FORCES, EPISTEMIC AUTHORITY, AND COORDINATION

Three crucial elements of our understanding of rating agencies as coordination services firms will be considered here. The first of these is the social basis of rating agencies. What social forces do rating agencies represent and which do they seem to oppose? This will shape our sense of what can be expected from rating agencies. The second part will introduce the notion of epistemic authority. This illuminates the nature and limits of the influence of rating agencies. The last part will consider the issue of coordination itself, and suggest that rating agency activity does not merely constrain other institutions, but contributes to the generation of market actors themselves.

Social Forces

Rating institutions are not conceived of here as "primitive units," about which we can know nothing. Instead, rating agencies should be understood as embedded in networks of social interest representation. These social forces, comprising classes and class fractions, compete for hegemony, or consent-based leadership over other groups, by constructing the strongest alliance of social forces, practices, and explanatory worldviews.[24] The most significant struggles within the contemporary world revolve around the different fractions of capital, as these strive to reinforce and recreate their social hegemony against claims from other social stakeholders. Capital, in the neo-Gramscian view advocated here, is not a pool of inert financial resources, but a social relation of privilege with regard to the ownership and control of productive (or rent-extracting) enterprise, and the creation and appropriation of a surplus. Part of this privilege, of course, is exercised through the state in a variety of different forms. Like the state, conceptions of the relationship between rating agencies and the power of capital are likely to be controversial. The argument made here is not so much about whether the agencies are representative of capital as a whole, but rather, which constellation of interests within this broad grouping of social forces they seem to represent more than others. The view advocated in this chapter is that rating agencies represent what Stephen Gill has called "globalizing elites."[25] These elites are a "directive, strategic element within globalizing capitalism."[26] They are tied to the promotion of market discipline and emerge from financial rather than real economy interests.[27] I do not argue that rating agencies and their officials are themselves part of this group of elites. Their social origins, educations, and incomes may put them outside these precincts. However, the agencies do seem to be places in which some of the most important thinking about the problems of capitalism is being undertaken. What we see here is a supporting fraction of technical analysts, of people with a track record of good judgment, which in an increasingly decentred society are gravitating closer to the center where strategic decisions and deferrals are made. Rating agencies do not represent the interests of globalizing elites in a conscious, conspiratorial fashion, battling the evil hordes of the welfare state and socialism. Representation of the interests of globalizing elites reflects a shared "operating system" as Lipschutz has written, drawing an analogy with computing.[28] In this sense, rating is an "ideology" in that its assumptions privilege a system of values and knowledge tied to particular social forces.[29]

Epistemic Authority

The ascendancy of rating agencies within the GPE relates closely to two resources. The first of these, as discussed, is the capacity to substitute for banks in disintermediated capital markets, and solve the information problem between those with funds and those seeking them. Here we see the rating agency as a go-between or agent, assisting the interface of different fractions of capital. Because rating agencies have inside knowledge of a local nature, and have expertise at credit assessment, there is a risk that rating agencies might, should they wish, abuse their role as agents, and transcend the service role attributed to their relationship to the investor fraction of capital.

Beyond this more narrow argument about potential "agency costs" is the broader question of the authority exercised by the agencies and its relationship to knowledge. The key thing to observe about rating agencies is that they do not seek to persuade, but to make judgments (i.e., ratings) as a feature of their authority. This epistemic authority can be understood to quell doubts and win the trust of audiences, not because of its content, but because of the relationship between the rating agencies in this case, and the fractions of capital that seek resources and those that have funds.[30] This peculiar form of authority emerges from the relations of asymmetry between the agencies and those who are subject to their judgments. This asymmetry is not of a personal nature, but emerges from the circumstances in which investment resources are allocated in the late twentieth century, the professional and local experience of the agencies, and their long accumulation of eminence. The agencies' epistemic authority is not impermeable or everlasting. Clearly, this is not the case because the authority of rating agencies has grown as a consequence of change in the nature of markets, especially the decline of banks as allocators of wholesale resources. My argument is that rating agencies have moved from influence to authority with the growth of capital markets. Influence implies a range of levels of respect. The latter, however, is bivariate in that authority either exists or is absent. Once established it is, by its very nature, hard to budge, as others are likely to discount the "mistakes" or epistemic failures of the agencies, given their stock of eminence. At some point, of course, these resources could be overwhelmed by a persistent record of perceived failure. But given the lack of a counterhegemony, in the form of alternative means for the production of judgments in disintermediated conditions, such a collapse is unlikely. Internet or other information-technology resources are not an alternative as the dispersal of information they represent precisely ignores the point that certain evaluations are worth more than others. Some are socially valorized and others are held to be mere conjecture.

An interesting feature of the epistemic authority of rating agencies is their relation to governmental institutions. Solving information problems in markets, being seen as highly eminent and to be deferred to, seem to be considerable resources for these private firms in their relations with states. They see themselves as "quasi-regulatory institutions," an elevated position considering their private status.[31] They are well placed to defer state challenges to their prerogatives, as the hesitancy with which any new effort to further pull them into official surveillance demonstrates. Indeed, the most significant aspect of their relationship with public authority is the tendency of government to use features of the quasi-regulatory output of the rating agencies as substitutes for their own action. This points to a curious dialectic in rating agency–state relations. States are happy to foster local rating agencies in order to develop capital markets. This has been common in recent years in East Asia where national governments have organized securities regulation around the requirement for the credit rating of debt issues.[32] Governments will also at times use the output of rating agencies against their enemies to demonstrate how well they are doing or to indicate to the public what sort of challenges they are confronted with.[33] However, when states are downgraded by the major global agencies they are often vocal in their denunciation of the judgments.[34] Another aspect of this relation to states is that the rating agencies—certainly the major ones—are American and represent the epistemic predilections domiciled in the United States. By this I do not mean that the agencies are mere tools of American domination, but that their authority has a special salience to it because knowledge emerging in the United States has a higher global valuation than that produced by a British, Canadian, or Japanese agency. The variety of interactions between states and rating agencies underscores the validity of Keohane's observation that it is the interconnections between state and transnational relations that are more important than whether it is states or non-state institutions that are dominant.[35]

Coordination

The idea of coordination in international political economy seems to have fallen between the two poles of mainstream theory. In this view of how to understand the GPE, power and authority are understood to reside in governmental institutions exclusively, while exchange is thought to be a feature of the market alone. The reality of the GPE is that the social networks that ameliorated transactional uncertainty in the past are much reduced by the greatly increased social distance between market participants. Coordination can, at a minimum then, be viewed as an uncertainty-reduction device that allows transactions to go ahead without undue friction or costly creation of measures to prevent loss, in a market context of heightened social distance. We can think of this process as an intermediate or hybrid one, which is best viewed as at times consensual and at other times coercive. It is consensual when it gives rise to wide agreement or a hegemonic set of ideas about the basis for transactions. It is coercive when the coordinator must use sanctions (such as ratings) against other firms to bring behavior into line.

Coordination services firms play an infrastructural role, both greasing the wheels of capitalism through reducing uncertainty, and acting as gatekeepers when necessary. They are middle-level private forms of authority, equidistant on the one hand from the institutions characteristic of a private regime, and on the other, from informal industry practices.[36] However, like other forms of private authority, coordination services firms may comprise part of a broader structure such as a private regime, and it is also likely that they reinforce industry practices. CSFs are important because they are pervasive. Their ubiquity and infrastructural character gives their activities and judgments added legitimacy in relation to public institutions, in that their work can be presented as unproblematic, as part of everyday social constraints, rather than as processes of political organization.

Rating agencies should be understood, among other things, as CSFs. They help to solve the information problem between those with funds and those seeking them; they vet and judge practices, opportunities, forms of organization, whole fields of human enterprise. They adjust the ground rules inside capital markets and thereby shape the internal organization and behavior of those institutions seeking funds. Their views of what is acceptable shape the actions of the resource-deficient in anticipation. This anticipation effect, or structural power, is reflected in the minds of capital-market participants in terms of their understandings of the views and expectations of the agencies. In turn, this acts as a base point from which their business initiatives are developed. The coordination effect that stems from rating, considered in general, is to narrow the expectations of creditors and debtors to a certain well-understood or transparent set that is shared among themselves. Thus the agencies do not just constrain the capital markets, as neorealism sees anarchy doing to states, but actually provide significant pressures on market participants themselves, contributing importantly to their internal constitution as agents. Coordination, as conceived here, combines structure and agency.

There is a danger when thinking about coordination services firms like rating agencies in attributing the private authority evident here to some effect of economic function without contemplating the possibility of other influences. In the case of rating agencies, there is a lot of concern within the organizations about their reputation and the fragility of this resource. In other words, there is an understanding that the epistemic authority of the institutions rests on what is said and done, leading the analyst to think seriously about the extent to which the authority of rating agencies is constructed and not just derived from their "function."[37]

THREE ARGUMENTS

I now want to develop three arguments about features of rating coordination, in each case considering the likely effects for private firms and governments. The argument I made above about the effect of coordination services firms was that through a process of consent-generation and coercion they narrow expectations among agents to a common set upon which agreement exists, lowering the likely costs of transactions. This coordination effect is a reflection of the structural power of the agencies, the anticipation of the agencies' views by others and their action to meet these anticipated judgments. This structural power also reflects the epistemic authority attributed to rating agencies in the GPE. The three forms of coordination I identify exist at different levels of social action. Together, they comprise a shifting but coherent set of principles of coordination in the GPE.

The first form of coordination that rating agencies generate I will call information coordination. By information coordination, I mean in a narrow sense that the data or raw material upon which business (or governmental) activities are undertaken is increasingly made more transparent and reliable over time. The more overtly political sense in which we can understand this form of coordination is in terms of a displacement of local practices and information systems by those imported from outside.

The significance of information coordination can be seen a number of ways. In the United States this form is of less interest as most firms report publicly as it is and thus a lot is known about them through regular financial statements and annual reports. Equity and bond analysts compare and contrast these as their stock in trade. However, the situation is more complex outside the United States. One can, of course, anticipate many positive results of pushing firms to be more transparent, such as a reduction in fraud and bribery. However, using different assumptions in financial reporting generates starkly different prognoses from those previously considered valid.[38] Moreover, exposure of different rates of return on investment, say, in Germany, compared to the global average, as reported in the rationale for a rating, might embolden particular social forces to seek change in what had been considered acceptable as far as German business performance was concerned. This could have profound effects over time on differently institutionalized forms of capitalism, subjecting them all to the expectations inherent in the American model.[39]

My second argument is about risk coordination. What I refer to by this term is a process of evaluating and making judgments about the degree to which firms and governments have in place mechanisms to cope with risks such as litigation, exchange rate movement, interest rate change, or market risk. Rating agencies are also acutely aware of sovereign risk, in particular, the power that states retain to control foreign exchange earnings.[40] Means of risk abatement include contingency funds, insurance, forward cover for foreign exchange, derivatives strategies, and similar activities. The best way to understand these risks and risk strategies is as features of the much greater speed and volatility inherent in the GPE.

Risk coordination is important because it generates pressures that further the synchronic disembedding of productive activity in the GPE. The synchronic is a conception of time as the present, a universalization of current patterns and structures. Synchronic ways of thinking assume social institutions are the way they are because of the functions they serve. This view tends to ignore the diachrony of development processes, the maturation and the learning that have gone before the appearance of institutions in their current form. This reductive view of the world tends to devalue forms of planning and embedded production, and fosters a mercantile, speculative worldview that seeks opportunities for short-term profit rather than sustainable growth.[41] "Embedded" here refers to the complex of human relations outside market transactions based on rational maximization, but that nonetheless support human exchange, such as expectations, trust, and obligation.[42] Implicit in this view is the understanding that material life has—through most of human history—been generated in social networks and directed toward growth and the development of productive capacity. In an effort to meet what they perceive as the challenges of the GPE, bond-rating agencies further the polar opposite of embedded structures of habit and thought, as they encourage the more innovative financial technologies.[43] Perhaps the most extreme example of this disembedding effect are structured financings. These mechanisms for selling bonds are a way for the issuers of debt to obtain a rating well beyond what they would get without the innovation. It involves securing the bonds by a lien on specific assets such as credit card receivables that stand ahead of other rights on liquidation.[44]

The final argument I wish to make is about the coordinating effects of the centralized consideration of the strategies and plans of firms. This is strategic coordination. My argument is not that rating agencies conspire to bring about a particular structure to an industry like J. P. Morgan is understood to have done in steel and railroads.[45] The argument is that rating agencies are inherently conservative about firm strategy, look backwards, and are in effect always applying the lessons of the last growth model to the future. Now, this may not have been a problem in the boom years of the postwar era when prosperity was widespread.

Fordist models of productive organization produced both good wages and high profit levels. Unfortunately, this model spluttered to an end sometime in the 1970s and has been replaced by the austere circumstances of the GPE. I am not suggesting for a moment that rating-agency officials are unaware of such change. They tend to be thoughtful and focused individuals with an excellent grasp of the wider economic world. Despite this, the rating agencies are still largely organized on a sectoral basis that reflects the Fordist model. My argument is that the agencies are caught in something of a paradox. On the one hand, they have acquired a greatly heightened scope to exercise authority because of disintermediation outside the United States. On the other hand, though, they face a rapidly changing, vastly differentiated range of industries and services characterized by niche production, rather than the standard assembly line, about which it is much harder to think comprehensively and with a sense that things are predictable. The existence of rating agencies necessarily assumes this last factor. This suggests proportionally more and greater problems ahead for the rating agencies if they are to maintain a role in the new economy.

CONCLUSION

This chapter has considered bond-rating agencies as a form of private authority in the GPE. It identified the origin of coordination in the information problem between fractions of capital with resources and those with opportunities to deploy them. Agencies and investors are clear that the agencies serve the investors, the principals, as their agents. Securities issuers, however, do not necessarily ascribe to this view, giving rise to an ongoing tension among rating participants.

The epistemic authority of the agencies provides a counterbalance to state authority, delegitimizing its intervention to a great extent in the capital markets. However, it is the interaction rather than the competition between state and private power that is the most important consideration.

Coordination, as achieved by the agencies, was defined as a narrowing of the expectations of the different social elements of capital to a shared, transparent set. Three brief arguments about different aspects of this coordination process were proposed. Coordination in this form, by being infrastructural in its nature, avoids the costs of political contestation to a great degree. Despite this strength, which is reinforced by the expansion of disintermediated markets for capital, rating agencies are challenged by the shattering of the postwar growth model just as OECD governments have been. This raises questions about their long-term prospects.

An important feature of coordination services firms evident in the example of bond-rating agencies is their epistemic authority and closely related structural power, rather than direct "power wielding." The reason for this is that authority and structural power are built upon a certain base of consent. This is a more robust structure upon which the social forces associated with coordination can generate legitimacy for their view of the world, for their approach to problems and their distribution of payoffs to allied social interests. Epistemic authority and structural power are, however, much harder to specify than the variables international political economists are used to. Not only is authority seemingly more intangible, it is also constantly being both constructed and worn away.

NOTES

1. For comments on an earlier version of this paper I am indebted to the editors, Sol Picciotto, and the workshop participants.

2. Stephen Gill and David Law, *The Global Political Economy: Perspectives, Problems and Policies* (Baltimore: Johns Hopkins University Press, 1988).

3. See the introduction to this volume, pp. 10–11.

4. Much of the following section draws on Timothy J. Sinclair, "Passing Judgement: Credit Rating Processes as Regulatory Mechanisms of Governance in the Emerging World Order," *Review of International Political Economy* 1.1 (Spring 1994) 133–59; and Timothy J. Sinclair, "Guarding the Gates of Capital: Credit Rating Processes and the Global Political Economy" (Ph.D. diss., York University, Toronto, 1995).

5. "Recalled to Life: A Survey of International Banking," *The Economist*, April 30, 1994, p. 11.

6. Ibid.

7. Ibid.

8. "Time to Leave: A Survey of World Banking," *The Economist*, May 2, 1992.

9. For an argument for the continued role of bank intermediation, especially in the European context, see Colin Mayer and Xavier Vives, "Introduction," in Colin Mayer and Xavier Vives, eds., *Capital Markets and Financial Intermediation* (Cambridge: Cambridge University Press, 1993), pp. 7–8.

10. John W. Pratt and Richard J. Zeckhauser, *Principals and Agents: The Structure of Business* (Boston: Harvard Business School Press, 1985).

11. *Moody's Investors Service: Consistency, Reliability, Integrity* (New York: Moody's Investors Service, undated), p. 3.

12. George Foster, *Financial Statement Analysis*, 2nd ed. (Englewood Cliffs, N.J.: Prentice Hall, 1986), p. 498.

13. Standard & Poor's, *Ratings Handbook* 1.5 (August 1992): 183.

14. Interview with Leo C. O'Neill, President, Standard & Poor's, New York City, August 18, 1992.

15. Interview with Edward Z. Emmer, Executive Managing Director, Corporate Finance, Standard & Poor's Ratings Group, New York City, August 17, 1992.

16. Rupert Bruce, "Debt-Rating Agencies Fill the Gap," *The International Herald Tribune*, November 14–15, 1992, p. 11.

17. "The Would-Be King of Credit Ratings," *The Economist*, August 16, 1997, p. 74.

18. Susan Greenberg, "New Rating Agency Causes a Stir," *The Guardian*, February 13, 1993.

19. Richard Waters, "Rating Agencies Complete Merger," *The Financial Times*, October 21, 1992.

20. Interview with Joanne Rose, Vice President and General Counsel, Standard & Poor's Ratings Group, February 1993.

21. Lynne Kilpatrick, "Debt-Rating's Flaws," *The Financial Times of Canada*, March 30–April 5, 1992, p. 1.

22. For details on use of ratings in U.S. regulation, see Richard Cantor and Frank Packer, "The Credit Rating Industry," *Federal Reserve Bank of New York Quarterly Review* 19.2 (Fall 1994): 6.

23. "S&P Opposes Ratings Disclosure in Prospectuses," *Standard & Poor's Canadian Focus*, January 1995, pp. 7–8.

24. For a discussion of these elements and others of the neo-Gramscian toolkit, see Robert W. Cox with Timothy J. Sinclair, *Approaches to World Order* (Cambridge: Cambridge University Press, 1996), pp. 124–43.

25. Stephen Gill, "Structural Change and Global Political Economy: Globalizing Elites and the Emerging World Order," in Yoshikazu Sakamoto, ed., *Global Transformation: Challenges to the State System* (Tokyo: United Nations University Press, 1994).

26. Gill, "Structural Change," p. 179.

27. On the real economy and financial speculation, see Cox with Sinclair, *Approaches to World Order*, pp. 174–88.

28. Ronnie D. Lipschutz, "Reconstructing World Politics: The Emergence of Global Civil Society," *Millennium* 21.3 (Winter 1992): 407.

29. Jorge Larrain, *The Concept of Ideology* (Athens, Ga.: University of Georgia Press, 1979), pp. 172–73.

30. On epistemic authority, see Bruce Lincoln, *Authority: Construction and Corrosion* (Chicago: University of Chicago Press, 1994).

31. O'Neill interview.

32. "Insatiable: A Survey of Asian Finance," *The Economist*, November 12, 1994, pp. 13–15.

33. See examples from state politics in Australia in David Hayward and Mike Salvaris, "Rating the States: Credit Rating Agencies and the Australian State Governments," *Journal of Australian Political Economy* 34 (December 1994): 1–26.

34. "Combative Keating Counters the Jabs and Jibes," *Euromoney*, April 1989, pp. 27–33.

35. Robert Keohane, review of Susan Strange, *The Retreat of the State*, *Millennium* 26.1 (1997): 226.

36. See the introduction to this volume, pp. 9–15.

37. On the other hand, this concern with reputation may reflect the possibility of competition from other rating firms rather than other ways in which uncertainty might be reduced in the capital markets.

38. For example, when Daimler-Benz sought listing on the New York Stock Exchange they had to follow New York state rules producing a major loss where German rules had generated a profitable result.

39. Michel Albert, *Capitalism vs. Capitalism* (New York: Four Walls, 1993).

40. David Stimpson, ed., *Global Credit Analysis* (London: IFR Books/ Moody's Investors Service, 1991), p. 138.

41. On the synchronic and diachronic, see Robert W. Cox, *Production, Power, and World Order: Social Forces in the Making of History* (New York: Columbia University Press, 1987), pp. 1–9. Also see Timothy J. Sinclair, "Global Governance and the International Political Economy of the Commonplace," paper presented to the International Studies Association, Toronto, March 1997.

42. For a sustained discussion of embeddedness, see Mark Granovetter, "Economic Action and Social Structure: The Problem of Embeddedness," in Mark Granovetter and Richard Swedberg, eds., *The Sociology of Economic Life* (Boulder, Colo.: Westview Press, 1992).

43. On these issues, see Cox with Sinclair, *Approaches to World Order*, pp. 174–88.

44. *S&P's Structured Finance Criteria* (New York: Standard & Poor's, 1988), pp. 19–20.

45. Ron Chernow, *The House of Morgan: An American Banking Dynasty and the Rise of Modern Finance* (New York: Touchstone, 1990).

CHAPTER 7

Multinational Corporations as Agents of Change: The Globalization of Intellectual Property Rights

Susan K. Sell

If war is much too important a subject to leave up to generals, as Bismarck said, the rules of international commerce are far too important to leave up to government bureaucrats.
—James Enyart, Director, International Affairs, Monsanto Agricultural Company[1]

This chapter begins with a simple question: How did a small group of corporate executives of U.S.-based multinational corporations succeed in making intellectual property policy for the rest of the world? Twelve chief executive officers formed this group, the Intellectual Property Committee (IPC), representing: Bristol-Meyers, CBS, Du Pont, General Electric, General Motors, Hewlett-Packard, IBM, Johnson & Johnson, Merck, Monsanto, and Pfizer,[2] in March 1986, six months before the Punta del Este meeting launching the Uruguay Round of GATT negotiations. The IPC sought to develop international support for improving the international protection of intellectual property (patents, copyrights, trademarks, and trade secrets). The IPC, in conjunction with its counterparts in Europe and Japan, crafted a proposal based on existing industrialized country laws and presented its proposals to the GATT Secretariat. By 1994, the IPC had achieved its goal in the Trade Related Aspects of Intellectual Property (TRIPs) accord of the Uruguay trade round.

The 1994 TRIPs accord codifies a trade-based conception of intellectual property (IP) protection that binds signatory states, requires them to enact implementing domestic legislation, and adopt enforcement measures. The agreement provides IP owners with a twenty-year monopoly right, and subjects signatory states to the threat of trade sanctions if they fail to comply with the TRIPs provisions. This agreement would have been unthinkable without the concerted efforts of U.S.-based corporate executives.

The impetus for an IP agreement came from U.S. corporations for which IP constitutes valuable assets. A variety of export interests, including pharmaceutical, software, and entertainment industries, banded together to press for changes in U.S. trade laws and practices to strengthen global protection of IP. They achieved their legislative goals through, among other measures, amendments to Section 301 of the U.S. Trade and Tariff Act. They also pressed for inclusion of a trade-based conception of IP protection in the Uruguay Round of GATT negotiations. These corporations played a significant role in mobilizing domestic support for the TRIPs agreements and in shaping the content of U.S. negotiating proposals.

Intellectual property protection used to be the province of a small group of highly trained intellectual property lawyers, but now policymakers in industrialized countries have identified it as a key factor affecting their ability to compete in the global economy. No consensus exists about the merits of IP protection. Many argue that higher levels of IP protection promote innovation and the diffusion of new technology. Yet others insist that excessive IP protection retards socially beneficial innovation by providing monopolies to property owners.[3] The United States, and ultimately the parties to the GATT negotiations, accepted the particular vision articulated by the IPC.

The U.S.-based proposal to globalize a commitment to stronger IP enforcement was surprising, given the fact that domestically the U.S. enforcement of IP rights was relatively lax until about 1982.[4] In a very short time period, the United States changed its domestic approach to IP, then sought to globalize this commitment by incorporating IP into its trade policy instruments in both 1984 and 1988 amendments to domestic trade laws. The United States has pursued an aggressive approach by threatening targeted countries with trade sanctions for inadequate IP protection. Multilaterally, the incorporation of IP protection in both the North American Free Trade Agreement (NAFTA) and the TRIPs accord will have profound effects on those countries that do not yet share the American commitment to IP protection. These developing countries are hoping to achieve rapid industrialization and technological development by emulating the Japanese and East Asian models, which were not based on high levels of IP protection. Thus, the TRIPs accord may have negative distributional effects. Since the agreement is so new, the jury is still out and developing countries have been granted grace periods ranging from five to eleven years before they are required to adopt implementing legislation. However, in the meantime, IP protection is certain to provoke political conflict between U.S.-based private sector actors and developing countries.

What is new in this case is that industry identified a trade problem, devised a solution, and reduced it to a concrete proposal that it then advanced to governments. These private sector actors succeeded in getting most of what they wanted from an IP agreement, which now has the status of public international law.

The first section of the chapter addresses the sources and nature of private authority and presents the argument. Section two provides the background to the private actors' efforts in the United States, the President's Advisory Committee on Trade Negotiations and the formation of the IPC. Section three describes the IPC's efforts to mobilize its European and Japanese counterparts, and the development of a negotiating consensus. Section four discusses the negotiating process at the GATT, and the outcome of the TRIPs accord. The concluding section summarizes the argument and addresses the normative and distributive implications of this case.

THE ARGUMENT

The globalization of the world economy increasingly has blurred the boundaries between states and societies, domestic regulation and international commerce, public and private sectors. The TRIPs case contributes to a more general understanding of the role of private authority in the process of shaping the rules of international commerce that determine winners and losers in the world economy. By tracing the evolution of the TRIPs accord and examining the interaction between domestic structures, the private sector's role in the redefinition of U.S. interests, transnational coalition mobilization, and international organization, this chapter contributes to theorizing about the relationship between private authority, state policy, and international affairs.

In the TRIPs case, private actors worked together, exercised their authority and achieved a result that effectively narrows the options open to sovereign states and firms, and extends the opportunities of those firms that succeeded in gaining multilateral support for a tough IP instrument.[5] State-centric accounts of the Uruguay Round are at best incomplete, and at worst, misleading, obscuring the driving forces behind the TRIPs agreement.[6] Restricting the focus to the intergovernmental level, state-centric analyses obscure as much as they reveal and are ill-equipped to address the role of private authority. The TRIPs process was far more complex than a state-centric account would lead us to believe. In the TRIPs case, private actors pursued their interests through multiple channels and struck bargains with multiple actors: domestic interindustry counterparts, domestic governments, foreign governments, foreign private sector counterparts, domestic and foreign industry associations, and international organizations.

In effect, twelve corporations made public law for the world. The combination of the increasing openness of the United States system to private influence and the changing structural position of the United States in the world economy provided an opening for corporate influence. These were necessary, but not sufficient, conditions for the TRIPs outcome. As Mizruchi suggests, "the business community, despite its potential for power due to its huge accumulation of resources, will be a politically powerful actor only to the extent that it is capable of mobilizing as a politically unified force."[7] Powerful firms organized among themselves, through their industry associations and with their European and Japanese counterparts, to construct a transnational coalition favoring tough multilateral IP rules.

Domestically, the most active private sector participants were corporations working through their industry associations. By contrast, transnationally, U.S. corporate executives bypassed their industry associations and directly engaged their European and Japanese counterparts to press for a TRIPs agreement in the GATT. The transnational leadership of these U.S.-based corporations was decisive in the achievement of the TRIPs accord.

To explain the nature and exercise of private authority, one needs to examine the fluid relationships between private authority and state policy. According to Strange, "states may provide a framework of legal rights and duties within which other actors influence outcomes. Or they may be merely the arena, the stage or circus roof beneath which the action is played out."[8]

Conceptually, the relationship between state and private authority can vary considerably; private actors may see the state as an adversary, an ally, or irrelevant to the pursuit of its interests. Private actors may succeed in altering states' interests to conform to their private interests, thereby making the state an ally. Private actors may prompt the state to expand the framework of legal rights and duties by "persuading others to share fundamental beliefs about society and economy or to decide what knowledge is sought for and acquired and by whom."[9] In the IP case, firms began to see the state as an ally, once the state had accepted the private sector's trade-based conception of IP. According to Yoffie, "as the U.S. economy became more internationalized, many firms saw government as a potential ally against foreign companies. . . . Firms became politically active because the government had influence on critical uncertainties in the firm's environment."[10] One of these uncertainties was the extent to which foreign governments would protect U.S.-held IP. Private authorities saw the U.S. government, and by extension the international institution of the GATT, as a potential ally in its quest to expand international rules covering IP. In this case, private actors seeking to globalize their preferred conception of policy needed international institutions to further and legitimize the private actors' goals, monitor compliance, and enforce policy. Since these actors sought the protection of their IP, the GATT ultimately facilitated the achievement of their goals and helped empower this transnational coalition at the expense of others who fundamentally disagreed with its position.

Private actors may pursue their interests through state structures—political institutions, organizational routines, legal procedures, and norms defining appropriate conduct.[11] The concept of domestic structure underscores the importance of institutionalized access channels through which private actors press their demands. The private actors in this case appealed to both the legislative and executive branches in their quest for globalizing IP protection. The state is not a neutral broker of interests, and it structures private sector participation. For example, the executive branch established the Advisory Committee on Trade Negotiations (ACTN) to solicit private sector views in the shaping of U.S. trade policy. The ACTN proved to be an important vehicle for the globalization of the private interests of its member corporations. The state plays both a "dependent and intervening role, its initiatives [are] continually shaped by corporate preferences. Those preferences [are] ultimately dominant because of the structural relationship between multinational firms and foreign economic policy."[12]

Corporations are not like other interest groups. The "playing field" is far from level. As Lipson points out, "major corporations play a structurally privileged role, including a hegemonic role in establishing political norms and public agendas."[13] The corporations that formed the IPC were even more privileged than most; for example, eight of the member corporations are among the top fifty U.S. exporters.[14] They have access to resources unmatched by most other interest groups.

The sources of the IPC corporations' private authority are multiple and varied. Their prominent role in both production and knowledge structures gives them a larger voice as authority shifts from states to markets. Their sheer economic power is recognized by states, and authority is conferred upon them when governments give them an explicit policymaking role. The private authority of leading firms in IP derive "in part from their mastery of technology, in part from their financial resources and developed systems of marketing and distribution. But it has also depended on the support and collaboration of states in the promotion of an ideology of property rights."[15] Their expertise and access to information gives them an additional source of authority.

Corporations perform many essential functions for government,[16] not the least of which is to provide information. Their structurally privileged position contributes to what Lindblom refers to as "impairment" in the marketplace of ideas.[17] Yoffie suggests that large transnational enterprises are able to provide government officials with potentially useful information about foreign countries; "not all rivals can compete politically on these terms."[18] In IP, multinational corporations and their industry associations consistently have provided information about foreign governments' failures to provide adequate IP protection. Availing themselves of private policy networks, such as private law firms based abroad, these corporations have been the source of detailed substantive information about IP laws, practices, and infractions. The corporations have been vigilant in monitoring compliance in targeted states and have contracted law firms to report back to them. Corporations have committed considerable resources to the exposure of rampant piracy of IP abroad.

Furthermore, to determine the scale and scope of foreign piracy, the government has had to rely upon cost estimates provided by affected firms. For example, the first official quantitative estimates of distortions in U.S. trade stemming from inadequate IP protection abroad was based on data collected by the International Trade Commission (ITC), which sent out questionnaires to affected industries.[19] Firms interested in a trade-based approach to IP had plenty of incentive to overestimate the losses, especially "knowing that the ITC report would be used by politicians and economists in Washington when debating whether or not IP protection should become a major issue in international trade negotiations."[20] Subsequent independent estimates suggested that the ITC figures were wildly inflated.[21] Government reliance on information provided by a self-interested private sector stacked the deck in that sector's favor.

A further resource provided by the private sector is expertise in issue areas not well understood by government. In this regard, IP is especially unusual. IP lawyers are not like other attorneys. Most IP lawyers possess technical educational backgrounds in science, engineering, biochemistry, or chemistry. To a certain extent IP law is reminiscent of the Catholic Church when the Bible was in Latin. IP lawyers are privileged purveyors of expertise as was the Latin-trained clergy. IP law is highly technical and complex, obscure even to most general attorneys. The arcane nature of IP law gave additional advantages to the U.S. IP lobby;

its possession of technical and juristic knowledge was an important source of its private authority. The government had to rely on IP experts, who were also advocates, to translate the complexities into political discourse and make clear the connection between IP and international trade.[22] IP lawyers are socialized to promote the *protection* of IP, and uphold the ideology of private property rights. Thus, even though there are IP lawyers in the U.S. Commerce Department and the Patent and Trademark Office, they share a commitment to IP protection. Therefore, in this context, there is no neutral or objective group of civil servants in a position to counterbalance private demands.

When private actors need the state to promote their interests, private actors must present their interests in a way that appeals to policymakers in furthering the goals of the state. This is especially true in multilateral negotiations in which nation-states, not private actors, have standing. In this case, the IP lobby was particularly effective in translating their private interests into a matter of public interest. Conscious that the U.S. government was increasingly worried about its burgeoning trade deficit and its ability to effectively compete internationally, the IP lobby astutely packaged its demands as a solution to America's trade woes. IP advocates presented their industries as part of the solution and highlighted their strength as competitive exporters. They emphasized that they were the industries of the future, that would provide new American jobs into the next century. They further stressed that they were not seeking protection or special treatment of any kind, but sought the government's help in creating a fairer global trading order. Their success, in large part, was in their appeal to America's long-standing free-trade ethos and in pitching their cause in a way that captured the imagination of American policymakers as politically feasible. The way that the IP lobby presented its case to both Congress and the executive branch underscores the relationship between ideas and interests. Their efforts led the U.S. government to redefine its interests in IP, and endorse a trade-based approach to the globalization of IP. In this case, there would have been no multilateral TRIPs agreement without the concerted efforts of a handful of individuals. Prior to the 1986 Punta del Este meeting there was no enthusiasm for such an agreement outside the United States.

The story that follows illustrates the porous boundaries between domestic and international realms, public and private sectors, ideas and interests. This porousness reflects the complexity of a world in which multinational enterprises are the primary agents of internationalization, and are at the forefront of new forms of diplomacy and global regulation. According to Sally there are "issues of regulation and negotiation between MNEs, governments and other policy community/network actors that are distinctive and relate to the extraterritorial reach of the enterprise. Such trends are particularly evident in the 'new diplomacy' of MNE-government negotiating agendas—concerning firm-level advantages, national-level competitiveness, political and social goals."[23]

THE ORIGINS OF A TRADE-BASED APPROACH: THE ACTN AND THE IPC

Throughout the 1960s and 1970s, American businesses became increasingly politically active and involved in trade policymaking. Institutional changes adopted by the House of Representatives in the wake of the Watergate scandal paved the way for private actors to play a larger role in shaping trade policy. The decentralization of power in Congress and the opening up of legislative procedures made trade policymaking much more transparent. The reformers' goal "was to force policy choices out in the open by publicizing House actions and members' stands."[24] New House procedural rules made markups of bills open to the public and provided new opportunities for special interests to press their proposals.[25]

A number of developments in the late 1970s and early 1980s contributed to the increased influence of private sector export interests in U.S. trade policy and support for a new approach to trade. These included macroeconomic changes, such as the U.S. trade deficit and increasing pressure on the United States to be globally competitive, and the deindustrialization school of economic theory popularized by analysts such as Thurow, Reich, Magaziner, and Zysman and Cohen.[26]

The growing U.S. trade deficit, especially with Japan, engendered frustration in Congress. Advocates of a new approach to trade underscored the perceived lack of reciprocity between the United States and Japan, and laid the blame for America's trade woes abroad. Between 1980 and 1985, the U.S. trade deficit increased by 309 percent—from $36.3 to $148.5 billion.[27] Trade policy suddenly became the focus of U.S. aspirations to remain globally competitive. In response to the perception that the United States was in danger of losing the "race," both politicians and academics highlighted the fear of imminent deindustrialization. The U.S. preoccupation with competitiveness strengthened the hand of firms in shaping government policy.

The United States has wielded its market power through Section 301 of the Trade Act of 1974, which allows it to threaten trade retaliation to induce policy changes in targeted states. Section 301 gives the president the power to enforce U.S. rights under trade agreements and to eliminate policies and practices that discriminate or impose unjustifiable burdens on U.S. commerce. Amendments to Section 301 in the Trade Agreements Act of 1979 significantly expanded the scope of the private sector's participation in trade policy. The amendments allowed "private parties to take a significant and public step to enforce existing international agreements."[28] The act established the right of petitioners to seek governmental redress and required the federal government "to take account of the views of affected industry, effectively establishing a cooperative relationship between public and private sectors."[29] In the process of preparing for consultations and dispute settlement proceedings under Section 301, the U.S. Trade Representative (USTR) is required to seek information and advice from the petitioner and private sector representatives. Throughout the process of a Section 301 investigation, the USTR is expected to continue its consultations with the private sector.

In the late 1970s agricultural chemicals producers—Monsanto Agricultural Company, FMC, and Stauffer—acting through the U.S. government, engaged in bilateral talks with the Hungarian government in a quest to end the piracy of agricultural chemicals and strengthen Hungarian law.[30] The mobilization process began modestly, in the late 1970s, within the agricultural chemicals industry in the negotiations with the Hungarians. The initial efforts began within companies, such as Pfizer, FMC, IBM, and Du Pont. Activists, such as Enyart, within those companies persuaded corporate managers to dedicate resources to change foreign IP laws.[31] The mobilization process gained momentum as the agricultural chemicals industry joined forces with the U.S.-based International Anti-Counterfeiting Coalition (organized to protect trademarks in luxury and high fashion goods), and the Copyright Alliance to press for changes in U.S. trade policy. The scope of participation widened under the umbrella of the International Intellectual Property Alliance,[32] and soon patent interests were testifying before Congress in favor of copyright and trademark interests, which had heretofore been engaged in separate efforts. The IP activists realized that advocating enhanced protection of all forms of IP would help improve the climate for their particular interests, and thus banded together and united behind the common cause. As Chang Jae Baik points out, "protection of U.S. intellectual property rights became a dominating issue only after a few firms and industry organizations initiated an intellectual property lobby. . . . Through astute marketing of their demands, the lobby gain[ed] broad support from the business community and elicit[ed] support even from liberal trade–oriented Congressmen."[33]

In 1982, responding to industry pressure, the U.S. government engaged in numerous bilateral consultations with Korea, Mexico, Singapore, and Taiwan on their patent, copyrights, and trademark laws. As a result, Hungary, Taiwan, and Singapore took steps and enacted laws to ensure more vigorous protection.

These bilateral consultations were an important step in the evolution of the United States' new approach. Zalik points out that having U.S. trade officials (rather than intellectual property administrators) conduct these discussions with their foreign counterparts rendered the talks more effective because trade officials have more power to change policy.[34] Through these early successes U.S. industries realized that linking trade and intellectual property protection could be effective. Enyart emphasized that these early bilateral consultations convinced a large segment of U.S. high-technology and creative industries that exploiting the IP and trade linkage was a fruitful endeavor.[35]

Several other U.S. developments in intellectual property protection were overt in their intended international dimension, and the trend beginning in the early 1980s gained momentum. The United States began to expand its newly invigorated pro-patent approach to encompass international trade. As the former assistant general counsel of the Office of the U.S. Trade Representative argued, "the economic harm done to our industries today by the lack of adequate intellectual property laws abroad is staggering. . . . Our companies find they must compete with the unauthorized copies not only in the source country but in third countries as well."[36] Industries felt the pain, and U.S. industry representatives initiated a series of measures to try to reverse this trend.

Throughout the 1980s, the increasingly vocal IP lobby had played a larger role in the formulation of U.S. trade policy. Two corporate executives, Edmund Pratt, CEO of Pfizer Pharmaceutical, and John Opel, CEO of IBM, had long been lobbying the U.S. government to get serious about IP violators abroad. Both Pratt and Opel were involved in the U.S.-based International Anti-Counterfeiting Coalition (to protect trademarked high fashion and luxury goods) at the end of the Tokyo Round of GATT negotiations. Due to the nature of the IP produced by their companies, Pratt was primarily concerned with patent protection for pharmaceuticals, whereas Opel's focus was copyright protection and computer software.

From 1981, Pratt chaired the Advisory Committee for Trade Negotiations. The ACTN is the top of the private sector pyramid in terms of government representation. Members are presidential appointees who provide direct private sector consultation for trade policy. ACTN members played a major role in devising a trade-based IP strategy, and in shaping U.S. trade policy. Pratt and Opel pursued parallel efforts during 1983 and 1984 to advance their specific IP concerns to the administration. Largely as a result of their input, the President's Commission on Competitiveness report of 1983–84 included an addendum on IP protection as a competitiveness issue.

The sentiments of these private actors found formal expression in the reports of the ACTN's Task Force on Intellectual Property Rights. The heavy hitters of the private sector's campaign to secure better IP protection abroad were well represented on the task force. Among the participants of the eight-member task force were: John Opel, CEO of IBM; Fritz Attaway, vice president and counsel of the Motion Picture Industry Association; and Abraham Cohen, president of the International Division of Merck & Company Inc. (America's largest pharmaceutical corporation).

The U.S. government first officially linked IP protection and international trade in 1984. In January 1984, Gerald J. Mossinghoff, in his capacity as Assistant Secretary of Commerce and Commissioner of Patents and Trademarks, delivered a strong statement outlining the relationship between patents, trademarks, and international trade. He underscored the vital link between intellectual property protection and innovation, and American industry's capacity to compete globally. He concluded by emphasizing that "there is widespread bipartisan agreement that the protection of intellectual property worldwide is a critically important factor in expanding trade in high technology products. This Administration is committed to strengthen that protection as an integral component of our service to U.S. trade and industry."[37] In a classic example of the "revolving door" between government and the private sector, Mossinghoff left the government to become president of the U.S.-based Pharmaceuticals Manufacturing Association (PMA) in 1985—one of the most active associations in pressing for the linkage of IP and trade.[38]

Most significantly, Mossinghoff's statement signaled an end to the previous piecemeal treatment of intellectual property in the United States. Prior to late 1984 government agencies dealt with intellectual property problems on an ad hoc basis; U.S. embassies offered help to companies as problems arose.[39] Bipartisan support for this newly integrated approach emerged over a ten-year period in which private actors played an increasingly large role in focusing government attention on IP protection.

These private actors were in a good position insofar as they represented vigorous export industries that enjoyed positive trade balances. They successfully argued that foreign pirates, especially in East Asia and Latin America, were robbing them of hard-earned royalties. They pushed hard for a trade-based approach to intellectual property protection. Despite the fact that these corporate representatives had been busy trying to persuade foreign governments of the importance of providing adequate intellectual property protection, they argued that without the muscle and backing of the U.S. government, their efforts would continue to achieve weak results.

The particular ideas promoted by the industry associations laid the blame for the United States' growing trade deficit elsewhere by identifying an enemy (foreign pirates). They promised a more robust future for U.S. competitiveness and promoted themselves as viable and vibrant industries capable of leading the United States out of its economic doldrums. Furthermore, these industry associations united behind a trade-based conception. They elevated IP to the top tier of the U.S. trade agenda in a way that would permit the United States to maximize its leverage via access to its huge domestic market. Finally, their prescriptions offered an attractive alternative to mounting protectionist pressure, pressure that many policymakers found politically distasteful given the long-standing American free-trade ethos. Therefore, the ideas and solutions promoted by the private sector captured the imagination of U.S. policymakers as both feasible and politically desirable.

Congress adopted new amendments to the Trade and Tariff Act of 1984 that directly responded to the demands of the IP lobby. For the first time, the amended act included the failure to adequately protect IP as actionable under Section 301 and included IP protection as a new criterion for assessing developing countries' eligibility for nonreciprocal trade concessions under the Generalized System of Preferences (GSP) program. The section permits industries, trade associations, and individual companies to petition the United States Trade Representative to investigate actions of foreign governments. The 1984 amendments also gave the USTR authority to initiate cases on his own motion, which was helpful to companies in circumstances in which a foreign government might seek to retaliate against a company filing a 301 complaint.[40] Despite these legislative victories, the IP lobby continued to press the U.S. government to get tough with IP violators abroad.

In June 1984, a U.S. mission spent two weeks engaged in consultations on commercial counterfeiting with government officials in Taiwan and Singapore. The USTR, the State Department, the Patent and Trademark Office, the Copyright Office, and twenty private-sector participants representing ten industry associations, including the Motion Picture Association of America and the International Anticounterfeiting Coalition, participated. The Department of Commerce issued a memo about the trip, emphasizing that it expected "the continued close involvement of industry associations . . . in all follow-up activities."[41] Enyart points that the Taiwanese negotiations were striking in the breadth and diversity of U.S. industry representation, and that this expansion of actively involved industries was further reinforced by coalition work on the IP components of the Trade Act of 1984.[42]

In a statement before the Senate Finance Committee's Subcommittee on International Trade, Nicholas Veliotes, president of the Association of American Publishers, expressed his dissatisfaction with results in IP. He stated that the member organizations of the International Intellectual Property Alliance,

> came together . . . to press Congress and the Administration *first*, to recognize the critical importance to the United States of trade in goods and services dependent upon intellectual property protection worldwide, and *second*, to help forge the necessary legal tools enabling our trade negotiators to convince foreign nations to take action against massive and debilitating piracy and counterfeiting of U.S. books, music, records, films, computer software and other products. . . . There is no longer any question that improved protection for intellectual property is high on the U.S. government's list of trade priorities. It remains to be seen, however, whether this continued commitment can be translated into real success at the bargaining table. About 2 years after the enactment of these new laws [the 1984 amendments], we can report significant progress, but, as yet, no unqualified victories.[43]

In 1984, the USTR requested private sector input on the issue of including IP on the agenda of the upcoming GATT Round. John Opel commissioned Jacques Gorlin, an economist who had served as a consultant to ACTN and subsequently the IPC, to draft a paper for the USTR outlining a trade-based approach for IP. Gorlin's September 1985 paper, "A Trade-Based Approach for the International Copyright Protection for Computer Software,"[44] became the basis of the multilateral IP strategy that corporations soon pursued.

The year 1985 was a turning point in the private sector's quest for the globalization of its preferred trade-based conception of IP protection. Gorlin's contribution was his synthesis and extension of the more ad hoc lobbying requests and position papers that corporations and industry associations had presented to Congress and the executive branch throughout the early 1980s. His document provided the contours of a possible multilateral agreement for the GATT, as well as suggested strategies for consensus building. Not surprisingly, in October 1985 the ACTN Task Force on Intellectual Property Rights presented its report to ACTN and its recommendations appeared to be lifted wholesale out of Gorlin's document.[45]

Gorlin advocated a number of strategies including: a campaign to educate IP experts on the economic aspects of the issues; U.S. accession to the Berne Convention for the Protection of Literary and Artistic Works; the negotiation of an IP code with like-minded industrialized countries within the OECD or plurilaterally within the GATT, "to avoid the obstructionist tactics of the LDCs";[46] the recognition that the World Intellectual Property Organization (WIPO) would need to be consulted, and its resistance to the establishment of an IP code at GATT overcome;

and the continuation of complementary unilateral and bilateral efforts to combat piracy and weak enforcement abroad. According to Gorlin, the advantages of incorporating IP into the multilateral trade regime would include availability of a dispute settlement mechanism, the use of linkage to other trade and investment issues, and the greater political leverage of trade officials. As Gorlin summarized, developing a trade-based code "would help deal with the problems of piracy that are caused by governmental actions such as substandard legal protection and enforcement, by providing a forum with higher visibility, a tradition of finger-pointing, and a willingness to get involved in dispute settlement."[47] To build the necessary consensus, Gorlin advocated pursuing plurilateral simultaneous negotiations within the OECD and GATT.

In February and March 1986, USTR Clayton Yeutter asked Opel and Pratt for assistance in putting IP on the Uruguay Round agenda.[48] Yeutter pointed out that the European, Japanese, and Canadian governments were not getting any industry pressure for IP, and that without all of the big four on board (U.S., Canada, Europe, Japan) there was no chance of an IP deal in the Uruguay Round. To develop an IP code, Pratt and Opel needed a core of committed and actively engaged companies with international connections to secure U.S. governmental and foreign support.[49] At this point Opel and Pratt contacted their peers and convinced their fellow CEOs to form the IPC in March 1986. According to Enyart, the CEOs provided adequate funding and human resources to the IP effort, and provided added momentum by directly contacting their corporate counterparts.[50]

The IPC, rather than working through its respective industry associations, chose to bypass these associations in search of a quick consensus. The IPC sought rapid results; to maximize its impact it deliberately limited its membership, and insisted that member companies be represented by the top echelons of management to avoid cumbersome negotiations within the corporations. The IPC operated as a committee of the whole, and its streamlined structure was designed to get things done quickly. It represented a broad array of U.S. industries—chemical, computer, creative arts, electronics, heavy and consumer manufacturing, and pharmaceutical industries. As Enyart points out, "no existing U.S. trade group or association really filled the bill, we had to create one."[51]

That same month, March 1986, the ACTN's Task Force on Intellectual Property Rights issued a second report focusing on U.S. bilateral and unilateral efforts (USTR 1986). It, like Gorlin's 1985 paper, endorsed a carrot and stick approach by supporting efforts to provide technical training in IP issues to foreign officials, while also strengthening U.S. trade leverage over reluctant foreign governments. Among the sticks were making the renewal of GSP benefits contingent on the effective protection of IP and the further strengthening of Section 301.

The task force also underscored the crucial role that the private sector had played in the expansion of a trade-based approach. According to the report, "the U.S. IP-based industries have already played a significant catalytic role in defining IP as a trade issue and in having U.S. trade officials accept IP as part of their agenda."[52] The task force emphasized the continuing importance of private sector/government dialogue for shoring up domestic consensus on a trade-based approach.

Domestically, the IPC was far from idle.[53] It contacted the U.S. Chamber of Commerce and numerous industry associations to persuade them of the merits of a trade-based approach to IP. These organizations adopted IPC positions and endorsed the overall multilateral strategy. For example, in July 1986 the Joint Working Party on IP issues and the GATT of the International Chamber of Commerce recommended the inclusion of IP in the new GATT round.[54] Since the IPC member corporations were among the most active in their respective industry associations as it was, this was not a particularly hard sell.

IPC: MOBILIZING AN INTERNATIONAL COALITION; SHORING UP A CONSENSUS

Time was short; the IPC only had six months before the upcoming September Punta del Este meeting. From the time of its formation in March, the group wasted very little time in its quest to develop a prenegotiation consensus with the Europeans and Japanese. IPC members immediately contacted their peers in European and Japanese industry. In June 1986, the IPC met with the Confederation of British Industries, the BDI in Germany, the French Patronat and through them, with the Union of Industrial and Employers' Confederations of Europe (UNICE).[55] In July, the IPC went to Japan and met with the Japan Federation of Economic Organizations (Keidanren).[56]

In these meetings, the IPC stressed that the issue of IP was too important to leave to governments.[57] The group argued that industry needed to decide upon the best course of action and then tell governments what to do. The IPC convinced their European and Japanese counterparts of the merits of a trade-based approach to IP by emphasizing their common plight, and asking questions such as, "Don't you have problems with Brazil too?" The IPC emphasized the high costs of IP piracy, and the successes that had been achieved through bilateral trade negotiations. The IPC succeeded in forging an industry consensus with its Japanese and European industry counterparts, who agreed to work on it and pledged to present these views to their respective governments in time for the launching of the Uruguay Round. Pratt noted that this joint action by the U.S., European, and Japanese business communities represented a noteworthy breakthrough in the international business community's involvement in trade negotiations.[58] UNICE and Keidanren successfully advanced their cause to their governments in the short time remaining, because by the launching of the new trade round in September, the United States, Japan, and Europe were united behind the inclusion of an IP code in the GATT.

At the outset of the Punta del Este meeting, some Western delegations still endorsed a more modest approach to IP than that advocated by the IPC. They sought to revive a 1982 draft proposal on an Anti-Counterfeiting Code that had been developed in the wake of the Tokyo Round of GATT negotiations, and leave more comprehensive proposals on IP rights to later negotiating rounds. However, they soon abandoned this more limited strategy "for fear that a successful Anti-Counterfeiting Code might take the momentum out of the negotiations for a broader, all-inclusive code."[59]

U.S. industry, and the IPC in particular, had a potent ally at the Uruguay Round. Pratt was an advisor to the U.S. Official Delegation at the Uruguay Round meeting in his capacity as chairman of ACTN. This was auspicious because the private sector has no official standing at GATT.

In the United States, the IPC worked closely with the International Intellectual Property Alliance to coordinate and promote its positions to the government. The Patent and Trademark Office (PTO) and the USTR also worked closely together to push the U.S. IP agenda. Mike Kirk, the chief U.S. TRIPs negotiator was "very supportive."[60] Throughout the process the IPC continued to consult with the U.S. administration and Congress, and a 1988 IPC report indicated that the IPC's close relationship with Commerce and the USTR permitted it to shape both U.S. negotiating positions and specific proposals throughout the course of the negotiations.[61]

The IPC, UNICE, and Keidanren agreed to continue to work together to devise a consensual approach to an IP code at the GATT. Industry representatives met in October and November 1986, and worked on producing a consensus document to present to their respective governments and the GATT Secretariat. During this process of devising a concrete proposal for a GATT code, participants worked hard to fairly represent the diverse forms of intellectual property and the various industries involved.[62] In June 1988, this "trilateral group" released its "Basic Framework of GATT Provisions on Intellectual Property."[63] The contents were very similar to the concrete proposals of Gorlin's 1985 paper, and became the basis of the eventual TRIPs agreement.

As a consensus document, it included some compromises. For example, the U.S. pharmaceutical industry was not entirely satisfied with the provisions on compulsory licensing; but the United States conceded the issue to keep the Europeans and Japanese on board. Having produced this consensus proposal, the IPC, Keidranen, and UNICE returned to their home countries to pitch the trilateral approach to other industries and companies.[64] This process was not particularly difficult for the IPC, which faced a very receptive home government. In fact the U.S. government requested 100–150 copies of the June 1988 proposal and sent it out as reflecting its views.[65] Furthermore, the oft-noted differences in government-business relations in the United States, Japan, and Europe did not seem to make much difference in the ability of this trilateral group to secure governmental support for its proposals. By November 1987, the Europeans and Japanese tabled concrete negotiating proposals for an IP agreement, and thereby gave the TRIPs effort considerable momentum.[66]

Between 1986 until April 1989, IP issues stalled in the trade negotiations. Developing countries, led by India and Brazil, vehemently protested the inclusion of IP in the GATT. Meanwhile, the United States increased the pressure by adopting new amendments to U.S. trade laws.

In 1988 the United States strengthened its trade-based approach to IP. Motivated by industry lobbying, Congress pressed the administration to use Section 301 more vigorously. Congressmen bemoaned the fact that the executive branch shied away from trade retaliation "because of the desire to use trade to barter for other nontrade issues."[67] On August 23, 1988, Congress enacted H.R. 4848, the Omnibus Trade and Competitiveness Act of 1988 and adopted new amendments to Section 301. The 1988 amendments effectively transferred substantial authority from the president to the USTR. According to Representative Bill Richardson (D.–New Mexico), the change was "intended to enhance USTR's position as the lead trade agency and to make it less likely that trade retaliation would be waived because of foreign policy, defense, or other considerations."[68] In effect this change codified the elevated niche that trade had come to occupy in U.S. foreign policy—that trade issues should not be subordinated to issues traditionally conceived of as "high politics." The new act transferred to the USTR authority under Section 301 to determine whether foreign government practices are unfair and to take action.

The 1988 act strengthened the IP components that were originally incorporated in 1984. It required the USTR to annually identify IP priority countries, defined as those whose acts, policies, or practices deny effective and adequate intellectual property protection as well as those that deny fair and equitable market access to U.S. parties that rely on IP protection. Once the USTR had identified a priority country, it was required to self-initiate an investigation within thirty days. Within six months of initiating an investigation the USTR had to determine whether the priority country's activities were actionable, and if so, what action to take. Once the USTR had determined that action was warranted, it had thirty days to implement 301 action.[69]

The 1988 amendments were important because they indicated that the United States would continue to pursue the carrot-and-stick approach in trade policy and fortified the connection between IP and international trade. The tight time deadlines and requirement for public identification of violating countries reflected the expressed desires of the private sector to toughen U.S. resolve. The new procedures institutionalized the participation of the private sector by providing that, "before taking any action, the USTR shall consult with the petitioner and domestic industry and provide an opportunity for public views."[70]

The private sector secured the changes that it sought and proceeded to use these new weapons in its arsenal—swift retaliation and a more credible threat—particularly against newly industrializing and developing countries. Significantly, the recalcitrant Brazil immediately bore the brunt of the United States' aggressive strategy. The Pharmaceutical Manufacturers Association initiated a Section 301 case against Brazil for its failure to provide patent protection for pharmaceutical products. After Brazil refused to alter its domestic IP policy, in 1989 the U.S. placed a 100 percent retaliatory tariff (totaling $39 million) on imports of Brazilian pharmaceuticals, paper products, and consumer electronics.[71] Brazil filed a GATT complaint, charging that U.S. trade retaliation was GATT-illegal, but "withdrew its complaint when the actions were dropped [in summer 1990] in exchange for Brazil's patent commitments."[72]

THE GATT NEGOTIATIONS AND THE TRIPs ACCORD

Despite the fact that progress on the TRIPs negotiations had stalled, the IPC continued to pursue its multilateral efforts. The IPC worked to keep its business coalition together, and also focused its efforts on the GATT Secretariat. IP was a new issue for the GATT Secretariat. Some members of the secretariat recognized the inherent tension between free trade and the monopoly privileges of IP, yet did not systematically analyze TRIPs in this light but rather "responded to the 'imperatives of the negotiations.'"[73] Furthermore, taking a page from the 1985 Gorlin paper, negotiators worked in enclave committees to achieve plurilateral consensus—just as the IPC had done in its discussions with its European and

Japanese counterparts. The IPC replicated its consensus building approach within the GATT, and two subgroups—a "Friends of Intellectual Property" group, and the QUAD (the most powerful enclave committee)—significantly contributed to developing the TRIPs text.[74]

By April 1989, leading NICs/LDCs had accepted that GATT could have jurisdiction in IP, and that the TRIPs group could negotiate a comprehensive code of all trade-related aspects of IP rights. At the April 1989 Geneva meeting the delegations adopted a declaration endorsing continuation of the negotiating round and the applicability of GATT principles to intellectual property issues.[75]

There were several reasons that formerly intransigent developing countries went along. First of all, they were experiencing escalating pressure from the United States via Section 301 and GSP actions. Besides the Brazilian case, in May 1988 East Asian NICs were officially dropped from the U.S. list of developing countries and became ineligible for GSP benefits. Many developing countries hoped that cooperation on TRIPs might ease the 301 pressure. India had received considerable bilateral pressure from the United States to drop its opposition to the TRIPs agreement. Also, the United States, Canada, and Mexico had successfully negotiated NAFTA, which included stiff IP requirements. Many Latin American countries, hoping eventually to join considered IP commitments as part of the admission price.[76] For smaller countries that had not been targeted by 301 actions, NAFTA and the proliferation of similar regional trading blocs posed a different set of concerns that led them to support TRIPs and the Round as a whole. Not being parties to any preferential regional agreements, they came to endorse a strong liberalizing outcome to counter discriminatory trade practices emanating from the regional blocs, recognizing that broad market access was imperative for their economic well-being.[77]

Another factor was the glaring asymmetries in experience and expertise on IP issues. India and Brazil had formulated numerous counterproposals during the negotiations, stressing issues such as the public interest, shorter patent terms, and the obligations of IP owners to "work" their inventions in developing countries. However, corporate counsel from U.S. industry with extensive experience in IP and licensing critically evaluated these proposals. As Drahos points out, "once they had passed an opinion the enclave committee structure within the GATT, groups like the IPC and IIPA, the business triumvirate and the developed countries coordinated to criticize and reject the proposals."[78] Drahos stresses that the rejection of the counterproposals cannot be explained simply in terms of power, and that developing countries' representatives were novices with regard to IP and licensing expertise. Authority deriving from technical and juristic expertise enabled industrialized country negotiators to "pull rank" and subject developing country negotiators to "the disciplining effect of expert knowledge."[79]

Thus, by 1989 developing-country resistance had finally been overcome. Yet in 1990, the Uruguay Round negotiations collapsed in Brussels over agricultural issues.[80] This spelled an end to the so-called "green room" process in which thirty-five countries or so engaged in "horse-trading." In April 1990 the Latin Americans walked out. At this point, the GATT director general, Arthur Dunkel, took over the process. There would be no more horsetrading, but Dunkel took stances on controversial issues for countries to react and respond to. Lars Anzell was in charge of the IP drafts, and presented his own in March–December 1990. According to Gorlin, 1991 was a tense time in the negotiations. The IPC deliberately ceased its lobbying activities and left the process to official U.S. negotiators. The IPC did not want to seem underhanded, or acting behind the backs of the U.S. negotiating team. Agriculture and services were particularly thorny issues. The GATT talks resumed in September 1991, and, eager to move the negotiations forward, in December Dunkel produced a draft that he proposed be rejected or accepted as a whole. Negotiating parties finally reached agreement on the so-called "Dunkel Draft" and the Uruguay Round was successfully concluded on April 15, 1994.

The IPC succeeded in getting most of what it wanted in the TRIPs (Trade Related Aspects of Intellectual Property, Including Trade in Counterfeit Goods) agreement in the recently concluded GATT round. According to Gorlin, except for the lengthy transition periods for developing countries, the IPC got 95 percent of what it wanted.[81] The IPC was particularly pleased with the enforcement provisions. The industry representatives' demands are reflected clearly in the final agreement. For example, the TRIPs agreement affirms the principle of national treatment and mandates a twenty-year minimum period for exclusivity of patent rights from the date of filing the patent application.[82] Chemical and pharmaceutical producers gained by the provision in the TRIPs agreement that reverses the former burden of proof in process patent infringement cases; before the burden of proof of infringement rested with the patent holder, now the alleged infringer must demonstrate that the process used is substantially different.[83] Furthermore, the agreement restricts the issuance of compulsory licenses by forbidding exclusive licenses and sharply reducing the conditions for and scope of such licenses.[84] This is significant, because in the past, a number of developing countries reserved the right to issue exclusive compulsory licenses—authorizing a third party to work an invention and excluding the property owner from exploiting the resource. Policymakers in developing countries suspected that many foreigners filed patents solely to block the use of the patented invention in the country or to promote importation of that article by the patent holder. In order to protect themselves from paying above-market rates for patented technology due to an import monopoly, many developing countries believed that the threat of exclusive compulsory licensing was a powerful tool for ensuring that foreign IP holders put their IP to productive use rather than abuse their monopoly rights. This tool is no longer available to TRIPs signatories.

In a departure from GATT precedent, the TRIPs accord does not merely circumscribe the range of acceptable policies that a government may practice, but "obliges governments to take positive action to protect intellectual property rights."[85] The short-term impact of stronger global IP protection will be a significant transfer of resources from developing-country consumers and firms to industrialized-country firms.[86]

However, the TRIPs agreement includes some major concessions for developing countries. Articles 65 and 66 grant developing countries and least-developed countries five- and ten-year grace periods respectively, before they are obligated by the terms of the agreement. Furthermore, Article 27(2) stipulates that:

> members may exclude from patentability inventions, the prevention within their territory of the commercial exploitation of which is necessary to protect *ordre public* [emphasis added] or morality, including to protect human, animal or plant life or health or to avoid serious prejudice to the environment, provided that such exclusion is not made merely because the exploitation is prohibited by domestic law.[87]

Article 27(3) exempts from patentability diagnostic, therapeutic, and surgical methods for the treatment of animals, or humans; Article 27(4) exempts plants, animals, and their biological processes from patentability. These provisions will allow developing countries to continue to pursue conscious policies of drug patent exemption.[88] Additionally, agricultural chemicals may also fall under these exceptions, "provided the prevention of their commercial exploitation could be linked to a higher public order goal, such as the provision of an adequate food supply for the population."[89] The "*ordre public*" criterion is open to a variety of interpretations, and enhances the role of state discretion in determining patentability.

NORMATIVE ISSUES AND CONCLUSION

In intellectual property protection, cause-and-effect relations are still contested. While the North claims that stronger intellectual property protection will benefit developing countries, this relationship has yet to be demonstrated in either economic theory or empirical proof.[90] Referring to a user-oriented strategy for technological innovation, van Wijk and Junne suggest that, "as international competitiveness is not so much determined by the *production* of new technologies but rather by the *application*, technology policy actually puts increasing emphasis on the *diffusion* of new technologies to their users."[91] This raises questions about the social value of providing inventors with a twenty-year monopoly right, as established in the TRIPs accord. In an era of rapid technological change unimpeded diffusion has much to recommend it; otherwise, "strong protection of a key innovation may preclude competitors from making socially beneficial innovations."[92] Furthermore, safeguarding these monopoly privileges provokes justifiable fears among technological latecomers seeking to emulate the Japanese strategy of the "fast second" by reverse engineering and rapidly commercializing foreign technologies.

The hypothesis behind the TRIPs agreement is that stronger IP protection will lead to increased technology transfer, investment flows, and industrial development in less developed countries. As Donal O'Connor, the past president of the Licensing Executives Society (LES) of Britain and Ireland, pointed out in his candid assessment of the TRIPs accord, "this is a hypothesis that has not by any means been proven. It is one that we in LES wish to accept because it is one that we consider attractive."[93] Surendra Patel, a developing-country critic of the TRIPs agreement, observed that the U.S. TRIPs proposals were based on analyses and estimated loss reports provided by transnational corporate exporters and their industry associations. These reports were simply reproduced, without independent verification, in the government submissions. As he points out, "we now see a new paradigm: the losses of private companies are losses of the developed countries. And the losses of the developed countries are losses for all countries, for all peoples of the world."[94]

Despite this skepticism about the basis for the TRIPs accord, developing countries finally assented to its inclusion. Developing countries have limited leverage in the GATT forum, which is precisely why the United States found this venue more attractive than WIPO. Their shift to export-led industrialization makes access to Northern markets essential, and their participation in the WTO will provide benefits such as Most Favored Nation status. Yet their adherence to these new standards remains an open question and undoubtedly will be a continuing source of tension in the foreseeable future.

The TRIPs case raises some troubling normative issues. The TRIPs accord requires countries to make dramatic changes in their domestic IP policies. It raises the price of information and technology by extending the monopoly privileges of rights-holders, and requires states to play a much greater role in the enforcement of monopoly privileges.[95] It benefits the few at the possible expense of the many. Since the mobilization of corporate alliances for specific political purposes is the wave of the future, it is worth asking ourselves what the implications of this will be. Is what is best for twelve corporations best for the world? The industrialized countries built much of their early economic success on appropriating others' IP.[96] With the TRIPs accord, this option is foreclosed.

The Dispute Settlement Understanding (DSU) is elaborated in Article 64 of the TRIPs agreement, and instruments range from consultation and voluntary mediation to the suspension of trade concessions. The TRIPs agreement notwithstanding, the United States expects to preserve its right to pursue both 301 and GSP action against countries that fail to protect intellectual property. The Industry Functional Advisory Committee on Intellectual Property Rights for Trade Policy Matters takes the position that the United States can continue to pursue these actions, but acknowledges that the extent to which the sanctions of domestic law can be invoked are more limited if the GATT 1994 agreements are accepted.[97] Under TRIPs, the United States would have to submit complaints to the Dispute Settlement Body of WTO and abide by the WTO ruling. In its legislation on TRIPs, the U.S. House of Representatives stated that, "Nothing in this Act shall be construed . . . to limit any authority conferred under any law of the United States, including section 301 of the Trade Act of 1974, unless specifically provided for in this Act."[98] However, as Shrader suggests, "once the Dispute Settlement Understanding becomes fully effective in the year 2000, the extent to which unilateral action can be taken to remedy a trade practice may become a contentious issue for the United States."[99]

This is important because many of the U.S. industry representatives still are not fully satisfied with either the TRIPs or the NAFTA. Given the fact that they have been the most active in pressing for 301 action and GSP suspensions, one should expect this activism to continue. For example, even though industry associations praised NAFTA as the most comprehensive intellectual property agreement ever negotiated, the Business Software Alliance has complained that, "despite the NAFTA, Mexico has neither taken effective action against infringement of intellectual property rights, nor has it provided 'expeditious remedies' as effective deterrents to intellectual property violators."[100] Another commentator warned high-technology businesses that NAFTA offered little protection. He stated that "the failings of the Mexican system of intellectual property enforcement are an inheritance of past policies and a lack of understanding of the parameters of 'adequate' enforcement. . . . [Education and enforcement] efforts take far more time than simply changing the wording of laws."[101]

Industry representatives are even more dissatisfied with the TRIPs agreement, which is substantially weaker and less comprehensive than NAFTA. Industry associations have expressed dismay over the transitional period for developing countries, the lack of an obligation to protect against parallel imports (lawfully made goods that are not authorized for distribution in the country where importation is sought, also known as gray-market goods), the "public order" loophole, and weaker border enforcement of infringing articles than they desired.[102] Therefore, industry pressure to pursue 301 and GSP actions against infringing countries is unlikely to vanish.

This case illustrates the increasingly porous boundaries between public and private authority, domestic and international politics, and domestic regulation and international commerce. In the United States, corporate actors availed themselves of domestic institutional access to press their case and cultivated close working relationships with the legislative and executive branches of government. In the TRIPs case, corporate actors mobilized their private sector counterparts both at home and abroad to press their governments and the GATT to support and produce an IP code. They vigorously pursued their IP objectives at all possible levels and in multiple venues, successfully redefining IP as a trade issue. However, it was not merely their relative economic power that led to their ultimate success, but their command of IP expertise, their ideas, their information, and their skills in translating complex issues into political discourse. Not all ideas are equally privileged in political life; therefore, how one defines "interests," is central to understanding which sets of ideas affect policy. Furthermore, it is important to identify *who* is defining them. By promoting their particular vision as a solution to pressing American trade problems, the IP activists were able to capture the imagination of policymakers and persuaded them to adopt their private interests as American interests. Additionally, their initiative in producing concrete negotiating proposals significantly strengthened their hand.

The TRIPs accord is best understood as a product of the exercise of private authority. This chapter has examined the symbiotic relationship between the private sector and the state, but did not assume that private and public interests were synonymous. Instead it described the process by which private interests *became* public by examining domestic and transnational coalitions, domestic structures, and international institutions. While the globalization of the economy has enhanced the structural privilege of corporate actors in policymaking, one needs to examine the mechanisms through which this process is proceeding.

NOTES

I am grateful to A. Claire Cutler, Virginia Haufler, and Tony Porter, and the 1996 ISA Workshop on Private Authority participants for helpful comments on earlier drafts of this chapter.

1. James Enyart, "A GATT Intellectual Property Code," *Les Nouvelles* 25.2 (June 1990): 53–56.

2. Throughout the years 1986–1996, the IPC's membership fluctuated from eleven to fourteen corporations. In 1994 CBS, Du Pont, and General Motors no longer participated, but Digital Equipment Corporation, FMC, Procter & Gamble, Rockwell International, and Time Warner did.

3. Paul David, "Intellectual Property Institutions and the Panda's Thumb: Patents, Copyrights, and Trade Secrets in Economic Theory and History," in Mitchel B. Wallerstein et al., eds., *Global Dimensions of Intellectual Property Rights in Science and Technology* (Washington, D.C.: National Academy Press, 1993); R. C. Levin et al., "Appropriating the Returns from Industrial Research and Development," *Brookings Papers on Economic Activity* 3 (1987): 783–820, especially 788; Jeroen van Wijk and Gerd Junne, *Intellectual Property Protection of Advanced Technology: Changes in the Global Technology System: Implications and Options for Developing Countries* (Maastricht, the Netherlands: United Nations University, Institute for New Technologies, Contract No. 91/026, October 1992).

4. Robert Whipple, "A New Era in Licensing," *Les Nouvelles* 22.3 (September 1987): 109–10.

5. This rendering draws upon Susan Strange's conceptualization of private authority in telecoms, see Susan Strange, *The Retreat of the State: The Diffusion of Power in the World Economy* (Cambridge: Cambridge University Press, 1996), p. 100.

6. For an example of a state-centric analysis of the Uruguay Round, see A. Jane Bradley, "Intellectual Property Rights, Investment, and Trade in Services at the Uruguay Round: Laying the Foundation," *Stanford Journal of International Law* 23 (Spring 1987): 57–98.

7. Mark Mizruchi, *The Structure of Corporate Political Action* (Cambridge: Harvard University Press, 1992), p. 34.

8. Strange, *Retreat of the State*, p. 70.

9. Ibid.

10. David Yoffie, "Corporate Strategies for Political Action: A Rational Model," in Alfred Marcus et al., eds., *Business Strategy and Public Policy: Perspectives From Industry and Academia* (New York: Quorum Books, 1987), p. 45.

11. Thomas Risse-Kappen ed., *Bringing Transnational Relations Back In: Non-State Actors, Domestic Structures, and International Institutions* (Cambridge: Cambridge University Press, 1995), p. 19.

12. Charles Lipson, *Standing Guard: The Protection of Foreign Capital in the Nineteenth and Twentieth Centuries* (Berkeley: University of California Press, 1985), p. 256.

13. Ibid., p. 222.

14. James Aley, "New Lift for the U.S. Export Boom," *Forbes*, November 13, 1995, pp. 73–76.

15. Strange, *Retreat of the State*, p. 97.

16. Charles Lindblom, *Politics and Markets* (New York: Basic Books, 1977), p. 175.

17. Charles Lindblom, *Inquiry and Change: The Troubled Attempt to Understand and Shape Society* (New Haven: Yale University Press, 1990).

18. Yoffie, "Corporate Strategies," p. 49.

19. U.S. International Trade Commission, *Foreign Protection of Intellectual Property Rights and the Effects on the U.S. Industry and Trade*, USITC Pub. 2065, Inv. No. 332–245, February 1988.

20. Frank Emmert, "Intellectual Property in the Uruguay Round—Negotiating Strategies of the Western Industrialized Countries," *Michigan Journal of International Law* 11 (Summer 1990): 1324–25.

21. R. Michael Gadbaw and Timothy J. Richards, *Intellectual Property Rights: Global Consensus, Global Conflict?* (Boulder, Colo.: Westview Press, 1988).

22. In some respects, this conception mirrors issues raised by the "epistemic community" literature yet in this case my argument is broader. The relevant community of experts was hardly the image of scientists presenting their objective results in a persuasive manner. It included experts, advocates, lobbyists, and corporations who stood to gain quite a lot by prevailing.

23. Razeen Sally, "Multinational Enterprises, Political Economy, and Institutional Theory: Domestic Embeddedness in the Context of Internationalization," *Review of International Political Economy* 1.1 (Spring 1994): 177.

24. I. M. Destler, *American Trade Politics* (Washington, D.C.: Institute for International Economics, 1992), p. 68.

25. Ibid., p. 69.

26. Lester Thurow, *The Zero-Sum Solution: Building a World-Class American Economy* (New York: Simon & Schuster, 1985); Robert Reich and Ira Magaziner, *Minding America's Business: The Decline and Rise of the American Economy* (New York: Harcourt, Brace and Jovanovich, 1982); Robert Reich, "Beyond Free Trade," *Foreign Affairs* 61 (Spring 1983): 773–804; John Zysman and Stephen S. Cohen, *Manufacturing Matters* (N.Y. Basic Books, 1987).

27. Dale Hughes, "Opening Up Trade Barriers With Section 301: A Critical Assessment," *Wisconsin International Law Journal* 5 (1991): 177.

28. Bart Fisher and Ralph Steinhardt, "Section 301 of the Trade Act of 1974," *Law and Policy in International Business* 14 (1982): 575.

29. Ibid., p. 605.

30. Enyart, "A GATT Intellectual Property Code," 54.

31. Ibid.

32. This umbrella organization consists of the following eight trade associations of: American Publishers, Inc.; American Film Marketing; Data Processing Service Organizations; Computer Software and Services Industry; Business Software Alliance; Computer and Business Equipment Manufacturers; Motion Picture Association of America; National Music Publishers; and Recording Industry of America. The IPC and IIPA worked closely together, and many of

the IPC members were quite active in their respective industry associations as well. However, for purposes of this chapter I will focus my discussion on the IPC. For a more detailed account of the role of industry associations in reforming U.S. IP laws and promoting a trade link, see Susan K. Sell, "The Origins of a Trade-Based Approach to Intellectual Property Protection," *Science Communication* 17 (December 1995): 163–85.

33. Chang Jae Baik, "Politics of Super 301: The Domestic Basis of U.S. Foreign Economic Policy" (Ph.D. diss., University of California at Berkeley, 1993), 147n56.

34. Alice T. Zalik, "Implementing the Trade-Tariff Act," *Les Nouvelles* 21 (December 1986): 200.

35. Enyart, "A GATT Intellectual Property Code," p. 54.

36. Zalik, "Implementing the Trade-Tariff Act," p. 199.

37. Gerald Mossinghoff, "The Important of Intellectual Property in International Trade," *Business America* 7 (January 1984): inside cover.

38. For further examples of the revolving door between government and the pharmaceutical industry, see Viveca Novak, "How Drug Companies Operate on the Body Politic," *Business and Society Review* 84 (Winter 1993): 58–64.

39. Zalik, "Implementing the Trade-Tariff Act," p. 200.

40. Ibid.

41. U.S. Department of Commerce, "Roger D. Severance Trip Report on Consultations with Taiwan and Singapore on Commercial Counterfeiting," International Trade Administration memorandum, June 6, 1984, p. 2.

42. Enyart, "A GATT Intellectual Property Code," p. 54.

43. U.S. Senate, Senate Finance Committee, *Intellectual Property Rights: Hearings before the Subcommittee on International Trade of the Senate Finance Committee*, 99th Congress, second session, May 14, 1986, pp. 162–64.

44. Jacques Gorlin, "A Trade-Based Approach for the International Copyright Protection for Computer Software," 1985, unpublished manuscript, obtained from the author.

45. U.S. Trade Representative, *Task Force on Intellectual Property, Summary of Phase I: Recommendations of the Task Force on Intellectual Property to the Advisory Committee for Trade Negotiations* (October 1985).

46. Gorlin, "Trade-Based Approach," p. iv.

47. Ibid.

48. This section based on author's interview with Jacques Gorlin, January 22, 1996, Washington, D.C.

49. Enyart, "A GATT Intellectual Property Code," p. 54.

50. Ibid.

51. Ibid.

52. United States Trade Representative, *Advisory Committee for Trade Negotiations Task Force on Intellectual Property Rights, Summary of Phase II: Recommendations of the Task Force*, March 1986, p. 8.

53. Author's interview with Gorlin.

54. Testimony of Kenneth Dam, Vice President, Law and External Relations, IBM Corporation, on behalf of the IPC, U.S. Senate, Senate Finance Committee, *Possible New Round of Trade Negotiations: Hearings before the*

Committee on Finance, 99th Congress, second session, July 23, 1986, p. 149.

55. UNICE is the official spokesman for European business and industry in European institutions; it is composed of 33 member federations from 22 countries with a permanent Secretariat based in Brussels.

56. Keidanren is a private, nonprofit economic organization representing virtually all branches of economic activities in Japan. It maintains close contact with both public and private sectors at home and abroad.

57. This paragraph based on author's interview with Gorlin.

58. Peter Drahos, "Global Property Rights in Information: The Story of TRIPs at the GATT," *Prometheus* 13.1 (June 1995): 6–19. See p. 13.

59. Emmert, "Intellectual Property," p. 1939.

60. Author's interview with Gorlin.

61. Drahos, "Global Property Rights in Information," p. 13.

62. Enyart, "A GATT Intellectual Property Code," p. 55.

63. IPC, Keidranen, and UNICE, "Basic Framework of GATT Provisions on Intellectual Property," 1988.

64. Enyart, "A GATT Intellectual Property Code," p. 55.

65. Author's interview with Gorlin.

66. M. Damschroder, "Intellectual Property Rights and the GATT: United States Goals in the Uruguay Round," *Vanderbilt Journal of Transnational Law* 21 (1988): 398.

67. Judith Hippler Bello and Alan Homer, "The Heart of the 1988 Trade Act: A Legislative History of the Amendments to Section 301," *Stanford Journal of International Law* 1 (Fall 1988): 1.

68. Ibid., p. 3n10.

69. Summary based on ibid., pp. 41–42.

70. Julia Christine Bliss, "The Amendments to Section 301: An Overview and Suggested Strategies for Foreign Response," *Law and Policy in International Business* 20.3 (1989): 519.

71. "Differences over Code on Patents," *Latin American Regional Reports—Brazil*, RB-91-04 (London: Latin American Newsletters, May 2, 1991), p. 4.

72. Mossinghoff, "For Better International Protection," *Les Nouvelles* 26 (June 1991): 77.

73. Drahos, p. 14.

74. Ibid.

75. Emmert, "Intellectual Property," p. 1374.

76. Drahos, p. 15.

77. John Whalley, "Developing Countries and System Strengthening in the Uruguay Round," in Will Martin and L. Alan Winters, eds., *The Uruguay Round and the Developing Economies* (Washington, D.C.: The World Bank, 1995), pp. 305–26.

78. Drahos, "Global Property Rights in Information," p. 15.

79. Ibid.

80. Author's interview with Gorlin.

81. Ibid.

82. See Office of the U.S. Trade Representative, The 1994 General Agree-

ment on Tariffs and Trade, Annex 1(C), "Agreement on Trade-Related Aspects of Intellectual Property, Including Trade in Counterfeit Goods," August 27, 1994, Articles 3(1), 27(1), and 33 of the TRIPS Agreement.

83. See C. Kent, "NAFTA, TRIPs affect IP," *Les Nouvelles* 28 (December 1993): 179; and TRIPS Agreement, Article 34.

84. TRIPs Agreement, Article 31.

85. Bernard Hoekman and Michael Kostecki, *The Political Economy of the World Trading System: From GATT to the WTO* (Oxford: Oxford University Press, 1995), p. 156.

86. Dani Rodrik, "Comments on Maskus and Eby-Konan," in Alan Deardorff and R. Stern, eds., *Analytic and Negotiating Issues in the Global Trading System* (Ann Arbor: University of Michigan Press, 1994), p. 449.

87. TRIPs Agreement, 1994.

88. Kent, "NAFTA, TRIPs Affect IP," p. 176.

89. Ibid., p. 177.

90. For a discussion of intellectual property protection's potentially negative effects on technological innovation, see R. C. Levin et al., "Appropriating the Returns," pp. 783–820, especially 788.

91. van Wijk and Junne, *Intellectual Property Protection*, p. 63.

92. Levin et al., "Appropriating the Returns," p. 788.

93. Donal O'Connor, "TRIPs: Licensing Challenge," *Les Nouvelles* 30.1 (1995): 17.

94. Surendra Patel, "Intellectual Property Rights in the Uruguay Round: A Disaster for the South?" *Economic and Political Weekly*, May 6, 1989, p. 983.

95. Drahos, "Global Property Rights in Information," p. 6.

96. Paul A. David, "Intellectual Property Institutions and the Panda's Thumb: Patents, Copyrights, and Trade Secrets in Economic Theory and History," in Mitchel B. Wallerstein, Mary Ellen Moore, and Roberta A. Schoen, eds., *Global Dimensions of Intellectual Property Rights in Science and Technology* (Washington, D.C.: National Research Council, 1993), pp. 19–61.

97. Dorothy Shrader, "Intellectual Property Provisions of the GATT 1994: The TRIPs Agreement," Congressional Research Service Report for Congress, Report No. 94–302 A, The Library of Congress, Washington, D.C., March 16, 1994, p. 13.

98. H.R. 5110, quoted in Sylvia Morrison, "How Will the Uruguay Round of GATT Affect the U.S. Computer Industry?" Congressional Research Service Report for Congress, Report No. 94–840–E, The Library of Congress, Washington, D.C., November 3, 1994, p. 3.

99. Shrader, "Intellectual Property Provisions," p. 13.

100. BSA, Business Software Alliance, "Fact Sheet: International Policies Governing the Software Industry," May 5, 1995, Washington, D.C., p. 4.

101. E. Einstein, "NAFTA: Little Protection for Technology," *Les Nouvelles* 30 (March 1995): 29.

102. On the issues of gray-market goods and border enforcement, see Dorothy Shrader, "Enforcement of Intellectual Property Rights under the GATT 1994 TRIPs Agreement," Congressional Research Service Report for Congress, Report No. 94–228 A, Library of Congress, Washington, D.C., March 3, 1994, p. 20.

CHAPTER 8

Self-Regulation and Business Norms: Political Risk, Political Activism

Virginia Haufler

What is the role of norms in guiding or shaping international affairs? This question has generated some of the most interesting research on the forces that influence state behavior of the past few years. It also has been a major impetus underlying the attention now paid to the role of nonstate actors in world politics, which often act as conduits for new norms that affect state behavior.[1] However, one glaring omission in this literature is any mention of the norms generated by the business community. There has been a distinct tendency to treat corporations as "different" from other nonstate actors.[2] Furthermore, the dominant models of corporate motivation view them as self-interested profit-driven actors, unprincipled and without any standards of behavior—and thus not a good place to look for the generation and promulgation of norms. Any differences among firms in terms of their preferences is seen as deriving from their market position or asset structure, which are the only determinants of what they consider to be appropriate behavior.[3]

In this chapter, I argue that corporate motivation today is quite complex, and that the behavior of the firm is at least partially guided by principles and norms. Such principles and norms affect the behavior of firms both at home and abroad, in their negotiations with each other, with home and host governments, and with international organizations. To the degree that corporate agreements negotiated among firms now govern extensive areas of international economic affairs and constitute a form of private authority, we must consider principles and norms drawn from the business community as constituent elements in how those areas are regulated. The widespread acceptance (or not) of particular ways of doing business and of relating to the social and political environment of a business organization can confer legitimacy upon the particular practices of an industry. Such legitimacy contributes to the ability of private associations to gain an authoritative voice over the governance of relevant issues.

There are two places where we can view how such norms have direct political effects: first, in business lobbying of governments on issues affecting them, such as trade policy or environmental regulation; and second, in business efforts at self-regulation. The former is the traditional perspective on the role of the firm in international political economy, which takes states as the primary actors in international affairs. The latter is the primary focus of the emerging literature on private regimes, private international law, transnational business networks, and strategic alliances.[4] The former type of analyses focus on the power of business in structural or interest-based terms, defining and measuring them in terms of material and financial resources, asset specificity, and other determinants of sectoral interests, and linking these interests to domestic political coalitions.[5] This chapter takes a different tack by examining the power of business norms in structuring the environment within which political action takes place, thus affecting both the direct participants in a business regime, and also structuring activity outside of it.[6]

The following section discusses the concept of corporate norms, their relationship to interfirm cooperation, and how they might affect global governance and authority. The following two sections provide cases illustrating the construction and effects of particular business norms. The case of international risks insurance outlines the ways in which industry norms regarding insurability have evolved over the past century, determining what is considered to be a public good and what is considered a private one. The definition of insurability is embedded within insurance industry associations and agreements, constituting a private international regime in which there is generalized consensus on appropriate norms within the majority of the insurance community. In this arena, the insurers have the primary authority in determining the structure of state/market relations. The case of environmental efficiency norms illustrates the way in which currently changing corporate norms regarding efficiency affect the firm's perspective regarding regulatory intervention by government. This area of construction of new norms has not yet reached a broader consensus and therefore cannot be described as a regime. But to the extent there is congruence or incongruence between these emerging norms and current regulatory proposals, they may affect the ability of governments to negotiate and implement international environmental agreements. These two cases are meant more to illustrate a potentially rich field of research on the modern global political economy than rigorously to test hypotheses.

CORPORATE NORMS AND GLOBAL GOVERNANCE

The majority of the literature on the firm ignores business principles and norms and discusses the preferences of firms as being driven by utility maximization, with utility measured by the goals of profit maximization, expansion of market share, and maximizing shareholder value.[7] The traditional economic focus in models of corporate behavior generally does not address the development of management preferences regarding exactly how to reach those goals. I argue the sources of those preferences do not come from some automatic and innate character to the task of producing and marketing a good or service, laying down the exact steps to reach corporate goals. Corporate management obviously responds to market signals, as in the neoclassical model, but the character of that response is not equally obvious. Instead, preferences regarding strategies derive from general practices in the industry, from technological and managerial knowledge, and from the society of which the firm and its managers are a part. Corporate preferences are driven in part by norms about the appropriate approaches to the business. In other words, they have principles, which are "beliefs of fact, causation and rectitude," and norms, which are "standards of behavior defined in terms of rights and obligations"—to quote Krasner.[8] (I will simply refer to corporate norms, with the understanding that this includes principles.)

Here, I am not addressing the literature on corporate governance, which analyzes how the structure of ownership of a firm determines, for instance, management relations with shareholders and workers. Nor am I assuming that corporate norms are the same thing as what we call "business ethics," which contains a moral judgment about socially acceptable behavior or the "social responsibility" of businesses.[9] I am not imputing to businesses anything necessarily "good" by describing them as having norms. However, I am at times addressing the "stakeholder" literature, which argues that firms have a "stake" in the economic, social, and political health of the surrounding society, and therefore should define their self-interest broadly and choose corporate strategies that do not undermine that society.[10] The degree to which corporate managers perceive this link is largely determined by the accepted norms within their industry.

Where do corporate norms come from? A number of factors influence the accepted practices of businesses. The majority are given fairly straightforwardly by the market itself, which signals through the price system what practices "work" and which do not. But this is only part of the story, since there exist alternative means of attaining the same economic goals. Norms derive from widespread principles of business, seen in business school curricula and management journals everywhere. Particular industries also construct and propagate their own sets of principles and norms through extensive contacts within their communities; in fact, we can refer to them as forming an "epistemic community," as Haas would call it.[11] Through industry associations, journals, and other forms of communication, information and knowledge about industry "best practices" can be transferred throughout the industry and become a standard for behavior. Finally, the larger society itself signals what is acceptable behavior and what is not, and to a certain degree these social norms are absorbed by management (sometimes by force, through the political-regulatory system, but sometimes through socialization).

What broader effects do industry norms have? Such norms determine the strategies firms pursue in two areas. First, they affect the manner of production. The manner in which a good or service is produced includes the organization of production (for instance, hierarchical or distributed; transnational, multinational or national), financing (credit, retained earnings), resource consumption and type of materials used (waste, toxicity), and working conditions (wages, health, and safety). Second, these norms affect the strategies of firms in their relations with "outside" forces, that is the political or regulatory system at the local or international level.[12] They may constitute a kind of international private law, as described by Slaughter and Cutler.[13] These strategies clearly have an impact on the distribution of resources, both material and human, and on the political system. Although we tend to treat corporations as separate, closed systems, in fact every firm is embedded and entwined within a larger system of social, political, and economic relations.

How do these two elements—norms and strategies—affect the international system? In this chapter, I will concentrate on the ways in which corporate norms can provide the foundation for a private international regime. Such a private regime is formed when there exists broad congruence across an industry regarding principles and norms, and these are institutionalized within industry associations and interindustry contracts and treaties. Through them, a sector may perform a self-regulating function in which firms that act against those norms are sanctioned by the industry itself, often through exclusion from the business itself. As the regime becomes more institutionalized, it reinforces accepted norms. These regimes may be legitimized and backed by state power, as private rules are incorporated into legal systems or as authority over an issue is explicitly delegated to the private sector.[14]

Empirical evidence for this discussion of corporate norms and international affairs will be drawn from two cases: first, the private regime for international risks insurance, which is largely based upon the insurers' definition of what is an insurable risk and what is not; and second, a less sector-specific emerging set of norms regarding environmental efficiency as a basis for production strategies. The former is an explicitly historical case that highlights the development and change of norms over time. The latter focuses on contemporary developments that may lead in time to the development of a private regime, or may affect the character and effectiveness of interstate regimes. Both of these cases demonstrate the strong effects of principles and norms upon business behavior and through it, the widening or narrowing of opportunities for other businesses, for social groups, and for governments.

THE INSURABILITY OF INTERNATIONAL RISKS

This section examines the international risks insurance regime that evolved over the course of the past century.[15] Here, I will concentrate on one set of important principles and norms: those regarding whether or not international political risks are insurable and, if so, who should insure them. The principles ("beliefs of fact, causation and rectitude") concern insurers' beliefs regarding what causes political risks and whether it is possible to establish probabilities for their occurrence. The norms of insurers ("standards of behavior defined in terms of rights and obligations") refer to their perceptions regarding their relations with customers, especially to what extent insurers are obliged to meet their customers' demand for political risks insurance, and the terms and conditions of the insurance contract. We can separate these two analytically, but in practice these norms and principles overlap.

This regime consisted initially almost entirely of private insurers and reinsurers, dominated by the London market. At the turn of the century, the major institutions structuring the regime included Lloyd's of London, the Association of British Insurers (which represents insurance companies), and various organizations dedicated to particular aspects of insurance, such as salvage. The dominant set of corporate norms respecting insurability could be enforced through the reinsurers, who act as "coordination services firms" for the industry as a whole by providing insurance to the insurers, and who generally adopt conservative definitions of insurability. Through these institutions, the insurers attempted to establish and enforce a particular view of insurable risk. The coherence of this view varied over time, but in general dominant regime norms can be identified. As these changed, so did the power of particular players within the regime, and significantly, so did the participation of the state.

Risks of all types can pose a significant barrier to international commerce, and the attempt to reduce or redistribute risks imposes major costs on participants. Any service that reduces such risks provides benefits not just to the actors involved, but also to the wider society, since it facilitates economic activity. The traditional response to *foreign* risks has been military action by the state to prevent losses to commercial actors, but sending in the army or navy to protect merchants is politically and financially costly. A different response to international risk has been to develop a means to redistribute the costs of any loss, and one of the primary means of doing so is through insurance.

The risks to international trading, lending, or investing may involve contending with the forces of nature, such as storms that sink ships; or they may be commercial risks, such as the failure to properly market a product to a foreign culture; but the most difficult risks to cope with are political risks, which are "[c]hanges in the operating conditions of foreign enterprises that arise out of the political process, either directly through war, insurrection or political violence, or through changes in government policies that affect the ownership and behavior of the firm."[16] The most dramatic and intractable of these is war. And insurers have debated for decades to what extent war risk is insurable.

In order to understand the particular dynamics of international risks, as opposed to domestic ones, we need to analyze essentially five types of insurance: specialized political risks insurance, marine insurance, export credit insurance, investment guarantees, and reinsurance. Political risk insurance covers losses due to actions or inactions by governments or other political entities; this has included, at various times, the risk of loss due to war, civil war, expropriation and nationalization, terrorism and kidnaping, inconvertibility of funds, contract repudiation, embargoes, and the calling of financial guarantees. Marine insurance covers ships and ship cargoes against both natural and man-made disasters. Export credit insurance covers loan defaults and payment delays for loans that are extended by a seller to foreign buyers, and that are often affected by political events. Investment guarantees cover political risks that are specific to direct investment. And reinsurance simply insures the risks of other insurers, including their international political risks.

The particular principles and norms that drive the international risks insurers are those concerning their understanding of what is an insurable risk. Insurance is an imperfect market, since not all kinds of insurance are offered at all times, and because the sellers (insurers) do not just sell a product or service, but also attempt to influence the behavior of their customers so as to reduce the risk of loss.[17] Therefore, the insurers have attempted to develop a regime that, in essence, regulates both their own and their customers' behavior in order to protect the insurers from excessive losses; to the extent the insurers suffer high losses they are unable to protect their customers from excessive losses.[18]

Insurance underwriting experience, backed by more and more sophisticated information-gathering techniques and analytical skills, has produced an increasingly refined standard insurance contract. These contracts define the exact relationship between the insurer and the customer, and attempt to determine all possible contingencies to which the contract might apply. They contain the exclusions and limitations that protect both the insurer and the insured by establishing the incentives that they hope will modify the potential for opportunistic behavior by either one. By putting some kinds of risk out of the normal range of insurance underwriting, the industry puts the onus for managing those particular risks back onto potential customers, which can lead them to pursue other strategies, including turning to their own governments for protection.

Up until the turn of the century, war risks were included in standard insurance policies. However, as political tensions increased among major powers such as Great Britain, the United States, Germany, France, and Russia, the insurers began to reconsider their automatic acceptance of war risks. In 1896, the London Assurance Company suggested in a letter to the Committee of Lloyd's that war risks should be specifically excluded from marine insurance policies. Lloyd's did not go along with this suggestion at first, concerned as it was with competition between Lloyd's and the other insurance companies. But doubts about the war risks business began to grow, as there were "signs of some uneasiness about what the next war at sea would be like and searching of hearts as to how far the ordinary machinery of insurance would stand the strain of modern war."[19] Given the losses to insured property in the Spanish American War and the Boer War, and given the increasing technological sophistication of military forces, the Committee of Lloyd's, which acted as the central administrative organ for the decentralized market that was Lloyd's of London, would change its mind.[20] In June 1898 they declared that henceforth all marine policies should exclude war risks unless a separate agreement to include them was signed, separating marine and war risks from each other. From that point on, marine and cargo insurance policies included the clause: "Warranted nevertheless free of capture, seizure, and detention, and the consequences thereof, or of any attempt thereat, piracy excepted, and also from all consequences of hostilities or warlike operations, whether before or after declaration of war" (referred to as the F.C. and S. clause).[21]

By removing war risks from the normal marine insurance policy, and making it therefore more difficult to obtain war risks coverage, the insurers established new norms regarding insurability. They essentially declared that war risks were not "normal" risks.

British politicians thenceforth would have to consider the serious potential consequences for shipping, and by extension, for British trade and security in general. Insurers designed marine insurance policies so as to increase the incentives for ship's captains to avoid conflict; on the outbreak of war all insured ships had to put in to the nearest protected harbor and stay there until the conflict ended. By the turn of the century, British officials were repeatedly debating what to do about the fact that one major effect of these new and strictly defined war risk insurance contracts was that all British ships would be sitting in safe harbors at the outbreak of any war.[22] Furthermore, they clearly anticipated that non-war risks insurance on shipping would experience a huge rate increase at the onset of any conflict. Increased insurance costs would strain the ability of shippers and cargo-owners to support their business, and would lead them to limit or halt their trade for the duration of the conflict. In the decade leading up to the outbreak of World War I, the British government formed numerous commissions to consider alternatives, such as further strengthening the Navy, convoying merchant ships, or providing direct government insurance for shipping during time of war. When World War I began, the government finally felt compelled to establish a government war risks insurance agency to supplement—and for a short time replace—the private market. War among the great powers simply was not considered to be a truly insurable risk, and the private sector withdrew.

After the Great War, the government closed down its insurance program. Over the course of the 1920s, the commercial insurers gradually became more willing to consider war risks insurance once again, beginning to expand how they defined insurability in response to their own increasing experience and techniques of calculating probabilities and designing insurance contracts. For instance, Lloyd's underwriters looked back on their World War I experience, in which they had realized great profits on a new form of insurance—for bomb damage. During the first year of the war, damage from bombing simply was not as extensive as they predicted. This experience led some underwriters after the war to insure war risks on property such as buildings (land-based war risks as opposed to marine war risks) around the world.

Many insurers eagerly sold insurance against the losses from the "civil commotion" in Spain beginning in 1936, both on land- and sea-based war risks. Many of the leading underwriters expanded their definition of insurability, and covered their customers against damage from the civil war, including full insurance against fire damage (a fairly common result of modern war-fighting). In 1937, news reports began to tell of high losses and mounting claims on war risks policies of all types. Many underwriters had insured ships trading with Spain against war risks because they counted on the ships' obtaining military protection from British naval vessels stationed in the Mediterranean.[23] In this case, their calculation of probabilities included an assessment of British political intervention, a calculation that proved incorrect. They also had tried to hedge themselves against losses by insuring ships from a wide range of countries, covering merchant ships from Britain, Spain, Norway, the Soviet Union, and others—all of which were attacked or appropriated by combatants. The new land-based war risks policies led to the most bruising losses, as innovations in warfare such as massive aerial bombardment of cities and towns destroyed lives and property that would not have been at risk in earlier wars. Modern technology and tactics made it increasingly difficult to delineate the line between the war zone and civilian territory.

Even as they had insured land war risks in Spain, many underwriters had also been insuring the same type of risk in England. As the scale of war damage in Spain became more well known, some British underwriters realized that a war in their own country, which was much more industrialized and densely populated than Spain, would be absolutely devastating. At this point, it became clear that land war risks insurance in particular had become a gamble, pure and simple.

In 1936, the chairman of Lloyd's, Neville Dixey, first raised the issue with the Committee of Lloyd's of excluding land-based war risks from all insurance policies. In order to work, such an exclusion clause would have to be accepted by all underwriters, both at Lloyd's and in the companies, both in Britain and abroad. Any free riding by insurers trying to gain a competitive advantage by offering land war risks insurance while others did not would lead to the collapse of the agreement. Dixey then opened negotiations with underwriters at Lloyd's and at the companies.[24] These negotiations occurred throughout a year when the claims for losses on land war risks in Spain kept piling up, keeping in front of insurers the potential for unsustainable loss if a truly major war broke out. The end result was a near total ban on land-based war risks insurance, implemented and enforced by the London insurance market.[25] Lloyd's of London convened a committee that, with support from the management of the largest British companies such as the Commercial Union, Royal Exchange Assurance, and Eagle Star, drew up and promoted what became known as the Waterborne Agreement. All major European insurance companies signed the agreement.[26] Sea-based war risks, however, could still be covered, since ships had the option of simply sailing out of harm's way.[27]

Demand for war risks insurance increased throughout the 1930s as conflict in Europe seemed more likely. The British government, anxious to maintain and expand the nation's trade and shipping industries, exerted pressure on the private insurance market in an attempt to influence policies and rates, and there was some discussion of the acceptance of war risks by Her Majesty's Government, somewhat similar to the pre–World War I debate.[28] As in that earlier debate, political leaders worried about the maintenance of trade in commodities, both to supply the war effort and to serve the populace as a whole. Eventually, the British Parliament authorized the Board of Trade to reinsure "King's Enemy risks," leaving the marine insurers themselves to handle the content and price of the direct insurance. When Germany invaded Poland, however, the government reverted to a program of direct war risks insurance. In 1939 it established a Commodities Insurance Scheme under the War Risks Insurance Act, followed two years later by the War Damage Act, which introduced direct compensation for damage to buildings, land and business from enemy acts. War among the Great Powers simply could not be considered insurable in the private sector. At the same time, the government considered such insurance a public good and stepped in to rectify a market failure.[29]

After World War II, the norms and principles of insurability regarding war risks remained in place for decades, with only occasional pressure on the limits. Foreign crises generated constant demand for coverage of risks; at the same time, new technology emerged that might have changed the insurers calculations. The nature of international risks changed, with nationalizations and expropriations threatening foreign investment in the 1960s and 1970s, although these declined dramatically by the following decade. It was only in the 1980s that insurers began to rethink what international risks were insurable, though the changes that occurred were not stimulated by anything so dramatic as before. War risks still remained separate from standard marine insurance policies, and the Waterborne Agreement remained in force. However, the insurers became more confident about their ability to insure a broader class of political risks.

The demand for political risks insurance shot up with the fall of the Shah of Iran, followed by the long Iran-Iraq War. The executives running transnational corporations began to accept the need to buy such insurance, and pressed their regular property insurers for expanded coverage. They asked their insurers to relax restrictions on specialty products, including insurance coverage for land war risks and financial guarantees.[30] Some Lloyd's underwriters and other insurers were willing and able to cover new forms of international risks. The category of political risk grew to include (at various times) war risks, terrorism, kidnap and ransom, currency inconvertibility, contract frustration and rejection insurance; contract frustration risks became one of the fastest-growing portions of the political risks market.[31]

Some underwriters began skirting the provisions of the Waterborne Agreement without directly repudiating it, in an effort to satisfy their customers' demands.[32] Nonsignatory firms and government agencies became more willing to cover some land war risks in selected regions of the world. In the mid-1980s, the Chubb insurance group covered land war risks, but only in conjunction with its property and casualty coverages.[33] By the middle of the 1980s, some underwriters openly urged that the agreement be reviewed, and certain brokers began asking underwriters to cover war risks on land, provided that nuclear war and major power war be excluded.[34] They argued that underwriters had become more sophisticated since the 1930s; they have more skill in setting the parameters of coverage and correctly establishing the price for a policy; they know more about how to control opportunistic behavior; and they now have much more experience upon which to calculate the probability of political risk itself. They also have become more adept at attracting customers to strictly limited contracts through providing ancillary services, such as information on business and political conditions in foreign countries, or training in loss prevention. Thus, the restrictions agreed to in the 1930s seemed outdated.

While many underwriters became more willing in theory to insure against war and other political risks, in practice it became more and more difficult for them to do so by the end of the 1980s. When the boom in political risk business began in 1979, the insurance market as a whole had become an extremely attractive source of profits. The financial deregulation that had begun in the United States stimulated a major boom in financial markets during the 1980s. Attracted by high returns and low barriers to entry in the insurance industry, too many new entrants quickly caused a problem of overcapacity and a competitive lowering of prices to untenable levels. Insurers discovered they could invest their large streams of premium income in financial instruments whose returns dwarfed anything they could obtain from selling insurance; high investment returns allowed insurers to push the limits of their business, increasing competition to new extremes as they drove prices downward, writing contracts that covered marginally insurable risks and lowering prices below their costs (referred to as "cash-flow underwriting").[35] The explosive growth and profitability of financial investments perverted the insurance market by turning it into a cash cow, to be milked of premium income that could then be invested.[36] The problem was particularly acute for the reinsurers, which reportedly had a 100 percent overcapacity in 1982 and thus would be particularly vulnerable in a downturn.[37] And a downturn did indeed arrive, inevitably.

The London political risk market began to tighten due to mounting claims for losses, reduced reinsurance capacity, and a weakened world economy.[38] In the wider insurance markets, the softening of prices was accompanied by extensive and unanticipated losses, especially from product and pollution liability claims. Up until about 1985, "the most important single factor concerning the world insurance market has been overcapacity."[39] But the increased capacity chased too little premium income and produced heavy underwriting losses in every country. By 1985, the industry as a whole was reaching financial exhaustion.[40] Two years later, potential customers expressed concern that both the U.S. and London markets were shrinking in terms of the number of political risk underwriters, even as contract terms became quite restrictive.[41]

Self-regulation of the industry, leading to more restraint in defining insurability, came through the important role played by the reinsurers. Reinsurers provide insurance to other insurers, which increases their capability to cover large risks. This gives reinsurers significant influence over the industry. The major reinsurers, such as Lloyd's, Swiss Re, and Munich Re, tend to define insurability conservatively and generally have been reluctant to cover political risks.[42] In 1984, when the demand for political risks insurance was at its height, CIGNA could not assume new political risk business in the Philippines and some Latin American countries because its reinsurer would not cover it under its reinsurance treaty limits.[43] In the mid-1980s, many reinsurers pulled back from covering certain kinds of insurance, including political risk insurance, as interest rates dropped, investment income declined, and losses mounted.[44] As a result, the supply of private sector insurance for political risks began to contract. When CIGNA attempted to write a policy insuring Citibank's loans to five developing countries, the reinsurers claimed this violated the terms of their reinsurance treaty, and made it impossible for CIGNA to conclude the deal.[45] The large size of many current transactions requires the direct insurance underwriters to obtain every bit of reinsurance possible. On truly expensive deals, the lack of even some small but crucial reinsurance percentage can scuttle the deal, and for esoteric specialties with narrow markets the lack of reinsurance can close down that business. In this case, direct insurers were willing to define insurability broadly, but the reinsurers insisted on a more narrow norm with regard to political risks.

During the same decade, government agencies that supplied political risks insurance in the form of export credit insurance and investment guarantees expanded substantially, largely in response to the limits on private sector insurance. The commercial insurers did not consistently cover all political risks, and usually were only willing to do so for short-term transactions and under strict contract limits. The combination of debt crisis in the developing world and heightened economic competition among the developed countries put pressure on governments to promote exports and foreign investment. One means of doing this was through their insurance and guarantee programs.

The managers of government agencies found themselves under conflicting pressures from their political masters to expand their services, but without generating the losses of typical government-subsidized insurance programs.[46] The British Export Credit Guarantees Department and the U.S. Overseas Private Investment Corporation and Export-Import Bank implemented increasingly commercial practices in the operation of their programs, carefully judging the insurability and probability of loss for different projects and countries based largely on the principles and norms established by the private sector. A further development was the establishment of a new World Bank partner agency, the Multilateral Investment Guarantee Agency, dedicated to providing investment guarantees to reduce the risks facing investors in developing countries and promoting foreign direct investment. The idea of such a multilateral investment guarantee agency had been discussed for decades, and even had been part of the original proposal for the World Bank itself. States agreed to establish it finally through a number of converging factors: the debt crisis; the perceived decline of U.S. power and influence; the activism of dedicated World Bank bureaucrats; and the increased ability to convince developing countries to commit to investment protections, which would make large risks more insurable. The purpose of these unilateral and multilateral efforts on the part of governments was to establish a stable investment climate for business.[47]

Overall, we can see that the decisions of insurance underwriters regarding the insurability of political risks, especially war risks, varied over time and across insurers. The definition of insurability had to be mutually agreed upon and negotiated among insurers, due to the strong collective action problem inherent in the notion of not supplying a particular kind of insurance. In a period of high demand for war risks insurance, for instance, as often has happened, there is a great temptation to pursue weak underwriting standards and bend or even break the accepted norms. The few who accept those risks may make huge profits—this time. But if there are excessive losses instead, this harms the insurance industry as a whole in a number of ways. First, the reputation of the industry, which is extremely important, may be damaged if the insurer cannot make good on claims. Second, many big risks (which international ones typically are) involve more than one insurer; other insurers may have to make good on the claims. And third, to the extent that high losses are common in the industry or very severe, the entire industry sees its capacity to cover risks of all types shrink; when an insurer loses too much money it may withdraw from a number of markets at once in response.

BUSINESS AND THE ENVIRONMENT

The second case discussed here considers the emergence of new norms within environmental issue areas. A striking element of these issues is the huge role played by nongovernmental organizations (NGOs), which have been active in agenda setting and monitoring on an international basis.[48] Many such NGOs now have standing at international negotiations. One interesting development has been the emergence of a sector of the business community equally willing to be activists on environmental issues. This raises new questions about the role of corporate norms in influencing the strategies chosen by business in achieving the standard goals of increasing profits, market share, and shareholder value. The following discussion introduces preliminary evidence of changing corporate norms. I do not argue here that this is a private regime. Instead, I indicate signs that a certain degree of governance of corporate behavior is emerging with regard to the environment, and that changing corporate norms in this area affect what states are able to accomplish in domestic and international arenas.

In the past decade, numerous associations, books, and journals have touted the new movement toward "corporate social responsibility" or "corporate ethics."[49] The business community itself is clearly divided on these social-political issues, and part of the division rests on different perceptions about what kinds of corporate behavior produce sufficient profits and competitiveness in the modern capitalist economy. In other words, the principles and norms upon which they base their strategic decision-making vary based upon the degree to which a firm believes that it is possible to "do well while doing good."

One way of exploring these (potentially) changing norms is to examine the adoption of preferences based upon what might be called "eco-efficiency." The field of environmental economics has emerged in the past decade or so as a source of new knowledge about the links between environmental problems and economic ones.[50] While most of this literature examines the interaction of natural and economic systems, some of it has begun to address the more practical issues facing corporate managers. In particular, there is now increased attention paid to redefining a core goal of corporate management: increasing efficiency.

Traditionally, efficient management has meant that costs must be kept to a minimum, leading to the intensive exploitation of the least costly factor of production. The result often has been a high level of waste by-products and the destruction or degradation of the natural environment, since most natural resources are either very cheap or costless to the firm (the "commons" problem). There exist two ways in which the incentives for such behavior might be changed: the imposition of incentives or costs by external forces, that is, the government, in order to force corporations to internalize the costs of environmental degradation; or a change in norms due to internal forces that lead managers to reformulate what they consider to be efficient and appropriate behavior. Both of these are extremely important elements in changing behavior, but for this chapter, I will concentrate on the latter.[51]

In the past decade, increasing numbers of businesses have begun to experiment with and in some cases dedicate themselves to more sustainable practices in the way they produce their goods and services. A significant number of business leaders are beginning to view sustainable practices as a contribution to bottom-line profits, instead of as an extra cost. On a relatively small scale, Ben and Jerry's, The Body Shop, and Smith and Hawken have all made a virtue—and marketing success—of their dedication to progressive environmental principles. Alone, these firms are too small and unique to be considered influential; however, they are simply the most visible face of a larger trend. On a larger scale, the Business Council for Sustainable Development (now the World Council for Sustainable Development), led by Stephen Schmidheiny, publicized case studies of eco-efficiency in *Changing Course: A Global Business Perspective on Development and the Environment*. The council itself is an international organization of transnational corporations that had a visible and controversial presence at the U.N. Conference on the Environment and Development (UNCED, or the Rio Conference).

This change in attitude among some companies can be attributed in part to the increasing demand by consumers for ecologically acceptable products; companies that successfully anticipate changing global consumer demand have a competitive advantage.[52] For instance, the contemporary clothing retailer Esprit is launching a "green" product line, which will be marketed as fashionable, environmentally friendly, and cutting-edge in the use of new technologies.[53] Large numbers of businesses are jumping on the bandwagon, although sometimes in the most superficial ways.[54]

Evidence from the past few years indicates a surprising increase in the pace of change in corporate culture. For example, the chemical industry eventually participated in developing strict international notification procedures for toxic exports, a significant break from their earlier unyielding negotiating position.[55] In agriculture, even some major growers formerly wedded to traditional practices are beginning to implement organic techniques, as we can see in the California grape growing industry.[56] Various world industry associations now recommend their members use environmental technologies and finance research and development in new procedures for ecological audits and life-cycle analysis.

A 1992 survey by the United Nations Centre for Transnational Corporations found that many businesses have established corporate environmental policies that actually exceed national standards.[57] Other corporations have rectified their practices even prior to the implementation of any government regulation, and sometimes even before any lobbying for change occurs. The World Resources Institute recently published a volume describing a number of company environmental programs in order to highlight and directly encourage what its editor views as a "sea change" in corporate environmental understanding.[58] The experiences related suggest there is much more room for shaping investment in environmentally favorable ways than is popularly supposed.

These changes reflect both a response to transformations in the wider society of which business is a part, and also a rethinking of what it means to be an "efficient" corporation. Traditionally, efficiency has been perceived as the maximum use of the least costly factor in the production process. This generally meant extremely intensive use of relatively cheap resources, especially water and air. True efficiency, however, is the minimum consumption of all factors per unit of output, as those businesses most aggressively pursuing environmental practices have discovered. Their example holds out hope that depletion and degradation of resources will not expand exponentially into the future, but will be restrained by changes in the management of business itself.[59] The question is how to facilitate and hasten those changes; the answer lies in policy developments at both the national and international level.

More systematic evidence concerning the spread of norms of eco-efficiency can be found indirectly in the fact that investment remains strong even in countries with strict environmental regulations. Approximately two thirds of foreign investment continues to flow into Europe, Japan, and the United States; these are the major markets, it is true, but it is surprising given the expectation that investors will seek out pollution havens.[60] Curtis Moore and Alan Miller, in *Green Gold*, even point to strict regulations in Germany and Japan as stimulating the development of environmental technologies that are a source of competitive advantage in world markets.[61] A recent analysis indicates that among U.S. industries, those that are heavily regulated actually did quite well in international trade, remaining competitive despite their regulatory "burden."[62]

The new norms emphasizing eco-efficiency are being enforced in a number of ways. First, through what might be called "shaming." Corporations declaring adherence to environmental policies often sign international business agreements, and are monitored by other businesses and business associations. In order to continue in good standing, they must maintain and implement acceptable policies. If they do not, their failures are publicized, both within the industry and without, and other businesses may decline to work with them. Second, "green" firms may develop incentives for others to adopt good environmental practices. In an interesting twist, some insurers are becoming strong enforcers of corporate environmental policy, since they often hold ultimate liability for cleaning up pollution or making medical payments to victims. The major reinsurers are even showing up at climate change conferences. They have been making large payments in the past decade for severe weather damage, and to the extent climate change causes severe weather and humans cause climate change, the insurers have an interest in changing human behavior. Third, the state obviously plays a role in enforcing newly emerging societal norms with regard to the environment.

This discussion of changing corporate norms with regard to environmental issues indicates the existence of a growing number of corporations with norms that differ substantially from the mainstream, and from our common perception of what motivates firm behavior. Those holding similar norms in common are beginning to form associations, such as the Business Council for Sustainable Development; they also are developing common principles, such as the Caux Principles on business behavior; and they are generating a new literature of books and journals that speak their common language. All of this may lead to the construction of an environmentally oriented business epistemic community. The impact of this network of like-minded corporate leaders may be felt in the actual results of their actions in reducing ecological degradation; in their effects on the behavior of other businesses, as they hold others to their new standards; and in their acceptance of national and international regulation of economic activity in the name of protecting the environment. In this case, the norms established by a portion of the business community affect the wider international community both directly and indirectly.

CONCLUSION

These two cases have shown us well-established norms that have changed over time, and newly emerging ones that have yet to be institutionalized (if they ever will be). Neither case fully conforms to the liberal notion that firms merely respond directly to market signals. The private international regime for international risks is based on a collective notion of insurability. Insurers define insurability based on their own experience, emerging underwriting techniques, and changes in the social and political environment. All of these determine how they believe insurance works, and what their responsibilities are toward customers. A pure market model would assume that insurers would always be willing and able to sell a policy, so long as the price was high enough. But insurers are willing to ignore demand for a particular kind of insurance and withdraw entirely from the market, and even cooperate in common institutions to enforce that withdrawal on all insurers. Corporate norms regarding insurability are further reinforced by the degree to which reinsurers are willing to insure the portfolio of risks the direct insurer has contracted.

The absence of international risks insurance generally leads to a political debate over the appropriate role for government in ameliorating foreign risks, and the degree to which this type of service is a public good. Governments over the course of the twentieth century expanded their export credit and investment guarantee programs in the belief these would stimulate economic growth through expanding exports and foreign investment. Government programs accepted many, though not all, of the same contractual practices and determinations of insurability found in the private sector. Currently, the British government has withdrawn from most forms of international risks insurance (though not all) and the United States has cut back its programs. At the same time, new investment guarantee programs have been established multilaterally, through the World Bank subsidiary Multilateral Investment Guarantee Agency (MIGA) and the new bank for Eastern European projects, the European Bank for Reconstruction and Development (EBRD). The debate over what is considered to be an insurable risk and how it will be divided between private markets and public efforts has been shifted to the global level. Interfirm cooperation among insurers in setting standards has directly influenced the shape of government programs.

The environmental case is more ambiguous, contradictory, and counterintuitive. In this case, new corporate norms regarding eco-efficiency are being institutionalized and transmitted by a growing epistemic community within the wider business community. These norms have been selectively adopted, primarily by consumer-oriented firms where customer demand for "green" products has the most influence; yet it is not restricted to these industries alone. We cannot say that a regime is in place here, and yet some elements of interfirm cooperation and self-governance are perhaps emerging. Various agreements among businesses, such as the Caux Principles, set a standard for behavior, even though they are not strictly enforced. Perhaps no private regime will form in the end, but these norms may have an important effect on the ability of governments to conclude and implement regulatory regimes for the environment, both domestically and internationally, that would not otherwise be possible.

This is a preliminary overview of the interaction of business norms, interfirm cooperation, and international politics through brief explorations of the norms of insurability within the insurance industry, and the norms of efficiency within the manufacturing community. International business can construct a regime around strong norms and principles that they have developed; these norms open or close alternatives for others, including governments, and therefore have a real impact on politics. Further research needs to determine in more detail what drives changing corporate norms, and how changes in them affect domestic and international regulatory regimes. Areas in which we might be able to examine corporate norms are labor policy (for instance, Levi's Corporation has established a global policy regarding the treatment of workers) and biodiversity (the example of Merck Pharmaceuticals and its ground-breaking agreement with the Costa Rican government on exploring the rainforest for genetic raw materials).

NOTES

1. Audie Klotz, "Norms Reconstituting Interests: Global Racial Equality and U.S. Sanctions against South Africa," *International Organization* 49.3 (Summer 1995): 451–78; Judith Goldstein and Robert Keohane, eds. *Ideas and Foreign Policy: Beliefs, Institutions, and Political Change* (Ithaca: Cornell University Press, 1993); Martha Finnemore, *National Interests and International Society* (Ithaca: Cornell University Press, 1996); Paul Wapner, *Environmental Activism and World Civic Politics* (Albany: SUNY Press, 1996).

2. Virginia Haufler, "Crossing the Boundary between Public and Private," in Volker Rittberger, ed., *Regime Theory and International Relations* (Oxford: Clarendon Press, 1993).

3. Helen Milner, *Resisting Protectionism: Global Industries and the Politics of International Trade* (Princeton: Princeton University Press, 1988); Jeffry Frieden, *Debt, Development and Democracy: Modern Political Economy and Latin America, 1965–85* (Princeton: Princeton University Press, 1991).

4. For a skeptical view of the role of business in the contemporary international economy, see Susan Strange, *The Retreat of the State: The Diffusion of Power in the World Economy* (Cambridge: Cambridge University Press, 1996); see also Debora Spar, *The Cooperative Edge* (Ithaca: Cornell University Press, 1994); Lynn Mytelka, ed., *Strategic Partnership: States, Firms and International Competition* (Rutherfield, N.J.: Fairleigh Dickinson University, 1991); Tony Porter, *States, Markets and Regimes in Global Finance* (New York: St. Martin's Press, 1993); A. Claire Cutler, "Canada and the Private International Trade Law Regime," in A. Claire Cutler and Mark W. Zacher, eds., *Canadian Foreign Policy and International Economic Regimes* (Vancouver: University of British Columbia Press, 1992); J. Rogers Hollingsworth and Robert Boyer, *Contemporary Capitalism: The Embeddedness of Institutions* (Cambridge: Cambridge University Press, 1997); Virginia Haufler, *Dangerous Commerce* (Ithaca: Cornell University Press, 1997).

5. Milner, *Resisting Protectionism*; Robert Keohane and Helen Milner, eds., *Internationalization and Domestic Politics* (Cambridge: Cambridge University Press, 1996).

6. See Martha Finnemore, *National Interests in International Society* for a sociological approach to international relations that takes norms seriously, examining states and international organizations. In addition, the Gramscian approach to international political economy acknowledges the influence of business norms, though without framing it in these terms. The "historic bloc" of Gramscian analysis pays attention to the cultural hegemony of particular modes of thought generated within society by capitalist forces—modes of thought that are akin to what we mean by norms, including a civil society of which the business community is a part. See Stephen Gill, ed., *Gramsci, Historical Materialism and International Relations* (Cambridge: Cambridge University Press, 1993); Craig Murphy, *International Organization and Industrial Change: Global Governance since 1850* (New York: Oxford University Press, 1994).

7. Scott R. Bowman, *The Modern Corporation and American Political Thought: Law, Power, and Ideology* (University Park Pa.: Pennsylvania State University Press, 1995). The relative weight of these three goals varies in the estimation of different studies, and is determined in part by the structure of the firm (whether or not it is publicly owned, for instance). For instance, Japanese corporations often favor market share over profit, compared to American corporations, which tend to focus on share value.

8. Stephen Krasner, ed., *International Regimes* (Ithaca: Cornell University Press, 1993), p. 2.

9. Note that business ethics has become part of the required curriculum in most American business schools today. A recent newspaper article, for instance, noted that Harvard Business School is overhauling its MBA curriculum to emphasize business ethics, among other things. See Lynnette Khalfani, "Business Tries to Keep the Wolves Out of the Flock," *The Washington Post*, August 11, 1996, p. H4. This is one source for transmitting particular norms—to the extent that business students take these courses seriously.

10. The concept of stakeholder has gained recent prominence, especially in Britain; see, for instance, Gavin Kelly, Dominic Kelly, and Andrew Gamble, eds., *Stakeholder Capitalism* (New York: St. Martin's Press, 1997). The stakeholder literature essentially argues that particular capitalists must take into account the stability of the social system in order to attain their own self-interests, broadly defined.

11. Peter Haas, *Saving the Mediterranean: The Politics of International Environmental Cooperation* (New York: Columbia University Press, 1990).

12. The institutional context within which business operates within a country has a great effect on the character and operation of their norms. For instance, the degree to which industry and government are antagonists in debates over regulatory policy varies across political systems; see, for example, David Vogel, *National Styles of Regulation: Environmental Policy in Great Britain and the United States* (Ithaca: Cornell University Press, 1986). This chapter does not address directly these variations, but any larger examination of the issues raised here would have to do so in such a comparative context.

13. A. Claire Cutler, "Global Capitalism and Liberal Myths: Dispute Settlement in Private International Trade Relations," *Millennium: Journal of International Studies* 24.3 (1995): 377–97; Anne-Marie Slaughter, "International Law in a World of Liberal States," *European Journal of International Law* 6 (1995): 503–38.

14. See Slaughter, "International Law in a World of Liberal States," for a model of international law in which individuals and groups are the main actors who choose norms, though these are facilitated by states.

15. For a full analysis, see Virginia Haufler, *Dangerous Commerce*.

16. David A. Jodice, compiler, *Political Risk Assessment: An Annotated Bibliography* (Westport, Conn.: Greenwood Press, 1985), p. 5.

17. See Carol Heimer, *Reactive Risk and Rational Action: Managing Moral Hazard in Insurance Contracts* (Berkeley and Los Angeles: University of California Press, 1985). The particular types of opportunistic behavior by customers that insurers must control are the threat of moral hazard and adverse selection.

18. Haufler, *Dangerous Commerce*.

19. D. E. W. Gibb, *Lloyd's of London* (London: Macmillan, 1957), p. 221.

20. Lloyd's of London has a unique and odd structure. Underwriters sign insurance contracts on their own behalf, and not on behalf of Lloyd's as a whole. In order to facilitate business, however, they eventually formed some common administrative and policymaking bodies, though to this day they are not a corporation in the traditional legal sense. This type of organization historically has been a strength of Lloyd's, providing flexibility. Today, it is a liability that is perceived as partly at fault in the recent spate of scandals over fraud and mismanagement.

21. United Kingdom Public Records Office (PRO), Admiralty papers, no. 1/8913 120982.

22. The Admiralty pondered the question: if the Straits of Dover and entrance to the Thames were closed at night during war, what would be the effect on the Port of London? The Admiralty representative stated that ships would remain in "any place of safety in which they might be, or which they could reach, until they could proceed under protection of adequate insurance, or until absence of danger was so obvious that such protection was unnecessary." United Kingdom PRO, Admiralty papers, ADM no. 8913, p. 2.

23. United Kingdom PRO Index to Foreign Office Correspondence, 1933–37, vol. II, no. 120987.

24. Gibb, *Lloyd's of London*, p. 232.

25. The agreement excluded the United States and Canada, which at the time were out of bombing range. In addition, American law forbade the companies from concluding foreign agreements.

26. United Kingdom PRO Board of Trade papers, "War Risk Insurance," 1937, BT 58/304 119531, p. 1.

27. In almost all insurance contracts of every kind, the coverage is terminated in case of war among the Great Powers. A. A. Cassidy, "Underwriting Political Risks," *C. I. I. Journal* 6.2 (April 1982): 86.

28. United Kingdom PRO Index to Foreign Office Correspondence, vol. II, 1936, no. 332.

29. Bringing in the concept of market failure may seem to go against the argument presented here about the importance of corporate norms. However, there are important distinctions to be made here. Great Power war is indeed uninsurable in the private sector and generates a failure of the market; commercial firms simply do not have the financial capacity to pay the level of claims expected from such a major, destructive war. In the absence of Great Power war, however, war risks may indeed be insurable. The question then becomes whether the private sector will be willing to supply war risks insurance (and other types of political risks insurance). This depends on prevailing norms regarding the insurability of those risks.

30. Lee Coppack, "Insurers under Pressure over Political Risks," *Lloyd's List*, December 24, 1982.

31. Contract frustration insurance covers the cancellation or repudiation of contracts due to political tensions or government interference. Kidnap and ransom insurance covers risks of kidnaping, extortion, and hostage takings; corporations now routinely seek such insurance for their executives abroad.

32. The chairman of Mutual Marine Office Ltd., in trying to drum up support for land war risks, said "It should be fun, and it could be rewarding." "Cover Proposed for Land War Risks," *Business Insurance*, October 15, 1984, p. 48.

33. Stephen Kobrin, "Description and Analysis of the U.S. Market for Political Risks Insurance for Overseas Investments in Developing Countries," *OPIC*, April 24, 1986, p. 17. Other firms often insist on keeping political risks products separate from their other insurance business.

34. Stacy Shapiro, "Insurers Consider Land War Risks," *Business Insurance* November 12, 1984, p. 96.

35. As a report in *The Economist* stated, "The stupidity of cash-flow underwriting and its threat to the industry is clear to all and sundry." "Slow: Danger Ahead," September 25, 1982, p. 6.

36. The UNCTAD in the late 1980s grew concerned that many foreign reinsurers active in developing countries were inexperienced, unreliable, and viewed reinsurance underwriting "merely as a vehicle for developing investment funds at a time characterized by extraordinarily high interest rates." Developing-country insurance markets relied heavily on outside reinsurers, and thus were quite vulnerable to any disruptions. United Nations Conference on Trade and Development, "Invisibles: Insurance, Reinsurance Security," Study by the UNCTAD Secretariat TD/B/C.3/221, February 3, 1987, p. 3.

37. "Slow: Danger Ahead," *The Economist*, September 25, 1992, p. 6.

38. Stacy Shapiro, "London Political Risk Market Tightens," *Business Insurance*, October 15, 1984, pp. 47–48.

39. Antony M. Baker, "Liberalization of Trade in Services—The World Insurance Industry," in Orio Giarini, ed., *The Emerging Services Economy* (Oxford: Pergamon Press, 1987), p. 199.

40. John W. Milligan, "Coping with the Rigors of a Tough Market," *Institutional Investor*, April 1985, pp. 159–67.

41. Michele Milone, "Political Risk and Lloyd's: Still a Pair," *National Underwriter* (Property/Casualty Edition), September 28, 1987, pp. 40–41.

42. Most reinsurance contracts are placed by international brokers, such as Kemper and Prudential, which are often viewed by reinsurers as being much too influential.

43. Taravella, "Political Risk Cover Taking Off in U.S. Market," p. 46. The contracts between direct insurers and their reinsurers are called treaties, as if these firms were sovereign entities.

44. Kobrin, "Description and Analysis," p. 12. UNCTAD raised concerns about reinsurance security and its impact on developing countries throughout this period. Developing country representatives complained of discriminatory terms granted by western reinsurers to business in developing states, and believed that reinsurers struggling with losses in the OECD countries were unfairly raising rates in the non-OECD countries in response. See "Report of the Committee on Invisibles and Financing Related to Trade of the Second Part of its Twelfth Session," UNCTAD 14 May 1987 TD/B/C.3(XII)/Misc.4.

45. Kobrin, "Description and Analysis," p. 15. When news leaked about CIGNA's unusual policy, banks questioned other political risk underwriters about their willingness to underwrite inconvertibility risks; most turned it down, partly due to concerns about insurability and partly due to concerns about lack of capacity. Shapiro, "London Political Risk Market Tightens," *Business Insurance*, October 15, 1984, pp. 47–48.

46. Government export credit and investment guarantee agencies serve numerous purposes, with straightforward insurance only one of them. They are often used to promote foreign policy goals, including development aid. They typically include some subsidy in the rates charged customers.

47. See Charles Lipson, *Standing Guard: Protecting Foreign Capital in the Nineteenth and Twentieth Centuries* (Berkeley and Los Angeles: University of California Press, 1985). The expansion of multilateral guarantees constitutes a strengthening of the international investment regime. There is some talk also of putting investment on the table for WTO discussions. There is disagreement, however, on whether regulating investment should be considered a trade issue at all. To the extent that the investment regime is strong and effective, we can expect insurers to be more willing to define insurability of international risks broadly.

48. See, for instance, Wapner, *Environmental Activism and World Civic Politics*.

49. See Thomas Donaldson, *The Ethics of International Business* (New York: Oxford University Press, 1989); William Baumol, *Easy Virtue: Business Ethics and the Invisible Hand* (Cambridge, Mass.: Basil Blackwell, 1991); David Braybrooke, *Ethics in the World of Business* (Totowa, N.J.: Rowman and Allanheld, 1983).

50. Nick Hanly, Jason Shogrun, and Ben White, *Environmental Economics: In Theory and Practice* (New York: Oxford University Press, 1997); Anil Markanya and Julie Richardson, *Environmental Economics: A Reader* (New York: St. Martin's Press, 1992).

51. For a critique of the efficiency view of the government role in social regulations, including the environment, see Mark Sagoff, *The Economy of the Earth: Philosophy, Law and the Environment* (New York: Cambridge Univer-

sity Press, 1988). He argues that workplace, consumer product, and environmental problems are "primarily moral, aesthetic, cultural and political and that they must be addressed in those terms" (p. 6).

52. Gene Pokorny, of Cambridge Reports/Research International, presents evidence that consumers today are less likely than previously to trade off environmental values for other values. "Going Green," *Coal Voice* 16.1 (January 1, 1993): 12. A recent issue of *The Economist* reported that 42 percent of Britons claimed they consciously shopped for green products, twice as much as a year ago (October 20, 1990, p. 88)

53. As heard on National Public Radio, "Morning Edition," November 3, 1993.

54. There have been accusations of "greenwashing" the corporate image through public relations expenditures. Steve Sawyer et al., "How Green Is Green?" *Communication World* 9.5 (April 1992): 22–27. See also "DuPont: Friends of the Earth Assails TV Campaign," which reports the accusation of "green fraud." *Greenwire*, August 28, 1991.

55. See the excellent analysis of the development of international regulation of the pesticide industry by Robert L. Paarlberg, "Managing Pesticide Use in Developing Countries," in Peter M. Haas, Robert O. Keohane, and Marc A. Levy, eds., *Institutions for the Earth: Sources of Effective International Environmental Protection* (Cambridge: MIT Press, 1993).

56. Some California grape growers originally pursued organic farming to appeal to customers concerned about toxics in the food supply. They discovered, after initial investments and a move up the learning curve, that organic methods are productive and cost-effective (report on "Morning Edition," National Public Radio, November 1, 1993).

57. United Nations Centre on Transnational Corporations, *Benchmark Survey* (New York: United Nations, 1992).

58. Bruce Smart, *Beyond Compliance: A New Industry View of the Environment* (Washington: World Resources Institute, April 1992).

59. No matter how fast this change occurs or how widely it becomes an accepted norm, many environmental activists would argue it will be too little, too late.

60. This is not to say that pollution havens do not exist. This also may not indicate any changing norms at all if we see at the same time a lowering of standards due to the pressures of competition for that foreign investment, in which governments are tempted to weaken their regulations to attract investors. The evidence on this is mixed at the moment.

61. Curtis Moore and Alan Miller, *Green Gold: Japan, Germany, the United States, and the Race for Environmental Technology* (Boston: Beacon Press, 1994).

62. Michael Porter, "America's Green Strategy," *Scientific American*, April 1991.

CHAPTER 9

Embedded Private Authority: Multinational Enterprises and the Amazonian Indigenous Peoples Movement in Ecuador

Pamela L. Burke

In April 1992, over 10,000 Amazonian indigenous peoples under the direction of the Organization of Indigenous Peoples of Pastaza (OPIP) marched from the rainforest to the national government of Quito, Ecuador, in response to the development of their land by multinational oil companies. Following the march, OPIP was granted an unprecedented communal land title of 1,115,574 hectares. In December 1993, OPIP organized the Villano Assembly for three days to discuss the future of oil exploration in the Ecuadorian Amazon. As a result, OPIP and ARCO oil company articulated plans for resource extraction measures that would satisfy both parties. In each of these cases, multinational oil companies were actors involved in dialogue not only with national governmental leaders, but directly with local indigenous peoples.

The direct participation and communication between multinational oil companies and indigenous peoples challenges the traditional economic, private nature of multinational enterprises (MNEs) and suggests a quasi-public role for MNEs in the global system. Furthermore, the inclusionary behavior of oil MNEs with indigenous peoples demonstrates a change in MNE behavior from that of a private, autonomous actor, uninvolved in local/societal affairs, to that of a quasi-public actor that has direct impacts upon the mobilization and collective action strategies, and ultimately policy outcomes, of indigenous peoples. This chapter asserts that MNEs are quasi-public actors that function on multiple levels within the international system, including subnational, national, and transnational.

List of Abbreviations

CONAIE	Confederation of Indigenous Nationalities of Ecuador
CONFENIAE	Confederation of Indigenous Nationalities of the Ecuadorian Amazon
FOIN	Federation of Indigenous Organizations of Napo
IGO	International Governmental Organization
INGO	International Non-Governmental Organization
MNE	Multinational Enterprise
NGO	Nongovernmental Organization
NRDC	National Resources Defense Council
ONHAE	Organization of the Huaorani Nation of the Ecuadorian Amazon
OPIP	Organization of Indigenous People of Pastaza
PVO	Private Voluntary Organization
RAN	Rainforest Action Network

In order to analyze these transnational processes, MNEs must be examined as dynamic actors that have networks of communication and information with other transnational actors, such as international nongovernmental organizations (INGOs) and intergovernmental organizations (IGOs); national actors, such as governmental leaders; and subnational/societal actors, including social movement organizations (SMOs) and national nongovernmental organizations (NGOs). Through a comparative case study of four indigenous organizations and geographic locations of petroleum development in the Ecuadorian Amazon, this chapter will examine the change in MNE behavior and its impacts on indigenous peoples' collective action strategies and policy outcomes. Based on this analysis, it will offer some observations about the quasi-public nature and behavior of MNEs.

International relations literature recognizes the authority of actors via the dichotomy of state sovereignty and the anarchic international system. Therefore, authority in international relations has been examined as "legitimate authority as involving a process of mutual recognition among the society of sovereign states."[1] However, this state-centric notion of authority neglects the analysis of nonstate actors and the authority that they may possess in the international system. The recent mobilization of transnational actors and successful policy changes in response to issues such as human rights, the environment, women's rights, and indigenous rights suggests that nonstate actors do possess a level of authority within the international system. Moreover, the globalization of trade, finance, technology, and industry suggests that private, nonstate actors at the international, national, and subnational levels possess an authority outside of the state system that warrants further analysis. As Philip G. Cerny noted, "From international regimes to cross-cutting local pressures, new circuits of power are emerging."[2]

This chapter utilizes conceptions of public and private authority in order to analyze the international system. Notions of public and private permit nonstate actors to be significant, authoritative elements of the international system, while still recognizing the international system of states and their sovereign authority. Authority, based on the framework provided by Claire Cutler, Tony Porter, and Virginia Haufler, is defined as the "power to influence or command thought, opinion, or behavior."[3] As Cutler cogently argues, liberalism establishes a dichotomy of space between public and private, such that public concerns the political, and private concerns the economic.[4] Public legitimate authority is "wielded by officials of the government who have gained that power to influence or command through any number of political means, most notable via elections."[5] Private authority is perceived as neutral or apolitical, having to do with the natural economic cycle.[6] The *problematique* of this project is the ability of private actors to obtain and maintain authority on the international level. This chapter discusses the boundaries between public and private authority and the difficulty of distinguishing between the two regarding oil MNEs in Ecuador. Furthermore, the authority of MNEs impacts not only the state level or international level, but also the societal level. Thus, the observations of this chapter challenge future researchers to analyze subnational impacts of transnational public/private authority.

THE FRAMEWORK FOR ANALYSIS

One perspective of international authority is derived from regime analysis. Based on the widely accepted definition by Stephen Krasner, regimes are "sets of implicit or explicit principles, norms, rules, and decision-making procedures around which actors' expectations converge in a given area of international relations."[7] Regimes possess a level of authority in the international system with regard to international cooperation and multilateral resolution of problems. However, the rise and decline of regimes, as well as their maintenance, has been attributed to states.[8] Although scholars have acknowledged the significance of norms[9] and networks of knowledge communities ("epistemic communities"),[10] states are viewed as the key actors of authority within a regime.

For the purposes of this analysis, the regime approach offers foundations upon which to build. Regimes affirm the notion of authority within the international system. They also point to the significance of ideas, norms, and networks of knowledge and information within the international system. Furthermore, the empirical evidence upon which regime theory is based suggests that multiple actors in the international system can coordinate interests in order to form an authoritative position and implement policies. These conceptions are fruitful in operationalizing notions of interfirm cooperation, or "private regimes," but they are not useful in analyzing the consequences and nature of this authority on a subnational level.[11]

Like Susan Strange,[12] I concur that regime analysis lacks precision in identifying the dynamics of the international system. Strange argues that regime analysis is a "state-centric paradigm that limits the vision of a wider reality."[13] Regime analysis does not provide a clear account of relations between subnational actors and transnational actors or their influence upon specific issue areas.

Virginia Haufler points out that the definition of regime does not necessarily preclude an important role for nonstate actors. She notes that private regimes "institutionalize agreements among nonstate actors and regularly negotiate their conflicts."[14] Haufler describes private actors as firms and private voluntary organizations (PVOs), such as the International Planned Parenthood Federation, both of which have played key roles in transnational policy coalitions that influenced national policies, but through different resources. PVOs are unlikely to form regimes, but rather operate through domestic coalitions and information exchange. Firms, on the other hand, may "operate through the domestic political system to influence inter-state regimes."[15]

Haufler observes that corporate private regimes cooperate beyond price and market share. Rather, these firms "institutionalize agreements among non-state actors and regularly negotiate their conflicts."[16] Furthermore, she remarks that PVOs are not always without private motivations and that information exchange and transfer of norms takes place between social forces and firms, in addition to the traditionally studied exchange between PVOs and societal forces. The conceptualization of nongovernmental organizations as PVOs facilitates a distinction between NGOs as "purposive" rather than "principled" actors. By categorizing international nongovernmental organizations as "principled," we lack an understanding of the diverse interests and goals of these groups.[17]

The notion of "private voluntary organizations" (PVOs) is significant to this project. It further identifies actors of private authority within the international system. Thus, while firms are the concentration of this project and this chapter, they interact with other private actors in the international system and these interactions may influence the behavior of MNEs and shape private authority in the international system. Adding to the identification of private actors, this chapter also considers societal actors as forces of private authority within the international system.

The activation of networks of communication and information exchange among private actors may form a private regime, or "an integrated complex of formal and informal institutions that is a source of governance for an industry or economic issue area as a whole."[18] However, if the private actors involve PVOs, social movement organizations (SMOs), or other private, social forces, it is more likely that the result will be networks and alliances based on common goals and interests. These networks and alliances fall into the second category of institutionalization of private authority as defined by this project. When these networks and alliances form based on an issue area, such as human rights or the environment, private actors may take on quasi-public roles in order to implement policy change. Thus, the activation of transnational networks may politicize a private actor and convert a once private authority to a position of public actor. The case of oil MNEs in Ecuador illustrates this situation in which private actors, oil MNEs, have formed networks with PVOs and SMOs, thus changing their behavior toward indigenous peoples as well as changing their nature to that of a quasi-public authority.

Margaret Keck and Kathryn Sikkink have developed the term "transnational issue network," meaning, "the set of relevant actors working internationally on an issue who are bound together by shared values, a common discourse, and dense exchanges of information and services."[19] Although Keck and Sikkink have identified means of communication and linkage among multiple levels of actors, they have not included MNEs in the transnational issue network framework. MNEs can be targets of transnational issue networks, but they also can be active participants in this melange of private actors, as will be illustrated through the case of oil MNEs in Ecuador.

M. J. Peterson offers a corrective for this approach. She includes individuals, interest associations, societal groups, *and* firms in her conception of "international society."[20] The private authority of MNEs cannot be ignored in a complete account of international relations theory. Thus, this chapter intends to broaden the concept of a transnational issue network to include firms and to provide preliminary observations of the quasi-public nature of firms.

Alison Brysk provides a model for including societal forces in the analysis of transnational relations. She incorporates the literature of social movements and regime theory to analyze the transnational organization of indigenous groups in Latin America. Brysk asserts that indigenous organizations and national nongovernmental organizations have formed networks with the international human rights and environment regimes.[21] These regimes have utilized their private authority to influence national policy change for indigenous peoples. This chapter analyzes the interactions between MNEs and other transnational actors in order to clarify the private/public nature and behavior of firms.

In conceptualizing the nature of a multinational enterprise, we must also account for its global nature, such that it is part of a larger global society and is impacted by global ideas. Cerny asserts that "the logic of collective action is becoming a heterogeneous, multilayered logic, derived not from one particular core structure, such as the state, but from the structural complexity embedded in the global arena."[22] Although the global society is founded upon a system of states, this system evoked networks among nonstate actors. Global economic life of private actors also facilitates networks among actors. These private, economic networks may have derived from market activity, but the results of these interactions among actors may "give way to social relations that are not themselves driven by economic incentive."[23] Thus, MNEs are not outside of the influence of transnational ideas and can be part of a transnational network that motivates the MNE to become a quasi-public actor.

Haufler notes the embeddedness of firms in global civic culture. She asserts that in business areas that "social groups perceive a strong ethical or moral content," such as "conservation of biological diversity," firms operate within a larger cultural context.[24] Stopford and Strange refer to the embeddedness of a firm in the societal culture as the "good citizen."[25] For instance, firms have changed their policies to incorporate ecological safety measures. Ecuadorian MNEs have changed their behavior to include indigenous peoples in their policymaking processes and to clean areas of the rainforest and its rivers contaminated by petroleum. The role of MNEs has expanded to include negotiation not only on business policies, but also environmental plans, social plans, and in some cases, talks of profit-sharing between MNEs and indigenous organizations have emerged. MNEs have also provided resources for indigenous organizations. Thus, direct negotiations with MNEs have not only affected the Amazonian indigenous social movements, but have also challenged our perceptions of the functions of MNEs in the global system.

This research, in concurrence with Haufler,[26] finds that goals of protection of indigenous rights and their environment are not "completely incompatible" with profit and development of the MNE. Furthermore, the change in behavior of MNEs suggests that private actors are not immune to the discourse and ideas within the global arena, and may, in fact, be motivated to act on these ideas. In the case of Ecuador, the oil MNEs that did act upon the notion of indigenous rights and ecological protection altered their role to that of a more public nature. This may be generalized to other MNEs that become embedded in a society and are compelled to act as "citizens" in that society, rather than private, autonomous actors.

Although the state is not always the authoritative actor in the international system, the global system was founded upon a system of states that still influences interactions within the global arena. As discussed earlier, all states are subject to penetration by the global economy and transnational actors.

This framework suggests that weak states that are dependent upon the resources of a firm are more penetrable to private authority and actors than are strong states that do not depend upon the resources of a firm. As Stopford and Strange[27] posit, governments are faced with new challenges due to changing world structures. Moreover, multinationals are not "monolithic" actors and managers are increasingly becoming statesmen. Thus, the role of states is significant, but they are actors in the global arena bargaining for authority over other transnational, private actors.

States have a close interaction with private actors, societal and transnational. Peter Evans[28] argues that firms and states have shared economic interests. Economic transformation is most likely to occur when states have achieved a level of "embedded autonomy," in which the state and private actors are connected, yet the state is insulated from domination by private actors. Eduardo Silva[29] asserts that these dense networks of communication between firms and government leaders are crucial for influencing the private sector's confidence to commit resources for development programs. While both of these conceptions are useful, they do not account for a state that does not represent the majority of its societal forces, such that alliances with firms only facilitate economic success, but not social representation and equity. In cases where the state is struggling to maintain legitimacy over a population in which some elements may be challenging it, alliances with firms and not social forces could exacerbate potentially violent societal actors.

In *these* cases, the state is being challenged from private actors from below and from above. Rather than conceiving of the state as an authoritative sovereign actor or a partner with economic, private actors, I view the state as a mediator.[30] The state as a mediator seeks to interact with both private actors from transnational and subnational levels. At times, it is in the interest of a state to remain out of negotiations between transnational actors and societal actors, such as cases in which the state can place blame on private actors or the state does not have the resources to be involved (i.e., technological, knowledge-information, etc.). At times when state sovereignty is challenged, or the legitimacy of the regime is challenged, the state has greater incentive to be involved in actions and negotiations between transnational and subnational actors. As Roger Normand, policy director of the Center for Economic and Social Rights, commented on the situation between oil MNEs, the state, and indigenous peoples, "Ecuador's indigenous and environmental organizations have pushed human rights groups to re-examine their exclusive focus on government actors."[31] Furthermore, an attorney for the Sierra Club Legal Defense Fund commented that government institutions are so underfunded and understaffed that most monitoring responsibilities remain in the "hands of the corporations themselves."[32] Thus, states may abdicate their responsibilities and authority to private actors under certain conditions.

This also implies that states are facilitating the private authority of actors. Rather, states are actors in a bargaining process in which firms, transnational organizations, and societal forces are a part. It may be the case, as based on these observations, that certain issue areas preclude the state from having an authoritative role. These issue areas would be those of "strong moral or ethical content," similar to those that were previously asserted to influence a firm.[33] Therefore, states may have restraints on their authority on issues such as environmental protection, human rights, or ethnic conflict. These restraints allow other transnational actors (private and public) to influence state and substate policies and actions.

This framework utilizes the literatures of regime analysis, transnational relations, and state–firm bargaining in order to operationalize the notions of private and public authority in multiple levels of analysis. Each of these literatures provides a basis for analyzing actors at various levels in the international system, national, transnational, subnational. However, private authority pervades each of these levels and is likewise influenced by actors at each of these levels. Thus, a complete understanding of private authority must not be conceived as static, but rather as a dynamic, transnational process.

ECUADORIAN BLACK GOLD:
THE EVOLUTION OF PUBLIC AND PRIVATE AUTHORITY

In order to analyze the complex nature and behavior of oil MNEs in Ecuador, it is necessary to understand the evolution of their roles from private actors to quasi-public actors and their historical relationships with the Ecuadorian national government. Moreover, oil MNEs in Ecuador have changed their behavior with regard to indigenous peoples and environmental standards in response to pressures from other private actors including indigenous organizations, PVOs, and state actors. The change in MNE behavior from exclusionary toward indigenous peoples and low environmental standards to inclusionary and elevated environmental standards, warrants further investigation of their impacts on indigenous peoples and policies within Ecuador.

Oil MNEs have a history of having substantial private authority in the international system. The 1971 signing of the Teheran Agreement, passing the authority of pricing and production control from multinationals to OPEC, is an example of the private regime formed by oil MNEs throughout recent history. Following the dissolution of Standard Oil Company in 1911, seven oil companies developed and remained authoritative private actors into the present period. Two of the "Seven Sisters" played significant roles in the evolution of the Ecuadorian petroleum industry, Gulf and Texaco. These "Seven Dinosaurs," as referred to in Ecuador, dominated the oil policies in many of the host countries from which they were extracting resources. One observer referred to Ecuador and other host countries as "virtual colonies of the oil companies."[34]

However, the late 1960s and early 1970s witnessed a change in host country policies—nationalization of the oil industry. It was at this time that oil MNEs became less autonomous and began establishing a public space in host countries. Thus, private authority and the evolution of a public space for oil MNEs is nothing new. The *new* aspect of this story is that oil MNEs have begun to change their behavior not just with regard to policies that affect their own profit, but also with regard to policies toward social actors. They have joined a new quasi-public space in which they have joined networks with other private actors in order to impact the political policy process and policy outcomes. Furthermore, oil MNEs have taken on quasi-public roles, such as providing for social services, health services, and education, that are traditionally associated with state/public responsibilities.

The observations from this case study of Ecuador are intended to provide empirical evidence of the relationships between oil MNEs, the state, transnational actors, and social forces. These observations can be applied to other developing countries that are experiencing similar pressures from above and below the level of the state, such as Mexico, Venezuela, Bolivia, Peru, Colombia, Nigeria, Zaire, Tanzania, Burma, Indonesia, and Papua New Guinea. In each of these cases, private firms not only impact national policy, but also impact the lives of social actors and the policies by which they live.

Prior to 1992, Ecuador was one of two Latin American nations that belonged to the Organization of Petroleum Exporting Countries (OPEC), and was its second smallest producer. Although Ecuador is small in comparison to other oil-producing countries, the petroleum industry within Ecuador is vital to the economy. Because of the economic strength of this industry, its representatives hold influential status in the national policy process. As Catherine Conaghan and John Malloy note, throughout Ecuador's history, oil MNEs have remained private actors that tried to influence public decisions. For example, throughout the 1980s, business interest groups developed lobbying capabilities and influenced much of the neoliberal economic reforms.[35] They note that presidents often rely on professional economic advice from industry representatives, rather than political party members or government officials. This reliance on actors outside of government is due largely to the volatility of Ecuador's twenty-three political parties. Since the petroleum industry is so significant within the Ecuadorian economy, networks between oil industry members and government leaders were established.

Large reserves of petroleum were discovered in subsoil deposits in the Amazonian region in 1967. In August 1972, petroleum development began and a 313–mile trans-Andean production pipeline that was built from Lago Agrio in the Amazon across 12,000–foot mountains and down into the Pacific Ocean. Production of petroleum quadrupled from 1972 to 1977, increasing the GNP from $2.2 billion in 1971 to $5.9 billion in 1977. Based on the increase in national income, petroleum revenues were utilized for education, rural loans, and infrastructural development. The petroleum industry became a significant actor within Ecuadorian economic and political policymaking.

Throughout the 1970s, Ecuador struggled to nationalize the oil industry. This struggle was made more difficult by the private consortium of oil MNEs, led by Gulf and Texaco, who acted together to deter nationalization. In 1972, the Corporación Estatal Petrolera Ecuatoriana (CEPE) was established, which was largely responsible for petroleum policy and execution. The goal of the Ecuadorian government during this time period was complete state ownership of all subsoil deposits. In August 1973, Texaco began petroleum production in the Amazon, with CEPE reaping 25 percent of the subsidiary stock over the next four years. This relationship is an example of the public/private partnership between oil MNEs and the state in Ecuador.[36]

General Jarrín, Minister of Natural Resources, was highly criticized for the inefficiency of the CEPE. In September 1974, Texaco and Gulf were actively engaged in promoting Jarrín's removal from office. They initiated a private press campaign against the general.[37] Multinational oil companies involved in production in the Amazon were pressuring the government to open its market to the international system and to allow for further exploration. In 1976, Texaco and Gulf formed a consortium of multinational oil companies against the Ecuadorian National Government in response to their nationalistic oil policies.[38] This consortium signifies the private authority that oil MNEs had in the global and domestic arena.

During the late 1970s, Ecuador opened its domestic market to foreign oil companies for the development of petroleum reserves primarily in its Amazonian region, and tried to lure foreign investment that it may have turned away in the earlier part of the decade. As in many developing countries, Ecuador did not have the technology, training, or knowledge for petroleum extraction in this region. Thus, private authority is also a function of the control of information, resources, and knowledge in a specific area.

In 1979, Ecuador transitioned to a democratic, civilian-led government. With this change, the state increased oil exploration in the Amazon for foreign oil companies. In 1980, Texaco reinvested in petroleum development in the Amazon.

However, as oil prices dropped by $2.00 per barrel from 1980 to 1981, Ecuador's oil boom came to an end. Ecuador was forced to explore more land for petroleum reserves. As one incentive to increase investment and production, the 1982 Oil Law decreased the taxes that foreign companies had to pay. In 1985, the government negotiated new terms for petroleum exploration with Occidental, Belco, British Petroleum, and Esso/Hispanoil. By June 1987, further negotiations were reached with multinational corporations and several corporations purchased drilling rights in several blocks within the Amazon. These corporations included, Occidental, Exxon, British Petroleum, Conoco, ARCO, Unocal, and Tenneco. Oil revenues are not only important to Ecuador's domestic economic stability, but they also provide funds for payments of its $8.3 billion foreign debt. Thus, pressures to develop petroleum derive from both domestic and international forces.[39]

The current president, Sixto Durán Ballén, was elected in 1992 and has implemented economic reforms, including privatization of the petroleum industry. In December 1992, Ecuador quit its membership in OPEC. In 1993, Durán Ballén opened the Amazon for further exploration. Both the Cuyabeño National Park and the Yasuní National Indigenous Reserve were included in the areas of exploration.[40] In November 1993, Maxus Oil Company (USA) announced plans for an investment of $743 million to explore and produce oil over the next twenty years. Exploration investment has increased under Durán Ballén due to his relaxation of the hydrocarbon laws and reform of crude oil laws to encourage "participation contracts," which allow foreign firms to freely sell their crude oil rather than receive a fixed compensation by the state.[41]

Currently, Ecuador's challenges in the Amazon are not only from the multinational oil companies; there are also pressures from indigenous groups and environmental activists to create better resource development policies. Environmental policy began with the formation of the environmental bureau, the Dirección General de Medio Ambiente (DIGEMA), in 1984 by the Ministry of Energy and Mines. In 1990, a new environmental department was designed, the Subsecretario de Medio Ambiente (SMA). The government has increased funding for and development of environmental preservation projects in petroleum development areas throughout the 1990s. For example, environmental impact reports must be filed yearly with the government. Furthermore, the government has introduced more stringent environmental protection policies with regard to oil production and exploration. Multinational corporations have also increased their funding of environmentally safe exploration and production.

Much of the environmental policy in the Amazon has been created in response to the protests of indigenous peoples and the pressure of international NGOs. Most oil policy that was formulated throughout the 1970s and 1980s did not take into consideration the impacts of petroleum development upon indigenous peoples and their land.

However, the 1990s has witnessed new relationships between oil MNEs and indigenous peoples. In addition, oil policies have changed toward negotiation and incorporation of indigenous demands. Through the inclusion of indigenous peoples in the oil policy process, petroleum development and policy has taken a new form. This policy impact has recently been witnessed through the formation of a new indigenous political movement, Pachakutik, and the election of three indigenous leaders to the National Congress.

Since the political organization of indigenous peoples and organized national protests in the mid-1980s and early 1990s, MNEs in the Amazonian region have consulted with indigenous peoples in the policy planning of petroleum reserves in indigenous areas. Moreover, oil MNEs have initiated social programs for indigenous groups in the areas in which petroleum is developed. For example, Maxus, Conoco, and Texaco have all initiated health care, education, and fishery development programs for indigenous peoples. MNEs have taken on the role of the government in this sense, since they are providing social programs for indigenous peoples. Negotiations between indigenous peoples and MNE representatives highlights the complexity of the role of MNEs within a host country and their impacts upon societal groups.

THE INDIGENOUS PEOPLES OF THE AMAZON

Although they initially remained isolated, Amazonian peoples organized in response to religious missionaries and colonists who were settling in their regions. Organization in response to oil development on their traditional homelands is relatively recent. This organization has developed since the original organizations of the 1960s with Salesian missionaries (the Shuar Federation) characterized by small, local groups to its current stage of development with large regional councils, participating under a national organization, which negotiate with oil MNEs and government officials. This section will briefly trace the evolution of organization and mobilization of the Amazonian peoples.

Indigenous people comprise about 40 percent of the Ecuadorian population, or 4,728,000 people.[42] Indigenous peoples of the Amazon encompass 2.5 percent of the total indigenous population (1.0 percent of the total population), or about 120,000 people.[43] The Shuar and the Quichua, numbering over 100,000, are the two largest groups in the region. The other groups are the Achuar (2,500), the Siona-Secoya (600), the Cofán (460), the Huaorani (600), and other small indigenous groups.[44] Despite their small percentage of the total indigenous population, Amazonian peoples are leaders of the indigenous rights movement and maintain the highest level of contact with private, transnational actors.

In 1964, the first Indian federation formed through the aid of Salesian missionaries, called the Federation of the Shuar Centers. This group of Ecuadorian Indians established programs for their communities outside of state programs. These programs included bilingual education, health care, and improved technologies for cattle ranching. This organization was founded to strengthen indigenous organization and communities due to the new influence of oil companies and employees in the Amazon.

In the 1970s, the Federation of the Indigenous Organization of Napo (FOIN) and the Organization of the People of Pastaza (OPIP) formed, which together represent over sixty Quichua communities. There are provincial indigenous organizations throughout the Amazonian region. They combine the indigenous traditions of shamanism with more western forms of organization, such as a president, a vice-president, and a secretary. These groups were primarily concerned with struggles for land. They have currently assumed leadership positions within the national organization of indigenous peoples, and have expanded their demands to include the environment, education, health care, and increased political participation on a national level.

In 1980, the groups of the Amazon joined together to form the Confederation of Indigenous Nationalities of the Ecuadorian Amazon (CONFENIAE). This regional organization contains members of the

TABLE 9.1
Indian Organizations of the Ecuadorian Amazon

Organization	Ethnic Group	Year	Province
Shuar Federation	Shuar & Achuar	1962	Morona & Zamora
AIPSE	Shuar & Achuar	1963	Morona
FOIN	Quichua	1969	Napo
FCUNAE	Quichua	1976	Napo
OPIP	Quichua	1977	Pastaza
FOISE	Quichua	1980	Sucumbios
CONFENIAE	Multi-ethnic	1980	Amazon region
OISSE	Siona-Secoya	1986	Sucumbios
COFÁN	Cofán	1990	Sucumbios
ONHAE	Huaorani	1990	Napo

Source: Fernando Serrano, "The Transformation of the Indian Peoples of the Ecuadorian Amazon into Political Actors and its Effects on the State's Modernization Policies" (Master's thesis, University of Florida, 1993), p. 4.

TABLE 9.2
The Effects of MNEs on Indigenous Peoples'
Mobilization and Policy Outcomes

Indigenous Group/ MNE Behavior	Group Organization	Int'l. NGO Contact	Mobilization	Policy Outcome
CONFENIAE/ Exclusionary	Strong	Moderate	Moderate	
CONFENIAE/ Inclusionary (1990)	Strong	High	High/Strategy change	Land; education; resources
ONHAE/ Exclusionary	Weak	Low	Low	Yasuní Reserve
ONHAE/ Inclusionary (1991)	Medium	Moderate	Moderate; Strategy change	Education; resources
OPIP/ Exclusionary	Strong	Moderate	Moderate	
OPIP/ Inclusionary (1989)	Strong	High	High; Strategy change	Land; resources
COFÁN/ Exclusionary	Weak	Low	Low	Cuyabeño Reserve
COFÁN/ Inclusionary (1994)	Strong	Moderate	Moderate; Strategy change	Resources

Shuar and Quichua peoples in leadership positions, in addition to members of the Achuar, Huaorani, Cofán, Siona, and Secoya tribes. Through this alliance, the organization has brought their issues to the public attention and to the political agendas of national and international groups. They also have formed alliances with environmental and human rights organizations, in addition to bringing "oil companies and the government to the negotiating table, particularly regarding development practices in the Amazon."[45] Most importantly, the regional association has struggled and protested for land rights, and continues to do so.

The national indigenous organization of Ecuador is CONAIE. It was first formed by the union of ECUARUNARI (the Sierra indigenous council) and CONFENIAE in 1980 and originally called the Coordinating Council of Indigenous Nationalities of Ecuador (CONACNIE). Following this union, the coastal Indian communities formed a regional group, COICE (Coordinator of Indigenous Organizations of the Coast of Ecuador), and it joined the two former groups to form the current day CONAIE. Amazonian peoples participate in the CONAIE, which has aided and supported them in negotiations with the government and oil companies.[46]

OVERVIEW OF CASES

Through an analysis of the CONFENIAE, OPIP, ONHAE, and the Cofán indigenous organizations and corresponding geographic locations of oil development, this chapter will elucidate the significance of the change in MNE behavior on the level and type of mobilization of indigenous peoples, and the inclusion of indigenous peoples within the policy process.[47] Furthermore, it illustrates the evolution of the quasi-public nature of MNEs and their level of embeddedness not just within the national landscape, but also within societal arenas. The activation of private, transnational networks between MNEs, PVOs, and indigenous organizations has politicized the role of MNEs within Ecuador and the larger global arena.

Indigenous group organization will be categorized as: (1) strong, (2) medium, or (3) weak. Strong organization implies that a group has considerable resources, has sustained the organization for a long time period, and has support of a large majority of the group that it claims to represent. Weak organization implies that a group has few resources, has recently organized, and has little support from the group for that it claims to represent. Medium organizational level includes aspects of strong and weak organization, such that it has not sustained organization over a long time period, but does have the support of 50 percent or more of the group that it claims to represent.[48]

The concept of transnational actors will be broken down into international NGO contacts and MNE behavior to assess the significance of MNE behavior and its function distinct from international NGOs. CONFENIAE and OPIP will be characterized as strong group organizations. Both have high levels of contact with NGOs (national and international) and have been included in the MNE policymaking process. Since their inclusion within the MNE policymaking process and the state policy process, both groups have experienced high levels of mobilization among members and their strategies of mobilization have changed from local and regional to national and international.

ONHAE, the Huaorani organization, and the Cofán indigenous peoples have weaker organizations. Both organizations are relatively new, although their common identities, shared communities, and networks are not. However, their resources are less than those of the other two groups, including contact with NGOs. Both of these groups have experienced lesser degrees of inclusion in the policy process of MNEs and the state. However, after MNEs changed their behavior toward these groups, indigenous group mobilization strategies changed, expanding from issues of land demarcation to environmental protection and profit-sharing. Currently, the Huaorani and the Cofán utilize transnational strategies, such as e-mail and international media, to attract attention and support for their organizations. The change in the level of mobilization and strategies, and inclusion within the policy process (or policy change) in all four groups after MNE inclusionary behavior suggests that MNE behavior is significant in the collective action process.

The networks between private actors, as mentioned above, implies that authority in the international system does not solely derive from states. The cases below provide evidence of networks of private actors that influence each other's behavior. Oil MNEs play prominent roles in these networks because of the large amount of resources that they provide. However, firms are part of the broader global society of ideas and norms. Based on these cases, oil MNEs have been influenced by the norms of these private transnational and societal actors, and have in turn changed their nature and behavior in response to new motivations.

CONFENIAE, the Huaorani, and Conoco

CONFENIAE has been a strong regional organization since its foundation in 1980. It has cultivated contacts and resources from international and national NGOs and has aided in the local organization of indigenous peoples in the Amazon. ONHAE, the Huaorani organization, on the other hand, is a relatively new group. It has not yet cultivated the transnational contacts of the CONFENIAE, nor has it successfully sustained mobilization of its members. However, in both cases, as will be illustrated with regard to Conoco Oil Company, direct negotiations and inclusionary MNE behavior increased the level of mobilization and changed the strategies of CONFENIAE and ONHAE.

The demarcation of 66,570 hectares of land to the Huaorani people and another 250,000 hectares for the Yasuní National Reserve, under President Hurtado in 1982 was supported by an alliance between CONFENIAE and international and national NGOs. CONFENIAE was in its beginning stages of mobilization during the early-1980s. However, in the mid-1980s, oil companies began exploration of the lands that had been demarcated to the Huaorani. Until this point, the Huaorani had not officially organized, in a western style (although they have been living in shared communities for hundreds of years), and their connections with international and national NGOs were primarily through CONFENIAE, the regional Amazonian organization.

Throughout the mid-1980s, CONFENIAE built strong alliances with national and international NGOs to protest oil development in the Amazon. In 1986, Conoco, a DuPont subsidiary, successfully bid for exploration rights of block 16, located within the Yasuní National Reserve. Environmental NGOs and CONFENIAE organized in response to Conoco's announcement of profitable oil deposits and plans for extraction. The major international NGOs that were involved in the affair with Conoco were: CARE, Cultural Survival, the Nature Conservancy, the Natural Resources Defense Council, Wildlife Conservation International, the Sierra Club, and the Rainforest Action Network.[49] While some links were made directly with the Huaorani, most links between international NGOs and the Amazonian indigenous peoples were made through CONFENIAE and its president, Valerio Grefa.

Throughout 1988 and 1989, international environmental NGOs worked with Ecuadorian NGOs and CONFENIAE to formulate alternative oil and environmental policies for the Yasuní Reserve. These NGOs organized press conferences, newspaper editorials, seminars, and international forums to make other aware of the situation in the Amazon. Through these transnational links, Yasuní was designated a Biosphere Reserve by UNESCO in 1989, and a world center for plant diversity and endemism under the IUCN-WWF (World Wildlife Fund) Plants Conservation Program.[50]

In 1990, the National Resources Defense Council (NRDC), a U.S.-based international nongovernmental organization specializing in the environment, became directly involved in the Conoco affair through its interactions with Judith Kimerling, an environmental attorney working in the Amazon, and Valerio Grefa of CONFENIAE. Robert Kennedy Jr.

and Jacob Scherr, the director of the NRDC's international program, asked Kimerling to show them the Amazonian region in question with Conoco. After their visit to the Amazon, they hired Kimerling and wrote to Edgar Woolard, the chairman of DuPont, to criticize Conoco's exploration plans. In November 1990, Conoco and the NRDC had a meeting in New York City without indigenous representatives. After the meeting, Kennedy and Scherr agreed to a compromise with Conoco.[51] Following negotiations and pressure from CONFENIAE, in coordination with NRDC and other NGOs, Conoco agreed to endorse a ten million dollar nonprofit foundation for indigenous peoples.

In March 1990, Kennedy and Scherr of NRDC coordinated efforts with the Amazonian indigenous peoples through CONFENIAE, and its president, Valerio Grefa. Grefa, Kennedy, and Scherr met with Conoco officials to discuss a compromise on the Yasuní Reserve exploration process. Grefa, on behalf of CONFENIAE, proposed that indigenous peoples receive one dollar per barrel of oil in block 16, or about $211 million. NRDC supported the CONFENIAE proposal.

About the same time, ONHAE, the Organization of the Huaorani Nation of the Ecuadorian Amazon, was formed. Until this point, the Huaorani were not part of any negotiations with regard to Conoco. Following the negotiations with Conoco, the Huaorani organized its people. ONHAE incorporates Huaorani community standards with western styles of organization including a vice-president, secretary, and treasurer named Moi, Amo, and Enqueri respectively. ONHAE mailed a letter to the Rainforest Action Network, protesting the exploration for petroleum within their territory.[52]

Previous to the formation of ONHAE, there were reports of Huaorani seizing oil-drilling sites, and attacking or stealing from oil company employees. The Taegeri, the most remote and isolated Huaorani, have been reported to have killed any outsiders who have tried to contact them. However, most protest and mobilization against the oil MNEs were locally organized and were not sustained over time.

Due to the letter from ONHAE and the international protest against the Conoco petroleum development plans, Conoco sent an anthropologist, James A. Yost, to speak with the Huaorani living in and around the area of land that they were to develop. At this point, the Huaorani had changed their mobilization strategies from violent protest to transnational contacts and efforts at negotiation with Conoco. Yost concluded that many of the Huaorani had had experiences with nonindigenous peoples due to oil exploration on their land. He reported that the Huaorani had seemed to absorb their environmental change with little change to their communities, however further loss of land would disturb their community living standards.[53] This was Conoco's first official contact with the Huaorani.

It is unknown exactly how many Huaorani ONHAE represents. Based on reports from Kimerling and Joe Kane, ONHAE has received few funds from international NGOs, and their leadership has remained unstable since its foundation in 1990. However, after Conoco included the Huaorani in its discussions of oil development in the Yasuní territory, the mobilization strategies of the Huaorani changed. While there were still local protests reported around oil development sites, ONHAE united the demands of its members and bargained directly with Conoco.

In 1991, direct negotiations among ONHAE, CONFENIAE, and international and national NGO's including NRDC began. Prior to negotiations, NRDC consulted with international NGOs, including Cultural Survival, National Wildlife Federation, and the Sierra Club. It also worked with national NGOs in Ecuador, including CORDAVI, Fundación Natura, and the Campaña Amazonia.[54]

In February 1991, Nanto and Moi of ONHAE, Kennedy and Scherr of NRDC, and Grefa of CONFENIAE, met with Conoco officials directly. In mid-May, Grefa tried to convince ONHAE to agree to the proposal of Kennedy and Scherr, allowing oil development for a percentage of the profits, but ONHAE refused. During the summer, CONFENIAE negotiated directly with Conoco without the aid of the NRDC. There have been no reports though of final agreements between CONFENIAE and Conoco. In September 1991, the Ecuadorian government approved the contract for Conoco's development of block 16. On October 11th, Conoco announced its withdrawal from the development project in block 16.[55] It sold its shares to Maxus Energy, a Dallas-based oil MNE.[56]

Maxus has utilized inclusionary policymaking with the Huaorani. They have directly contacted the Huaorani and have provided funds for health care facilities and bilingual education centers, and have vowed to improve their environmental standards to meet those of the Huaorani. For example, Maxus funds a secondary school in Toñampare. Furthermore, Maxus employs an anthropologist, Rossana Faieta, who contacts Huaorani members to understand their demands and issues. Since the Conoco affair, other oil MNEs have created positions and departments that deal directly with indigenous concerns, such as Petroecuador, Arco, and Texaco.

ONHAE has continued its strategy of direct MNE negotiations with Maxus. In May 1992, Nanto and Moi of ONHAE met with the general manager of Maxus, William Hutton, to discuss the Huaorani position on development of their lands. They also utilized new tactics such as newsletters and tape recordings of conversations to relay their information to other actors, including transnational NGOs.

However, since the change in MNE behavior toward indigenous peoples, mobilization strategies have not only changed, but protest has increased. In November 1992, Maxus constructed a road in Huaorani territory (the Yasuní Reserve). In protest, ONHAE organized 200 Huaorani to march from the Amazon to the Maxus offices in Quito. They camped outside the offices for two weeks. Violence increased to the point of assault against the Maxus anthropologist, Rossana Faieta. In August 1993, Maxus reached an agreement with ONHAE. Maxus would not release the agreement, but did state that it provided educational, health care, and other benefits to the Huaorani in return for development on their land.[57]

A recent report in the Multinational Monitor signifies an increase in the quasi-public nature of Maxus in this area of the Amazon. Reports state that critics of Maxus "worry about ceding it such fundamental government functions as health and education."[58] Neil Popovic, an attorney for the Sierra Club Legal Defense Fund, commented, "It's no longer clear who's supposed to do what. The Ecuadoran government has abdicated its responsibilities to private companies and has made no effort to regulate them."[59] In this case, oil MNEs have not only changed their behavior and influence indigenous organizations, but they have also changed their nature from private to public actors in the Ecuadorian landscape. Although government officials were present in negotiations with oil MNEs and indigenous peoples, the state is more of a mediator in this situation than an authority figure.

More recently, in July 1995, 200 Huaorani protested and stopped work at a Maxus installation. They demanded $3.00 per barrel for the 30,000 barrels pumped daily from their lands in the Yasuní Reserve. Negotiations between Maxus and ONHAE representatives are still taking place.[60]

Throughout their negotiations with Maxus, ONHAE increased their mobilization, suggesting that change in MNE behavior not only changes strategies, but also stimulates group mobilization. However, group organization is also a significant variable in the framework for analyzing collective action. Group organization must be strong to effectively negotiate with MNEs and sustain collective action.

ONHAE remains at medium level of organization due to internal problems. Moi and Nanto, its former leaders, do not agree on strategies. Amo, another former leader, died in 1991. Enqueri supports the strategy of compromise, while Moi supports violent protest. Prior to 1989, the Huaorani had a weak organization, few contacts with international and national NGOs, and MNEs excluded them from policymaking. Since the formation of ONHAE in 1990, the Huaorani have strengthened their organization to a medium level, and have increased their contacts with international NGOs. Furthermore, they directly participate with oil MNEs with regard to development of their land, education, and health care.

The inclusionary policies of Conoco and Maxus legitimated the role of ONHAE within the political policy process. Furthermore, ONHAE changed its strategies. It utilized transnational actors to disseminate information to the international community, and it utilized international NGO funds to travel within Ecuador, mainly to Quito, and to the United States. In 1994, for example, Moi traveled to Washington, D.C., through funding by the Sierra Club Legal Defense Fund to testify on behalf of the Huaorani before the Inter-American Commission on Human Rights, of the Organization of the American States (OAS).[61] The Huaorani have increased their resources, changed their strategies toward transnational linkages (including direct negotiations with MNEs), and have mobilized transnationally. MNEs played an integral role in their transformation. An assessment of the collective action of the Huaorani cannot overlook the significance of MNEs within the process. Currently, Maxus and ONHAE are establishing new educational programs and negotiating possibilities of profit-sharing.[62]

CONFENIAE, founded in 1980, was a strong organization prior to the 1989 Conoco proposals. It has a strong leadership, high membership, high levels of international NGO contact and resources (although they will not disclose figures), and has been included in many policy discussions between indigenous peoples in the Amazon and oil MNEs. CONFENIAE also has been legitimated as a political actor through its transnational linkages with international NGOs and oil MNEs. Its strategies have changed since its direct contacts with MNEs. CONFENIAE is not just located in the Amazon, but also has a national headquarters in Quito, with a professional staff, which regularly lobbies the government for changes in policy toward indigenous peoples. It has professionalized its mobilization from local and regional marches to international newsletter, e-mail connections, and media coverage. Because MNEs included CONFENIAE in the oil policy process, the national political role of CONFENIAE has been strengthened.

Aside from strategies, CONFENIAE has increased its levels of protest. CONFENIAE is a strong actor within the national indigenous organization, CONAIE. It has participated in protests with CONAIE in 1990, 1992, 1993, and 1994. These were national marches that shut down the country and blocked roads for as long as two weeks. In June 1994, CONFENIAE helped organize with CONAIE a blockage of over fifty-six access roads to oil-drilling sites, causing oil shortages within the country. Thus, the legitimation of the indigenous movement by transnational actors, including MNEs, has changed the mobilization strategies of CONFENIAE, but it has also provided new policies regarding indigenous peoples in the Amazon, such as better educational facilities, environmental protection regulations, and health care facilities, which are all negotiated by and provided by MNEs (in this case, Maxus).

OPIP

The Organization of Indigenous Peoples of Pastaza (OPIP) was founded in 1977 in response to the colonization of their lands since the early 1960s by oil companies and oil company employees. OPIP is comprised of Quichua indigenous peoples of Pastaza. There is a strong sense of identity among members and social networks among members are dense. Moreover, OPIP has received much national and international attention due to its organization of a march from the Amazon to Quito in 1992. Its resources from transnational actors are greater than those of the Huaorani and its links with transnational actors are close. Like the Huaorani and CONFENIAE, OPIP has directly negotiated with ARCO, the oil MNE developing resources in Pastaza. OPIP is the strongest member of CONFENIAE and is in the executive position of the national indigenous organization, CONAIE.

Direct negotiations with the government and oil MNEs also affected the mobilization and policy outcomes for OPIP. In May 1989, there were ten days of discussion between government officials, ARCO and Petroecuador representatives, and indigenous organizations, led by OPIP. The discussions took place in Sarayacu, an OPIP stronghold and one of the most politically active Quichua communities. OPIP blocked the air strip until an agreement was reached. The agreement was called the "Sarayacu Accords." The accords called for the cessation of oil exploration in the OPIP lands until they received compensation from oil companies for environmental destruction to the lands. It included a promise from the state to stop further exploration of natural resources that would harm the environment. The Sarayacu Accords presented the first step in negotiations between the state, indigenous peoples, and oil companies. OPIP had a major role in these meetings. It utilized the private power of oil MNEs and their relationships with the state to strengthen its role as a political actor during this time. Moreover, OPIP was aided through the resources of international and national NGOs.

Through the stature gained in the Sarayacu Accords, OPIP increased its mobilization. For instance, in 1990 the Borja administration opened a sixth round of oil exploration rights in block 10, the OPIP land. In response to this, OPIP organized a hunger strike by eighty-two people in the Santo Domingo Church in Quito, with CONFENIAE and CONAIE. The government surrounded the church, but by June 2, indigenous peoples in the Sierra, Napo, and Pastaza mobilized, blocked roads, and marched in the streets. On June 6, the Borja administration negotiated a settlement with CONAIE. By August 22, 1990, the Borja administration met with 120 indigenous leaders, including Leonardo Viteri, director of the Amazanga Institute, representing OPIP. The OPIP document demanded control over natural resources, including subsoil. It was rejected by the administration.[63]

Also in 1990, negotiations between ARCO and OPIP moved to San Francisco, California, which is the base of Rainforest Action Network (RAN). RAN began an international campaign of support for OPIP and organized international press releases and demonstrations against ARCO. RAN published the results of an environmental impact study of the OPIP area that denounced ARCO. In August 1991, ARCO asked for a meeting with RAN to debate the results of the RAN study. In this meeting, ARCO presented its results of an environmental impact study of block 10, which contradict those of RAN. As a result, OPIP proposed an independent study by the Center for Environmental Design Research of the University of California (CEDR), which ARCO and RAN accepted.

In March 1992, OPIP, ARCO, RAN, and Oxfam America met again in Berkeley to analyze the independent study results. CEDR concluded that ARCO's site was excellent, but not without environmental impact and gave a list of six suggestions in which ARCO could improve. ARCO accepted the criticisms and agreed to continue a dialogue with OPIP to prevent future conflicts. It also proposed another meeting in California with the same actors for June 1992 to discuss a second environmental evaluation.[64]

However, OPIP continued political action. On April 11, 1992, OPIP organized a march from Puyo in the Amazon to Quito of about 10,000 Quichua, Achuar, and Shiwiar peoples funded by Oxfam America and a grant from the Rainforest Action Network (RAN) of $20,000, among other NGO contributions.[65] In response to their protests, the Borja administration negotiated a land settlement with OPIP, granting their constituents 1,115,574 hectares of land, without subsoil rights. Again, this march, international support, and the land demarcation strengthened the organization and mobilization of OPIP.

In 1992, OPIP formed the Amazanga Institute, which provides a facility for negotiation between ARCO and OPIP representatives. The institute combines western and traditional technical support and research to develop environmental management plans for the Amazon, including satellite technology. They are also working with the oil industry to create environmental monitors in their area and train indigenous peoples to monitor their communities. In this case as well, OPIP has utilized the power and resources of oil MNEs to affect policy change in their region.

OPIP and ARCO have been engaged in dialogue to establish guidelines for further drilling of their land. A reserve of 700 million barrels of light crude was discovered in their territory. ARCO has accepted the criticisms of OPIP and has continued to negotiate with individual OPIP community leaders.[66]

In December 1993, OPIP called a general meeting at an oil well in Villano, the operating base of ARCO to protest ARCO's activities. About 400 members camped out in Villano for two nights. ARCO representatives met with indigenous leaders, thus affirming the strength of OPIP in the region. As a result of this meeting, Suzana Sawyer observed that "OPIP leadership and community members began to re-articulate the relations between multinationals and local communities and influence the particular pattern of resource extraction in their territory."[67] OPIP has continued its mobilization against oil development, such as its seizure of oil wells in the Lago Agrio area, near the Yasuní Reserve, in April 1995.[68] Currently, OPIP is continuing its research and work at the Amazanga Institute for further negotiation with ARCO.[69]

After the Villano meeting, ARCO invited four representatives of OPIP to meet with company executives in Dallas, Texas. The goal of this meeting was not just to discuss past events, but also future events, being that the Ecuadorian government had begun its seventh round of international licensing for blocks of land in the Amazon. As a result of this meeting, OPIP and ARCO agreed that ARCO would finance and complete two studies: one on the impacts of development and the other on socioeconomic impacts. To this date, this study has not been completed because ARCO has not received permission from the Ministry of Energy and Mines to build the pipeline that it needs for oil production.

Sixto Méndez, Manager of the Environment, Health, and Safety for ARCO, also noted that ARCO has invested in many social programs in the Pastaza community, such as medical clinics, more nurses and doctors, potable water, cattle-selling, and investment in Amazonian artisanship. ARCO's second phase of community development is to offer two university scholarships each year to Puyo residents and has already placed more teachers in the school system. Méndez commented that many times ARCO has more influence than the municipal governments with regard to demanding government programs. For instance, ARCO requested vaccinations from the Ministry of Health for the Pastaza province. He stated, "The government does not exist for indigenous peoples in this area."[70]

OPIP has increased its contacts with transnational actors since its inception in 1977. MNEs have also included OPIP in their policymaking processes, legitimating the political role of OPIP. Since ARCO has directly negotiated with OPIP, OPIP's organization and resources (transnationally and nationally) have strengthened. The change in MNE behavior has led OPIP to change its mobilization strategies. It now demands direct contact with ARCO representatives. It also has developed sophisticated facilities for researching oil development in the Amazon. OPIP has cultivated international newsletters and information dissemination through international NGOs, such as the RAN, Seventh Generation Fund, Oxfam America, the Inter-American Foundation, and the Coalition for Amazonian Peoples and Their Environment. Aside from inclusion within the oil policy process, OPIP has obtained land rights to its territory, which further strengthens its position in negotiations with oil MNEs.

The case of OPIP elucidates the significance of the private authority of oil MNEs in the global arena and at the social bases. Indigenous organizations recognize the resources to be gained from international and national NGOs, but also recognize the level of power to be gained through negotiations and programs with MNEs. Likewise, MNEs create social programs without state or local government aid, recognizing their role as public actors. Thus, MNEs have maintained their private nature and authority, while utilizing it in a quasi-public manner to improve conditions in Amazonian regions.

Cofán

The Cofán are a unique case in the Amazon because they have circumvented the state and filed suit against Texaco Oil Company in the United States. Although the Cofán are a small group and have fewer resources than others, they have utilized new, transnational strategies to change oil policy in their region. For instance, they have established an eco-tourism business in the Amazon through funding from international NGOs, such as RAN.

The Cofán indigenous peoples number from 460 to 1,200 peoples, depending upon various estimates. Their formal organization did not develop until 1990, in response to the alleged environmental destruction of their lands by Texaco oil company. The Cofán are represented in and act jointly with CONFENIAE. Prior to 1990, the Cofán had a strong identity, but low levels of mobilization and resources. However, since 1990, the Cofán have successfully mobilized and have gained transnational resources from U.S. law firms.

In November 1993, the Cofán filed a class-action suit in New York Federal Court against Texaco, seeking $1.5 billion in damages to be invested in a clean-up project. Cristóbal Bonifaz, of the law firm Khon, Nast, and Graf in Philadelphia, has donated his time and firm time and resources to their case. Judith Kimerling, an environmental attorney and author of *Amazon Crude*, has also joined the suit, aiding the Cofán.

This law suit challenges the national sovereignty of the Ecuadorian state. The Ecuadorian government has intervened on the side of Texaco, claiming that this lawsuit affronts its national sovereignty. Later, on November 25, 1996, the attorney general, Leonides Plaza, announced that the government was considering intervention on the plaintiff's behalf. The intervention of the state in this case points to two observations. First, the Ecuadorian state has lost some of its sovereignty to private actors. Second, the corporate power of Texaco is so important that the state intervened on its behalf. The state, at the same time, issued a general statement against ecological degradation by petroleum extraction. Thus, the state again must play the role of a mediator in this issue area.[71]

However, Judge Vincent Broderick has ruled that he will hear the case in New York if Texaco's decisions in the Cofán area were made in its New York offices. Since that time, Texaco has begun implementation of a clean-up program and has attempted to settle out of court with the Cofán. The following summer, 25,000 Peruvians also filed suit against Texaco for similar damages.[72] Thus far, all proposals have been rejected. The case is still pending.[73] The Ecuadorian case will be an example to other oil producing countries in the developing world.

Since this law suit, the Cofán have been consulted directly by oil companies about their land in the Cuyabeno Reserve. The state oil company, Petroecuador, has implemented negotiations to include the Cofán in drilling plans. Although the Cofán are a small group in the Amazon, their level of protest has increased since the inception of this law suit. For instance, in November 1993, members of the Cofán community forced workers off of a Petroecuador drilling site within the Cuyabeno Reserve.[74] Since making direct contact with MNEs, they have also changed their mobilization strategies to include transnational actors and to continue direct negotiations with oil MNEs, including Occidental, ARCO, Maxus, and Oryx.

SUMMARY AND CONCLUSIONS

Evidence from this chapter illustrates the significance of MNEs within the collective action process. Analysis of collective action cannot simply include MNEs in a framework as target actors. Rather, transnational actors must be analyzed individually, and their impacts must be measured based on their individual behavior with regard to societal actors and the state. In order to develop an understanding of the impacts of transnational actors upon societal actors and policy outcomes, MNEs must be examined as part of an exchange of transnational norms and information, in addition to the traditionally studied transnational actors, such as IGOs and international NGOs.

MNE behavior in the Ecuadorian Amazon is significant because a change in their behavior has also led to a change in indigenous mobilization and policies regarding indigenous peoples. The corporate power of MNEs, and their recognition of indigenous rights issues, opened the political opportunity of indigenous groups, nationally and transnationally.[75] Moreover, the change in MNE policies provided resources for indigenous peoples, such as educational and health care facilities.

After direct negotiations with MNEs, indigenous groups increased their level of mobilization and their level of political action, such as national protests, in addition to changing their mobilization strategies to frame their demands in terms of land demarcation and environmental protection. The tactics utilized for these strategies include international newsletters and direct proposals with MNEs. These once isolated indigenous actors became much more professional in their approach to the petroleum industry, establishing national offices in Quito (where oil MNEs are located) and e-mail connections. Recently, the indigenous communities of Ecuador have formed a new political movement, Pachakutic, and have won seats in the National Congress. They will also seek alliances with other political parties who share their principles. Thus, indigenous actors have become proactive in their mobilization and have utilized the power of oil MNEs in negotiations for social policies.

Some qualifications must be made however with regard to the level of inclusion and negotiation in the policy process of the state and MNEs. I do not assert that indigenous groups have been successful in the achievement of all of their goals with regard to oil development or oil MNEs, nor do I assert that they have been completely included in the state policy process. Rather, this chapter seeks to broaden the framework for analyzing the social impacts of MNEs. There have been reports of MNE policies aimed at dividing the leadership of indigenous groups, and unfulfilled promises of clean-up for oil spills in indigenous lands. Further analysis of the implementation of negotiated agreements is also needed. Moreover, a complete analysis of the indigenous movement in Ecuador cannot overlook the internal dynamics of the individual organizations and the relations between indigenous organizations. However, previous studies have assumed that MNEs were solely target actors, and have not examined their impacts directly upon group mobilization. Indigenous groups have moved toward negotiations with MNEs, which warrants further examination of MNEs as transnational actors participating in information exchanges.

Furthermore, MNEs have assumed the role of a quasi-public actor in the sense that they have been responding to policy requests from the indigenous Amazonian populations. Conoco, Maxus, ARCO, and Texaco have all participated in direct negotiations with indigenous peoples for environmental security and development, natural resource management plans, health care, education, and transportation and infrastructure. These issues are those typically associated with the public sphere.

Moreover, MNEs and indigenous peoples have negotiated without the presence of state representatives. Maxus has initiated its own environmentally safe policies since 1991. It also funds a bilingual school without government support. ARCO representatives and Quichua peoples have been developing resource management plans through the Amazanga Institute, and even met in California and Texas without state officials. Although the Ecuadorian government has tried to intervene, Amazonian peoples have filed suit against Texaco in the United States for environmental destruction of their lands. Maxus, ARCO, and Texaco all have representatives that act as liaisons between indigenous organizations and the MNE. The most striking example of the MNE as quasi-public is the fact that Amazonian peoples have politically acted with regard to two actors: the state and MNEs. They have focused their desire for policy change on both actors as well. Much of the mobilization has been focused on oil MNEs in the Amazon, as opposed to demanding state intervention. Thus, MNEs have acquired a role independent of the state in the Amazon.

This is not to argue that the state is insignificant in this analysis, but rather acts as a mediator in issue-areas where it does not have the resources or does not want the responsibility to act. Indigenous peoples and the environment are two issue-areas in which states are sensitive to penetration from transnational actors. In Ecuador, oil MNEs also maintain a high level of private authority that includes them in the debate over natural resource extraction. Thus, the struggle for indigenous rights, oil extraction, and the environment has compelled private as well as public actors to become involved. As Martin J. Scurrah asserts, "This partial abdication of the state's responsibilities means that the final outcome in the protection-exploitation trade-offs will be largely determined by the play of political and economic forces beyond its control and with results not necessarily to its liking."[76]

There is further evidence that the indigenous movement is expanding. For example, indigenous leaders from South America joined together at the Latin American Studies Association Meetings in Washington, D.C., in September 1995. In November 1995, Amazon indigenous representatives from South America, including Peru, Bolivia, Colombia, Ecuador, and Venezuela, gathered in the northeastern region of Ecuador together with INGOs from the Coalition in Support of Amazonian Peoples and Their Environment. The representatives spoke with

Amazonian leaders in areas greatly affected by oil development and exchanged strategies for negotiations with oil MNEs. This project will continue with a report of the oil MNEs that are present in each country.[77] Finally, people in Nigeria have followed the path of the Cofán and have filed suit against Shell Oil Company in the United States for environmental destruction of their lands due to petroleum development.[78]

Transnational links among private actors have been increasing in the international system. However, states are not the only actors affected by these links. We need to go beyond the level of analysis of the state to societal and international levels, recognizing links between the three levels. MNEs no longer negotiate solely at the state level. They too have influenced the level of societal actors. The case of indigenous peoples in Ecuador represents one example of societal change based not only on the domestic level, but also based upon the change in political opportunities facilitated by private, transnational actors, namely MNEs. Further analysis of MNEs and their impacts upon the societal level will increase our understanding of the embedded nature of private authority and its relationships with public authority in the international system.

NOTES

Part of the research for this project was conducted with funding from the Institute for the Study of World Politics (ISWP), Washington, D.C. I would like to thank the ISWP and La Universidad Andina de Simón Bolívar, Quito, Ecuador for their support during my field research investigation.

1. A. Claire Cutler, Virginia Haulfer, and Tony Porter, "Private Authority and International Regimes," paper presented at the Workshop on Private Power, Public Power, and International Regimes, San Diego, April 16, 1996.

2. Philip G. Cerny, "Globalization and the Changing Logic of Collective Action," *International Organization* 49.4 (1995): 329–39.

3. Cutler et al., "Private Authority," p. 8.

4. A. Claire Cutler, "Global Capitalism and Liberal Myths: Dispute Settlement in Private International Trade Relations," *Millennium: Journal of International Studies* 24.3 (1995): 377–97.

5. Cutler et al., "Private Authority," p. 8.

6. Cutler, "Global Capitalism."

7. Stephen D. Krasner, "Structural Causes and Regime Consequences: Regimes as Intervening Variables," in Stephen D. Krasner, ed., *International Regimes* (Ithaca: Cornell University Press, 1983).

8. See Robert Keohane, *International Institutions and State Power* (Boulder Colo.: Westview Press, 1989).

9. Donald J. Puchala and Raymond F. Hopkins, "International Regimes: Lessons from Inductive Analysis," in Stephen D. Krasner, ed., *International*

Regimes (Ithaca: Cornell University Press, 1983); Oran R. Young, "The Politics of Regime Formation: Managing Natural Resources and the Environment," in F. Kratochwil and E. D. Mansfield, eds., *International Organization: A Reader* (New York: HarperCollins, 1994).

10. Ernst B. Haas, "Words Can Hurt You; Or, Who Said What to Whom about Regimes," in Stephen D. Krasner, ed., *International Regimes* (Ithaca: Cornell University Press, 1983).

11. Virginia Haufler, "Crossing the Boundary between Public and Private: International Regimes and Non-State Actors," in Volker Rittberger, ed., *Regime Theory and International Relations* (Oxford: Clarendon Press, 1993).

12. Susan Strange, "Cave! Hic Dragones: A Critique of Regime Analysis," in Stephen D. Krasner, ed., *International Regimes* (Ithaca: Cornell University Press, 1983).

13. Ibid., p. 337.

14. Haufler, "Crossing the Boundary," p. 13.

15. Ibid., p. 10.

16. Ibid., p. 13.

17. See Margaret Keck and Kathryn Sikkink, "Transnational Issue Networks in International Politics," paper presented at the 91st meeting of the *American Political Science Association*, August 31–September 3, 1995.

18. Cutler et al., "Private Authority," p. 11.

19. Keck and Sikkink, "Transnational Issue Networks," p. 2.

20. M. J. Peterson, "Transnational Activity, International Society and World Politics," *Millenium* 21.3 (1992): 371.

21. Alison Brysk, "Acting Globally: Indian Rights and International Politics in Latin America," in Donna Lee Van Cott, ed., *Indigenous Peoples and Democracy in Latin America* (New York: St. Martin's Press, 1994), p. 371.

22. Cerny, "Globalization," p. 620.

23. Paul Wapner, "Bringing Society Back In: Environmental Governance and World Sociology," paper presented at the Annual Meeting of the International Studies Association, April 1996, p. 10. See also Ronnie D. Lipschutz, "Reconstructing World Politics: The Emergence of Global Civil Society," in *Millennium, Journal of International Studies* 21.3 (1992): 389–420, which examines the way in which transnational political networks link domestic and international actors.

24. Virginia Haufler, "Private International Regimes and Corporate Norms," paper presented at the Workshop on Private Power, Public Power, and International Regimes, San Diego, California, April 16, 1996, p. 12.

25. John M. Stopford and Susan Strange with John S. Henley, *Rival States, Rival Firms: Competition for World Market Shares* (Cambridge: Cambridge University Press, 1991), p. 225.

26. Haufler, "Private International Regimes."

27. Stopford and Strange, *Rival States.*

28. Peter Evans, *Embedded Autonomy: States and Industrial Transformation* (Princeton: Princeton University Press, 1995).

29. Eduardo Silva, "From Dictatorship to Democracy: The Business-State Nexus in Chile's Economic Transformation, 1975–1994," *Comparative Politics*, April 1996, pp. 299–330.

30. My thanks to Dr. Edward Comor, American University, for his helpful suggestions on this concept.

31. Chris Jochnik, "Amazon Oil Offensive," *Multinational Monitor* 26.1–2: Jan./Feb. 1995, p. 8.

32. Ibid., p. 8.

33. Thoughts on this subject are derived from Haufler, "Private International Regimes."

34. John D. Martz, *Politics and Petroleum in Ecuador* (New Brunswick, N.J.: Transaction Books, 1987), p. 41.

35. Catherine Conaghan and John Malloy, *Unsettling Statecraft* (Ithaca: Cornell University Press, 1994), p. 28.

36. Martz, *Politics and Petroleum*, pp. 105–9.

37. Ibid., p. 124.

38. Ibid., pp. 133–54.

39. Christopher Brogan, "The Retreat from Oil Nationalism in Ecuador, 1976–1983" in *University of London Institute of Latin American Studies Working Papers* (London: University of London, 1984), pp. 29–36.

40. Raymond Colitt, "Fueling Petroleum Output," *Business Latin America* 28: April 19, 1993, p. 6.

41. Raymond Colitt, "Business Outlook: Ecuador," *Business Latin America* 28: November 29, 1993, p. 5.

42. George Psacharopoulos and Harry Anthony Patrinos, *Indigenous Peoples and Poverty in Latin America* (Washington, D.C.: The World Bank, 1994), p. 28.

43. Jordan R. Pandor, "Desarrollo y Poblaciones Indígenas de América Latina y el Caribe," *Instituto Indígenista Americano and the FAO* (1990), applying UN Population Estimates from 1995.

44. "Las Nacionalidades Indígenas en el Ecuador: Nuestro Proceso Organizativo," *CONAIE* (Quito: Ediciones Abya-Yala, 1989), pp. 35–37. I estimate 120,000 people because exact numbers of these groups have not been surveyed. The numbers in parentheses are approximations based on academic studies.

45. Melina H. Selverston, "The Politics of Culture: Indigenous Peoples and the State in Ecuador," in Donna Lee Van Cott, ed., *Indigenous Peoples and Democracy in Latin America* (New York: St. Martin's Press, 1994), p. 136.

46. Ibid., pp. 135–36.

47. Please see table 9.2.

48. Ideas on the concept of group organization were derived from the work of Ted Robert Gurr and Barbara Harff, *Ethnic Conflict in World Politics* (Boulder, Colo.: Westview Press, 1994).

49. Joe Kane, *Savages* (New York: Alfred A. Knopf, 1995), p. 54.

50. Judith Kimerling, *Amazon Crude* (Washington, D.C.: National Resources Defense Council, 1991), pp. 33, 89.

51. Kane, *Savages*, p. 60.

52. Ibid., p. 62.

53. Ibid., p. 67.

54. "NRDC's Actions on Conoco's Proposed Oil Development in Ecuador," Natural Resources Defense Council, Washington, D.C., pp. 2–4.

55. Natural Resources Defense Council, "NRDC's Actions," pp. 2–4.

56. Joe Kane, "Letter from the Amazon," *The New Yorker* 69.31: September 27, 1993, p. 69.

57. Kane, "Letter," pp. 77–78.

58. Jochnik, "Amazon Oil Offensive," p. 8.

59. Ibid.

60. "Ecuador," *The Energy Economist*, July 1995, p. 14.

61. Joe Kane, "Moi Goes to Washington," *The New Yorker* 70.11 (May 2, 1994): 74.

62. Greg Barker, "Ecuador: Troubled Oil Sector," *Business Latin America*, April 19, 1993, p. 6.

63. Fernando Serrano, "The Transformation of the Indian Peoples of the Ecuadorian Amazon into Political Actors and Its Effects on the State's Modernization Policies" (Master's thesis, University of Florida, 1993).

64. Hector Villamil, President OPIP, from the Archives of Acción Ecológica (NGO), 1997.

65. Rainforest Action Network (RAN), "Protect-an-Acre Grants Given in the Amazonian Countries," Archives of RAN 1995.

66. "The Struggle of the Organization of Indigenous Peoples of Pastaza— OPIP Newsletter," *Seventh Generation Fund*, January 1994, pp. 1–3.

67. Suzana Sawyer, "Indigenous Initiatives and Petroleum Politics in the Ecuadorian Amazon," *Cultural Survival Quarterly*, Spring 1996, p. 27.

68. *The Energy Economist*, July 1995, p. 14.

69. Interview, Leonardo Viteri, Technical Consultant for OPIP and President, Amazanga Institute, March, 7, 1997.

70. Interview, Sixto Méndez, Manager, Health, Environment and Safety, ARCO Oriente, Inc., January 19, 1997.

71. Coalition for Amazonian Peoples and Their Environment, "Amazon Update #9," December 15, 1995.

72. Jochnik, "Amazon Oil Offensive," p. 5.

73. Glenn Switkes, "The People vs. Texaco," *NACLA Report on the Americas* 28.2 (Sept./Oct. 1994): 6–10.

74. Raymond Colitt, "Business Outlook: Ecuador," *Business Latin America* 28: November 29, 1993, pp. 4–5.

75. For more on the notion of political opportunity structures, see Charles Tilly, *From Mobilization to Revolution* (New York: McGraw-Hill, 1978); Sidney Tarrow, *Power in Movement: Social Movements, Collective Action, and Politics* (Cambridge: Cambridge University Press, 1994). I argue that private transnational actors, in this case MNEs, can alter political opportunity structures within the state or on a transnational level.

76. Martin J. Scurrah, "Lessons from Environmental Struggles in the Andes," paper presented at the 1995 Meeting of the Latin American Studies Association, Washington, D.C., September 28–30, 1995, p. 4.

77. Coalition, "Amazon Update #9."

78. See, *International Herald Tribune*, November 18, 1995, p. 12.

PART 4

The Evolution of Public and Private International Authority

CHAPTER 10

Hegemony and the Private Governance of International Industries

Tony Porter

Is there a pattern in the historical development of private authority internationally? This chapter suggests that there is, but that history does not display a smooth unilinear international growth in private authority over time. Rather the pattern is closely related to two cyclical features of the world economy: the rise and decline of British and U.S. hegemony and the rise and decline of the leading industries that fueled each hegemon's ascendance.[1] In this pattern, knowledge, as in other chapters, plays a key role in the production of private authority, as much for its role in structuring activity as for communicating information about existing conditions. In particular this chapter focuses on technological knowledge and its role in promoting cohesion of leading firms and in preserving their lead over other firms. This process of cohesion and control, an important aspect of private authority, varies along with the rise and fall of hegemony and of leading industries.

I develop these points by comparing certain organizational features of the international political economy at the time of the rise and then decline of British and U.S. hegemony respectively. In each case I begin with an examination of a particular leading industry that has come to be emblematic for ascendence of that hegemony—cotton for Britain and automobiles for the United States. These leading industries are significant not just because of their sizeable contribution to value-added in the hegemon's national economy, but also because they pioneered new forms of industrial and social organization upon which that hegemony was based: the industrial revolution itself is most closely associated with cotton and Fordism[2] with automobiles. Both industries were also closely associated with the hegemon's international presence.

257

In each case leading firms were initially able to exercise authority with respect to international markets with the help of a set of private social institutions centralized in the hegemon's territory. Technology flowed freely among these firms, contributing to the centralized critical mass of producers needed to sustain the new industry and the private authority associated with it. Geographic and social distances inhibited diffusion of technical knowledge to potential competitors in other countries, further enhancing the capacity of leading firms to maintain their lead and to exercise authority in international markets. The state's most important role with regard to these growing leading industries was to respond to the socioeconomic paradigm that they represented by undermining previous social institutions and sources of private authority.

In examining the more mature periods of each hegemony I shift to a more general analysis of the organization of international industries, reflecting the diminished importance of the leading industry that had fueled hegemonic ascendence. The strengthening of the patent regime as each hegemon declined is of particular interest. This strengthening involves a more prominent presence of the state that is closely related to the evolution of knowledge, hegemony, leading industries, and private authority. As the hegemon's leading industries mature, the tacit technological knowledge that previously had facilitated the cohesion of leading firms and their dominance of markets becomes more codified and is more easily disseminated. Leading firms from the hegemonic economy are no longer able to exert control by themselves. Private authority thereby diminishes. In the case of both British and U.S. hegemonic decline, however, private actors were able to have states strengthen the patent regime. This allows more explicit and formal control over knowledge flows and becomes the basis of renewed and more multilateral private cooperation, allowing the reinvigoration of private international authority. In the wake of British hegemony, this reinvigorated private international authority was evident in the cartel movement, for which the strengthened patent regime was an important tool for encouraging collaboration. Presently the proliferation of strategic alliances, which resemble the earlier cartels in some important respects, also works in conjunction with the strengthened intellectual property regime.

These patterns have some important implications for our understanding of private international authority and for policy more generally. *First*, as is evident from the other chapters in this book, markets are not simply composed of atomistic, competitive firms engaged in arm's length interactions. Rather, firms create private interfirm institutions and these allow them to authoritatively structure an industry. *Second*, an excessive emphasis on the novelty of private authority is problematic for both scholarly and practical reasons: it leads us to miss recurring patterns in the relationship between private and public authority and it obscures important policy lessons from the past. The case of U.S. antitrust policy, to which I devote some attention below, is illustrative. After World War II the United States vigorously used antitrust policy to delegitimize cartels, opening the field for the mode of socioeconomic organization associated with its leading firms, the oligopolistic but relatively autonomous multinational corporations. Fifty years later, antitrust policy was being modified to permit forms of interfirm collaboration that had been targeted previously, justified by the novelty of contemporary global competition. This chapter suggests that there are more similarities with the earlier period than is often recognized and that its negative lessons should be taken more seriously. The *third* implication of these patterns in the development of private international authority is for our understanding of interstate regimes. The strengthening of patent regimes had much less to do with the type of interstate interactions upon which international relations theory conventionally focuses than with a prior evolution of private authority.

I turn now to the cases, looking first at the emergence of cotton as a leading industry when British hegemony was ascendant, then at the period of British decline during which the patent regime was strengthened, in the late nineteenth century, and the cartelization movement, which reached its height in the interwar period. I then look at the organization of the automobile industry at the beginning of U.S. hegemony and the role of the U.S. state at the end of World War II in destroying cartels as a competing form of industrial organization. Finally, I turn to the strengthening of the patent regime in the Uruguay Round of the General Agreement on Tariffs and Trade and the growth of new forms of interfirm cooperation, indicating the similarities between this period and the evolution of private authority as British hegemony declined.

BRITISH HEGEMONY AND THE GOVERNANCE OF COTTON

In this section I will show that the organization of the international cotton industry during the period of British hegemonic ascendance was made possible by the private authority that emerged from a dense network of social institutions centred in Manchester and Liverpool. Cotton markets, then, were not simply an aggregate of atomized arm's length transactions, nor were they primarily organized by the state. In this early period, private authority was facilitated by an informal control of knowledge, enhanced by the geographic and cultural distance between the center of the cotton industry and potential competitors abroad, and by the novelty and lack of codification of the technology upon which the industry was based.

In his extensive study of the organization of Manchester merchants, Redford[3] confirms Adam Smith's famous comment at the time about the propensity of owners to engage "always and everywhere in a sort of tacit, but constant and uniform combination.[4] Edwards concludes after a narrative account of the relationships in this period that "it seems that the price of [cotton] yarn was determined by a few large spinners."[5] This did not just involve the domestic market:

> Naturally, the changes in industrial organization called for corresponding changes in commercial relations. The new industrial capitalists were manufacturing on a scale which demanded free access to world-wide markets; they early realized the necessity for organization in defence of their common interests.[6]

At the heart of this organization in cotton's innovative period were a sequence of Manchester and Liverpool associations. The most notable Manchester associations included the Manchester Committee for the Protection and Encouragement of Trade and the Cotton Manufacturers' Company (founded 1774), the Manchester Commercial Society (founded 1794), the Manchester Chamber of Commerce (founded 1820), and the Liverpool Cotton Brokers' Association (founded 1841). The two organizations founded in 1774 illustrate the role of these private associations in shaping the activities of both private and state actors. The Committee for the Protection and Encouragement of Trade conducted active campaigns to prevent the diffusion of technology to foreigners and to expand the access of the merchants to foreign supply of cotton by weakening state controls over shipping. While the Cotton Manufacturers' Company did not outlive the stress of the war with the United States, it did for a number of years seek to stabilize prices by purchasing cotton for the manufacturers as a whole. There is evidence that more informal price-fixing and market-sharing agreements continued to be well established in the first decade of the nineteenth century.[7] The Manchester Commercial Society sought to enforce proper business practices at home and abroad by developing a capacity for collective boycott of offending firms, to keep open the links between British, German, Swiss, and Italian markets during the war in Europe at the end of the century,[8] and to help collect foreign debts owed to British cotton merchants.

Although there were periods of difficulty for these associations the overall trajectory was toward increasing institutionalization. By the 1830s the Manchester Chamber of Commerce had a well-developed structure, between 230 and 320 member firms, and had become "a most influential body dealing with a wide variety of questions, concerning fiscal and financial policy, foreign and imperial trade, company law, and many other aspects of commercial life."[9] Perhaps the best-known campaign of the Manchester merchants was for free trade and the abolition of the Corn Laws, which was brought about in 1846.[10]

The Liverpool based institutions were focused on the supply of raw cotton and experienced a similar trajectory of institutionalization to the Manchester associations. Initially these institutions were informal but hardly atomized as is evident in the careful description by Ellison of the specific buildings that they met in, the few key families that organized the trade, and their distinctive dress. Even after the formation of the Cotton Brokers' Association in 1841 the informal norms continued to be important:

> For many years after the formation of the Association, the business of the market was conducted on the lines of an unwritten code, which clearly defined the functions, and plainly set forth the rights and duties, of both merchants and brokers, in their individual capacities and in their conduct towards each other.[11]

Brokers and their clients had exclusive mutual commitments to each other:

> it was against the etiquette of the market for any broker, buying or selling, to poach, as it was called, upon the ground of any fellow broker . . . guerrilla warfare in the manufacturing districts brought down upon the delinquents universal condemnation.[12]

Ellison, writing at the time, gives a detailed account of the formalization of these institutions as competitive pressures increased. Ultimately the monopoly of the brokers over the cotton trade was broken and a new set of arrangements governing the trade were administered by a dramatically reformed and renamed Liverpool Cotton Association with seventeen specific articles in its founding agreement. A similar process of institutionalization occurred with the payments system for cotton passing through Liverpool.[13]

This account of the evolution of cotton institutions in Manchester and Liverpool indicates that markets did not merely involve atomized individual actors engaged in arm's length transactions. On the contrary, elaborate private institutions were created to coordinate activity, enforce compliance, and achieve political goals. This relied on a blending of informal norms and formal rules, of voluntary compliance and the imposition of sanctions. In short, we see the emergence and deployment of private authority.

The above account primarily focuses on the role of private authority in organizing the leading firms and individuals in the cotton industry itself. We are interested as well, however, in the degree to which the emergence of this private authority extended beyond these actors. There are two indications that such influence was not negligible. The first of these is the ability of the cotton industry to use the British state to achieve its goals with respect to other actors. The dramatic success of the Manchester Chamber of Commerce, noted above, in bringing about free trade, is a key example, but the Manchester associations also waged a successful campaign to weaken competing older institutional arrangements for organizing international markets, the control of the state-chartered East India and Levant Companies over the Middle Eastern and Asian markets. These state-chartered companies were criticized as too sluggish. For instance, the East India Company's land and transport taxes were so onerous that they discouraged Indian farmers from supplying cotton to Manchester—a key policy goal of the British cotton producers and merchants who were wary of their increasing dependence on U.S. supply. Similarly, the East India Company was slow to institute steam-driven mail delivery, a key improvement in communications technology for the merchants. The Levant Company, until the Manchester merchants succeeded in having it abolished in 1825, controlled all access to the Turkish empire.[14]

Although information is not as plentiful on the relationship between the social institutions at the center of the cotton industry and the industry's periphery, there is good reason to suspect that the private authority generated by the former also extended to the latter. In part this would have been exercised by the dependence of peripheral firms on the Liverpool institutions for selling cotton. The centralization of the cloth market in London helped sustain international linkages as between a half and a third of London merchants were foreigners. The London merchants also traveled extensively abroad and set up retail establishments in distant locations such as Rio and Monte Video. Cross-border partnerships were common even in the first decade of the nineteenth century as with Kirkman Finlay of Glasgow, who had warehouses in Malta, New Orleans, New Providence, and the Bahamas, and, in 1803, a network of 700 correspondents in Europe. In short, the channeling of cotton products, from plantation to retail sale, through a set of institutional arrangements centered in Britain, facilitated the exercise of private authority by the Manchester and Liverpool merchants over the industry as a whole.[15]

The Role of Technology

Centralized private authority in the cotton industry was further enhanced by the processes by which knowledge was diffused among the leading firms and restricted from diffusing to other actors. The critical mass of cotton production that clustered around Manchester, which was needed to sustain the institutions discussed above, would not have developed without the diffusion of the new technologies. The flow of technology within and among British firms was primarily managed by informal private arrangements and not the patent system. Griffiths, Hunt, and O'Brien find that in the eighteenth century only 44 percent of 174 key inventions in the textile industry were patented.[16] Indeed a key upsurge in innovation occurred after the patents of the most famous innovator, Arkwright, were broken following a sustained effort by a private institution, the Manchester Committee for the Protection and Encouragement of Trade.[17] Firms attempted to control the diffusion of their technology by prohibiting the visit of competitors to their factories, but these were not very effective.

In contrast to this relatively free flow of information among British participants in the cotton industry, both the state and geographic distance acted to slow the diffusion of British technology to foreign competitors. The state enacted laws to prohibit the emigration of skilled craftspeople.[18] Attempts were made, as with domestic competitors, to prohibit factory visits by foreigners. It seems likely that the latter was more successful given the distance that foreigners needed to travel, and the absence at the international level of developed labor markets and other social institutions to offset the efforts to control diffusion. Over time, of course, the efforts to control the flow of technology were ultimately unsuccessful. Efforts to obtain knowledge of British production practices through the luring abroad of British workers and the smuggling of machines intensified in the first decades of the nineteenth century and the regulations that had sought to prevent technology transfer were scrapped for workers in 1824 and for machines in 1843.[19]

There are several indications that the Manchester cotton industry was losing its unique position and that competition was intensifying by the early 1830s. The records of the Manchester Chamber of Commerce in 1833 indicate increasing alarm among member firms as American firms began to interfere with their access to American raw cotton and displace British exports to Mexico and South America, and as lower-cost producers were expanding in France, Switzerland, Germany, Austria, and Italy.[20]

Looking overall, then, at the rise of the cotton industry at the time of British hegemonic ascendence, the presence of the institutionalized private arrangements that fostered the rise of private authority is evident. These extended their influence not just over leading firms and peripheral cotton firms, but also over the state, and consequently over actors outside the cotton industry. The free flow of knowledge at home and control over its international diffusion enhanced these arrangements by contributing to the construction of a geographically centralized community of firms in Manchester and Liverpool, and by forestalling the emergence of competitors from abroad. In the next section it will be apparent that these types of arrangements did not remain viable and a different relationship between state and private authority then developed.

THE ORGANIZATION OF INTERNATIONAL INDUSTRIES WITH THE WANING OF BRITISH HEGEMONY

In the second half of the nineteenth century the type of arrangements that had sustained the international exercise of private authority in the cotton industry had decayed, undermined by the proliferation of competing cotton producers in other countries, by the emergence of other industries vying for influence over the British and other states, and by the diminished stature of the British state in the world as a whole. In this section I contrast the international organization of private authority from 1869 to 1939 with the earlier case of private authority in the cotton industry. I focus in particular on differences in the way in which the regulation of the international diffusion of knowledge was used to sustain centralized private authority. There are two steps in this process. In the first, states were called upon by private actors to regulate the international flow of knowledge by the construction of a patent regime. Formalized, explicit rules provided by states therefore replaced the regulation of knowledge flows by informal procedures and by the effects of cultural and geographic distances. In the second step, following World War I, these new rules were used by private actors to construct powerful, multinational, and often very formal forms of private international organization—the cartels—leading to an unprecedented growth of international private authority.

The Nineteenth-Century International Patent Regime

Patents have always had an ambivalent effect with regard to the flow of technology. On the one hand they confer a temporary monopoly on the holder of the patent and thereby restrict the flow of technology. On the other hand they provide rewards to inventors and thereby stimulate the production of new knowledge. Moreover, some patent laws, such as compulsory working or licensing provisions, attempt to promote an orderly diffusion of technology.[21]

During the nineteenth century the balance of power between proponents and opponents of patent laws corresponded to the ascendance and decline of free trade and British hegemony. In the early part of the century country after country adopted patent laws, but by mid-century the opponents of patents had gained the upper hand. In England in 1869 the *Economist* predicted that patent laws would be abolished. Bismarck supported abolition and the Dutch repealed their patent laws from 1869 to 1910.

The tide turned decisively in favor of patent rights with the Vienna Congress of 1873 and the Paris Conference of 1878. The Vienna Congress was stimulated by the concern, most notably on the part of Americans, that participants in an Austro-Hungarian sponsored exposition of that year would not enjoy adequate protection for their inventions. The Congress was sponsored privately but 13 of the 158 participants were representatives of states. German participants predominated. The Congress established for the first time an international endorsement of patent protection, although this was qualified by support for compulsory licensing. It also set up a preparatory committee the work of which led to the convening of the Paris Conference five years later.

The Paris Conference of 1878, like the earlier Congress, was unofficial, although it was sponsored by the French government and included 11 representatives of states among its nearly 500 participants. The support for patent laws was much stronger than the earlier Congress. The principle of national treatment was established.

In 1880 in Paris this preparatory work culminated in the first official international conference on patent rights, involving nineteen governments. In in turn initiated a process of negotiation that culminated in the International Union for the Protection of Industrial Property of 1884, to which most countries acceded, including the United Kingdom and France in 1884, the United States in 1887, Japan in 1899, and Germany in 1903.

The posthegemonic dispersion of international economic activity across countries and economic sectors is a key factor in explaining the fluctuation in support for patent rights over the course of the nineteenth century. As was noted above with respect to cotton, British firms relied on informal institutions to manage the flow of technology and would therefore have felt little need for international patent protection. Indeed, their own growth had been stimulated by the breaking of Arkwright's patents. The export of British technology was embedded in the machinery, managers, or skilled workers that flowed abroad and the resulting income flows were allocated through the market or informal agreement. The interests of foreign firms, intent on acquiring British technology, would not have been served by strong international patent laws.

By the latter part of the nineteenth century, however, this configuration of private interests had altered significantly. The influential role of the United States in the Vienna Congress exemplified this: U.S. industry had developed to a point that exports were desired but the informal mechanisms earlier available to the British firms were not an option for U.S. firms. The British, while not the leaders in the negotiation of the regime, recognized its worth given the diminished organizational capacity of their firms. The prominent role of private actors, including the forty-eight Chambers of Commerce represented at the 1878 Paris Conference, indicates the degree to which states were being asked to provide a regime within which a new level of negotiated private arrangements could be brought about.[22]

International Cartels in the Interwar Period

In the period between World Wars I and II, firms joined international private formalized collaborative arrangements of an unprecedented number and complexity. In industry after industry cartels were set up that were governed by highly specific market-sharing commitments and were often consolidated by license sharing, formal international organization, joint production facilities, and mechanisms for monitoring and enforcing compliance.[23] Estimates placed the proportion of goods sold under cartel control in 1939 in the United States—hardly the center of cartel activity—at 87 percent for mineral products, 60 percent for agricultural products, and 42 percent for manufactured products.[24] In many industries virtually all international trade was controlled by cartels. As Stocking and Watkins put it, "even in those countries where economic liberalism had taken firm hold, notably England and the United States, businessmen were rejecting competition as a regulator of economic activity and turning with increasing frequency to cartels to temper competitive forces and diminish business risks."[25] The patent system was a key mechanism used to enhance cartel solidarity. As Hexner noted, "in addition to corporate controls and trademarks, patents were the only tie 'legitimate' all over the world which could be used to bind entrepreneurs in marketing controls."[26]

The cartel period marked an unprecedented growth in private international authority. Like the earlier experience of the cotton industry, this authority was fostered by the development of formal and informal institutions and by the control and diffusion of knowledge. The latter period was significantly more complex however. The cartels were multinational and were based to a much greater degree on formalized rules governing the flow of knowledge, rules that were in turn based on a patent regime negotiated, at the behest of firms, by states. This allowed the strong exercise of private authority over the leading firms involved in the cartels, but it also allowed those firms to influence states, and thereby to extend the private authority associated with the cartels to other actors. In many cases the division of markets, and thereby cartel solidarity, was secured by the acquisition by cartel members of high national tariffs. The exercise of authority went beyond influence over these industry-specific state policies however. Cartels began to be promoted by their participants, and were seen by many other citizens, as a beneficial new form of social organization that could contribute to world peace, to the stabilization of international markets, to ensuring orderly transfer of innovations, and as a rational way to cope with the negative effects of excess capacity.[27]

One might assume from this account that we are seeing a long-range and unilinear growth in institutionalization of all kinds at the international level. In the next section we will see that this was not the case. The automobile industry, contributing to and benefiting from the rise of U.S. hegemony, never adopted a cartel form of private international organization. Nor did it rely on patents to sustain private authority. As we shall see, it resembled in important respects the early cotton industry, suggesting that the changes I have discussed above are part of a cyclical patttern associated with the ebb and flow of hegemony.

U.S. HEGEMONY, AUTOMOBILES, AND INTERNATIONAL PRIVATE AUTHORITY

In this section I will start by looking at the early organization of the automobile industry during the period of U.S. ascendence, and then shift to a more general analysis of the role of the regulation of knowledge flows in the sustenance of private authority in a posthegemonic world. Like the early cotton industry, the organization of the automobile industry was initially faciliated by an informal sharing of technical knowledge among leading firms in a particular geographic location, reinforced by geographic, cultural, and social distance between these firms and potential competitors in other countries. Over time, however, this centralization of international private authority among a few leading U.S. firms was undermined by the diffusion of knowledge and the strengthening of competitors. In its place has emerged, as in the earlier period, more multilateral private arrangements: strategic alliances and joint ventures. Once again we see these arrangements facilitated by a strengthening of the patent regime by states—and also, in this later period, by a reversal of antitrust prohibitions on horizontal interfirm collaboration, prohibitions that had previously helped U.S.-style multinational corporations to displace cartels as the dominant form of international private authority.

The automobile industry, after a late-nineteenth-century European lead, was quickly dominated by U.S. firms. The sixth individual car ever produced by Ford was exported to Canada in 1903, before the company was even two months old.[28] Ford's first European plant was opened in Britain in 1911, followed by General Motors (GM) in 1923. By 1929 the United States controlled 85 percent of the world market for cars.[29]

Sharing of product technology was a key ingredient of the new industry's initial growth. Early German and French successes at manufacturing automobiles were facilitated by German legal rulings in 1884 and 1886 annulling the Deutz company's patent rights over the four-stroke principle.[30] Attempts by Selden in the United States and Lawson in Britain, neither of which were committed to expanding automobile production, to obtain a monopoly of patent rights to automobile technology set back development in their respective countries for a while.[31] In the first case Ford overturned Selden's monopoly, held by the Association of Licenced Automobile Manufacturers, through very costly legal action and subsequently American automobile producers established a practice of freely exchanging new product technology. This occurred in the form of a patent pool established by the major American automotive manufacturers under the auspices of the Automobile Manufacturers Association (AMA) formed in 1913: "patents were more or less disregarded and not considered of any special importance."[32] The AMA included all American automobile manufacturers, a total of thirty-four at the beginning of World War II.[33] In the United Kingdom, Lawson's monopoly was eventually eroded as well. His patents lost their value over time and the British courts eventually overturned the patents (since sold by Lawson) in 1907.[34]

The launching of automobiles as a new leading sector displays some important similarities to the case of cotton discussed above. As with cotton the sector began to expand rapidly only after key patents were overturned and technology began to flow more freely among the leading firms. In the case of automobiles this sharing of technology was explicit: the American cross-licencing of technology agreement, established in 1915, lasted until 1955.[35] Like cotton, replicating Ford's methods abroad was difficult because of the way in which they were embedded in local sociotechnical institutions.[36] European labor unions effectively resisted Taylorism and living standards were not initially high enough to sustain demand for mass production. "Ford permitted full observation of his processes, but to reproduce them took years, and the Highland Park factory was constantly improving its methods. Consequently, for a decade no company could match Ford production."[37] The adoption of the large hierarchical structure that was to become characteristic of U.S. MNCs further reinforced the control over technology of leading U.S. producers. As noted above, despite the popularity of international cartels for managing industries, there were never any international automobile cartels in the interwar period. As with cotton the industry was sufficiently concentrated in terms of geography and nationality for leading firms to exercise authority without formal international private institutions.

Despite these parallels between cotton and automobiles as new leading sectors, there is, at first glance, an important difference: the private institutions of U.S. automakers, such as the American Automobile Association, did not play as prominent a political role as did the Manchester cotton merchant associations. This might suggest that the private authority produced by the automobile industry was not comparable to that of the cotton industry. On closer examination, however, it becomes clear that enthusiasm for the form of industrial organization that the automobile industry exemplified motivated the U.S. state to carry out a sustained international campaign to demolish the major competing form of industrial organization—the cartels. While the link between the automobile industry and this political initiative is much less direct than the overt lobbying of the cotton merchants against the state-chartered companies, there is an important similarity: in both cases a vibrant new industry, closely associated with massive social, cultural, and urban transformation, provides a new form of industrial organization that the state then assists by undermining the organization of the older industries. I will examine this process in the next section.

The Destruction of the Cartels

Much as the British cotton industry worked hard to get the British state to weaken the great mercantile trading companies, the hierarchical form of MNC epitomized by the U.S. automobile companies did not displace the alternative economic arrangement—the cartels—without a political struggle. Following World War II the American state carried out a sustained and ultimately successful campaign to delegitimize cartels.[38] This was carried out, first, through the creation of new international rules in the United Nations, the European Economic Community, and other international institutions, and secondly through the military occupation and reconstruction of United States' two main competitors with respect to alternative corporate governance regimes: Germany and Japan.

In classic Gramscian fashion this U.S. effort involved an intertwining of power, coercion, and ideology. While coercion, as with the military occupations, and more subtle forms of power, as with political pressure in the UN, were both important, the delegitimation of cartels as a result of their association with German and Japanese militarism was also significant. In the interwar period, as noted above, interfirm cooperative arrangements were regarded positively by many. As the postwar U.S.-led campaign against cartels proceeded, however, cartels were broken up or forced underground and were so successfully delegitimized that the term itself has come to have exclusively negative connotations as in its association in U.S. political discourse with foreign oil or drug activities. The United States was able to successfully associate its prevailing domestic corporate governance regime—highly centralized oligopolistic nonfinancial corporations—with the powerful convergence of signifiers such as freedom, free markets, democracy, and competition that was at the heart of the discursive dimension of the postwar hegemonic order.[39]

This ideological campaign accompanied the effort to build strong antitrust measures into the International Trade Organization (ITO), and, when the ITO failed to come into existence, the General Agreement on Tariffs and Trade (GATT) and the Economic and Social Council (ECOSOC) of the UN.[40] Although neither the ECOSOC nor the GATT antitrust commitments resulted in identifiable alterations in national practices, they did help to define a post–World War II anticartel consensus. The Marshall Plan also provided useful leverage: "direct pressure was applied to recipient nations to do away with the cartel mentality as at least a formal condition of obtaining American aid."[41] Stronger antitrust provisions were agreed to in the European Coal and Steel Community[42] and the Treaty of Rome, which set up the European Economic Community.[43] The 1945 *Alcoa* case in the United States established the extraterritorial application of U.S. antitrust law to agreements conducted abroad by foreign corporations that had an effect on U.S. imports.[44] Vigorous extraterritorial application of U.S. antitrust laws continued through the 1950s despite protests by other governments.[45]

The occupations of Germany and Japan gave the United States an unprecedented opportunity to reshape the domestic corporate governance regimes of its two most important challengers.[46] As in the United States, the new German and Japanese legislation targeted horizontal interfirm cooperation rather than the vertical centralization of the U.S.-style MNC. Although critics of U.S. policy have noted the degree to which prewar concentrations of economic power were retained in these two countries, these occupation policies did substantially tilt the "playing field" in favor of U.S.-style autonomous MNCs and away from cartel forms of organization, despite the potential advantages of the latter for late industrializers with relatively small domestic markets.

A particular target of U.S. policy was the use of the patent system for constructing cartels.[47] As the tide turned against cartels the restrictive aspects of the patent system came under attack. A prominent 1942 proposal by *Fortune* magazine called for "abolishing the protection which the patent system gives to monopolistic practices" and perhaps even introducing compulsory licensing.[48]

In short, as with cotton previously, the firms from the world's leading economy initially neither required nor supported frameworks for negotiating private arrangements with their counterparts in other countries. Indeed the ascendancy of U.S. firms was assisted by the ability of the U.S. government to suppress the multilateral framework that had evolved in the wake of British hegemony. Powerful international intrafirm hierarchies, with head offices centralized territorially under U.S. jurisdiction, provided the new source of private authority for industry after industry. The technological lead of these firms and their bureaucratic structure were mutually reinforcing and initially had little reliance on the patent system that had earlier been so important.

CHANGES IN PRIVATE AUTHORITY
WITH THE DECLINE OF U.S. HEGEMONY

In the last quarter of the twentieth century, as signs of the relative decline of American hegemony began to proliferate, a shift in the international private arrangements for organizing industries began to occur that resembled closely the shift that occurred in the wake of British hegemony. As American technology diffused and firms from other countries built their own industrial capacity, the old highly bureaucratized and centralized U.S. MNCs began to enter into more complex negotiated arrangements with their foreign counterparts. States became more active in providing a strengthened framework for enhancing multilateral private arrangements. As in the interwar period interfirm linkages were facilitated by a strengthened international patent regime. The role of the state was most evident in the case of the United States, which reversed its previous linking of patents and antitrust policy: antitrust policy was weakened to allow the types of arrangements against which the United States campaigned in the 1950s and the United States became a vigorous supporter of strengthening international regimes for intellectual property rights. I will start with a brief examination of the fate of the U.S. auto industry, including its initial reliance on direct state protection and its subsequent move to develop new private interfirm arrangements domestically and with foreign competitors. I will then turn to the strengthening of the patent regime.

The U.S. share of world auto markets declined consistently from 82 percent in 1950 to 32 percent in 1973.[49] By 1992, the share held by U.S. firms had plummeted to 16.5 percent. Between 1973 and the early 1980s governments began to step in to negotiate and enforce a new type of market-sharing arrangement: voluntary export restraint agreements (VRAs) with Japan. In 1975 the British quota was set at just over 10 percent and the French at 3 percent, followed by West Germany's 10 percent quota in 1981.[50] A VRA with Japan was negotiated by the EC as a whole in 1991 and strengthened the following year. The first U.S. VRA was established in 1981, supported by all three big U.S. automakers. It was replaced in 1985 by unilateral restraints by Japan.[51]

While the threat and reality of state-initiated market-sharing arrangements have continued to play a role in the organization of the international automobile regime, particularly with respect to Europe, there are signs of a shift away from such arrangements to private ones. The most important evidence of this shift is the proliferation of strategic alliances and joint ventures between firms but a decline in enthusiasm on the part of the automakers for state intervention is also significant.

A full description of the increasingly complex entanglement of the world's automakers with each other goes beyond the scope of the present essay. Here I will simply cite some of the more important examples, which include equity arrangements such as GM's 34.2 percent ownership of Isuzu and, Ford's 25 percent ownership of Mazda, joint ventures for manufacturing, including GM's famous NUMMI joint venture with Toyota in California, as well as alliances between Volvo and Renault, Daimler-Benz and Mitsubishi, Ford's various production agreements with Volkswagen, Suzuki, BMW, Fiat, Mazda, and Nissan. GM has arranged to exchange components and parts with Renault, Honda, Toyota, Isuzu, Volkswagen, and Fiat, and similar arrangements link Volkswagen and Toyota, Chrysler and Renault, and Nissan and Peugeot.[52] In an industry in which, in 1987, twelve companies accounted for a 74.2 percent share of world markets,[53] such interconnections provide a strong basis for coordinated control of markets.

Indeed in the past few years there have been scattered explicit announcements by car makers of intentions to fix market shares. For instance GM announced in April 1988 that it would not seek to win back market share from Japanese companies in the United States.[54] Nissan made an explicit commitment to cut exports to the United States by 50 percent from the peak level of 1986, and both Honda and Toyota have pledged to export a fixed percentage of their production in the United States.[55] Given the antitrust provisions of U.S. and E.U. law it is not surprising that more explicit overall agreements on market shares are not made. Such agreements are unnecessary, however, given the widespread explicit coordination of production and marketing of particular products that is involved in the alliances cited above.

This strengthening of private arrangements among the leading auto makers has been accompanied by a shift away from reliance on state-initiated VRAs. Significantly the key accomplishment of President Bush's much publicized 1992 trip to Japan with the chairs of the big three U.S. firms was to expand the potential for private cooperation by insisting that Japanese plants use more U.S. components, and that Japanese dealers handle more American cars[56]—not to establish a new VRA.

In short, the U.S. firms, faced with the demise of the old arrangements by which they had dominated international markets, were turning to new forms of interfirm cooperation. Coordination of production decisions with former competitors promised to introduce a new orderliness into markets. A new form of private international authority was being constructed. Here I have focused on the automobile industry, but these changes were to be found across many industries in which U.S. firms faced similar challenges. There are significant parallels here to the construction of cartels in the interwar period. This point is reinforced by the changes in the antitrust and patent regimes to which I now turn.

Changes in Antitrust and Patent Regulations

In 1984 the U.S. Congress sought to encourage joint ventures in research and development by offering them significant protection from the traditional threat under U.S. antitrust law of treble damages.[57] This shift accelerated under the Bush administration: by 1989 U.S. Commerce Undersecretary Robert Mosbacher was stating "All American industries deserve the opportunity to form cooperative ventures that will enhance their international competitiveness without exposing themselves to unwarranted antitrust attack."[58] There is also an accelerating reversal of the New Deal separation of finance and industry.[59] In short, the U.S. state is constructing a domestic regime that embraces the types of cooperative arrangements between firms that it had so vigorously opposed both domestically and internationally in the interwar and immediate postwar period.[60]

This change in the U.S. domestic antitrust regime has been accompanied by a consistently declining enthusiasm in international regimes for the antitrust campaign that had been waged so vigorously in the immediate postwar period. As industrial and political capacity grew in overseas markets the desire and capacity of U.S. firms for greater participation in those markets led to a proliferation of joint-venture arrangements. Vigorous extraterritorial application of U.S. antitrust laws, termed in 1956 by one analyst "one of the most vexing problems confronting American business and industry today,"[61] made participation in these joint ventures by U.S. firms problematic.[62] Combined with increasing international interest in applying antitrust principles to restrictive business practices of U.S. MNCs in host markets and extraterritorially[63] these developments also contributed to a cooling of U.S.

enthusiasm for its own international antitrust campaign[64] as did the use by foreign governments of antitrust measures such as compulsory licensing to offset U.S. MNCs' control of technology.[65]

The most dramatic strengthening of the international regime for intellectual property rights (IPRs) has been the commitments made during the Uruguay Round of trade negotiations.[66] The agreement mandates most favored nation and national treatment principles with regard to IPRs, eliminating the ability of states to favor their own firms in their use of patents and copyrights. A uniform twenty-year standard was agreed and all World Trade Organization (WTO) members are bound to the provisions of the Paris Convention on industrial property and the Berne Convention on copyright (except for the latter's provisions for "moral rights") even if they had not previously adhered to it. Requirements of firms to work patents in domestic markets were effectively eliminated by providing patentees the right to supply imports. Compulsory licensing has been restricted to some degree. The agreement requires members to provide detailed enforcement procedures against counterfeiting. Providing legal provisions to protect trade secrets were also required of countries for the first time in an international agreement. Customs officials have been authorized to seize goods suspected of being pirated. Signatories are also expected to provide a domestic legal regime that would enhance the ability of foreigners to protect their IPRs, including detailed provisions regarding the discovery of evidence, rights to counsel, injunctions, damages, and temporary restraining orders. Finally disputes over IPRs can be taken through the WTO's dramatically strengthened dispute-resolution mechanism.

The WTO arrangements build upon previous bilateral agreements, as for example the agreements between the United States on the one hand and China (1992), Indonesia (1989), and Singapore (1987), which have led to tougher IPRs in those countries.[67] The United States has also linked strengthened IPRs to the preferential trade arrangements with LDCs including the General System of Preferences, the Caribbean Basin Initiative, and the Andean Trade preferences. The United States has used Section 301 of its Omnibus Trade and Competitiveness Act of 1988 to threaten countries that do not provide strong IPRs, as for instance in the cases of Mexico, India, and China, which reworked their laws after such threats. The North American Free Trade Agreement (NAFTA) has also been seen as a model for the protection of IPRs because of its strong provisions. These require, for instance, that Mexico further strengthen its criminal and civil remedies against violations.

These changes in antitrust and intellectual property policies mark a dramatic reversal for a waning U.S. hegemony from the corresponding policies in its period of ascendance. This reversal signifies an important change in the nature of private international authority. In the earlier period emerging leading industries, such as automobiles, were organized by a few oligopolistic multinational firms. The authority of the leading auto firms was enhanced by their sharing of technology among themselves, promoting cohesion and contributing to the critical mass needed to realize the industry's potential for stimulating economic and social transformation. Diffusion of this technology abroad was inhibited by geographic and social distance. In short, the bureaucratic organization of the multinational corporations provided a basis for the private authority need to organize the international industry. While the auto MNCs differ in their organizational capacity from particular cotton firms a century before, the two industries were similar in their reliance on private authority and in the way in which the diffusion and control of technical knowledge were carried out. The antipatent and anticartel mood under U.S. hegemony corresponded with the way in which private authority was organized in this period.

With the relative decline of U.S. hegemony, as in the earlier British case, these private arrangements, were no longer sustainable. Technologies and corresponding modes of social organization had diffused, leading to competition from other countries. The hierarchies of the U.S.-based MNCs could no longer retain control over the flow of knowledge. More complex negotiated private arrangements among firms of different nationalities been constructed in response. These have been facilitated by state initiatives such as the negotiation of VRAs in the 1970s and 1980s, in which threats to close off national markets to rising competitors reinforced a willingness of firms from different countries to collaborate—very much as tariffs in the interwar period complemented the cartel arrangements of firms. States have also acted to build and strengthen dramatically regimes for intellectual property rights as hegemony has waned, as was the case in the late nineteenth century. More formalized, state-negotiated mechanisms for regulating the flow of knowledge have replaced earlier informal and private arrangements. These complement the new private multinational collaborative private arrangements, such as joint ventures and strategic partnerships, in which leading firms effectively divide up new markets in the course of jointly developing the technology upon which these markets will be based. The parallels with the international cartels in the interwar period are evident.

CONCLUSION

The above sections have shown that the rise and decline of both U.S. and British hegemony have been accompanied by quite similar patterns of

change in the private arrangements for organizing international industries. In the early period of these hegemonies leading firms were able to
construct private arrangements for organizing markets. These were
faciliated by the location of the leading firms in a single country, by an
informal sharing of technology at home, by geographic and social barriers to the international diffusion of that technology, and by the assistance obtained from the hegemonic state in removing obstacles related
to the dominant private arrangements of an earlier period, thereby supporting the new form of social organization associated with the emerging leading sectors. With the maturing of these hegemonies new private
arrangements were negotiated: these were multilateral and were faciliated by new formalized rules, provided by states, to regulate the international flow of knowledge—a strengthening of the patent regime.The
present historical period, with its proliferation of international interfirm
arrangements and strengthened regimes for intellectual property, initiated by firms but supported by states, is not a novel feature of a post-
industrial or newly globalized economy, but rather repeats developments that were present in a previous period of hegemonic decline.

This chapter, then, has confirmed the importance of private institutions in understanding the governance of the international economy.
Sometimes these institutions have been quite formalized, as with the various organizations that were involved in organizing the cotton industry.
At other times they have been more informal as in the ties between the
British firms and American producers of cotton. They have, however, in
each case, been more important in launching and organizing new leading industries than were states. Yet by themselves these private institutions were unable to cope with the coordinating challenges that arose as
new firms began to undermine the arrangements of the leading firms.
States continue, then, to play an important part in providing a framework for the negotiation of private arrangements as a sector matures.
However, it would be difficult to adequately analyze these state initiatives without understanding the private arrangements that preceded
them.

NOTES

Research for this chapter was supported by the Social Sciences and Humanities
Research Council of Canada, Research Grant number 410-95-1023.

1. Thompson has correlated growth rates in hegemonic countries with the
rise and fall of leading industries. With the centralization of these industries in
their territories the hegemonic countries enjoyed both direct revenues and positive externalities, including backward and forward linkages to other industries

and the spread of technologies and modes of social organization. Yet the very pervasiveness of these effects produced inertia, and consequently problems of competitiveness, as the initial technologies matured and other countries built more up-to-date productive capacity. William R. Thompson, "Long Waves, Innovation, and Decline," *International Organization* 44.2 (Spring 1990): 201–33. In this chapter I primarily treat hegemony as involving such patterns in the international centralization of economic activity rather than variations in the exercise of political power by a leading state over other states.

2. Fordism refers to mass-production lines and to the raising of wages to stimulate consumption of mass-produced products, both of which Henry Ford pioneered.

3. Arthur Redford, *Manchester Merchants and Foreign Trade, 1794–1858* (Manchester, England: Manchester University Press, 1934), p. 1.

4. Smith quote from *Wealth of Nations*, bk. 1, ch. VIII, cited in Redford, *Manchester Merchants*, p. 1. Information on the Manchester institutions also is from Redford, and the Liverpool institutions from Thomas Ellison, *The Cotton Trade of Great Britain* (New York: Augustus M. Kelley, 1968[1886]).

5. Michael M. Edwards, *The Growth of the British Cotton Trade 1780–1815* (Manchester, England: Manchester University Press, 1967), p. 139.

6. Redford, *Manchester Merchants*, p. 1.

7. Edwards, *Growth of the British Cotton Trade*, pp. 140–41.

8. Redford, *Manchester Merchants*, pp. 22–48.

9. Ibid., p. 72.

10. Ibid., chapter 11.

11. Ellison, *Cotton Trade of Great Britain*, pp. 168–69, 272.

12. Ibid., 273.

13. Ibid., part II, chapters 4, 7, 8.

14. A similar but earlier pattern occurred in Africa: private British traders displaced the Royal African Company after its collapse in 1748. See Julia De Lacy Mann, "The Growth of the Cotton Trade in the Eighteenth Century," in Alfred Wadsworth and Julia De Lacy Mann, eds., *The Cotton Trade and Industrial Lancashire 1600–1780* (Manchester, England: Manchester University Press, 1931), pp. 111–208, especially 149. On the East India and Levant Companies, see Redford, *Manchester Merchants*, chapters 9 and 14, especially p. 90.

15. The information in this paragraph is based on Edwards, *Growth of the British Cotton Trade*, pp. 162–67. See also W. O. Henderson, *Britain and Industrial Europe 1750–1870: Studies in British Influence on the Industrial Revolution in Western Europe* (Leicester: Leicester University Press, 1965).

16. Trevor Griffiths, Philip A. Hunt, and Patrick K. O'Brien, "Inventive Activity in the British Textile Industry, 1700–1800," *Journal of Economic History* 52.4 (December 1992): 881–906, especially 884–85.

17. Given the current U.S. stance on intellectual property it is ironic that the transfer of cotton technology to the United States was facilitated by a 1790 federal copyright law that "legalized the American printing of foreign works [including technical manuals] without regard to their authors' literary property rights." David J. Jeremy, *Transatlantic Industrial Revolution: The Diffusion of Textile Technologies between Britain and America, 1790–1830s* (Oxford: Basil

Blackwell, 1981), p. 69. See also Ellison, *Cotton Trade of Great Britain*, p. 21 and Redford, *Manchester Merchants*, p. 5.

18. Jeremy, *Transatlantic Industrial Revolution*, chapter 2.

19. Ibid., p. 42.

20. The number of cotton factories in the United States increased from four to about 800 between 1803 and 1832. Redford, *Manchester Merchants*, p. 98. This did not immediately crowd the British producers out of the American raw cotton market: 77 percent of British imports of cotton came from the United States between 1815 and 1859, with some years registering dependence figures of up to 84 percent. D. A. Farnie, *The English Cotton Industry and the World Market 1815–1896* (Oxford: Clarendon Press, 1979), p. 15). See also Redford, *Manchester Merchants*, pp. 80–81.

21. This and the next several paragraphs are based on Edith Tilton Penrose, *The Economics of the International Patent System* (Baltimore: Johns Hopkins University Press, 1951).

22. International finance played an important role in this period that is consistent with this model but that cannot be developed here. As a history of the International Chamber of Commerce noted : "The capital of the world economic community before the war was London. Under the shelter of the liberal imperial authority at Whitehall, but never overshadowed by it, the City of London exercised the major control over the world's capital markets and through these markets over the great process of the production and distribution of wealth." George L. Ridgeway, *Merchants of Peace* (New York: Columbia University Press, 1938), pp. 13–14. Yet this control was to a large degree restricted to setting the broad parameters of interactions as, for instance, in the nature of the portfolio investment that characterized the international capital flows of that period. On financial innovation in this period and its relationship to hegemony see Tony Porter, "Innovation in Global Finance: Impact on Hegemony and Growth since 1000 AD," *Review* 18.3 (Summer 1995): 387–429.

23. As is well known, enforcement of cartel agreements is difficult because incentives to defect increase with the cartel's effectiveness. Many interwar cartels had provisions for arbitration under the auspices of the International Chamber of Commerce and for penalties. Hexner comments that once these provisions had to be invoked it was likely that the cartel was in trouble—in other words informal pressures were more important than formal ones in encouraging compliance. Ervin Hexner, *International Cartels* (London: Pitman, 1946), p. 80.

24. George W. Stocking and Myron W. Watkins, *Cartels in Action* (New York: Twentieth Century Fund, 1946), p. 5.

25. Ibid., p. 4.

26. Hexner, *International Cartels*, p. 73.

27. Sidney Dell, *The United Nations and International Business* (Durham and London: Duke University Press, 1990), pp. 4–5; Clemens Wurm, *Business, Politics and International Relations: Steel Cotton and International Cartels in British Politics, 1924–1939* (Cambridge: Cambridge University Press, 1993), pp. 181–82.

28. Mira Wilkins and Frank Ernest Hill, *American Business Abroad: Ford on Six Continents* (Detroit: Wayne State University Press, 1964), p. 1.

29. John Kenly Smith Jr., "National Goals, Industry Structure, and Corporate Strategies: German Chemical Cartels Between the Wars," in Akira Kudo and Terushi Hara, eds., *International Cartels in Business History* (Tokyo: University of Tokyo Press, 1992), pp. 139–58.

30. James M. Laux, "The Genesis of the Automobile Revolution," in Jean-Pierre Bardou, Jean-Jacques Chanaron, Patrick Fridenson, and James M. Laux, *The Automobile Revolution: The Impact of an Industry* (Chapel Hill: University of North Carolina Press, 1982), pp. 1–76, especially 75.

31. Martin Adeney, *The Motor Makers: The Turbulent History of Britain's Car Industry* (London: Collins, 1988) and Carl H. A. Dassbach, *Global Enterprises and the World Economy: Ford, General Motors, and IBM, the Emergence of the Transnational Enterprise* (New York and London: Garland Publishing, 1989).

32. George E. Folk, *Patents and Industrial Progress* (New York and London: Harper and Brothers, 1942), p. 23.

33. Ibid., p. 24.

34. Kenneth Richardson, *The British Motor Industry 1896–1939* (London and Basingstoke, England: Macmillan, 1977), pp. 17–19.

35. Laux, "Genesis," p. 44.

36. Carlota Perez, "Structural Change and Assimilation of New Technologies in the Economic and Social System," in Christopher Freeman, ed., *Design, Innovation and Long Cycles in Economic Development* (New York: St. Martins, 1986).

37. Wilkins and Hill, *American Business Abroad*, p. 52.

38. In part this U.S. campaign was driven by particular domestic political traditions rather than international rivalry. There are two ways in which a long-standing antipathy to concentrations of economic power in American political culture led to a particular form of corporate structure that at its emergence was unique among the industrialized countries. The first of these, most extensively and persuasively argued in the work of Mark J. Roe, is the New Deal proscription of the organizational function that was played by investment bankers until the 1930s and that continues to be played in other countries to a much greater degree. Mark J. Roe, "A Political Theory of American Corporate Finance," *Columbia Law Review* 91 (1991): 10–67. The second idiosyncracy was the uniquely pervasive impact of antitrust legislation. Up until World War II there was nothing comparable in other countries to the Sherman Antitrust Act of 1890 and related Supreme Court and executive branch initiatives. The act had, as Chandler notes, "a profound impact on the evolution of modern industrial enterprises in the United States. . . . Because the act forbade monopoly or any form of contract or combination in restraint of trade, close interfirm cooperation was defined as illegal collusion" (Alfred D. Chandler, *Scale and Scope: The Dynamics of Industrial Capitalism* [Cambridge, Mass.: Belknap, 1990]), p. 72. Ironically this did not prevent concentration of economic power but rather changed its form: the Sherman Act was followed by a wave of merger activity as legal intrafirm arrangements replaced the now illegal activities of cartels and trade associations (ibid., p. 75).

39. The U.S. Temporary National Economic Committee, created by Congress in 1938 in response to concerns about concentrations of economic

power, played a key role in mobilizing U.S. policymakers and the public against cartels. The TNEC's final report stated "the interchange of patents between American and foreign concerns has been used as a means of cartelizing an industry to effectively displace competition. The production of vitally important materials . . . has been restrained through international patent controls and cross-licensing which have divided the world market into closed areas. As a result, the capacity of American industry to produce these materials is not adequate to meet the needs of the defense program" (Folk, *Patents and Industrial Progress*, p. 62).

40. Sigmund Timberg, "Restrictive Business Practices as an Appropriate Subject for United Nations Action," *Antitrust Bulletin* 1.7 (December 1955): 409–40.

41. Thorelli, who goes on to note of the post–World War II shift in European antitrust policy that "all the antitrust laws concentrate on cartel arrangements. . . . European laws are not, as a rule, much concerned with single-firm monopolies or corporate combinations as such" (Hans B. Thorelli, "Antitrust in Europe: National Policies After 1945," *University of Chicago Law Review* 26.2 [Winter 1959]: 222–36, quote from 233). In other words the types of anticompetitive policies most likely to be pursued by U.S.-style MNCs were not restricted. U.S. pressure exerted through the Marshall Plan was supplemented with a series of bilateral Treaties of Friendship, Commerce, and Navigation that set out policies on restrictive business practices. For instance, separate treaties were concluded with Italy and Britain in 1948. E. Ernst Goldstein, "Effect of Foreign Antitrust Laws on United States Business," *Southwestern Law Journal* 12.4 (Fall 1958): 405–58.

42. Jean Monnet, the head of the European Coal and Steel Community (ECSC), commented that Articles 65 and 66 were "Europe's first major antitrust law" (Goldstein, "Effect of Foreign Antitrust Laws," p. 428).

43. Heinrich Kronstein, "Cartels under the New German Cartel Statute," *Vanderbilt Law Review* 11.2 (March 1958): 283.

44. An example of the impact of extraterritorial application of U.S. antitrust laws is evident in the payment by seven European and U.S. shipping corporations of $6.1 million in fines in response to 1980 charges that they fixed prices in trans-Atlantic shipping (M. A. Blythe, "The Extraterritorial Impact of the Anti-Trust Laws: Protecting British Trading Interests," *American Journal of Comparative Law* 31.1 [1983]: 99–129). For information on international antitrust efforts see Dell, *United Nations and International Business*, chapter 1; Samuel K. C. Kopper, "The International Regulation of Cartels—Current Proposals," *Virginia Law Review* 40.8 (December 1954): 1005–28 and Sigmund Timberg, "Conflict and Growth in the International and Comparative Law of Antitrust," *American Bar Association International and Comparative Law Bulletin* 4.3 (July 1960): 20–27. As noted below, U.S. enthusiasm for international antitrust machinery began to wane as it became clear that U.S. MNCs might be targets. Kopper, "International Regulation of Cartels," p. 1012.

45. Kurt E. Markert, "Recent Developments in International Antitrust Cooperation," *Antitrust Bulletin* 13 (Summer 1968): 355–72, and Timberg, "Conflict and Growth."

46. U.S. military authorities in charge of the occupation of Germany promulgated Law 56 in 1947. It called for the elimination of "concentrations of economic power as exemplified, in particular, by cartels, syndicates, trusts, combines, and other types of monopolistic or restrictive arrangements" (cited in John C. Stedman, "The German Decartelization Program—The Law in Repose," *University of Chicago Law Review* 17.3 [Spring 1950]: 441–57, quote on 441). It was agreed in the Paris Treaty between the Allies and Germany that the Allied cartel laws would remain until replaced by comparable German law. Such a law was enacted with the Cartel Statute of 1957. Kronstein, "Cartels," pp. 271–301. In 1945 the Supreme Commmander for the Allied Powers (SCAP) directed the Japanese government "to elimate and prevent private monopoly and restraint of trade" (Lester N. Salwin, "Japanese Anti-Trust Legislation," *Minnesota Law Review* 32.6 [May 1948]: 588–605, quote on 588). Salwin's title, Chief of the Antitrust Legislation Branch, Antitrust Division at SCAP, undermines his contention that SCAP was not directly involved in the details of the Diet's 1947 Act that carried out this directive. Japanese securities markets were also remodeled on U.S. lines.

47. Charles R. Whittlesey, *National Interest and International Cartels* (New York: Macmillan, 1946), p. 76.

48. L. G. W Bronson, "Cartels and International Patent Agreements," 1946, typescript, p. 92.

49. Jean-Jacques Chanaron, "The Automobile under Fire," in Jean-Pierre Bardou, Jean-Jacques Chanaron, Patrick Fridenson, and James M. Laux, *The Automobile Revolution: The Impact of an Industry* (Chapel Hill: University of North Carolina Press, 1982), pp. 272–90. See especially pp. 175, 178.

50. Peter F. Cowhey and Edward Long, "Testing Theories of Regime Change: Hegemonic Decline or Surplus Capacity?" in *International Organization* 37.2 (Spring 1983): 157–88; see 178.

51. Peter F. Cowhey and Jonathan D. Aronson, *Managing the World Economy: The Consequences of Corporate Alliances*, (New York: Council on Foreign Relations, 1993), pp. 98, 102–3.

52. John R. Munkirs, "The Automobile Industry, Political Economy, and a New World Order," *Journal of Economic Issues* 27.2 (June 1993): 627–38.

53. Norman Coates, "The Globalization of the Motor Vehicle Manufacturing Industry," *Planning Review* 17.1 (January 1989): 34–39.

54. Ibid., p. 39.

55. Cowhey and Aronson, *Managing the World Economy*, p. 114.

56. Ibid., p. 115.

57. Thomas M. Jorde and David J. Teece, "Competition and Cooperation: Striking the Right Balance," *California Management Review* 31.3 (Spring 1989): 25–37. Clark documents the progressive acceptance by the U.S. Supreme Court of the academic arguments for much wider acceptance by U.S. antitrust authorities of vertical and horizontal cooperative arrangements See Nolan Ezra Clark, "Antitrust Comes Full Circle: The Return to the Cartellization Standard," *Vanderbilt Law Review* 38.5 (October 1985): 1125–97.

58. Walter Adams and James W. Brock, "Joint Ventures, Antitrust, and Transnational Cartelization," *Northwestern Journal of International Law and Business* 11.3 (Winter 1991): 433–83, quote on 436.

59. The Federal Reserve gradually has been weakening the Glass-Steagall separation of commercial banks, investment banks, and industry over the past decade. The Riegle-Neal Interstate Banking and Branching Efficiency Act of 1994 finally overturned the New Deal–era McFadden prohibitions on interstate branching effective June 1, 1997.

60. Although international factors are acknowledged as important by analysts of these changes in U.S. antitrust policy they are part as well of a broader reversal of previous concern about concentrations of economic power. Taken as a whole the sea change in academic attitudes to antitrust is profound enough to have been labeled a "revolution" by one participant (Yale Brozen, *Concentration, Mergers, and Public Policy* [New York: Macmillan, 1982]). For a discussion of the "Chicago school" critics of antitrust activities and of their impact on the U.S. Supreme Court, see Clark, "Antitrust Comes Full Circle."

61. Sol M. Linowitz, "The International Businessman Meets the Anti-Trust Laws," *Cornell Law Quarterly* 41 (Winter 1956): 215–23, quote on 215.

62. Friedmann noted with regard to joint ventures that "it is therefore a matter of considerable concern that the Sherman Act, as currently interpreted, may, in an already extremely difficult international situation, impede the very form of American enterprise that is most acceptable to a majority of the less developed countries." Wolfgang G. Friedmann, "Antitrust Law and Joint International Business Ventures in Economically Underdeveloped Countries," *Columbia Law Review* 60 (June 1960): 780–91, quote on 781. See also Sol M. Linowitz, "Antitrust Laws: A Damper on American Foreign Trade?" *American Bar Association Journal* 44 (September 1958): 853–55.

63. Ironically, at the beginning of the 1970s there was widely publicized concern expressed within the U.S. that the EEC was beginning to expand its extraterritorial application of EEC antitrust law to U.S. firms. John Dietz, "Enforcement of Anti-Trust Laws in the EEC," *International Lawyer* 6.4 (1972): 742–70. See also Kopper, "International Regulation of Cartels," and Joel W. Howell III, "Extraterritorial Application of Antitrust Legislation in the Common Market," *Columbia Journal of Transnational Law* 12.1 (1973): 169–81.

64. Foreign protest at U.S. extraterritorial enforcement also contributed to an easing of this enforcement in the 1960s. Markert, "Recent Developments," p. 359.

65. Sigmund Timberg, "The Impact of Antitrust Laws on Multinational Licensing and Franchising Arrangements," *Antitrust Bulletin* 13 (Spring 1968): 39–52.

66. This paragraph draws on J. H. Reichman, "Universal Standards of Intellectual Property Protection under the TRIPS Component of the WTO Agreement," *International Lawyer* 29.2 (Summer 1995): 345–88.

67. This paragraph draws on Meredith A. Harper, "International Protection of Intellectual Property Rights in the 1990s: Will Trade Barriers and Pirating Practices in the Audio-visual Industry Continue?" *California Western International Law Journal* 25.1 (1994): 153.

CHAPTER 11

Private Authority in International Trade Relations: The Case of Maritime Transport

A. Claire Cutler

This chapter examines the regulation of private international trade relations, which provides a very rich and interesting example of the operation of private international authority. Private international trade law is concerned with the international sale, transportation, financing, and insurance of goods, as well as with dispute resolution.[1] These activities are generally identified as "private" because they primarily concern commercial transactions involving individual merchants or business corporations and not involving states. Public international trade law, in contrast, regulates interstate commercial activity and is generally regarded as the preserve of states. This chapter addresses the problematic nature of the private/public law distinction arguing that it serves to enhance the authority of corporate actors while simultaneously rendering such actions politically unaccountable. In developing this line of argument the chapter generates important insights into the nature of the relationship between private or corporate authority and public or state authority. It suggests that the relationship between private and public authorities is by no means uniform or static, but is complex. The balance between private and public authorities in the regulation of trade relations and their degree of integration have varied over both time and issue-areas. Moreover, private international trade law cuts across issue-areas, sectors, and industries and touches upon most of the subjects addressed by the other chapters in this volume. The laws governing international transactions involving intellectual property rights, commodity trade, and the corporate practices of international service industries, for example, are often embodied in laws that have their origin in private international trade law and practice. Indeed, the historic origins of international commercial law are to be found in the customs and practices of medieval merchants engaged in private commercial exchange.[2] Many of these customs and practices were inherited from still earlier ancient law and practice and were universalized throughout the European trading world by medieval merchants engaged in long-distance trade. Modern commercial practice has further extended the reach of international commercial law well beyond the European trading world to most every part of the globe.[3]

Private international trade law is thus foundational in an historic sense. However, it is also foundational in a normative sense in that it establishes the normative framework for international commercial relations. Indeed, private international trade law is today most accurately described as an attribute of modern capitalism and an essential element in the constitution of state/society relations under modern capitalism.[4] Private international trade law forms part of the juridical conditions of capitalism by establishing the rules of contract, property, and dispute resolution that define rights and establish standards of liability allocating the risks of commercial exchange and providing for stability of possession. Some of the norms are embodied in international conventions and are widely recognized by commercial actors as binding rules of international law. They are known generally as "hard law." Others operate as "soft law," in that as model laws or codes they depend upon the will of contracting parties to vest them with binding authority. Hard law is thus "binding," while soft law describes "instruments that are not legally binding though they affect the conduct of international relations by states and may lead to the development of new international law."[5]

There is tremendous variation in the sources and nature of the norms governing international commercial transactions. They derive from both domestic and international sources.[6] However, they are united in their role in structuring the expectations and the activities of commercial actors according to certain generally accepted principles. This normative framework provides a common language and a common set of values and procedures that unite those engaged in international commerce. In this sense, it is constitutive of the conditions of economic exchange; it provides the ground rules and protections that enable and facilitate exchange and is thus linked in a fundamental way to private international economic and commercial cooperation.

The view that private international trade law forms the foundation for international economic cooperation among private actors would generally find support from most analysts in the field. More controversial, however, is the assertion that private international trade law is also constitutive of the "political" foundations of capitalism—that it is central to the constitution of authority in international affairs. This position is controversial because "private" relations are deemed by liberal thought to be "apolitical" in content and effect, while the law governing them is generally regarded as operating neutrally among market participants assumed to be of equal bargaining power.[7] As a body of "private" law, private international trade law is regarded by experts in the field to be inherently "apolitical."[8] The distributional impact of the law is concealed by assumptions concerning its value-neutrality and its functional role in facilitating commercial exchange through the reduction of transaction costs and the promotion of certainty and predictability in commercial contracting and in dispute resolution. This chapter takes the position that private international trade law functions in a distributional way to determine "who gets what, when and how" and on what terms and is, thus, inescapably "political."[9] While assumptions of neutrality and equality in bargaining power may approximate relations among commercial actors from the developed world, they lose meaning for those involving parties from less developed parts of the world.[10]

Significantly, however, the "political" content and effect of the law is obscure and not well understood by students of international relations. A variety of explanations may be advanced to account for this obscurity,[11] but one important explanation lies in the historical development of the distinction between private and public international law. The distinction between public and private international law initially served to expand the scope of state authority over certain commercial transactions, which came to be the subject of public international trade law. Over time, it also facilitated the de facto expansion of corporate power and authority over other transactions that formed the foundation for private international trade law. Private transactions were deemed to be apolitical and neutral in nature and, hence, were regarded as beyond the reach of state authority. As apolitical concerns, private trade laws were considered inappropriate subjects of public authority.

In addition, the definition of "authority" implicit in the public/private law distinction creates obstacles to theorizing about the political authority of private actors. The association of "political" authority with the public sphere, occupied by governments, and the association of "apolitical" economic activity with the private sphere, occupied by individuals and nonstate corporate actors, creates a bar to conceptualizing private action as political action. Indeed, these associations obscure the political significance of private power and authority in international affairs and assume separations that are deeply problematic analytically and normatively. Moreover, the treatment of these separations as natural and inevitable incidents of liberal market-based societies neglects crucial historical differentiation in the content of the public and private spheres. This results in a static and unhistoric understanding of the evolution of political authority in international affairs.

The discussion proceeds in two parts. The first section examines the public/private distinction in international law and associates the distinction with liberal theories of international law and international relations. It makes a case for the growing inadequacy of notions of political authority that rest upon the distinction and suggests the need for an analytical revision of the foundational concept of personality in international law. This revision needs to reflect historical and contemporary variations in the actors who are regarded as acting authoritatively in international commercial relations and should, at the very least, impose greater accountability on the corporate sphere. The second part illustrates the historical constitution and reconstitution of authority in the area of maritime commerce, illustrating the analytical power and ideological significance of concept of private global authority. It shows that the concept provides assistance in explaining the historic evolution of significant international commercial norms governing maritime transport and their association with a variety of private and public authorities. The discussion concludes with some implications of private authority for international affairs, addressing some of the issues raised in the introduction to this volume.

DISTINGUISHING PRIVATE AND PUBLIC INTERNATIONAL LAW

This section describes the distinction between private and public international law and addresses its origins, operation, and significance for conceptualizing authority in international affairs.[12]

Describing the Private/Public Law Distinction

The private/public distinction is used in both domestic and international law. In domestic law, the distinction embodies a differentiation between matters that are properly regarded as the subject of state regulatory authority and those that remain the preserve of the individual. The public/private distinction has been used to differentiate between "open" and "intimate" in the context of privacy concerns.[13] It also informs the distinction between "work/government" and "social life/family," which is central to much feminist analysis.[14] In liberal theory it provides the foundation for the distinction between the "state" and "civil society," the latter including socioeconomic as distinct from political matters.[15] Liberal theories of international law and international relations are premised upon a number of dualisms or distinctions reflecting what Michael Walzer terms the "liberal art of separation."[16] According to Walzer, "liberal theorists preached and practiced the art of separation. They drew lines, marked off different realms, and created the sociopolitical map with which we are still familiar" and which includes distinctions between private and public life, home and work, civil society and political community, among others. "Liberalism is a world of walls, and each one creates a new liberty."[17] Duncan Kennedy less charitably observes that the "history of legal thought since the turn of the century is the history of the decline of a particular set of distinctions—those that taken together, constitute the liberal way of thinking about the social world."[18] These include distinctions between state and society, public and private, individual and group, subject and object, and freedom and coercion. The public/private law distinction is associated most closely with the following dualisms: politics/economics, state/society, government/economy, government/family, and subject/object. In most cases, one side of the dualism signifies what is properly regarded as the subject of public authority, while the other represents a sphere carved out of the regulatory ambit of the state as a privileged area of more-or-less individual or private authority.

In international law, the public/private distinction embodies differentiation in both subject-matter and legal doctrine.[19] Generally, public international law concerns the relations between states and to a very limited extent between international organizations and some nonstate actors. It includes the familiar concerns with the sources and subjects of international law, the application and enforcement of international law, the law of international organizations, the law of treaties, the laws of war, law of the sea, and a host of other subjects involving the international relations of states. In contrast, private international law regulates the international relations among individuals, ranging from family relations to international commercial transactions between and among private traders and corporations.[20] The latter includes the international sale of goods between private parties and ancillary services, like insurance, transportation, financing, and dispute resolution.[21]

Doctrinally, public and private international law are treated as separate fields. Public international law is generally regarded as deriving form the sources identified in Article 38 of the Statute of the International Court of Justice and includes international treaties and customary international law as the most significant sources. Private international law, in contrast, is of a more complicated doctrinal status, although many private international laws derive from municipal legal systems.[22]

However, most important for theorizing about political authority in international affairs are the actors or agents identified as the proper subjects of the discipline and regarded as "authoritative" in creating and enforcing commercial laws. This raises important and vexing matters concerning the meaning of "authority" and its relation to issues of identity and subjects of the law.[23] Indeed, as noted in the introduction, the meaning of authority raises the ontological issue of defining the very essence of politics and political activity. Controversy over its meaning "is invariably cast in the form of a dispute over the relation between the notions of authority, power, and legitimacy . . . the very question of what politics is and what the field and scope of political activity consists in."[24] However, recognizing that "authority" is "an elusive concept" and submits to "no single view . . . that can serve as the model for understanding all the different uses to which it is put," it is possible to identify the main elements of the concept of political authority as it is used in political and legal theory.[25] Joseph Raz identifies "political authority" with " a right to make laws and regulations, to judge and to punish for failing to conform to certain standards, or to order some redress for the victims of such violations, as well as a right to command."[26] Distinguishing between being "an authority" (as an expert, scholar, or specialist) and being "in authority" (as a political leader or commander), many theorists recognize the necessary element of trust and the general perceptions of legitimacy that vest both an authority and those in authority with the necessary qualities.[27] In asking "who speaks with authority?" one is asking who has "the capacity to perform a speech act that exerts a force on its hearers greater than that of simple influence, but less than that of a command?"[28] The idea is that at either extreme of persuasion or coercion, authority is extinguished. At one extreme, persuasion lacks the trust and acceptance that characterizes relations of authority. At the other extreme of coercion, authority shades into brute force.

> Authority is thus related to coercion and persuasion in symmetrical ways. Both of these exist as capacities or potentialities implicit within authority, but are actualized only when those who claim authority sense that they have begun to lose the trust of those over whom they seek to exercise it. In a state of latency or occultation, persuasion and coercion alike are constitutive parts of authority, but once actualized and rendered explicit they signal—indeed, they are, at least temporarily—its negation.[29]

For international legal thinkers, the concept of political authority is intimately related to notions of legitimacy and generally shared perceptions of authority. Myres McDougal and Harold Lasswell, founders of what is referred to as the New Haven approach, define authority in precisely these terms. They state that "[a]uthority is the structure of expectation concerning who, with what qualifications and mode of selection, is competent to make which decisions and by what criteria and what procedures." They distinguish authority from control: the latter designates "an effective voice in decision, whether authorized or not." Law exists at the meeting place of the authority and control: when there is a "conjunction of common expectations concerning authority with a high degree of corroboration in actual operation."[30] The idea that law is more than simply the operation of authority in that it also contains a behavioral or empirical element of effective control is instructive. It suggests that it is not enough to have shared expectations and perceptions of legitimate authority, but that those expectations must be translated into action and behavior through compliance with authoritative practices. It also suggests an analogy with customary international law, the existence and proof of which turns upon meeting both a behavioral/empirical test and a subjective/normative test. Under international law, a custom differs from a usage. As Ian Brownlie observes, a "usage is a general practice which does not reflect a legal obligation." He offers the examples of ceremonial salutes at sea and the practice of exempting diplomatic vehicles from parking prohibitions.[31] A custom, in contrast, reflects both uniformity and consistency in practice (the behavioral/empirical test) and the belief that the practice is obligatory: *opinio juris et necessitatis* (the subjective/normative test).[32] It is the second factor that differentiates legal custom from social usage, courtesy, or morality[33] and suggests that legitimate authority involves both actual compliance and shared recognition of authority.[34]

In a similar vein, Thomas Franck posits that legitimacy does not depend upon coercion, but upon state perceptions of the legitimacy of rules and the rule-making institutions.[35] These perceptions in turn depend upon a number of factors that influence the quality of the rules and institutions (including the determinacy or clarity of the rule, the authenticity of a rule, which is determined by symbols, rituals, and pedigree, the coherence of a rule with generally accepted principles, and adherence of the rule and institutions to right processes or procedures). Franck identifies others who link legitimacy to procedural and process-related issues, including Dworkin's requirements of fairness, justice, and integrity[36] or the adequacy of procedures relating to participation, consent, and openness in authority relations. With reference to the latter concerns, Franck cites Jürgen Habermas and the significance of discursive practices or processes in the validation of authority.[37]

Franck also identifies another more controversial link of direct relevance to theorizing about political authority. This is a link made by neo-Marxists between legitimacy and the justice of outcomes. Franck identifies what he terms operational and theoretical problems in associating the legitimacy of rules with the justice of their results and concludes by defining legitimacy in terms of the observance of proper processes and procedures. In doing so, Franck echoes Hedley Bull's reservations about the inability of achieving normative agreement or solidarity in a substantive or purposive way over the meaning of justice in a world comprised of a multiplicity of sovereign states.[38] To Bull, world justice is not attainable in contemporary world politics. It is only possible in the context of a world community or society capable of identifying the common good.[39]

> If, in the present condition of world politics, in which states are the principal actors, ideas of interstate or international justice play a dominant part in everyday discussion, and ideas of human justice play a smaller part, ideas of cosmopolitan or world justice play very little part at all. The world society or community whose common good they purport to define does not exist except as an idea or myth which may one day become powerful, but has not done so yet.[40]

To Franck, as well, "the system of states, which is the basic contemporary circumstance of the international community, vastly complicates the task of discerning applicable principles of justice."[41]

The very limited role that Bull accords to international law in influencing state behavior[42] complements Franck's belief that international legal-political authority operates only with regards to the legitimacy of processes and procedures and not in terms of the legitimacy of purposes or the justice of outcomes.[43] Franck like Bull regards the multiplicity of states in the world as a barrier to contemplating any sort of normative solidarity over the purposes or outcomes of political authority. For both, the constitution of political authority on the basis of the principle of the sovereign equality of states militates against the promotion of justice in international affairs. Franck identifies operational and theoretical impediments to associating political authority and legitimacy with the justice of outcomes. The operational problem stems from the impossibility of associating states with justice. Franck argues that justice attaches only to individuals and not to states, and thus is not a legitimate pursuit of political authority. He argues that "justice can only be said to be done to persons, not to such collective entities as states."[44] The idea of "justice among states" is a "misleading metaphor" because it is individuals who experience justice and injustice, "who, unlike states, are capable of pleasure and pain."[45] This operational problem is compounded by the problem of theorizing about state agreement and solidarity in the face of normative pluralism. As Franck observes, "[w]hen different belief systems contend, what can one say about the justice of rules?"[46] Bull is even more direct: a recognition of demands for justice are ultimately revolutionary and subversive of the state system. "Demands for world justice are therefore demands for the transformation of the system and society of states, and are inherently revolutionary."[47] Franck echoes this view in the comment that the "evolution of a system of global justice, therefore, must await, and go hand in hand with, the system's transformation from one based on states to one based on the primacy of world government and global citizenship."[48] For both, the legitimacy of political authority turns on the adoption of adequate processes and procedures to ensure the maintenance of a modicum of order in the contemporary states system.[49] Operational and theoretical problems deriving from the nature of the states system thus bar the association of political authority with substantive justice. Moreover, nonstate entities, be they individuals or corporations, are factored out of the ambit of political authority. Political authority relates only to states.

This view differs substantially from that of the New Haven school, which adopts an explicitly purposive and policy-oriented approach to international law and postulates "human dignity" as the central guiding principle for international legal authority.[50] For the New Haven scholars, normative pluralism does not act as a bar to entertaining questions of justice. Indeed, they "have freely acknowledged the necessity of making value choices . . . arguing that such choices are inevitable in all approaches, and that they should be made explicit by policy makers and scholars."[51] In addition, in positing that international legal authority operates in the context of a multiplicity of "participants," they carve out a space for individuals and, arguably, for other nonstate actors such as corporations in international affairs.[52]

Thus, for many theorists we see that trust and shared perceptions of legitimacy are regarded as important elements of political authority. Moreover, the proof or evidence of the operation of political authority, like legal authority and as opposed to moral or social authority, lies in actual compliance. Differences emerge, however, in the conditions that render an authority legitimate, including at least two major distinctions between legitimate purposes or outcomes and legitimate procedures.[53] These distinctions in turn are linked to underlying assumptions of authority, identity, and legitimate subjects that inhere in the public/private distinction and give rise to both analytical and normative concerns. As Steven Lukes notes, the nature of "authority" is both an analytical and a normative question.[54] It is an analytical issue when one considers how authority is structured, how it operates, how it is recognized and is distinguished from other manners of influence. It is a normative issue when one inquires into the justification for authority and questions who or what vests it with legitimacy and why should it be accepted as such. As will be discussed in the next section, the tendency to recognize the political identity of states but not of nonstate entities, be they individuals or corporations, when coupled with the inability to theorize about justice as an element of legitimate political authority, has rather troubling normative implications for the rights and obligations of both individuals and corporations. It is here that we must consider the historical origins of the private/public distinction in international law and the normative implications of its operation, for this distinction is an essential element of contemporary notions of political authority.

Origin, Operation, and Significance of the Distinction

The distinction between private and public international law is an essential element in the structuring of global political authority. The distinction serves to identify the agents and identities that are regarded as capable of exercising political authority, while simultaneously precluding the possibility of the exercise of such authority by others. Karl Klare observes that the "public/private distinction poses as an analytical tool . . . but it functions more as a form of political rhetoric used to justify particular results."[55] Indeed, I have argued elsewhere that in international law "the distinction is not reflective of an organic, natural or inevitable separation, but is an analytical construct that evolved with the emergence of the bourgeois state."[56] The distinction was articulated in the context of the move from the feudal to the modern political economy. This initially entailed the emergence of the European state system and the absolutist state as the dominant political authority structures. Later, with the advent of capitalism and the liberal state, state authority in many places emerged in democratic and republican forms. The private/public distinction was cast and has been recast, analytically, at different times as part of transitions in the dominant mode of production from feudal to capitalist and the resulting transformations in social relations.[57] Today, various postmodern and postcapitalist transformations are reconfiguring and relocating political authority, effecting changes in the content of the public and private spheres.

In feudal times, there was no distinction between public and private international law. Indeed, there was no real concept of international law in the modern sense of a distinct body of law regulating the foreign relations of states. There was a notion of the *jus commune,* which included the common law of medieval merchants. The latter is known generally as the law merchant (*lex mercatoria*) and is the medieval ancestor of modern private international trade law. The medieval law merchant attained such universality in the European trading world that it came to be known as part of the *jus gentium* or the law of nations.[58] Roman law had bequeathed the distinctions between local law and universal law and between civil law and public law to European states. However, it took the replacement of medieval political arrangements of ambiguous and overlapping authority structures by the states system and the transition from a feudal to a market or capitalist society to generate the domestic/international and private/public distinctions.

While Roman law specified different types of authority, they do not reflect the distinction between public and private authorities.[59] Three types relate to our modern notions of political authority, while the fourth does not. *Auctoritas patrum* or *auctoritas senatus* refers to the authority of the senate; *auctoritas principis* refers to the authority of the emperor; *auctoritas tutoris* refers to the authority of the trustee or guardian. The fourth type of authority is *auctoritas venditoris*, which refers to the authority of the commercial vendor and concerns the authority of one selling goods to pass on title and property in the goods to the purchaser. We see that there was a recognition of the distinction in authority relations between the governors and the governed and between buyers and sellers, but they were not yet articulated in terms of distinctions between government and economy or civil society.

In states where Roman law was never received, the distinction between the public and private realms developed in the context of the relations attending the emergence of the bourgeois state and the practices of constitutional and responsible government.[60]

The identification of the self-regulating market as a defining institution of the private sphere placed the public/private distinction at the heart of legal discourse in the nineteenth century and marked an important transition from feudal to capitalist relations.[61] It also marked the beginning of the association of political authority with the public sphere of governments and the association of "apolitical" relations with the private sphere of markets and individuals. Moreover, these associations conferred identity and identified legitimate subjects. They represented a differentiation between authoritative and nonauthoritative actors and actions; between actors who evoke trust and who can and do legitimately bind others and those who cannot; between actions that are authoritative and actions that are not. The public sphere was recognized as the domain of legitimate political authority and authoritative judgment, while the private sphere related to private and politically nonauthoritative judgment. Significantly, as Friedman observes, "'[p]rivate judgment' is *not* a judgment exercised on private matters such as family life or business affairs; it is not a privatized or apolitical judgment. It is rather a nonauthoritative judgment, which may be highly political in content but which is nevertheless not entitled to prescribe behaviour."[62]

The authority of the market in ordering private relations was grounded in legal theory and liberal political economy, which provided the rationale for the private and "nonauthoritative" regulation of individual, corporate, contractual, and tortious (wrongful) activities. Horowitz notes that "[j]ust as nineteenth-century political economy elevated markets to the status of the paramount institution for distributing rewards on a supposedly neutral and apolitical basis, so too private law came to be understood as a neutral system for facilitating voluntary market transactions and vindicating injuries to private rights."[63]

In political theory, the free market was and still is regarded as an integral component of liberal theorizing. The market is represented as the "sphere of economic competition and free enterprise, the market in commodities, labor, and capital . . . the buyers and sellers of commodities are entirely at liberty to strike any bargain they wish, buying anything, selling anything, at any price they can agree upon, without the interference of state officials."[64] While contemporary liberals have long recognized important imperfections in market operations, they continue to regard market activity as an integral part of international relations.[65] However, there is a great degree of controversy over the nature of the relationship between the market and the state; between the private and the public spheres.[66] The extent to which states control markets or, conversely, are driven by them forms a central debate in international political economy today.[67] Much of this controversy stems from the axiomatic nature of the associations of states with political activity and of markets with economic activity, with the private/public distinction.[68]

In international law, the public/private distinction formed the foundation for establishing the dominant authority structure as that of the territorial state and the states system, eliminating any potentially rival claims to identity and authority coming from individuals or from corporate entities. As Mark Janis notes, "[n]ineteenth century positivists promoted the notion that the individual was not a proper subject of international law . . . public international law went to matters affecting states, while private international law concerned matters between individuals."[69] International lawyers refer to this as the doctrine of international legal personality. This doctrine identifies who or what is a "subject" of the law and, hence, who is authoritative. It determines who possesses "rights and duties enforceable at law. . . . Legal personality is crucial. Without it institutions and groups cannot operate for they need to maintain and enforce claims."[70] Shaw elaborates on the doctrine:

> One of the distinguishing characteristics of contemporary international law has been the wide range of participants performing on the international scene. These include states, international organizations, regional organizations, non-governmental organizations, public companies, private companies and individuals. Not all such entities will

constitute legal persons, although they may act with some degree of influence upon the international plane. International personality is participation plus some form of community acceptance.[71]

The identification of states as the proper "subjects" of international law is generally associated with legal positivism, which attributes the binding force of international law to states and state consent. It contrasts with and followed on natural law theories,[72] whose assumption of a universal moral order transcending time and place fit more comfortably with a more inclusive notion of the subjects of international law.[73] Legal positivism developed along with the emergence of the modern states system and is associated with the works of Johann Jacob Moser (1701–85), Emerich Vattel (1714–67), Richard Zouche (1590–1660), John Austen (1790–1859), Hans Kelsen (1881–1973), and H. L. A. Hart (1907–92).[74] Historically, legal positivists provided the legal equivalent of the statist political theories advanced by Jean Bodin and Thomas Hobbes.[75] Today, the modern doctrine of international legal personality continues to run parallel to territorial/statist conceptions of international relations.[76] Only states are recognized as full members of the United Nations and the degree of legal personality possessed by international organizations is determined by and derived from their member states.[77] Only states may bring contentious proceedings before the International Court of Justice.[78] Only states are entitled to claim the right of territorial integrity, a basic right recognized in the Charter of the United Nations. The international legal status of transnational corporations, which are probably the most visible private global actors today, has been likened to the status of the individual under international law. Both are *objects* and not *subjects* of the law: they have no original rights or liabilities at international law; the only rights or liabilities they possess is derivative as nationals of a state, under the principles governing nationality.[79] Moreover, such rights or liabilities can only be asserted or assumed by the state on behalf of the individual or the transnational corporation.[80] As one legal theorist notes, "[t]he law recognizes as 'international corporations' only those entities which are constructed by international law, that is by treaty. . . . This format is not available to the private commercial enterprise which must content itself with stringing together corporations created by the laws of different states."[81] Another notes that the transnational corporation lacks "concrete presence in international law . . . it is an apparition . . . its actuality sifted through the grid of state sovereignty into an assortment of secondary rights and contingent liabilities.[82] Yet another legal scholar observes the "awkward," but well-established assimilation of corporate nationality to the nationality of individuals.[83] The result is the "invisibility" of the transnational corporation under international law, as corporate power and responsibility is filtered through the state.

While few international relations analysts would go so far as to declare transnational corporations to be "invisible" in terms of their political significance, there is a dominant tendency to regard corporate power as ultimately linked to and conditioned by state power. This is particularly evident in the comment by Stephen Krasner that "it is states or polities that structure the basic environment within which transnationals must function: the nature of the legal system; the specification of legitimate organizational forms . . . the determination of acceptable modes of political action."[84] Indeed, a key aspect of the debate between neoliberals and neorealists is the relative significance of state and non-state/economic actors and activities to international relations. Both accept "states as the dominant actors that seek to maximize their own utility."[85] However, neoliberals accord much more scope for mutual interests among states and arguably suggest greater scope for economic actors and activities to influence international relations.[86]

The symmetry in legal and political approaches to the issues of identity and authority in international law and international relations illustrates the symbiotic development and interrelated nature of the legal and political theories that formed the foundation for the emergence of territorially individuated political authority. It also suggests that both disciplines are slow to react to postmodern and postcapitalist developments that call into question the analytical vigor of the distinction between private and public international law. These developments are effecting a shift in authority structures, reconfiguring state and corporate authority and control. In some cases they are challenging, modifying, and eroding the political authority of states and enhancing corporate power. In other cases, corporations are working with states in corporatist associations and enhancing state authority and control. Although some, like the New Haven scholars, explicitly reject a "state-centric" approach to international authority and identify the important actors as "participants," the singular association of states and governments with public authority remains very powerful.

In domestic law, the public/private distinction came under attack in the past by those concerned about the growing concentration of capital[87] and the fear that "so-called private institutions were acquiring coercive power that had formerly been reserved to governments."[88] According to Horowitz, it became a "sign of legal sophistication" to recognize the problems with the private/public distinction in domestic law. However, today the distinction is being reasserted with new vigor in the privatizing and deregulatory ethos of domestic elites and has almost unchallenged legitimacy in international law and among international corporate elites. For example, there appears to be a great deal of recognition of the enhanced power of transnational corporations, but this is unaccompanied by commensurate efforts to regulate them.

> The obvious importance of private corporate activities to the international legal system is yet to be accommodated in legal theory, which still equates them with the individual. As participants, certain multinational enterprises control resources more extensive than many states, and their decisions contribute to the shaping of the political structure of national and international regimes. As put by one observer, "the international combine has wrested the substance of sovereignty from the so-called sovereign state." Their effective power permits them to negotiate and agree as equals with governments.[89]

Numerous efforts by international organizations, regional organisations, business and industry associations have produced guidelines, codes, recommendations, and other "soft law" norms in the attempt to regulate the activities of transnational corporations.[90] It was hoped that the Draft Code of Conduct produced by the Commission on Transnational Corporations[91] would be a major contribution to the development of a regulatory framework, but a consensus over the draft was never achieved. Other failed international efforts "affirm rather than challenge the assumption that it is a state's prerogative to deal with TNCs [transnational corporations] through its national legal systems."[92] This poses a major normative problem of ensuring corporate accountability. There is no guarantee that a state will assume responsibility for the actions of corporations having its nationality. Often the place of nationality is only remotely connected to corporate operations, functioning in many cases as a tax haven.[93] As the United Nations Centre on Transnational Corporations observes: "[a] number of factors . . . conspire to make purely national control systems variously evadable, inefficient, incomplete, unenforceable, exploitable, or negotiable . . . with respect to transnational corporations."[94] One solution is the recognition of the transnational corporation as a legal subject, bearing rights and responsibilities directly under international law. However, this faces major problems in states' unwillingness to "relinquish their traditionally dominant position in international law, or to acknowledge the effectiveness of law in the absence of a sovereign."[95]

The continuing influence of the association of political authority with states and the tenacity of the private/public distinction are significant in light of the development of new corporate structures that blur the distinction between private and public activities. Significant developments associated more generally with late- or post-capitalism are enhancing the authority of additional private actors, like business, industry, and trade associations.[96] In some cases, new corporate forms are emerging as a response to processes of economic globalization. Wyn Grant defines economic globalization as "a process in which transactions across the borders of nation-states increase in importance relative to those within nation-states; and whereby national boundaries cease to be a significant impediment to the movement of goods and services."[97] He argues that globalization has created the need for improved economic coordination transnationally, but that adequate "mechanisms of governance" have not been developed. Grant identifies intra- and interfirm developments as the "best developed mechanisms of governance that exist at the supranational level." These include "coordination within the new 'stateless firms'" and "through such devices as joint ventures and cartels."[98] Stateless corporations are businesses in which ownership, in terms of share holdings, is internationalized. Wynn notes that this is generally reflected in the composition of the board of directors.[99] Stateless corporations are emerging as a result of changes in patterns of foreign direct investment and shifts in production associated more generally with economic globalization.[100] They pose a particularly acute problem for notions of corporate accountability because they have the potential of even greater invisibility than traditional multinational corporations whose nationality can at least be linked relatively unambiguously to a single state.[101]

Similarly, Susan Strange observes that the proliferation of interfirm relationships, like "partnerships, production-sharing arrangements, collaborative research and networking . . . have begun to blur the identity and indirectly undermine the authority of the state."[102] Corporate mergers, acquisitions, strategic alliances, and networking between firms add further complexities. She notes that when "partners in the network operate and are registered in several countries, it is impossible even to guess the 'nationality' of the whole network. Yet much media comment and much academic analysis still assume that each transnational corporation has a national identity and that governments can identify and then support their own national champion."[103]

The development of novel corporate arrangements, which render transnational corporations more difficult to locate nationally, compounds their virtual "invisibility." Under international law, their activities are by definition nonauthoritative; they only become authoritative if a state decides to enforce their claims or to assume state responsibility for their actions. We have seen that, in theory, they cannot be authoritative because, as private actors, they lack international legal personality. They do not possess identity as subjects of the law. Moreover, liberal thinking works against recognizing the authority of private actors, such as transnational corporations or private business associations. The liberal faith in free economic markets and in representative democracy presents barriers to conceiving private relations or entities as politically authoritative or representative. Johns notes that "both of these institutions require international law to abdicate responsibility for the TNC. . . . The TNC is a creature of private law—'a typically democratic method of law-making . . . characterised as the sphere of private autonomy'."[104] To impute political authority and accountability to this private, market activity would be to turn representative democracy on its head. It would be "inconsistent with the liberal belief that the processes of democratically-elected government ought to be the only legitimate means of curtailing individual liberty."[105]

Moreover, the recognition of the identity of corporations and business associations as subjects of the law, as for individuals, runs up against the operational and theoretical problems raised by Franck. It means broadening the domain of political authority to include private actors which opens up the possibility of linking legitimate authority with concerns about justice. This risks Bull's greatest fear of promoting revolutionary demands for justice and human dignity over the systemic need for order.

Ironically, it is the transnational corporate elite who is pushing vociferously for the establishment of a global business regulatory order.[106] But it is an order of a particular sort—one consistent with a renewed emphasis on neoliberal values concerning the superiority of the private ordering of global corporate relations.[107] Global corporate actors are not trying to undo the "liberal art of separation" that draws the "map of the social and political world" by separating the economy and civil society from the political community and was meant to "mark off" "free exchange" from "coercive decision making."[108] They are not trying to harness private power through state regulatory controls. Rather, driven by intensified global competition, corporations and states are attempting to reposition themselves in a manner consistent with the move from the welfare to the competition state. As Philip Cerny observes, states can no longer focus on welfare as a purely domestic problem. "As the world economy is characterized by increasing interpenetration and the crystallization of transnational markets and structures, the state itself is having to act more and more like a market player, that shapes its policies to promote, control, and maximize returns from market forces in an international setting."[109] Furthermore, "[i]n a globalizing world, the competition state is more likely to be involved in a process of competitive deregulation and creeping liberalization."[110] In the corporate law world, this trend is evident in what is variously referred to as the "race to the bottom," "lowest common denominator," and "regulatory meltdown" as states engage in competitive deregulation of corporate activities.[111] Moreover, Robert Cox suggests that "economic globalization . . . may prove to be the underlying factor in the constitution of future political authorities and future world order." He further observes that

> [t]he key criterion today is competitiveness; and derived from that are universal imperatives of deregulation, privatization, and the restriction of public intervention in economic processes. Neoliberalism is transforming states from being buffers between external economic forces and the domestic economy into agencies for adapting domestic economies to the exigencies of the global economy. So now the market appears to be bursting free from the bonds of national societies, to subject global society to its laws.[112]

In a similar vein, Stephen Gill identifies the globalization of the state with the "restructuring of state and capital on a world stage towards a more globally integrated and competitive market-driven system" that transforms the state "so as to give greater freedom to the private aspects of capital accumulation in the extended state at the local, national and transnational levels."[113] But the enhanced power of private capital is rendered virtually "invisible" by the dominant ways of thinking about political authority. The problem of private global authority is at least twofold. In the first place, conventional notions of authority that associate authority with the state do not lend themselves easily to notions of private governance or "governance without government." As we have seen, both international relations and international law have trouble in theorizing about private authority. In the second place, the *a priori* status accorded the public/private distinction by liberal theory defines private/economic transactions out of existence as political concerns.[114] Private global authority, in a word, is an ontological impossibility. A review of the historical evolution of laws governing maritime trade, one of the earliest examples of private international law, illustrates that this is simply an inaccurate depiction of authority in the global political economy. Private actors, including merchants, corporations, and business associations have been intimately involved in creating and enforcing merchant laws for over a millennium, although their authority has weakened at times. Merchant laws have operated authoritatively in gaining the trust, the general perceptions of legitimacy and a high degree of compliance from the merchant community. The discussion will turn to review this significant instance of private global authority.

AUTHORITY IN MARITIME TRANSPORT

The generation of norms governing maritime transport illustrates a significant instance of private global authority. This significance stems, in part, from the general importance of international shipping to the global economy. Mark Zacher with Brent Sutton note that although international air transport has grown in recent years, "[s]hipping continues to dominate the movement of goods internationally."[115] They observe that in the late 1980s about two thirds of all international trade by value was transported by ship and they explain the more general significance of maritime transport thus:

> Shipping has been crucial to the growth of the world economy for two related reasons. First, as world production expands, international transportation services are required to carry many raw and intermediate goods to manufacturing plants and finished goods to consumers. Second, shipping is a more cost-effective method than land and air transport for moving most bulk goods between states. Without inexpensive, efficient oceanic transportation, world trade would not have grown as fast as it has because higher transportation costs lessen opportunities for exploiting comparative and competitive advantage.[116]

However, the development of maritime transport laws and practices is also significant as an example of the earliest private international trade law. It is possible to identify the historical origins of the distinction between public and private international law in the evolution of the authorities regulating marine transport. Edgar Gold observes that "[a]s an industry, marine transport evolved as a fiercely independent and private enterprise and over the years proved to the public interest, through its own achievements, that it could work that way. Its development was thus left to its own devices and its own rule making."[117] While maritime transport was regulated privately for a great deal of its early history, increasingly certain activities came to be regulated by national governments, public policymakers, and more recently international organizations. As Gold notes, the *commercial* and *industrial* aspects of maritime transport remained the preserve of private regulatory undertakings, while the *ocean use* aspects of maritime trade became increasingly the concern of governments and public policymakers. By the 1960s and 1970s, these two "monoliths," as represented in private and public international laws, respectively, "would address each other in language neither could understand nor comprehend."[118] The history of this development illustrates the processes by which political authority over maritime transport was constituted and reconstituted over time by private and public actors. This is a rich history revealing a growing multiplicity of and variation in actors involved in the creation and enforcement of maritime transport laws. It is also a history of "private protectionism" and the construction of what Susan Strange refers to as the "curtain of silence" around collusive industrial and corporate practices.[119] This history reveals the way in which the predominantly private authority structure reconfigured itself over time, illustrating both the historical specificity of the public/private distinction and the chameleon-like nature of private corporate power.

Trade law experts usually identify three general phases in the evolution of private international trade law.[120] These phases reflect the development of merchant laws, customs, and disputed settlement procedures over roughly a millennium. The first phase is the medieval period, from the eleventh to the sixteenth centuries. The second phase is the period of state-building and the establishment of the European state system, from the seventeenth to the nineteenth centuries. The third phase is the modern phase, which involves twentieth-century developments relating to the development of international organizations. Generally, these phases reflect the evolution of maritime transport law from its origins in ancient sea laws and private medieval merchant customs, through a phase of state-building and a growing differentiation between public and private regulatory orders, to the contemporary period with its complex mix of private and public regulatory authority of national, international, and transnational origins. A brief review of these phases illustrates how the authority structure for maritime transport has evolved from a basis in private family-based organizations and merchant customs, to increasing institutionalization in private industry and trade associations, corporations, and cartels, and finally, to an international regime comprised of a hybrid of private and public national, international, and transnational authorities. The authority structure exhibits considerable differentiation in the identity and number of actors involved in creating and enforcing maritime transport laws over time. In addition, it reveals significant changes in the balance between public and private authorities and their degree of integration in law creation and enforcement. These developments reflect more generally interrelated trends toward greater institutionalization, specialization, internationalization, and politicization of maritime transport issues.

Phase I: Medieval Sea Laws

Historically, private traders developed customs establishing the terms upon which maritime trade was conducted. Many of these customs were inherited from ancient maritime customs and from Roman law.[121] They attained universal application throughout the European trading world through the activities of consuls and specialized merchant courts that settled disputes in markets and ports. Some of the customs came to be codified in merchant laws and codes that obtained great currency. Institutionally, the laws were created and enforced privately and autonomously:

maritime transactions were independent from local legal systems in that they were recognized and enforceable only in merchant courts. However, this does not mean that there was no involvement of the local political authorities. Indeed, they were involved in maritime commerce, but in a very limited fashion in terms of regulating piracy and in providing merchants with safe conduct. As Gold argues, this involvement reflected the earliest beginnings of what was to become the distinction between public and private maritime law.[122] Public authorities, such as they existed at the time, and their local laws regulated matters concerning sea and ocean use. Initially, this included the regulation of piracy; later, the enforcement of freedom of the high seas; and still later, the regulation of the territorial seas, fisheries, and other ocean uses. This was to become the foundation of public international maritime law. In contrast, merchants regulated matters concerning the ship, crew, cargo, and transport. This was later to become the domain of private international maritime law. Medieval merchants developed a rich assortment of instruments and procedures to structure their transactions. Early merchant laws dealt with the various types of agreements and contracts by which maritime adventures were launched and goods were shipped. Many arrangements were devised by merchants to allocate transport risks and costs and to settle disputes. The medieval *commenda* and *societas* were forms of maritime loans and partnerships in use from the tenth century, which contained specific rules allocating the costs and risks of transportation.[123] The bottomry contract functioned as a mortgage on a ship given by the owner to a financier to pay for the costs of the voyage, the owner pledging the keel or bottom of the ship as security for repayment of the loan. *Respondentia* contracts, in contrast, were loans secured by the ship's cargo. These maritime loans functioned to raise capital and to disperse risks among lenders, merchants, and shipowners.[124] As early as the thirteenth century, bills of lading transferring to the holder a title to the document and to the goods and having the character of negotiable instruments were in use.[125] Merchants also devised rules regulating charter parties and regulating the payment of freight and obligations relating to unloading, delivery, loss upon jettison of the goods, shipwreck, or collision and the consequences of breach of contract. The earliest principle of insurance law, contribution to the general average, was developed as a means of apportioning the risks of maritime adventures.[126] The costs of losses resulting from actions taken for common safety, like jettisoning the goods in a storm, were apportioned among the parties to the adventure. In contrast to the very limited commercial law of the local judicial systems, the medieval law merchant is renowned for its ingenuity, adaptability, and efficiency.[127]

At the beginning of this phase around the eleventh and twelfth centuries, a number of cities emerged as important centers for the development of maritime laws. Venice, Amalfi, Trani, Pisa, Genoa, Marseille, Jerusalem, and Oleron were all important centers with commercial courts and systems of commercial law.[128] Merchant laws and transactions were universalized through the European trading world through the offices of legal consuls who traveled with merchants arbitrating disputes as they arose.

Powerful families in these cities controlled maritime trade.[129] However, as commercial power began to shift away from the eastern Mediterranean west and northwest, the family operation was replaced by trading corporations that contributed to greater specialization in ocean trade.

> In commercial terms, there was a discernable intensification of international commercial intercourse, which not only sharpened competition between rival maritime city-states but also, for the first time, between individual traders and ship owners. The result was greater specialization in ocean trade and the offer of commercial incentives to shippers and manufacturers. At the same time, the tight framework within which maritime cities carried on their business was enlarged— at times even broken up completely. Also, for the first time marine transport and maritime trade began to evolve and to be conceived of separately. The old-style "family" shipping/trading business now became a body corporate with interregional organization and international business relations.[130]

The Italian trading companies, such as Bardi, Peruzzi, and Acciaiuoli, had branches throughout the Mediterranean, in northern France, Flanders, and England.[131] By the fourteenth and fifteenth centuries Mediterranean trade centered in the western Mediterranean with Spain in control. Gold identifies this as the first "great internationalization of marine transport," wherein "[s]hippers and consignees cooperated with little consideration of nationality, borders, or sovereignty. Ship owners, masters, merchants, and sailors became a truly international group, which took the place of the old family concern."[132] New maritime codes were produced in the port of Barcelona, known as the Consolato Del Mare, and enforced by private adjudicators known as *consules maris*. Meanwhile, in the North Sea and Baltic, the Hanseatic League, a multinational enterprise comprised of some sixty to eighty merchant towns, ports, and cities at its height, came to dominate northern trade. Initially, the Hanseatic League adopted the Sea Laws of Wisby, which were modelled on the older Laws of Oleron, but later developed its own maritime code, known as the Hansa Towns Shipping Ordinance.[133] These merchant courts and associations contributed to such uniformity in merchant law that it became known as an integral aspect of the common law or *jus commune* of the day. Significantly though, it was not created or enforced by states or sovereigns, but by autonomous merchants and merchant associations and corporations.

As we move toward the end of the first phase, we see the Hansa League gradually displaced by English trade and the growth of Anglo-Dutch rivalry for control of the oceans. We also see the emergence of a clear distinction between private and public international law developing against the backdrop the emerging state system. For public international law, jurists like Hugo Grotius began to formulate the foundations for modern international law. In maritime law, this translated into rules regulating ocean use. The doctrine of freedom of the seas became the *grund norm* for public maritime law.[134] For private international law, nationalization and codification rendered maritime transport laws very much a part of national legal systems, undermining the universality of merchant laws and more or less replacing merchant autonomy with state authority.

Phase II: Expansion of the Public Sphere; Neutralization of the Private Sphere

With the development of centralized, sovereign states, many of the merchant codes and practices were incorporated into national commercial laws. Merchant laws ceased to exist as autonomous bodies of law as they were incorporated into domestic commercial legal regimes. The growing influence of legal positivism displaced the central role of customary mercantile laws with laws enacted by national legislators, while many merchant courts disappeared or were incorporated into the domestic legal systems and replaced by national courts of law. The process of nationalizing commercial law occurred in the United States, England, France, Germany, and in other European countries.[135] With national codifications of commercial law, maritime transport laws came to be increasingly isolated from public international law. As Gold notes "all the stages of the shipping pro[c]ess were affected—the building, loading, routing, and discharging; the bills of lading; the marine risks; the crew; the navigation rules, port customs, wharfage, banking, and brokerage; the laws of purchase and sale of ships."[136] These became the domain of national regulation and private international trade law. This translated nationally, Gold argues, into the benign neglect of the shipping industry.[137] These aspects of maritime transport were privatized: they became the preserve of private shipping companies, maritime insurers, and mercantile associations, and lawyers schooled in private international law. In contrast, the political foundation of public international law was expanding as states asserted new and more ambitious territorial claims to the seas and to ocean resources.

Importantly, maritime transport was not only privatized, but as a matter of "private" law, it was neutralized as a potentially "political" concern. It was rendered "invisible," along with other invisibles, like multi- and transnational corporations and mercantile associations engaged in maritime trade. Moreover, later in this period, in addition to being privatized and rendered invisible, maritime transport was also gradually being denationalized. As Gold notes, maritime transport came to be regulated by powerful private associations and interest groups "whose interests were conceived as international rather than national. In the various maritime countries, these groups—consisting mainly of shipowners, merchants, bankers, and insurers—found that regardless of national persuasion, they were united by vital common interests, over-riding the diversities of national laws."[138] In this regard, significant pri-vate institutional developments occurred with the establishment of transnationally organized shipping cartels, shipping or liner conferences, and shipowner and other mercantile associations.[139]

> Since 1880 the international shipping industry has been dominated by transnationally organized cartels. Today, in the bulk sector, multina-tional firms control raw-materials markets; control of cargoes enables these firms to dominate, albeit not control totally, the transportation of raw materials. In the liner sector, shipping conferences hold sway, although their power has weakened somewhat in recent years.[140]

Shipping or liner conferences involve the association of shipping lines for the purpose of regulating freight rates, allocating market shares, and sometimes revenue pooling.[141] They emerged as an industry response to surplus capacity and have remained, as Stephen Krasner notes, a "durable feature" of the industry. "They are, in effect, cartels that maintain their position by using customer rebates, stipulating con-tractual liabilities for shipping with non-conference members, and giv-ing low priority to goods from 'disloyal' shippers."[142] By 1900 there were some 100 shipping conferences; by 1970 there were around 360, which controlled about 90 percent of international liner shipping.[143] Cafruny notes that in the postwar period, the conference system regu-lating liner shipping, "was dominated by the Europeans and Japanese firms." In contrast, bulk trade was dominated "through ownership, financing, or long-term charters" by "American banks and multina-tional corporations" shipping under flags of convenience.[144] A flag of convenience is the flag, and hence the nationality of a ship, that is not of a state with which a ship is most closely connected. As the name sug-gests, they were developed to avoid taxation and other regulatory mea-sures, such as labor and safety legislation. As Stephen Krasner notes, they offer shipowners a number of advantages, "including low taxation, unrestricted capital movements, and lower operating costs."[145] While in use after World War I, flags of convenience became significant in bulk trade after World War II. Their use was promoted by the United States and U.S.-based multinationals involved in the extractive industries, but opposed by European states and trade unionists who supported the abilities of states to regulate labor relations and other areas.

In addition to shipping cartels and conferences, a number of shipowners associations and clubs were created in the nineteenth century to regulate maritime transport. The Liverpool Steam Shipowners Association was created in 1858 and included those operating out of British ports. The Chamber of Shipping of the United Kingdom was created around the same time and became an advisor to the British government on shipping matters. A number of Protection and Indemnity (P&I) Clubs were also created in the nineteenth century to regulate maritime transport insurance. Significant also, is the central role that Lloyd's of London came to play in regulating marine insurance.

The important point about liner conferences, cartels, and these shipping and insurance associations is that they "illustrate the tendency toward greater organization of the shipping industry at the private, nongovernmental level."[146] Moreover, they functioned authoritatively among their members with the full support of states.[147] However, despite the substantial coordination of shipping brought about by these powerful private organizations, they were unable to avert the tendency toward national differentiation in maritime transport laws resulting from this phase of nationalization. Such differentiation eroded the universality of merchant laws and generated a movement for the unification of maritime transport laws in the third phase and contemporary phase.

Phase III: Internationalization or
Transnationalization of Maritime Transport?

The unification movement involves both public and private actors, reflecting a hybrid of public and private authority. Unification efforts are underway in a number of arenas, both international and transnational, evidencing different degrees of institutionalization. However, in general, there has been a progression institutionally from informal industry practices, to increasing institutionalization through trade associations and self-regulatory organizations, and, finally, to an international regime comprised of a hybrid of private and public authorities. These arrangements correspond to the forms of private global authority identified in the introductory chapter. Today, the regime governing maritime transport embodies "a degree of collective identity," "routinized discussions of collective policy, [. . .] networks of organizational linkages," and an efficacious sanctioning system based upon a combination of private and public enforcement, that "enable us to speak of an internationalization of political authority."[148] However, the collective identity of the maritime transport regime is increasingly best described in terms of *disembedded liberalism* and the transnationalization of political authority. Private and public elites operating both nationally and transnationally and committed to deregulation and privatization are strengthening the tendency toward the denationalization of norms anticipated by earlier institutional developments. They are expanding the domain of private international maritime law to include commercial activities formerly regarded as part of the public law domain. In so doing, as they "pool their de facto authority over transnational space, they remove it from direct democratic control."[149] This suggests that we are no longer witnessing the *internationalization* of authority so much as the *transnationalization* of authority structures, as transnational commercial interests tighten existing controls and assume new ones.

A brief review of the most significant unification efforts shows that the unification of maritime transport laws began as a private engagement of commercial actors from Western European states. They functioned very much in a "clublike" environment, bound together by a shared commitment to facilitating trade through uniform laws and procedures.[150] However, with the growing internationalization of authority brought about by the creation of the United Nations system, the increasing politicization of transport issues by new states emerging from colonial pasts, and with the intensification of competition in the shipping industry brought about by technological changes and new entrants to the industry, the unification movement was transformed into an undertaking of global and universalist pretensions. These goals, however, have not been achieved and today unification is taking place in the context of deregulation and privatization, which is enhancing the influence of private transnational authority.

The earliest modern unification efforts were undertaken towards the end of the nineteenth century by the Comité Maritime International (CMI), a private organization of international maritime lawyers and insurers founded in Belgium in 1897.[151] The purpose of the CMI is to promote the unification of maritime law and practice. It has engaged in numerous unification efforts in various areas, including marine collisions, shipowners liability, salvage, freight, navigation safety, insurance of enemy property, maritime mortgages and liens, bills of lading, maritime insurance, ship arrest, carriers' liability, stowaways, penal jurisdiction, registry of ships, and international maritime arbitration.[152] Twenty CMI conventions have been adopted and are in force or have been replaced by other conventions.[153] As the CMI lacks international legal personality,[154] it operates though the Belgium state. Typically, the CMI prepares a draft convention in consultation with its member national maritime law associations. After often lengthy private proceedings, the Belgium government convenes an international conference where the convention is reviewed and ultimately adopted by participating states. As Gold notes, the CMI operated like a "private club," "strictly separate from the public sector. . . . The public sector came involved only after the subject had been thoroughly discussed, dissected, revised, and redrafted over a period of years, and only after careful lobbying of governments to gain support of the political factor in each country concerned. Only then was a diplomatic conference called—only then did private and public sectors meet."[155]

Other significant private associations of note at the end of the nineteenth century include the National Association for Social Sciences, which was founded in London in 1857 to review issues of maritime insurance (general average) and produced the first code on the general average in 1864. The International Law Association (originally the Association for Reform and Codification of the Law of Nations) was founded in 1873 and took over the work on the general average, producing the York-Antwerp Rules of 1890.[156] The Institut de Droit International, founded in Belgium in 1873, also engaged in the unification of maritime laws.

A number of private maritime transport associations formed in the early twentieth century, but Gold notes that their unification efforts are fragmentary. The International Chamber of Shipping (ICS) was formed in 1921 and is comprised of about forty national shipowner's associations, and deals with technical shipping standards, while a number of other private organizations are of mixed success in promoting unification. They include the International Shipping Federation, the Council of European and Japanese Shipowners, the International Chamber of Commerce, the EEC Shipowners Association, the Hongkong Shipowners Association, the Baltic and International Maritime Conference, the International Association of Independent Tanker Owners, the Oil Companies' International Marine Forum, and the International Union of Marine Insurance. The CMI continues to be the most influential private association in the development of marine transport laws, however, the International Chamber of Commerce (ICC) has made significant contributions as well. Indeed, the ICC is today regarded as one of the preeminent sources of maritime customary law.[157] Due to its private nature and what is regarded as a preoccupation with narrowly technical matters, the ICC does not attract much attention in the literature. However, the ICC is famous for revising the most authoritative statement of the terms of trade governing maritime transport, known as Incoterms 1980. As private legislation, they are not regarded as "hard" rules of international law. They are generally regarded as "soft" law, although many argue that their use is so widespread that they constitute customary international law.[158]

What is noteworthy is that these terms of trade have clear distributional consequences, but this is obscured by their highly technical nature. For example, Cafruny identifies the trade term *f.o.b.*, which provides that goods are to be loaded *free on board*, as creating a barrier to entry into bulk trading markets for less developed states.[159] Under the *f.o.b.* contract, the importer chooses the shipowner. In contrast, under *c.i.f.* contracts (cost, insurance, and freight), the exporter selects the vessel. Britain expanded its merchant marine by contracting the sale of coal *c.i.f.* and the import of cotton and oil, *f.o.b.* In each case, British shipowners were selected. Long-term contracting[160] and standard form contracting[161] too can work against market access, but again the highly technical nature of the problem contributes to its obscurity and to a general lack of understanding of the asymmetrical relations built right into commercial contracts. Moreover, these problems are addressed in forums known generally for their "practical" and "apolitical" orientations. Indeed, this is often cited as the strength of private law-creating agencies and of the modern law merchant in general.[162]

With the creation of the United Nations, efforts were undertaken to create an intergovernmental maritime organization. The Inter-Governmental Maritime Consultative Organization (IMCO) emerged as the first intergovernmental body to be solely concerned with maritime transport. However, state fears that IMCO would encourage new entrants to the shipping industry and, thus, interfere with existing shipping markets and monopolies, prevented the organization from operating for a decade. Zacher with Sutton observe that it was only after the traditional maritime states were assured that the role of the organization would be "technical" and not "political" was there sufficient state support to bring the convention creating the organization into force.[163] The suspicion that maritime states had about IMCO was evident in their push for the CMI and not IMCO to deal with pollution liability following the Torrey Canyon disaster in 1967 when an oil tanker sank off the British coast.[164] IMCO won that battle and has been very successful in producing conventions unifying maritime transport in matters dealing with safety at sea and marine pollution.[165] In 1982 it was renamed the International Maritime Organization (IMO).

Significantly, there was no representation in the CMI of less developed states until after the Second World War. It operated not only as a private-sector club, but one with a very limited membership. The IMO, too, was initially regarded by developing countries as a "'shipowners' club' controlled by and operated for the benefit of the world's major shipping states with little power, competence, or even concern for other interests in international maritime transport."[166] The commercial and economic policy objectives of the organization were diluted, and as Gold notes, states whose interests diverged from those of the major shipping states, such as cargo states, coastal states, and less developed states, had to look elsewhere for a forum "for a more equitable division of the international-shipping cake."[167]

This, however, was to change with the development of the Group of 77 comprised of new states emerging from colonial pasts and their articulation of demands for a New International Economic Order. These demands were presented in the institutional context provided by the United Nations and its specialized agencies, politicizing many matters considered the preserve of private law. New intergovernmental institutions were developed to address these concerns, the most significant being the United Nations Conference on Trade and Development (UNCTAD), and the United Nations Commission on International Trade Law (UNCITRAL).

UNCTAD I convened in 1964 to address the commercial concerns of developing states. These concerns related to what they regarded as barriers to entry into the shipping industry and laws and practices that endorsed discriminatory rates and fixed market shares. The developing countries focused on four main sets of issues: the unilateral fixing of freight rates; discriminatory practices of shipping conferences; the inadequacy of existing shipping services; and inequities in existing shipping legislation.[168] These issues brought them face-to-face with the private sector of the major shipping states, which had monopolized the regulation of commercial and economic aspects of shipping.

> The economic and commercial aspects of shipping were almost virgin territory at the time of the Geneva conference [UNCTAD I], a forbidden land into which neither international organizations nor the developing countries had easy access. On the international scene it was one of the several untouched strongholds of anachronistic private enterprise and its credo of laissez-faire, with liner conferences enjoying all oligopolistic privileges. Generally, data was scarce and there was a dearth of published material on the economics of ocean transport. This was primarily due to the secrecy which shrouded the practices of liner conferences, price fixing and costs. The absence of reliable figures prevented developing countries from fully substantiating their grievances and suspicions about certain shipping practices.[169]

Developing countries challenged the unilateral and, they argued, discriminatory fixing of freight rates by shipping companies. They challenged the activities of the liner conferences that prevented competition and blocked the entry of developing countries into the shipping market. They criticized the reliability of existing shipping services and made the case for the development of national shipping lines to service their own needs. Finally, they focused on inadequacies in existing maritime transport laws relating to bills of lading, marine insurance, charter parties, shipowner's liability limitations, and flags of convenience. These laws, they argued, were written by the major shipping states, like the United Kingdom, and favored the interests of shipowners over those of shippers. As Gold notes, the demand for the international regulation of what was basically a private industry "astonished" the major maritime states, who perceived it as a "direct attack on the 'law merchant,' Adam Smith, the Protestant ethic, and free enterprise."[170] However, as has been noted before, the private regulation of maritime transport was far from laissez-faire. Indeed, liner conferences, for example, are highly regulated organizations.[171]

The private sector maintained the liberal mystique of laissez-faire to rationalize continued self-regulation, while liner conferences were rationalized as necessary discriminatory practices to stabilize the industry. On the whole it was a successful effort. While some developing countries have entered the shipping industry, they have not been very successful in reformulating maritime transport laws.[172] For example, their concerns about flags of convenience were watered down. Cafruny notes that "the capitulation of the 'unholy alliance' of European shipowners and international seamen's unions to the United States government and multinational corporations on the issue of flags of convenience" deflected attention away from their existence to their effects.[173] Objections from developing states to the use of flags of convenience, which they argued blocked their efforts to participate in bulk shipping, began to build up in UNCTAD. To the relief of shipowners and OECD states, bulk shipping was not on the agenda at UNCTAD I. This subsequently came to be a major component of the Group of 77s shipping policies. However, opposition from OECD countries and multinational oil and minerals corporations blocked significant change of the flag of convenience system, while the Group of 77 was split with Liberia, one of the most significant flag of convenience states, breaking ranks.[174]

With regard to the matters of shipping legislation, the major maritime states moved at UNCTAD II in 1968 to have shipping legislation transferred to the newly created UNCITRAL.[175] UNCITRAL was created in 1966 and charged with the unification of private international law. International shipping was identified as a major area of concern and adopted as part of its program of work. The transfer of shipping legislation to UNCITRAL was opposed by developing states who regarded it as a move to further isolate the issues of maritime transport by charging them to a body whose mandate was said to be technical and not policy-oriented. It is fair to say that further isolation has been achieved. Developing states have generally been unsuccessful in UNCITRAL in bringing about significant reform in shipping legislation. UNCITRAL, in consultation with UNCTAD, did produce a set of rules governing bills of lading that are more accommodating of the concerns of developing countries (the Hamburg Rules), thus reflecting a victory for the developing states. However, it is only a partial one.[176] So few states have adopted the rules that most of world trade continues to be governed by earlier rules said to favor the interests of shipowners (the Hague Rules and the Hague-Visby Rules).

While UNCITRAL's mandate is to "further the progressive harmonization and unification of the law of international trade" with a view to representing "the principal economic and legal systems of the world, and of the developed and developing countries,"[177] a number of factors conspire against the effective representation for the developing countries. The highly complex and technical nature of commercial contracts and arrangements renders them intelligible only to legal specialists and those trained in the maritime industry. A very select group of international lawyers, government officials, and industry representatives control the workings of UNCITRAL. They are generally supportive of maintaining a basically self-regulatory order and, while UNCITRAL officials espouse concern about the development needs of many countries, such concern remains largely at the level of rhetoric. UNCITRAL advances the commitment to the superiority of the private ordering and self-regulation of commercial activity. It's officials support the value of private regulation through self-regulating contracts, merchant custom, and private dispute settlement through international commercial arbitration.[178] Increasingly, the products of unification are "soft" and optional law, consistent with the neoliberal commitment to regulatory norms that facilitate and supplement the private ordering of commercial relations.[179] UNCTAD has been marginalized by developed states who support the expansion of UNCITRAL's jurisdiction. UNCITRAL has expanded its activities to include more commercial activities, extending beyond maritime transport, that are of concern to developing countries.[180]

Other forces, too, are at work reconfiguring the authority structure for maritime transport. As Zacher with Sutton note, liner conferences have declined in strength, not because of developing countries' concerns,[181] but because of technological advances in containerized and multimodal transportation and the entry of new nonconference lines into the market. Container and multimodal transport introduced competition among different modes of transport, weakening the hold of liner conferences. However, they have also led to the concentration of transport services in a few very large, capital-rich corporations, pushing out pure shipping companies and creating new barriers to entry. They report that in the North Pacific, "trade went from forty-two liner companies in 1985 to ten joint ventures or consortia in 1993."[182]

Today, the unification of commercial law is taking place in an increasingly transnational context in which deregulation and privatization are the operative norms. A transnational corporate elite comprised of individual merchants, merchant associations, like the ICC, transnational insurance and shipping corporations and cartels are cooperating with governments and international organizations, such as UNCITRAL and UNCTAD, in an increasingly competitive climate. The growing transnational aspects of maritime transport are identified by Gold as major challenges facing the shipping industry. He argues that "[p]rivate maritime law can no longer simply service the needs of what is essentially a powerful minority" in light of the serious impact of its operations on broader community interests, like the marine environment.[183] The likelihood, however, of the maritime community or national communities taking on community obligations is questionable in the present deregulatory climate and in light of commitments to maintaining the private/public distinction. Moreover, the growing concentration of shipping in a "supercartel" under the Transatlantic Trade Agreement signed by the twelve major shipping companies in Atlantic trade, suggests that private protectionism is a well-entrenched norm.[184] According to Susan Strange:

> The conclusion seems clear that, while the rhetoric of free enterprise and open competition is necessary to the full integration of a world economy operating on a market principle, the rhetoric is often, in reality, empty of meaning. Both in the United States and in Europe, let alone Japan, the war against restrictive cartels is pretty much of a farce. In steel, in shipping, and probably in most chemicals, aluminum, electrical products, authority over the market is exercised by associations of firms organized in overt or covert cartels to rig prices in favor of the members—"conspiracies against the public" in effect. And in political terms, since the regulators are blind, inert or impotent, such cartels constitute "regimes within regimes."[185]

CONCLUSION

The history of private international trade law and the laws and practices governing maritime transport provides a rich source of data on the nature of private authority in international affairs. It shows that merchants and their associations and corporations have exercised an historic influence on maritime transport laws. They have functioned authoritatively in gaining the trust of fellow merchants, in achieving broadly based perceptions of legitimacy inside and outside the merchant community, and in securing the actual compliance of that community with merchant laws and practices. Their autonomy from state authorities, however, has varied over time and over issue-areas. Merchants functioned autonomously in the medieval phase in law creation and enforcement. This autonomy, however, was circumscribed and, in some cases, went underground in the second phase as states engaged in statebuilding incorporated the law merchant and its courts into national legal orders. At this time, the increasing differentiation between public and private maritime law served to isolate certain aspects of maritime trade from public authority as "private" law matters. This isolation preserved elements of merchant autonomy and provided the initial foundation for the future denationalization and transnationalization of authority. Other aspects, however, became part of governments' public policy concerns.

Merchant autonomy from state regulation is being reasserted in the third phase in the context of renewed commitments to the superiority of merchant custom as a source of legal regulation and private arbitration as the preeminent method for settling disputes. The success of the ICC's Incoterms 1980 is attributed to their origin in merchant custom. Unification efforts are shifting focus from state-sponsored international conventions, to "soft" law statements of principle favored by transnational merchants and the most powerful national commercial elites. These developments are occurring against the backdrop of the advent of the competition state and adjustments to intensified economic competition through deregulating and privatizing corporate and commercial practices.

Private international authority functions economically to structure commercial expectations and actions according to generally accepted principles. Merchant law provides a common language and set of values reflecting shared commitments to the facilitation of exchange. This is achieved through creating and standardizing legal instruments that manage the risks of maritime transport, like the insurance principle of the general average, and that allocate the costs of doing business, such as Incoterms 1980 and bills of lading, and that provide for ownership rights and liabilities, such as charter parties and partnerships. But private authority also operates politically to ensure that certain activities do not engage public regulation, scrutiny, and review. Private protectionism in the form of maritime cartels and private associations ensure limited entry to those who are not members of the maritime "club" by creating "invisible" barriers to entry. Indeed, the distributional consequences of rules that purport to operate in the common interest of providing greater certainty in transactions, like Incoterms 1980, are rendered invisible by their private, and hence, "nonauthoritative" origin.

The concept of private international authority is thus powerful analytically and ideologically. Analytically, it renders visible the activities of transnational corporations, business associations, and organizations that structure international commercial activity and determine outcomes in terms of controlling market access and market shares and regulating the entire process of transacting (contracting, transporting, financing, insuring, and resolving disputes). Ideologically, the concept reveals the private interests being served by the legal regime and raises the issue of corporate accountability. These concerns touch upon some of the questions raised in the introduction. There the editors ask whether the concept of private authority can be reconciled with state-centric approaches to international relations. This chapter suggests an ambiguous response. In law, corporate accountability is theoretically impossible because corporations lack international legal personality as subjects of the law. Legal doctrine and liberal political theory work against the recognition of corporate personality and, hence, accountability. However, in practice we see that corporate actors operate in a privileged, private sphere carved out for them by governments. Today, that sphere is being reconstituted as more content is given to the private realm through the competitive deregulation of corporate activities. Legal and political fictions about the "apolitical" nature of private commercial relations are presented as postulates of liberal theory, serving to render the corporate world legally and politically "invisible" and, hence, unaccountable.

The introduction also questions how private authority affects the distribution of power between states and impacts, domestically, on state-society relations. Here, it is instructive to recall Robert Cox's observation that "[t]heory is always *for* someone and *for* some purpose."[186] In carving out a private space for corporate activities, liberal legal and political theories clearly privilege commercial activity. They serve the interests of the most powerful commercial states, and within those states create a privileged corporate sphere. In maritime transport, private authority operates protectively to preserve the influence of the most powerful maritime states. Less powerful states are generally unable to effect major changes to shipping laws. While UNCTAD and UNCITRAL provide greater institutional access for less powerful states to decision-making procedures, this access does not translate into much influence over the outcomes. The control that the most powerful maritime states exercise over the activities of these international organizations severely limits the achievement of substantial change. The Code of Conduct for Liner Conferences did not radically alter protectionism in liner shipping, which in any case is being overtaken by container traffic and a new supercartel. Less developed countries scored no success in challenging the use of flags of convenience, while their success in the revision of rules governing bills of lading is marginalized by the lack of support from major trading states who continue to operate under the old rules. Finally, there are maritime rules, like Incoterms 1980, whose distributional consequences remain "invisible" and are thus not even recognized as matters in need of reform.

Private international authority, thus, gives rise to troubling normative implications. It operates undemocratically to privilege some states over others and, within those states, to privilege corporate interests over other societal interests. It supports the private sphere of capital accumulation and neutralizes and renders invisible the instruments serving those ends. Private international authority is incapable of providing justice of outcomes in any substantive way. At most it can provide more equitable procedures, but it is ultimately private power that determines the justice or injustice of the outcome.

NOTES

1. See generally J.-G. Castel, A. L. C. de Mestral, and W. C. Graham, *International Business Transactions and Economic Relations: Cases, Notes, and Materials on the Law as It Applies to Canada* (Toronto: Emond Montgomery Publications, 1986).

2. See generally, A. Claire Cutler, "Global Capitalism and Liberal Myths: Dispute Resolution in Private International Trade Relations," *Millennium: Journal of International Studies* 24.3 (1995): 377–97.

3. See A. Claire Cutler, "Public Meets Private: The International Unification and Harmonization of Private International Trade Law," forthcoming in *Global Society*, for a discussion of contemporary globalization of international commercial law.

4. A. Claire Cutler, "Artifice, Ideology and Paradox: The Public/Private Distinction in International Law," *Review of International Political Economy* 4.2 (Summer 1997): 261–85.

5. Hugh M. Kindred, J.-G. Castel, William C. Graham, Linda C. Reif, Donald Fleming, Armand L. C. DeMestral, Ivan A. Vlasic, and Sharon A. Williams, *International Law: Chiefly as Interpreted and Applied in Canada*, 5th ed. (Toronto: Emond Montgomery Publications, 1993), p. 78. And see Paul Szasz, "General Law-Making Processes," in Oscar Schachter and Christopher C. Joyner, eds., *United Nations Legal Order*, vol. 1 (Cambridge: Grotius Publications, Cambridge University Press, 1995), pp. 45–47 for discussions of hard and soft law. Examples of soft law include the United Nations Commission on International Trade Law's Model Law on International Commercial Arbitration and the International Chamber of Commerce's *Incoterms 1980*. The former have

been voluntarily adopted by many states and transformed from "soft" into "hard" law through national legal implementation. The latter are given legal force by voluntary incorporation into private contracts. Other examples of "soft" law include the Helsinki Accords and the Organization for Economic Cooperation and Development's Guidelines for Multinational Enterprises.

6. Private international trade law operates as both a *domestic* conflict of law system, identifying the applicable law when there is uncertainty as to what state's laws should govern an international transaction, and as a system of *internationally* negotiated rules and procedures. See generally, Cutler, "Artifice, Ideology and Paradox."

7. For fuller treatment of liberal mythology concerning the neutral and apolitical nature of legal regulation, see Cutler, "Global Capitalism and Liberal Myths," and see also Morton Horowitz, "The History of the Public/Private Distinction," *University of Pennsylvania Law Review* 130 (1982): 1423–28.

8. See Clive M. Schmitthoff, "Nature and Evolution of the Transnational Law of Commercial Transactions," in Norbert Horn and Clive M. Schmitthoff, eds., *The Transnational Law of International Commercial Transactions* (Deventer, The Netherlands: Kluwer, 1982), pp. 20–21 and Leon E. Trakman, *The Law Merchant: The Evolution of Commercial Law* (Littleton, Colo.: Fred B. Rothman, 1983) for this view.

9. This is Harold Lasswell's oft cited definition of politics. For a contemporary and similar definition of politics in the context of the global political economy, see Susan Strange, "Political Economy and International Relations," in Ken Booth and Steve Smith, eds., *International Relations Theory Today* (University Park: Pennsylvania State University Press, 1995).

10. For examples of the conflicting interests between developed and less developed states in the area of international sales law, see Elizabeth Hayes Patterson, "United Nations Convention on Contracts for the International Sale of Goods: Unification and the Tension between Compromise and Domination," *Stanford Journal of International Law* 22 (1986), pp. 263–303. See also Gulya Eörsi, "Contracts of Adhesion and the Protection of the Weaker Party in International Trade Relations," in International Institute for the Unification of Private Law (UNIDROIT), ed., *New Directions in International Trade Law*, vol. 1 (New York: Oceana Publications, 1977). For conflicts involving nonmarket economies, see Alejandro M. Garro, "Reconciliation of Legal Traditions in the UN Convention on Contracts for the International Sale of Goods," *The International Lawyer* 23.2 (1989): 443–89.

11. Joel Paul, "The Isolation of Private International Law, "*Wisconsin International Law Journal* 7 (1988): 149–78, identifies disciplinary and doctrinal reasons for the isolation of private international law.

12. This section draws in part on the analysis of historical origins and ideological significance of the private/public distinction in Cutler, "Artifice, Ideology, and Paradox."

13. See Karl Klare, "The Public/Private Distinction in Labour Law," *University of Pennsylvania Law Review* 130 (1982): 1358–1422.

14. See Celina Romany, "Women as *Aliens*: A Feminist Critique of the Public/Private Distinction in International Human Rights Law," *Harvard*

Human Rights Journal 6 (1993): 87–125; Stephen Rosow, "On the Political Theory of Political Economy: Conceptual Ambiguity and the Global Economy," *Review of International Political Economy* 1 (1994): 465–88, and Hilary Charlesworth, "The Public/Private Distinction and the Right to Development in International Law," *Australian Yearbook of International Law* 12 (1992): 190–204.

15. Klare, "The Public/Private Distinction in Labour Law," pp. 1358–59n2.

16. "Liberalism and the Art of Separation," *Political Theory* 12.3 (August 1984): 315–30. For a review of the liberal foundations of international law, see M. W. Janis, "Jeremy Bentham and the Fashioning of International Law," *American Journal of International Law* 78 (1984): 405–18, and for examples of liberal international relations theories, see Robert O. Keohane, *After Hegemony* (Princeton: Princeton University Press, 1984) and March W. Zacher with Brent Sutton, *Governing Global Networks: International Regimes for Transportation and Communications* (Cambridge, Cambridge University Press, 1996).

17. Walzer, "Liberalism and the Art of Separation," p. 315.

18. Duncan Kennedy, "The Stages of the Decline of the Public/Private Distinction," *University of Pennsylvania Law Review* 130 (1982): 1349.

19. See Joel Paul, "The Isolation of Private International Law," and Cutler, "Artifice, Ideology, and Paradox," for a more in-depth analysis of subject-matter and doctrinal distinctions between public and private international law.

20. Castel et al., *International Business Transactions and Economic Relations*, p. 521.

21. The following are some examples of the subjects covered by private international trade law: export sales, licensing, distributorships, joint ventures, choice of law, international arbitration and enforcement, and the extraterritorial application of tax, antitrust, and securities laws. See Cutler, "Artifice, Ideology and Paradox," 282n5 for a fuller account of its subject-matter.

22. See Cutler, "Artifice, Ideology and Paradox," for discussion of the contested doctrinal status of private international law that is attributed to disagreement over whether it constitutes an autonomous legal order or is merely an extension of domestic legal authority.

23. Identity here refers to the actors who are identified as the "subjects" of international law, a matter that will be taken up in the next section. Briefly, though, sociologists provide some interesting insights into the links between the concepts of authority, identity, and subjectivity. Burkhart Holzner and Roland Roberston, in "Identity and Authority: A Problem Analysis of Processes of Identification and Authorization," in Roland Robertson and Burkart Holzner, eds., *Identity and Authority: Explorations in the Theory of Society* (Oxford: Basil Blackwell, 1980), p. 5, observe that "the terms identity and authority are mutually implicative. No conception of authority makes sense unless we speak also of the ways in which units are identified and identify themselves. By the same token, identity implies authority in that the identification of self and others involves the problems of *authorship* and *authorization*." Moreover, the concept of identity involves the attribution of identity "in the sense of entitivity" as subjects or objects (p. 2). In that same volume Rainer C. Baum, "Authority and Identity: The Case for Evolutionary Invariance," p. 62, notes the "inevitable,

indissoluble, and, by now, obvious links between the concepts of authority and identity. It is interesting that the link so "obvious" to sociologists, is only being discovered by a few students of international relations, as evident in the work of contemporary postmodernists. See for example R. B. J. Walker, *Inside/Outside: International Relations as Political Theory* (Cambridge: Cambridge University Press, 1993).

24. This volume, Introduction, quoting R. B. Friedman, "On the Concept of Authority in Political Philosophy," in Joseph Raz, ed., *Authority* (Oxford: Basil Blackwell, 1990), p. 56.

25. R. B. Friedman, "On the Concept of Authority in Political Philosophy," in Raz, ed., *Authority*, 57. And see Stephen Lukes, "Perspectives on Authority," in that same volume for the variations in perspectives on authority.

26. "Introduction," in Raz, ed., *Authority*, p. 2.

27. See Friedman, "On the Concept of Authority in Political Philosophy."

28. *Authority: Construction and Corrosion* (Chicago: University of Chicago Press, 1994), p. 2.

29. Lincoln, *Authority*, p. 6.

30. "The Identification and Appraisal of Diverse Systems of Public Order," reprinted in Robert J. Beck, Anthony C. Arend, and Robert D. Vander Lugt, eds., *International Rules: Approaches from International Law and International Relations* (New York and Oxford: Oxford University Press, 1996), p. 120.

31. *Principles of Public International Law* 4th ed. (Oxford: Clarendon Press, 1990), p. 5.

32. See Brownlie, *Principles of Public International Law*, pp. 4–11 and M. N. Shaw, *International Law*, 3rd ed. (Cambridge: Cambridge University Press, 1991), chap. 3.

33. Shaw, *International Law*, p. 63.

34. For a good discussion of compliance, see Oran R. Young, *Compliance and Public Authority: A Theory with International Applications* (Baltimore: Johns Hopkins University Press, 1979).

35. Thomas M. Franck, *The Power of Legitimacy Among Nations* (New York and Oxford: Oxford University Press, 1990), p. 16.

36. Franck here cites Dworkin, *Law's Empire* (Cambridge, Mass: Belknap Press, 1986), chap. 6.

37. Franck cites Habermas, *Communication and the Evolution of Society* (Boston: Beacon Press, 1979).

38. *The Anarchical Society: A Study of Order in World Politics* (New York: Columbia University Press, 1977).

39. *The Anarchical Society*, p. 85.

40. Bull, *The Anarchical Society*, p. 85. Bull differentiates between international or interstate justice, individual or human justice, and cosmopolitan or world justice. The first are moral rules that confer rights and duties on states and nations. The second relate to moral rules conferring rights and duties upon individuals, while the third are the rules relating to the world common good—"an imagined *civitas maxima* or cosmopolitan society to which all individuals belong and to which their interests should be subordinate," p. 84.

41. Franck, *The Power of Legitimacy among Nations*, p. 233.

42. Bull differentiates between solidarist and pluralist conceptions of political/legal authority. The former posits the possibility for agreement among states concerning the standards governing state action. In contrast, the latter posits only minimal agreement among states, "which fall short of that of the enforcement of the law." Hedley Bull, "The Grotian Conception of International Society," in H. Butterfield and Martin Wight, eds., *Diplomatic Investigations* (London: Allen and Unwin, 1968), p. 52. And see A. Claire Cutler, "The 'Grotian Tradition' in International Relations," *Review of International Studies* 17 (1991): 53–58 for further discussion of solidarist and pluralist views of authority.

43. Franck in *The Power of Legitimacy*, pp. 17–18 actually identifies what he regards as three different formulations of the conditions attached to legitimacy: *process* in a Weberian sense of "a narrowly specific *process* . . . set out in a superior framework of reference, rules about how laws are made, how governors are chosen and how public participation is achieved"; *procedural-substantive* matters that look at how the authority is exercised in terms of openness, participation, and equality; and, *outcomes* in terms of the fairness, equity, justice, and freedom of the result. However, the first condition tends to shade into the second and so I prefer the more simple distinction between purposes and procedures, as advanced by Hedley Bull and Oran Young.

44. *The Power of Legitimacy among Nations*, p. 208.

45. Ibid., p. 209.

46. Ibid., p. 211.

47. *The Anarchical Society*, p. 88.

48. *The Power of Legitimacy among Nations*, p. 233. Franck here cites Robert Keohane's observation in *After Hegemony*, p. 249, that "states cannot be considered independent subjects of moral theory; a justification of the morality of states . . . must ultimately be made in terms of the rights and interests of individual human beings."

49. See Bull, *The Anarchical Society*, chaps. 4 and 6 and Franck, *The Power of Legitimacy among Nations*, chap. 13.

50. See Beck et al., eds., *International Rules*, p. 111.

51. Ibid.

52. See Rosalyn Higgins, "Conceptual Thinking about the Individual in International Law," in Richard Falk, Friedrich Kratochwil, and Saul H. Mendolvitz, eds., *International Law: A Contemporary Perspective* (Boulder and London: Westview Press, 1985), pp. 476–94.

53. The focus on legitimacy and trust and shared belief in the validity of procedures is also evident in Terry Nardin's conception of legitimacy. Nardin, too, is skeptical about the prospects for achieving normative solidarity over substantive matters and limits his notion of legitimate authority to agreement over procedures. See *Law, Morality, and the Relations of States* (Princeton: Princeton University Press, 1983).

54. "Perspectives on Authority," in Raz, ed., *Authority*, p. 203.

55. "The Public/Private Distinction in Labour Law," p. 1361.

56. "Artifice, Ideology and Paradox," p. 261.

57. For a good synopsis of these developments, see R. J. Holton, *The Transition from Feudalism to Capitalism* (New York: St. Martin's Press, 1985).

58. See René David, "The International Unification of Private Law," in *International Encyclopaedia of Comparative Law: The Legal Systems of the World, Their Comparison and Unification*, vol. II (The Hague: Martinus Nijhoff; Tübingen, Germany: Mohr, 1972), chap. 5, and Frederick Pollock and Frederick W. Maitland, *History of English Law*, vol. I (Cambridge: Cambridge University Press, 1898).

59. Lincoln, *Authority*, pp. 2–3.

60. See Cutler, "Artifice, Ideology and Paradox," for further analysis of these developments.

61. For a classic account of the origin of the separation of public and private authority in terms of the disembedding of the self-regulating market from its social and political context, see Karl Polanyi, *The Great Transformation: The Political and Economic Origins of our Times* (Boston: Beacon Press, 1944).

62. Friedman, "On the Concept of Authority in Political Philosophy," pp. 78–79.

63. "The History of the Public/Private Distinction, pp. 1425–26.

64. Walzer, "The Liberal Art of Separation," p. 316.

65. See for example Mark W. Zacher with Richard A. Matthew, "Liberal International Theory: Common Threads, Divergent Strands," in Charles W. Kegley, ed., *Controversies in International Relations Theory: Realism and the Neoliberal Challenge* (New York: St. Martin's Press, 1995). And see Robert Gilpin, *The Political Economy of International Relations* (Princeton: Princeton University Press, 1987), pp. 15–24, for the significance of the market to international political economy.

66. See for example the different views reflected in J. Rogers Hollingsworth and Robert Boyer, eds., *Contemporary Capitalism: The Embeddedness of Institutions* (Cambridge: Cambridge University Press, 1997). And see Susan Strange, *States and Markets* (London: Pinter, 1988).

67. See David A. Baldwin, ed., *Neorealism and Neoliberalism: The Contemporary Debate* (New York: Columbia University Press, 1993) for a collection of papers that investigate the nature of the relationships between state power and economic considerations. Also, see Herman M. Schwartz, *States versus Markets: History, Geography, and the Development of the International Political Economy* (New York: St. Martin's Press, 1994), chap. 2, for a good illustration of differences in analysis of the relationship between states and markets under neoclassical economics, world systems theory, and a group referred to as agnostics, which focuses on internal class or state-based politics. See also Robert Gilpin, *The Political Economy of International Relations* and Stephen Gill and David Law, *The Global Political Economy: Perspectives, Problems and Policies* (Baltimore: Johns Hopkins University Press, 1988) for rather different interpretations of the nature of the relationships between states and markets.

68. J. Rogers Hollingsworth and Robert Boyer, "Coordination of Economic Actors and Social Systems of Production," in Hollingsworth and Boyer, eds., *Contemporary Capitalism*, pp. 14–15, refer to the "conventional and overdone polarization between states and markets." They identify a number of social relations that are involved in governing and coordinating productive relations, including markets, communities, networks, associations, private hierarchies, and states.

69. "Individuals as Subjects under International Law," *Cornell International Law Journal* 17.1 (1984): p. 62.

70. Shaw, *International Law*, p. 135.

71. Ibid., p. 137.

72. See Beck, et al., eds., *International Rules*, chaps. 2 and 3 for good reviews of natural and positive law theories of international law, respectively.

73. Inclusive of the individual, at least. See Cutler, "The 'Grotian Tradition' in International Relations," for the view that natural law theories are more accommodating of the individual as a subject of international law than are positive law theories.

74. Beck et al., eds., *International Rules*, chap. 3.

75. Shaw, *International Law*, p. 25.

76. For a very good discussion of the territorial nature of state sovereignty and of contemporary challenges to territorial conceptions of political authority, see John Agnew, "The Territorial Trap: The Geographical Assumptions of International Relations Theory," *Review of International Political Economy* 1 (1994): 53–80.

77. *Reparations for Injuries Suffered in the Service of the United Nations Case* [1949] International Court of Justice Rep 174, 180.

78. Article 34(1), *Statute of the International Court of Justice.*

79. Nationality is defined as "the bond that unites individuals with a given state, that identifies them as members of that entity, that enables them to claim its protection, and that also subjects them to the performance of such duties as their state may impose on them." Gerhard von Glahn, *Law among Nations: An Introduction to Public International Law*, 7th ed. (Boston: Allyn and Bacon, 1996), p. 147. He notes further (158–59) that the traditional Anglo-American approach to determining the nationality of a corporation was the place of incorporation (domicile) and for unincorporated businesses, the state in which the governing body met or was located. In contrast, European states tended to use the state where the corporations home office was located or where its principal business was carried on. However, the approaches to corporate nationality shifted during the First World War in the context of determining the enemy status of corporations to focus more on the nationality of those who exercised control of the corporation. See too Brownlie, *Principles of Public International Law*, pp. 421–24.

80. There are some exceptions to the limited personality of individuals and private corporations, which might suggest some movement in legal practice that has yet to be reflected in legal theory. Notable exceptions include the status of individuals before the European Court and the status of private transnational corporations that have entered into contracts with states that are "internationalized" by provisions that bring the contract under the purview of public international law. On the individual, see Rosalyn Higgins, "Conceptual Thinking about the Individual under International Law," and concerning transnational corporations, see Fleur Johns, "The Invisibility of the Transnational Corporation: An Analysis of International Law and Legal Theory," *Melbourne University Law Review* 19 (1994): 893–923.

81. Detlev F. Vagts, "The Multinational Enterprise: A New Challenge for Transnational Law," *Harvard Law Review* 83 (1970): 740. According to Shaw,

International Law, p. 172n143, the Restatement (Third) of Foreign Relations Law of the United States provides that, "the transnational corporation, while an established feature of international life, 'has not yet achieved independent status in international law'." Ian Brownlie, *Principles of Public International Law*, pp. 68–69, cautions against "facile generalizations on the subject of legal personality" and notes that there are numerous entities possessing personality for limited purposes. He identifies Eurofima as an example of an intergovernmental corporation established by treaty involving fifteen states in 1955. The treaty established the corporation under Swiss private law, but it is given international privileges, including an exemption from Swiss tax laws. Shaw, *International Law*, p. 171 identifies INTELSAT, created in 1973 as an intergovernmental body for global commercial telecommunications satellites and the Bank of International Settlement, created in 1930 by a treaty among five states and Switzerland as examples of corporate entities exhibiting various elements of international personality.

82. Johns, "The Invisibility of the Transnational Corporation," p. 893.

83. Brownlie, *Principles of Public International Law*, pp. 421–22.

84. "Power Politics, Institutions, and Transnational Relations," in Thomas Risse-Kappen, ed., *Bringing Transnationals Back In: Non-State Actors, Domestic Structures and International Institutions* (Cambridge: Cambridge University Press, 1995), p. 279. Note, however, as does the volume's editor, that the various selections in the volume illustrate the oversimplification of the "state-centred" versus "society-centered" approach to the significance of transnational corporations. See Thomas Risse-Kappen, "Structures of Governance and Transnational Relations: What Have We Learned?" p. 281.

85. Zacher with Sutton, *Governing Global Networks*, p. 18.

86. See Zacher with Sutton, *Governing Global Networks*, chap. 2, and Keohane, *After Hegemony*, chap. 2.

87. See Cutler, "Artifice, Ideology and Paradox," for discussion of these trends.

88. Horowitz, "The History of the Public/Private Distinction," p. 1428.

89. Kindred et al., *International Law*, p. 50, notes omitted.

90. Johns, "The Invisibility of the Transnational Corporation," p. 897nn21–22 identifies ECOSOC, the European Union, the ICC, the World Bank, OECD, UNCTAD, UNFAO, ICFTU, Japanese Business Council, and the Japanese MITI Council on Industrial Structure as institutions that have attempted to regulate TNCs.

91. The commission was created in 1974 by ECOSOC and given the mandate to prepare a code of conduct for governments and TNCs. Drafts were produced in 1978, 1983, 1988, and 1990. Consensus over the draft was never achieved and in 1992 United Nations Centre on Transnational Corporations, Secretariat to the Commission, was dismantled and its functions were transferred to a new Transnational Corporations Management Division within ECOSOC.

92. Johns, "The Invisibility of the Transnational Corporation," p. 899.

93. For an interesting analysis of measures taken by the Australian authorities to prevent the manipulation of the Australian tax system so as to shield corporate profits from taxation by integrating the profits of offshore subsidiary cor-

porations with the profits of the Australian-based parent company, see John Azzi, "Historical Development of Australia's International Taxation Rules," *Melbourne University Law Review* 19 (1994): 793–813.

94. Quoted in Johns, "The Invisibility of the Transnational Corporation," p. 896.

95. Johns, "The Invisibility of the Transnational Corporation," p. 900.

96. For the analysis of some of these developments, see Fredric Jameson, *Postmodernism or, The Cultural Logic of Late Capitalism* (Durham: Duke University Press, 1991); David Held, *Democracy and the Global Order: From the Modern State to Cosmopolitan Governance* (Stanford: Stanford University Press, 1995); Susan Strange, *The Retreat of the State: The Diffusion of Power in the World Economy* (Cambridge: Cambridge University Press, 1996); and Strange, *States and Markets.*

97. "Perspectives on Globalization and Economic Coordination," in Hollingsworth and Boyer, eds., *Contemporary Capitalism,* p. 320. See Paul Hirst and Grahame Thompson, "Globalization in Question: International Economic Relations and Forms of Public Governance," also in that volume, for the depiction of a fully globalized economy as an ideal type against which the authors measure the present word economy and conclude it is not a fully globalized economy, but an international economy.

98. "Perspectives on Globalization and Economic Coordination," p. 319. Note, though, that cartels have operated with varying degrees of effective control over their members for some time historically. See for example Debora L. Spar, *The Cooperative Edge: The Internal Politics of International Cartels* (Ithaca and London: Cornell University Press, 1994) and the selections by Porter and Webb in this volume.

99. "Perspectives on Globalization and Economic Coordination," p. 323.

100. For a discussion of these developments, see Strange, *The Retreat of the State,* chap. 4.

101. Wynn, "Globalization and Economic Cooperation," p. 324 identifies ICI (Imperial Chemical Industries) and ABA (Asia Brown Bovari) as examples of "stateless corporations," noting that the "world of the stateless company has not yet arrived, but it is an incipient phenomenon which is worth attention."

102. "Global Government and Global Opposition," in Geraint Perry, ed., *Politics in an Interdependent World: Essays Presented to Ghita Ionescu* (Aldershot, Hants, England: Edward Elgar, 1994), p. 26.

103. She here cites the work of C. A. Michalet, "Strategic Partnerships and the Changing Internationalisation Process," in Lynn Mytelka, ed., *Strategic Partnerships: States, Firms and International Competition* (London: Pinter, 1991). And see the selection by Mytelka and Delapierre in this volume.

104. "The Invisibility of the Transnational Corporations," p. 912, quoting Hans Kelsen, *Pure Theory of Law* (Berkeley: University of California Press, 1967), p. 282.

105. Johns, "The Invisibility of Transnational Corporations," p. 913.

106. See ibid., 896; Detlev Vagts, "The Multinational Enterprise," p. 764.

107. This is evident in terms of the Multilateral Agreement on Investment being negotiated in the Organization for Economic Cooperation and Development

(OECD), which restricts the regulatory ambit of states over foreign investment activities. It is also evident in the shift in corporate legal preferences for "soft law" agreements over "hard law" ones. See Cutler, "Public Meets Private," for a discussion of the appeal of soft law norms governing international commercial contracting.

108. Walzer, "Liberalism and the Art of Separation," pp. 315, 321.

109. *The Changing Architecture of Politics: Structure, Agency and the Future of the State* (London: Sage, 1990), p. 230.

110. Philip G. Cerny, "The Dynamics of Political Globalization," *Government and Opposition* 32.2 (Spring 1997): 273.

111. In the context of European deregulation, see David Charney, "Competition among Jurisdictions in Formulating Corporate Law Rules: An American Perspective on the 'Race to the Bottom' in the European Communities," *Harvard International Law Journal* 32.2 (Spring 1991): 423–56.

112. "Critical Political Economy," in Björn Hettne, ed., *International Political Economy: Understanding Global Disorder* (Halifax, Nova Scotia: Fernwood Publishing, and London and Atlantic Highlands, N.J.: Zed Books, 1995), p. 39.

113. "Theorizing the Interregnum: The Double Movement and Global Politics in the 1990s," in Hettne, ed., *International Political Economy*, p. 85.

114. Justin Rosenberg makes this point very nicely in *The Empire of Civil Society: A Critique of the Realist Theory of International Relations* (London: Verso, 1994).

115. *Governing Global Networks*, p. 36.

116. Zacher with Sutton, *Governing Global Networks*, p. 36.

117. *Maritime Transport: The Evolution of International Marine Policy and Shipping Law* (Lexington: Lexington Books, and Toronto: D.C. Heath and Company, 1981), p. 363.

118. *Maritime Transport*, p. 363.

119. *The Retreat of the State*, p. 148.

120. See Cutler, "Global Capitalism and Liberal Myths."

121. See generally, Herold Berman and Colin Kaufman, "The Law of International Commercial Transactions (*Lex Mercatoria*)," *Harvard International Law Journal* 19 (1978): 221–78.

122. *Maritime Transport*, chap. 1.

123. See William Mitchell, "Early Forms of Partnerships," in C. Gross, ed., *Select Cases Concerning the Law Merchant*, vol. I (London: Bernard Quaritch, 1908).

124. Shepard Clough, *The Economic Development of Western Civilization* (New York: McGraw-Hill, 1959), p. 111.

125. Frederic C. Sanborn, *Origins of Early English Maritime and Commercial Law* (London: Century Co., 1930), p. 98.

126. William Vance, "The Early History of Insurance Law," in *Selected Essays in Anglo-American Legal History*.

127. See Berman and Kaufman, "The Law of International Commercial Transactions (*Lex Mercatoria*)."

128. The Sea Law of Rhodes, originating in ancient and local customs, is regarded as the first collection of maritime laws of the late Roman Empire and

furnished the foundation for many later collections. It contained provisions regulating jettison general average contributions, unloading, collisions, salvage, among other matters. The Sea Laws of Trani, Amalphi Code, and the merchant court of Pisa adopted rules from the Rhodian Sea Law, as modified by commercial custom. The merchant court in Pisa, in particular, is noted as the source for a variety of transport documents, including bills of lading, charter parties, contracts of affreightment, *commenda*, and bottomry contracts. Many of the rules embodied in the Sea Law of Rhodes were adopted in the Laws or Rolls of Oleron in almost identical form and dealt with matters including liabilities upon shipwreck or jettison and duties to the crew and safety of the cargo. Derivatives of the Laws of Oleron are found in the Sea Laws of Wisby.

129. Gold, *Maritime Transport*, p. 25.

130. Ibid..

131. Ibid.

132. Ibid., p. 26.

133. See ibid., pp. 26–29.

134. Hugo Grotius, *The Freedom of the Seas* (Mare Liberum), trans. Ralph Van Deman (Magoffin, N.Y.: Oxford University Press, 1916).

135. See generally, Berman and Kaufman, "The Law of International Commercial Transactions (*Lex Mercatoria*)."

136. *Maritime Transport*, p. 107.

137. Ibid., p. 109.

138. Ibid., p. 108.

139. See Trevor Heaver, "Canada and the Evolving System of International Shipping Conferences," in A. Claire Cutler and Mark W. Zacher, eds., *Canadian Foreign Policy and International Economic Regimes* (Vancouver: University of British Columbia Press, 1992), pp. 215–36, for an excellent review of the nature, function, and history of liner conferences.

140. Alan W. Cafruny, *Ruling the Waves: The Political Economy of International Shipping* (Berkeley, Los Angeles, and London: University of California Press, 1987), p. 14. Bulk shipping transports raw materials, liquid (oil), and dry bulk commodities. Liner shipping transports manufactured and packaged goods.

141. See generally Gold, *Maritime Transport*, p. 115 and Zacher with Sutton, *Governing Global Networks*, pp. 65–78.

142. Stephen Krasner, *Structural Conflict: The Third World against Global Liberalism* (Berkeley, Los Angeles, London: University of California Press, 1985), chap. 8, attributes their durability to intense competition from low barriers to entry, inelastic supply, and very high ratios of fixed to variable costs.

143. Zacher with Sutton, *Governing Global Networks*, p. 68.

144. *Ruling the Waves*, pp. 120–21 and 114.

145. *Structural Conflict*, p. 223.

146. Gold, *Maritime Transport*, p. 117.

147. See ibid., pp. 118–21, for a good discussion of the delegation of regulatory authority over marine insurance to Lloyd's. And see Zacher with Sutton, *Governing Global Networks*, p. 65, for state support for liner conferences.

148. This discussion draws on Alexander Wendt's analysis of the internationalization and transnationalization of political authority in "Collective Iden-

tity Formation and the International State," *American Political Science Review* 88.2 (1994): 393.

149. Wendt, "Collective Identity," p. 393.

150. Zacher with Sutton, *Governing Global Networks*, identify the facilitation of exchange as a dominant regime value.

151. See Gold, *Maritime Transport*, pp. 126–30; Zacher with Sutton, *Governing Global Networks*, pp. 39–40 and A. Mankabady, "International and National Organizations Concerned with Shipping," *Lloyd's Maritime and Commercial Law Quarterly* 3 (1974): 274–85.

152. Gold, *Maritime Transport*, pp. 153–55, 207, 246, 292, 359.

153. Zacher with Sutton, *Governing Global Networks*, p. 40.

154. Gold, *Maritime Transport*, p. 157n11 observes that it is administered as a sideline by a firm of marine insurers/lawyers in Antwerp.

155. Ibid., p. 155.

156. Ibid., p. 127. The general average is an insurance principle allocating risks and loss that can be traced back to the earliest ancient sea laws.

157. See Michael C. Rowe, "The Contribution of the ICC to the Development of International Trade Law," in Norbert Horn and Clive M. Schmitthoff, eds., *The Transnational Law of International Commercial Transactions* (Deventer, The Netherlands: Kluwer, 1982), pp. 51–60.

158. Jan Ramberg, "Incoterms 1980," in Horn and Schmitthoff, eds., *The Transnational Law of International Commercial Transactions.*

159. *Ruling the Waves*, pp. 58 and 261.

160. Ibid., p. 261.

161. These contracts are also known as contracts of adhesion and are widely used in maritime trade. See Eörsi, "Contracts of Adhesion and the Protection of Weaker Parties in International Trade Relations."

162. See the references cited above in note 8.

163. *Governing Global Networks*, p. 242n12.

164. Michael M'Gonigle and Mark W. Zacher, *Pollution, Politics and International Law: Tankers at Sea* (Berkeley: University of California Press, 1979), p. 67.

165. See ibid.

166. Gold, *Maritime Transport*, p. 260.

167. Ibid.

168. Ibid., pp. 278–80.

169. B. Gosivic, *UNCTAD: Conflict and Compromise* (Leiden: Sijthoff, 1971), p. 138.

170. Gold, *Maritime Transport*, p. 280.

171. Zacher with Sutton, *Governing Global Networks*, p. 40, make this point about the shipping industry in general.

172. So conclude Gold, *Maritime Transport*, pp. 282–83 and Zacher with Sutton, *Governing Global Networks*, p. 40.

173. *Ruling the Waves*, p. 247.

174. See also Zacher with Sutton, *Governing Global Networks*, pp. 66–67, for discussion of bulk shipping and the interests of the developing countries.

175. Gold, *Maritime Transport*, p. 348.

176. Developing states were not the only ones to challenge the justice of the existing rules. Other developed cargo states, like Canada, did so as well.

177. General Assembly Resolution 2205(21), 17 December 1966, *Official Records of the General Assembly*, Twenty-First Session, Annexes, agenda item 8, UN Doc. A/6396 and Add. 1 and 2, reprinted in *UNCITRAL Yearbook*, p. 1.

178. See Cutler, "Public Meets Private."

179. The trend toward unification through "soft," non-legislative means is noted in the Introduction to UNIDROIT, ed., *Principles of International Commercial Contracts* (Rome: UNIDROIT, 1994).

180. Summaries of the current unification and harmonization efforts of UNCITRAL may be found in the annual *UNCITRAL Yearbook*.

181. Far from challenging liner conferences, the UNCTAD Liner Code (1974) supports liner conferences. See Zacher with Sutton, *Governing Global Networks*, p. 75.

182. *Governing Global Networks*, p. 73. In addition, they identify intensified competition from the emergence of nonwestern shipping companies from Taiwan, South Korea, Hong Kong, and the People's Republic of China.

183. Gold, *Maritime Transport*, pp. 363–64.

184. Susan Strange, *The Retreat of the State*, pp. 154–55 discusses the supercartel and identifies the twelve parties to the agreement as Sea-Lamd (US), Atlantic Container (Sweden), Hapag-Lloyd (Germany), Moller-Maersk (Denmark), DSR-Senator (Germany), P&O and OOCL (UK) as well as Swiss, French, Dutch, and Polish firms.

185. *The Retreat of the State*, p. 160.

186. "Social Forces, States, and World Orders: Beyond International Relations Theory," reproduced in Robert W. Cox with Timothy Sinclair, *Approaches to World Order* (Cambridge: Cambridge University Press, 1996), p. 85.

PART 5

Conclusion

CHAPTER 12

The Contours and Significance of Private Authority in International Affairs

A. Claire Cutler, Virginia Haufler, and Tony Porter

In this chapter we focus on the key lessons about private international authority that have been drawn out by the preceding case studies. We start with the assumption that private authority does matter and that it is revealed by examining cooperative relationships among firms. In each of the cases it is clear that firms do not act as atomistic competitive units, driven solely by an economic imperative to maximize individual profits. On the contrary, firms, singly and jointly, construct a rich variety of institutional arrangements that structure their behavior. Through these arrangements they can deploy a form of *private authority* whose effects are important for understanding not just the behavior of firms, but also for analyzing the state and its policies. As noted in our introductory chapter, the very presence of the type of structuring effects that our cases have discussed, resembling in many respects the structuring effects of states, raises intriguing political questions. Do these reinforce state policies or undermine them? Do they exacerbate or ameliorate interstate conflict? What is their significance for democracy and for political conflicts associated with the distribution of economic resources? Before we address these issues, however, we need to explore three related but prior questions: (1) Why does private authority emerge? (2) How, practically, does it operate? and (3) How can we understand, theoretically, the production of authority from private action?

WHY DOES PRIVATE AUTHORITY EMERGE?

The Conceptual Relationships among Cooperation, Institutions, and Authority

While we explore more fully the conceptual features of private authority below, here we wish to start with a preliminary discussion of the relationships among the concepts of cooperation, institutions, and authority as a prelude to our analysis of the emergence of private authority in international affairs.

As noted in the introduction, international cooperation among firms is widespread, and in certain cases this cooperation may develop into private authority. Following Keohane, we defined cooperation as requiring active adjustment of behavior to reach mutual goals, and we highlighted as well the sense of obligation "that extends cooperation into the future and gives it the mantle of authority." Authority involves a surrendering of individual judgment, an acceptance of its dictates based not on the merits of any particular pronouncement but on a belief in the rightness of the authority itself. As such, authority lies between negotiation, where action is shaped by the payoffs produced by particular bargains, and coercion, where compliance results from fear rather than respect or faith. We have suggested, therefore, that a key source of private authority is the process by which interfirm cooperation is routinized and institutionalized over time.

Not all forms of interfirm cooperation produce authority—short-term cooperation involved in a particular one-off transaction, for instance, may not. Moreover the strength of the authority that arises from interfirm cooperation may vary widely. In some cases authority may be limited to the industry in which it is produced, as is the case, for instance, with the interwar cartels analyzed by Porter or the mineral markets analyzed by Webb. In other cases the exercise of private authority may alter the conduct of states, firms in other industries, and citizens in general, as is the case with debt-rating agencies or the Intellectual Property Committee. We explore such variations in private authority below. Here we wish to emphasize that it is important to analyze both persistent cooperation among private actors and the forms of private authority to which such cooperation gives rise.

Our reference above to the institutionalization of cooperation highlights the connection between cooperation, institutions, and authority. Cooperation that derives primarily from a rational calculation of the direct payoff from adjusting one's behavior in a particular strategic situation may not involve authority. Authority requires a basis in trust rather than calculation of immediate benefit, and therefore cooperation must involve the development of habits, norms, rules, and shared expectations—cooperation must be institutionalized. Young provides a typical definition of institutions as "social practices consisting of easily recognized roles coupled with clusters of rules or conventions governing relations among the occupants of these roles." He goes on to note that "the rules that link institutionalized roles and, therefore, form the superstructure of institutions, ordinarily encompass sets of rights or entitlements . . . as well as sets of behavioral prescriptions."[1] This reference to rights and prescriptions indicates an intersection with the concept of authority since authority could be defined as a right to prescribe. The concepts differ in two key ways, however. First, institutions are more comprehensive since they include nonauthoritative roles. Second, authority requires both a sense of trust or obligation toward an occupant of a role, and the corresponding capacity of that occupant to shape the behavior of others. Authority is thus associated with a particular and very important type of role that deserves distinctive analysis. At the same time the emergence of a supporting social institution is a precondition for the emergence of authority. The importance of this point will become evident below when we analyze the institutions with which the emergence of private authority is associated.

Interfirm and Firm–State Interactions

As noted in the introduction, we see private authority as emerging both from the interactions of firms and from the interactions between firms and the state. Firms may produce authority quite independently of the state. The influence of the bond-rating agencies analyzed by Sinclair, the Internet's private regime analyzed by Spar, and the Intellectual Property Committee analyzed by Sell are examples. In other cases firms may draw more heavily on the capacities of the state in constructing private authority, or the state may delegate or confer authority, as for example in Salter's chapter on the standards regime or Webb's account of the mineral study groups. Relatedly, the emergence of private authority where none existed previously may involve the displacement of arm's length impersonal market relations among firms or it may involve a displacement of public authority and public institutions by private authority and private institutions.

A distinctive feature of the present volume's focus on private authority is the way it highlights the interconnectedness of state practices and interfirm institutions. Usually these are treated as distinct, as in the business literature's analysis of strategic alliances among multinational corporations and the international relations literature's analysis of interstate regimes. In our cases, by contrast, this separation is shown to be illusory in two respects. First, the two types of actors are often heavily involved in directly influencing the internal operations of the other. This is evident in the way the firms organized in the Intellectual Property Committee essentially produced U.S. policy for the Uruguay Round, and in the way the state has been involved in setting international standards for the operation of firms. Second, the types of regulatory institutions produced by states and self-regulatory institutions produced by firms often complement or substitute for each other as has been the case in the organization of mineral markets. The importance of the patent regime constructed by states for reinforcing solidarity in the cartels in the interwar period, or the parallel efforts to produce maritime trade terms in both private and UN fora are other examples. The interconnectedness of state practices and interfirm institutions forces us to eschew explanations of private authority that rely on *a priori* assumptions about the relative importance of states and markets. Such assumptions can give coherence to research programs and policy advocacy, as in the realist insistence that states organize international markets, or the celebration by some neoclassical economists of constraints imposed by global markets on the exercise of state power. In the present volume, however, we wish to treat the relative influence, and even the distinctiveness, of state and market institutions as a research question to be addressed in each specific case.

Explanations for Private International Authority

The social sciences, including international relations, have provided sharply differing types of explanations for social phenomena, explanations that are linked to differing conceptions of the nature of society itself. One mode of explanation, which has been called rationalistic, treats individual utility-maximizing actors as the fundamental unit upon which analysis should be based.[2] Adequate explanations of social phenomena from this perspective stress the preferences and capacities of actors in explaining outcomes. In the study of international relations the actors to which rationalistic approaches have referred have included individuals, firms, and states. Other approaches have seen actors as less fundamental, as perhaps merely an effect of deeper structures, more holistic systemic or social factors, or longer-range historical dynamics. These approaches, bearing labels such as structuralist, constructivist, historicist, and reflectivist, base explanations of social phenomena on links to the larger structure, system, or historical dynamic upon which the approach focuses.[3] Still other approaches blend these rationalistic and social approaches in a wide variety of ways.

In this section we provide explanations for the emergence of private authority from both rationalist and more social approaches. We divide these into three general types, which we briefly introduce and then, below, describe in more detail. The *first* and most rationalistic category, which we label efficiency approaches, suggests that the social institutions from which authority emerges succeed because they reduce transactions costs and provide information for individuals, firms, and states. Rational actors either anticipate the benefits of such instititutions and therefore act to construct them, or such institutions emerge because there is a Darwinian competitive struggle in which those who choose the most efficient institutional arrangements win out. Analysis of the capacity of institutions to reduce transactions costs has been a key focus of a large scholarly literature, referred to as the *new institutional economics*.[4] While efficiency approaches focus on explaining the creation of institutions and not on the emergence of authority, they can be extended by viewing authority as an efficient solution to problems of collective decision-making. North and others typically use this framework to explain the emergence of state institutions as a response to particular social, political, and technological contexts, but this can be useful in explaining the emergence of private institutions and private authority also. Under certain conditions, endowing private actors with authority provides more efficiency gains than relying solely on public authorities. This may be particularly true for international transactions, which occur in a weak institutional environment.

The *second* type, which we call power approaches, suggests that social institutions function to enhance the capacity of some actors to exercise power over others. Thus, in an actor-centered approach, private authority may be created deliberately by powerful actors in order to bolster their position. In a structural power approach, social institutions are viewed as systematically advantaging some actors over others. Power and authority therefore can become cumulative based on these persistent inequalities, solidified and reproduced through time by the inertia of institutions. This occurs on an international scale with the emergence of global markets. Particular private actors, typically multinational corporations, become authoritative as a means to increase their ability to shape and profit from market activity; they are structurally advantaged by the spread of liberal institutions and global capitalism. The role of power in explaining the organization of economic transactions has been a key focus of Marxist, realist, and mercantilist approaches in the field of international relations.[5]

A *third* type, which we label historical trends, can be used to trace the emergence of international private authority from larger epochal or systemic changes. We look at three overlapping trends: the expansion of market forces, globalization in general, and the pace of technological change. This third category of historical trends is not entirely distinct from the efficiency and power-based explanations described above. For instance, an expanding imperative of efficiency or a cumulative structural inequality can be treated as aspects of the long-range expansion of market forces. However, in the first and second categories we seek more immediate and contemporary links to efficiency and power than in this third one. Indeed, efficiency and power can be used to explain the emergence of market forces, but market forces themselves can become causally important in creating private authority at different times and in different ways. As we noted in the introductory chapter, we are not arguing here that the emergence of private authority is unique to the late twentieth century, but we do argue that it differs from earlier patterns in significant ways.

Although in the foregoing paragraphs we have laid out three separate analytical categories, it is not always possible to disentangle them in practice. For instance, actors may accept the rule of private authority even if it creates advantages (and thus power) for others if that authority enhances the efficiency of transactions to such a degree that it produces net aggregate benefits for all.[6] Alternatively, when one group seeks to exploit another it will attempt to devise and deploy institutions that facilitate the most efficient pursuit of power. Discerning the relative importance of efficiency and power in the emergence of private authority is clearly difficult empirically. Complicating this is the fact that assessing whether an interaction is exploitative or beneficial requires the analyst to draw on principles of justice and fairness involving never-finished controversies that are fundamental to human sociality.

Efficiency-based explanations, power-based explanations, and historical explanations can be applied to both interfirm and firm-state interactions. In table 12.1 we attempt to summarize these, with illustrative examples provided for each cell.

Efficiency Gains and Private Authority

In this section we use efficiency gains as a basis for explaining the emergence of private authority, first focusing on interfirm interactions, and then on firm–state interactions. The efficiency gains we see as most important are those that reduce transactions costs, which are the costs involved in contracting for and carrying out the transaction itself. Here, the transactions we are concerned with are economic in nature. Echoing Keohane's analysis of interstate regimes, we distinguish among three types: (1) costs associated with information and uncertainty; (2) costs more directly associated with negotiation; and (3) enforcement costs.[7] Informational costs include, for example, measuring the attributes of a

TABLE 12.1

Varieties of Explanations for the Emergence of Private Authority

What Are the Causes?	*Who Interacts?*	
	Interfirm Interactions	*State-firm Interactions*
Efficiency gains	Institutions may reduce transactions costs among firms	States delegate regulatory functions to a more efficient private sector
Power and domination	Firms use institutions to control markets and exclude new entrants	Firms use institutions to capture state regulators, undermine regulations, or to enhance their ability to use the state against other actors
Epochal, systemic, or historical change	A long-range expansion of markets increases the demand and capacity for persistent interfirm cooperation, and thus private authority	Globalization undermines the authority of the state and enhances the demand and capacity of firms to produce new forms of private authority in its place

product, determining your counterpart's intentions in a negotiation, or monitoring compliance with a contract. Negotiation costs include, for example, determining with whom to negotiate, the appropriate terms to discuss, and even such practical details as where and when to meet. Enforcement costs are those involved in establishing the conditions and instruments for punishment when a contracted transaction is not completed; such costs also include measures that prevent the need for actual enforcement, such as reducing risk by the prior establishment of predictable behavior.

Private authority can reduce information-related costs by establishing standards for measuring and certifying the reliability of information and actors. By establishing recognized and widely accepted parameters and sites for interactions, private actors with authority can increase the efficiency of the negotiating process. Private authority also can be used to reduce enforcement problems by establishing recognized norms of behavior for which generalized compliance is expected, perhaps designing self-enforcing agreements. In economic transactions, firms would comply with the wielding of private authority because they have determined that it is reducing their costs of doing business. This may be reinforced by the perception that the private authority is based on expertise that contributes to efficiency. If this authority enhances efficiency, then those firms subject to it will enjoy a competitive advantage over others and will, over time, displace firms operating in its absence.

In order to understand the relationship between efficiency gains and the emergence of private authority, we need to compare and analyze transactions in a pure market setting; transactions that have been governed by public authority; and transactions governed by private authority. First, why might private authority reduce transactions costs below what is found in arm's length markets? The ideal operation of arm's length markets depends on the absence of transactions costs, and all exchange is based on supply and demand mediated by prices. Therefore, such "pure" markets simply do not have any institutional capacity to address information, negotiation, and enforcement problems. The development of institutional economics directly refutes the idea of such frictionless markets, and argues that institutions are a necessary concomitant to the development of markets. Second, why might private authority reduce transactions costs better than public authority? Here, we distinguish the "unique competitive advantages" of states and firms in the negotiation and management of governance arrangements. If we assume that these governance arrangements function to reduce transactions costs, then one would expect the degree to which states and firms participate in them corresponds to the degree to which their particular attributes effectively address such costs.[8] We list five considerations in table 12.2.

Enforcement is a key consideration in determining the relative advantages of states and firms. States are by definition the main enforcers, given collective legitimacy in the use of coercion. This is significantly attenuated, however, at the international level. Firms also have some enforcement capability, especially as technological developments increase interdependence among them, which provides them with leverage over one another. States also have an advantage in terms of the scale of their operations, with efficiency gains in regulating multiple industries and issues; governance arrangements among firms tend to be narrowly industry-based and limited in the number of issue areas covered. States also have an advantage in terms of the very principle of their existence—sovereignty. In international negotiations, states negotiate with other states and not with firms, and in certain commercial transactions state-owned industries have a decisive advantage. On the other hand, firms by definition are closer to the market and thus have an advantage in terms of familiarity with market participants and their business practices. Finally, states obviously have a greater capacity to govern by virtue of their ability to raise the funds to provide public goods through taxation. On the other hand, the development of contemporary global financial markets and the development of new technologies provides private sector actors with the capability to undertake the provision of large-scale private *and* public goods.

TABLE 12.2
The Competitive Advantages of States and Firms in Governance

Consideration	Advantage of State	Advantage of Firms
Enforcement	States have legal system, monopoly of legitimate violence at domestic level. Problem is weakness of legal system and lack of monopoly of violence at international level.	Firms have interdependence that provides leverage, extensive information about market actors at both domestic and international levels. Problem is reliance on state courts/coercion.
Factors related to number of industries/ issues	States have scale and scope economies in regulation across industries/issues at domestic level. Problem is need for interstate cooperation to accomplish this internationally.	Firms develop solidarity through joint practices specific to a particular industry, may be able to respond more flexibly to rapid change. Problem is narrowness of governance.
Factors related to type of actors	States are sovereign actors and recognize sovereignty as basis for negotiation, even for commercial transactions.	Firms are market actors and recognize market imperatives/business practices as basis for negotiation.
Ability to legitimize norms and rules to citizenry	State accorded legitimacy by society, represents collective expression of norms and the center of rule-making. Problem is lack of legimate public authority/society at international level.	Firms develop norms and rules that do not need broader legitimization, or that are legitimated by industry participants. Problem is narrowness of applicability.
Capacity	States have power to tax, provide public goods efficiently. Problem is fiscal constraints on state.	Firms have access to financial markets, technology.

In general, table 12.2 indicates that the state is likely to continue to enjoy a decisive advantage in governance where transactions are characterized by large-scale risks, or where they involve multiple industries or issue areas. States continue to enjoy their traditional advantage in enforcement and legitimation of policy domestically, but this is less the case when transactions are international or are restricted to private firms operating in single industries. In all respects the advantages that states enjoy relative to firms in the domestic economy are substantially reduced at the international level, where there is no centralized political authority and interstate cooperation remains difficult.[9]

Our cases offer numerous examples of how private authority can be regarded as reducing transactions costs, although not all authors would agree that efficiency considerations are a significant explanatory component of their cases. Spar argues that commerce on the Internet reduces transactions costs by removing intermediate steps (such as the need for retail distributors), but it also increases them by removing "many of the rules and institutions that have developed over time to support modern commerce." Property rights are poorly defined and difficult to enforce on the Internet, and e-cash as a means of payment is still quite risky. Private authority, in the form of the carving out of a rule-governed secure and controlled community by private service providers such as America Online, reduces such transactions costs. Sinclair's analysis of debt-rating agencies demonstrates that these private sector actors carry out more efficient monitoring and assessment of borrowers than would be possible for dispersed investors: "coordination can, at a minimum then, be viewed as an uncertainty reduction development that allows for transactions to go ahead without undue friction or measures to prevent loss in a market context of heightened social distance."[10] Haufler presents the development of norms of insurability as a means to reduce the need for industry participants to engage in costly case-by-case assessment of each risk, and the prohibition of lucrative but excessively risky insurance maintains the reputation and financial viability of the industry as a whole. Salter's standards organizations reduce uncertainty both for producers (by confirming technological trajectories) and for consumers (by measuring product performance). The establishment of maritime trade terms, as described by Cutler, reduces the need to engage in costly negotiations about particular shipments; private international trade law in general reduces uncertainty and enhances enforcement. The tendency of the oil MNCs and indigenous organizations in Ecuador, analyzed by Burke, to bypass the state and deal directly with each other could be viewed as substituting a more direct and efficient set of interactions for a state-mediated process that may not suit the needs of either party. Webb's mineral regimes operate, in part, to reduce uncertainty from excessive price volatility and the accompanying wasteful over- or under-investment. The interwar cartels analyzed by Porter and the knowledge-based oligopolies analyzed by Mytelka and Delapierre have been justified in similar terms. Finally, the Intellectual Property Committee, as analyzed by Sell, is an efficient organizational means of mobilizing the business community to promote the international regulation of intellectual property rights, as this well-connected set of those corporations with much at stake would be more effective than a more comprehensive trade association or individual lobbying.

The cases display considerable variation in the relative importance of state authority and arm's-length markets as alternatives to private authority. In insurance, knowledge-based oligopolies, and debt rating, the authority of states has always played a secondary role relative to market-initiated solutions. In the case of mineral markets, standards, maritime trade terms, and intellectual property rights, states have, in particular historical periods, been an important alternative, supplement, or counterpoint to private authority. For instance, in mineral markets it was the heightened activism of Southern states that undermined the private regimes of the 1950s, but states also played an important role in buttressing private efforts, either by threatening to impose trade measures against the states or firms that resisted private efforts at coordination, and, in some cases, by encouraging the formation of public/private study groups. International standards have been designed primarily by firms, but the international regime has been supported by states. In maritime trade law, states work with firms through the United Nations Commission on International Trade Law (UNCITRAL) or the International Institute for the Unification of Private Law (UNIDROIT) and build on previous private efforts such as those promoted by the International Chamber of Commerce. Through the IP agreements in the Uruguay Round, states provided a formalized response to firm demands for heightened intellectual property protection. In the case of interwar cartelization, states enhanced the ability of firms to build trust and enforce commitments by negotiating a prior strong patent regime. Trends in the relative importance of state authority and arm's-length markets vary: states have consistently low involvement in debt rating and insurance, are becoming relatively less important in mineral markets, standards, the Internet, and the domestic interactions of oil MNCs in Ecuador, and relatively more important over time in trade terms and intellectual property rights enforcement.

These variations in the relative importance of private and state authority can be explained in part with reference to the unique competitive advantages of states and private firms in the production of authority. Both maritime trade terms and intellectual property involve the extension of authoritative rules well beyond their architects, a task for which the state, with its unique capacity to make binding and legitimate laws, is better suited than firms. Relatedly both these issue areas are multisectoral, since many different industries ship goods or create intellectual property. State involvement in the governance of mineral markets can similarly be accounted for by the fact that states were very active as commercial transactors, thereby increasing the need for other states to get involved in the regime to satisfy the requirement of the sovereign states system that states only recognize each other in law. Similarly the growing displacement by private authority of public authority can be partially explained in this manner. The IPC was better able to initiate IP negotiations than were states because of their small number, their intense interest in the issue area, and their common experiences—IPC negotiations could be seen as more efficient than interstate negotiations at this early stage. Strong private authority in the standards regime can be explained in similar terms. As noted above, the growing importance of direct MNC–indigenous negotiations in Ecuador were stimulated in part by the desire to reduce the unnecessarily complicating presence of the state.

We should regard all the above points about the role of efficiency considerations in explaining private authority with caution, however. In the next section we qualify these conclusions to take into account the role of power. Indeed, most of our contributors would see power as out-weighing efficiency in a satisfactory explanation of private authority.

Power and Private Authority

The desire of leading firms to organize themselves to control markets and thereby enhance their own profitability has been a well-recognized feature of capitalism from the beginning, as evident in Adam Smith's famous comment about the propensity of owners to engage "always and everywhere in a sort of tacit, but constant and uniform combination."[11] In the liberal tradition the antidote to this tendency has been to encourage competitive markets and to prohibit excessive concentration through the development of antitrust policies. The Marxist tradition generally views collusion among firms as an inherent feature of capitalism, carried out through the controlling role played by banks and other financial institutions,[12] through organizations such as the Trilateral Commission,[13] or through mergers and acquisitions. Contemporary Schumpeterian and business literatures suggest that firms can dominate markets and extract rents by obtaining a succession of temporary monopolies by controlling new technologies. These analyses of the role of power and domination in interfirm relations urge us to regard with skepticism the implication of the transactions costs approach that private cooperative arrangements, by promoting efficiency, contribute to an increase in global welfare.

There are similar analyses of the power relationship between leading firms and states. Regulatory capture theory, for instance, suggests that enhanced private organizational capacity is used to ensure that regulations benefit the regulated industry at the public's expense.[14] Marxist analysis suggests that such capacity is used to influence or control the state more generally in the interest of capitalists or capitalism as a whole. Neo-mercantilist and strategic trade theories note the ability of large states and leading firms to improve their competitive positions, in part through enhanced collaboration among firms with the encouragement of the state.[15] Policy network theories analyze variation in the relative influence of private and state institutions across industries in terms of political and institutional factors.[16]

Two distinct roles played by power in private authority can be discerned. The first, an *ex ante* consideration, is the role of power in making it possible for firms to establish private authority in the first place. The adoption of a particular instititional arrangement may have much more to do with the power of its architects than its merits on efficiency grounds. The second, an *ex post* consideration, is the importance of the power produced by private authority once it is established. Actors with power create private authority, and private authority creates power. Anticipations of the power derived from private authority can motivate actors to build the institutions needed to produce it.

Our cases provide numerous examples of the importance of power in creating private authority. The knowledge-based networked oligopolies analyzed by Mytelka and Delapierre are built to an important degree on the legacy of privilege from traditional oligopolies enjoyed by their participants.[17] Webb, similarly, demonstrates that the management of mineral markets by private producers was built on oligopolistic market structures—structures that enhanced the organizational capacity of those producers. Once these were undermined by new players and heightened competition, the private regime collapsed. The increased prominence of the London Metals Exchange, with its damaging speculation, was due more to the weakening capacity of producers relative to traders and to institutional investors than to the LME's greater efficiency. For Sinclair the ratings agencies do much more than efficiently process information for decentralized investors: they represent a particular social force, the "globalizing elites" that are at the strategic center of contemporary capitalism. Sell too suggests that the success of the IPC in developing and exercising its authority had as much to do with the "structurally privileged position" of its twelve member corporations as with the efficiency of the IPC as a form of organization—although the IPC's efficiency could be seen as assisting its members in more effectively deploying their power. Salter notes that "standards reflect the priorities of their expert developers, who undoubtedly reflect the interests of their own governments and of the multinational firms who sponsor their participation and contributions"; smaller firms and developing country governments shape their own technological trajectories to conform with the standards developed by their more powerful counterparts. In the case of the Internet as well, power cannot be ignored in explaining the private character of its governance. In this case it is not so much the power of existing leading firms that accounts for the preeminence of private authority as that there is strong political opposition by "netizens" to government regulation, as evident in the failure of the Clipper chip. The opponents to government regulation also enjoyed a type of "structural power"—the decentralized nature of the Internet makes government prohibitions difficult to enforce but allows private firms to create enclosed, rule-governed spaces. The exclusion of the state from the interactions of MNCs and indigenous organizations in Ecuador, as analyzed by Burke, can similarly be attributed to their increased relative power vis-à-vis a weak state as well as to their greater efficiency.

The questions of information and enforcement that are central to efficiency explanations also have important linkages to the role of power in explaining the emergence of private authority. The cases demonstrate that information is not simply a neutral expression of existing industry conditions. On the contrary, information can be used to structure the behavior of industry participants, consolidating relationships of dominant firms and reducing the capacity of new entrants and states to participate, thereby reducing their potential to threaten the dominant firms. This is the case with the establishment of technological trajectories, as evident in Mytelka and Delapierre's account of knowledge-based networked oligopolies and Salter's standards regime. Consistent with efficiency considerations, coordination among leading firms is useful to reduce or share risks or costs, or, as Salter notes, because "some new technologies must be connectable and connected in order to be marketable at all." Yet such cooperation also allows leading firms to retain their lead, to have competitors adjust to the standards and technologies that the leading firms have developed. As Mytelka and Delapierre point out, this can also have consequences for public policy, as when profit considerations led to the relative neglect of tropical diseases by the pharmaceutical industry. Moreover, as she notes, traditional antitrust tools may be inadequate in dealing with the ability of firms to use knowledge to engage in restraint of trade. The use of knowledge to promote the interests of leading firms is not restricted to high-tech industries: Webb points out that the information produced by study groups in mineral markets, information that highlighted the potential for overcapacity, is also a precondition for coordinated cutbacks in production or other oligopolistic market practices.

Information can also be used to exclude certain actors from a policy process. Sell, for instance, notes that "most IP lawyers possess technical educational backgrounds in science, engineering, biochemistry, or chemistry. To a certain extent IP law is reminiscent of the Catholic Church when the Bible was in Latin. IP lawyers are privileged purveyors of expertise as was the Latin-trained clergy." Control over information can also involve the power to define what information is relevant, reinforcing particular perspectives that may benefit some at the expense of others.[18] In the case of IP, technical knowledge was inextricably bound up with a commitment to promote its protection. This gave the leading firms in the IPC a decisive advantage over states and other actors in the Uruguay Round negotiations. Cutler identifies a similar effect in maritime trade law due to its complexity. This was reinforced by the shifting of maritime trade term negotiations from the United Nations Conference on Trade and Development (UNCTAD) to UNCITRAL and UNIDROIT, as well as the treatment of international trade law as "private" and nonpolitical. Once again, these had more to do with the desire of leading shippers and their states to offset the challenge from new entrants and redistributive demands from developing countries than with the greater efficiency of the new forums.

Information is important with regard to the role of power in explaining the emergence of private authority, not just as a resource that can account for the successful pursuit by the architects of private authority of their own interests, but also because of its centrality for the phenomenon of authority itself. This is most directly addressed in Sinclair's chapter, in which he points to the contribution of ratings agencies' specialized knowledge to epistemic authority. A similar effect is evident in the standards regime, in maritime trade law, and in the IP negotiations.

Information is relevant to both roles of power distinguished previously—that is, prior possession and use of knowledge can explain the capacity of private actors to establish private authority, but also anticipation of the empowering effects of the knowledge that will be acquired once private authority is established can explain the motivation of the architects of private authority. Thus the ability of bond raters to produce specialized knowledge not only explains the inherent capacity of the ratings agencies to exercise epistemic authority, but also explains the incentive for powerful globalizing elites to make use of this particular institutional arrangement. Information and knowledge can be an effective motivator not only for the power that is gained from their structuring effects, but from their related commercial value. Knowledge is of value to knowledge-based networked oligopolies, for instance, both because it allows its possessors to structure markets and technological trajectories, and because it can be profitable to sell. Similarly, new knowledge about IP, or about e-cash on the Internet, is not passive—it simultaneously orients those absorbing it to new patterns of interaction, new commercial practices, and begins to constitute a new product.

For some of our cases it is difficult to separate out the first and second roles of power in the establishment of private authority: powerful actors build private authority to reinforce or extend their existing power. This need not necessarily be the case, however. For instance, the architects of private authority on the Internet are not building on a prior market dominance, in this case it is the motivational effect of the stakes that is most relevant: as Spar notes, "business is not simply going to walk away from the dazzling promise of the Internet." One could regard this promise as no more than an appropriate return for the riskiness of the product provided—as just an expression of the efficient operation of markets—but that would underestimate the political dimension of the displacement of the original private regime based on a principle of open access by a commercial private regime in which the principle of property rights in information is established and enforced. The two principles are incompatible, and prices are unlikely to capture adequately the values produced by the original regime so that it would be difficult to argue that we are simply seeing a shift to a state of relatively greater efficiency. Rather, in part, the shift reflects a struggle between two communities, each deploying a variety of political and commercial resources. A similar point could be made about the IP negotiations.

Historical Trends and Private Authority

In this section we explore the historical dimensions of private authority. The balance between public and private authority in international governance has varied over time, exhibiting both continuity and discontinuity and reflecting important material and ideological developments. These dimensions are significant complements to efficiency and power-based explanations of private authority. Both efficiency and some power-based explanations of private authority draw on rationalist premises and, as such, can be criticized for being of limited assistance in understanding the significance of deeper historical-sociological influences on international governance.[19] Keohane notes that rationalist theory can "be used to explore the conditions under which cooperation takes place, and it seeks to explain why international institutions are constructed by states."[20] However, he acknowledges that, among other deficiencies, such theory needs to be contextualized, both historically and sociologically. Rationalist theory, he argues, lacks an historical view: it does not "extend its vision back into history."[21] It has not been very successful in depicting what Fernand Braudel identifies as long-term history—civilizational and structural changes over *la longue durée.*[22] Others, too, share the sense that something is changing in key elements of the Westphalian system, but that the transformation occurring is obscured by rationalist theory.[23] Zacher with Sutton notes that rationalist-based neorealist and neoliberal theories "are basicaly time-bound to our present historical era."[24] They observe that these theories do not address the general structures, normative framework, or transformational developments in the Westphalian system.

The idea that something is changing challenges the beliefs that "[t]he texture of international politics remains highly constant, patterns recur, events repeat themselves endlessly,"[25] that the history of international relations is characterized more by continuity than by change, and that material rather than ideational factors are determinative.[26] Many express the need for a more historical and sociological approach that is sensitive to the epistemic or ideational and normative dimensions of international governance.[27] Moreover, there is a general sense that we are in the midst of a structural transformation that is simply not captured by state-centric analysis. Indeed, John Ruggie suggests that we need a whole new language—a new generative grammar that historicizes international relations and enables the contemplation of epochal change.[28] Ruggie emphasizes the shift in "the modern system of rule" from medieval to modern authority relations[29] and argues that we are presently in the midst of a transformation from modern to postmodern structures of authority.[30] This change is of the order of the transformation that occurred with the emergence of the modern market society analyzed by Karl Polanyi.[31] Forces of globalization, deregulation, and privatization are disembedding national economies[32] and generating a new mode of production and authority relations consistent with postmodern material and epistemic conditions.[33] Some speculate that this is causing a "redistribution of power among states, markets, and civil society,"[34] while others stress the new role that states are taking on as active participants in globalization.[35] However, there is a shared sense that we lack the "perceptual equipment"[36] to understand this transformation.

The historical and sociological insights into the emergence of private authority complement efficiency and power-based explanations by providing needed historical, societal, and ideational contexts. Our analysis of efficiency and power-based explanations of the emergence of private authority illustrate the capacity of rationalist theory to incorporate ideational and normative variables. The role of epistemic authority, for example, is stressed in a number of the papers. Haufler describes the insurance industry as an "epistemic community" characterized by technical and managerial expertise and united by shared corporate norms. She also analyzes the incipient eco-efficiency norm that appears to be developing in the environmental area. Spar's analysis clearly suggests that authority on the Internet is following closely on the heels of technological expertise. Bound by their own technological norms and experience, dispersed communities of Internet users have repeatedly repelled the regulatory advances of the state. Salter notes that the highly technical nature of the knowledge involved in standards works in favor of private regulatory arrangements, an observation also made by Cutler about the regulation of commercial and maritime relations. Sell too notes how expertise and control over information privileged the position of private actors in the determination of the norms governing the intellectual property regime and enabled the private sphere to shape the definition of the public interest for the United States. Some of the chapters in this volume associate private authority with broader historical trends in the development of the world capitalist economy and the states system. Others focus more on contemporary developments that associate private authority with globalization, and the related expansion of market forces and increased knowledge-intensity of production. While Sinclair notes the importance of epistemic authority in terms of the analytical capabilities and local knowledge possessed by bond raters, he associates this with deeper structural power emanating from the role of bond raters as a "gobalizing elite." Cutler too associates the authority of corporate actors over maritime transport with neoliberal ideology and the historical structural separations of public and private international law and practice. Both authors suggest a link between private authority and deeper historical trends associated with developments in the structure of global capitalism. These developments include the globalization of finance and production, privatization, deregulation, and the emergence of "competition states, " as states adjust to the changing terms of international competition.[37] Cerny has argued that globalization is a process of structuration that challenges us to "rethink history" in order to capture the way in which politics is being reshaped by a range of developments, including the emergence of the competition state as an active agent of globalization.[38] The incentives for private actors to develop norms enabling them to better adjust to intensified international competition is evident in the private authority wielded by corporations over intellectual property rules, while Mytelka and Delapierre place the emergence of knowledge-based networked oligopolies in the context of shifting terms of competition. Cutler argues that the neoliberal commitment of the most powerful actors to the private ordering of legal commercial and maritime regimes is premised on the belief that private regulatory arrangements are the most efficient and thus most desirable means for adjusting to increasing international competition. Here, historic trends in the development of global capitalism intersect with efficiency and power to produce the normative position that private ordering is the most appropriate way of dealing with intensified global competition.

One large-scale historical trend, the expansion of markets, is clearly a central feature of globalization as a multidimensional process involving political, ideological, and economic changes. The expansion of markets can also be seen as somewhat distinct from globalization, as independently transforming local interactions, for instance, or as expanding *intensively* (in the range of things that are tradable and in the intensity with which market dynamics govern those exchanges) as well as *extensively* (to new areas of the world). As alternative forms of social organization, such as family, community, or state, are displaced by markets, the authority associated with those alternatives diminishes and authority associated with market-based activity is enhanced. The displacement of the old Internet community by a commercialized regime, the commercialization of knowledge that stimulated the campaign for intellectual property rights and the superceding by market principles of redistributive principles in mineral markets could be seen as expressions of the long-range historical expansion of markets.

Similarly, the expansion of knowledge can be viewed both as a feature of globalization and as a distinct long-range historical trend. Rosenau has associated the growth of knowledge with the diminished authority of states in international affairs,[39] and although he has seen this as due to citizens in general being empowered by their increased knowledge, the decentralizing effect of easily accessible knowledge is likely also to empower firms relative to states. Knowledge can coordinate social action, and Lash has argued, "receding social structures are being largely displaced instead by *information and communication structures*."[40] When the production and transmittal of knowledge is increasingly carried out by private firms, as is the case with most of the industries discussed in this book, and in other areas of contemporary life, this expansion of knowledge can contribute to the emergence of private authority.

Two caveats are important to make with regard to the contribution of epochal change to the emergence of private authority. First, one should not overstate the novelty or the linearity of these changes. As Cutler and Porter point out in their chapters, private authority has existed in previous historical periods. Indeed, what appears to be rapid expansion of private authority now may be in part one phase of a more cyclical pattern. Cutler's account of private trade law, for instance, highlights a certain similarity in the way in which trade rules were established privately in earlier periods and in our current era, a continuity that was interrupted by two centuries of enhanced state authority. Porter suggests that private authority may rise and decline in particular industries as those industries emerge and mature. Skeptics of globalization have pointed out that in important respects the late nineteenth century was more globalized than now: time series that start with the mid-twentieth-century zenith of centralized state power mistakenly portray a return to earlier trends as an entirely novel and unilinear change.[41] Even in the post–World War II period some industries have witnessed a decline in private authority, as is the case with mineral markets analyzed by Webb in which private regimes were more influential in the 1950s and 1960s than they are today. A second and related caveat is that historical does not mean inevitable. The more actor-centric factors upon which our discussion of power and efficiency focused continue to offset the inertia or momentum of historical dynamics.

The Emergence of Private Authority

This section has explored three types of explanations for the emergence of private authority in international affairs. *Efficiency*-type explanations suggest that private authority may be effective at reducing transactions costs relative to atomistic arm's-length markets where no such authority exists, and relative to public authority based in states and interstate institutions. For instance, in atomistic markets the emergence of private authority can allow firms to better cope with strategic interdependence by enhancing commitments to joint activities or by providing sanctioned behavioral prescriptions around which coordination can occur. Private authority can mobilize firms to jointly press for public policy changes that would be unobtainable for firms acting individually. Private authority can establish, monitor, and even enforce performance standards that may enhance the confidence of an industry's customers. These efficiency advantages of private authority can bring its production about either by firms recognizing these advantages and acting to construct or comply with authority, or by a competitive process whereby interactions subject to authority displace those that are not. We suggested also that efficiency considerations may similarly explain the displacement of public authority by private authority, as for instance when firms in a particular industry need to coordinate their activity and find they tend to trust, deal easily with, and feel obligated to comply with private authority more than would be the case with public authority.

Power-based explanations emphasize the degree to which contemporary private authority may build on past dominance of markets or issue areas by the firms that construct it. Private authority may be more a way for such firms to reproduce their dominance than to enhance the efficiency of transactions. Private authority may allow firms to alter public policies to their own advantage, irrespective of the effects of such alterations on global welfare. Private authority may displace public authority not because the former is more efficient, but because powerful firms find it easier to pursue their particular goals without demands for accountability or the need to interact with other stakeholders that are associated with public authority. Private authority may not just be constructed by firms that have traditionally been dominant—it may also be a way for skillful private interests to achieve dominance, particularly in new industries where leaders have not yet emerged.

Historical explanations suggest that the emergence of private authority may be related to longer-range epochal shifts in the international political economy. The related processes of globalization, rapid technological change, and the expansion of markets all have been cited by some theorists as enhancing the power of private firms relative to states. In part historical explanations simply see efficiency or power-based factors as being more persistent and ubiquitous than would the explanations discussed under those labels above—but establishing the link between enhanced private authority and epochal change can open up analytical connections that would be obscured by a shorter time frame or a narrower focus. We have noted, however, that a historical approach can also point out the degree to which private authority in international affairs is not a new phenomenon, and thus we should regard suggestions that it is linked to epochal changes with caution.

We have emphasized that the above three types of explanations for the emergence of private authority are complementary rather than incommensurable. Often institutions enhance efficiency while also reinforcing differentials in power. While variation across issue areas and industries precludes any overall conclusion about the relative importance of efficiency, power, and historical trends for explaining the emergence of private authority in international affairs, it is important to attempt to make an assessment in any particular case, a task that our contributors have taken up in their respective chapters.

HOW DOES PRIVATE AUTHORITY OPERATE?

In this section we move beyond the question of why private authority emerges in international issue areas where there was no authority previously, or where public authority was preeminent, to ask how private authority operates once it is established. A goal here is to explore the significance of the varied instititutional arrangements that sustain private authority, as demonstrated in our case studies. We are also interested in clarifying some of the dimensions along which private authority can vary.

Institutional Features of Private International Authority

In our introduction we set out six types of cooperative arrangements between firms: (1) informal industry norms and practices; (2) coordination services firms; (3) production alliances, subcontractor relationships, and complementary activities; (4) cartels; (5) business associations; and (6) private regimes. We suggested that these were ordered to some degree from least to most institutionalized or comprehensive, and that integration between these various types of private arrangements in a particular industry or issue area could be a source of private authority. In this section we reassess these points in light of our contributors' case studies.

Examples of all six types of private arrangements are evident from the case studies. Haufler's analysis of the insurance industry provides a useful illustration of the impact of informal industry norms and practices: notions of which risks were insurable and which were not have had a structuring effect on the industry that went well beyond what could be accounted for by formal organizations issuing codified rules. Similarly Spar notes the role of informal norms in the governance of the Internet, particularly in its earlier period.

Of the case studies, Sinclair's discussion of debt-rating agencies focuses most directly on coordination services firms. The agencies do much more than offer passive information in exchange for money. By drawing on abstract models that define appropriate behavior and by transmitting through the market concrete applications of these models to particular cases the agencies are able to structure the behavior of both private and public borrowers. Our other cases, while not focusing as directly upon coordination services firms, provide evidence of their effects. Sell, for instance, highlights the influence of intellectual property lawyers on the Uruguay Round negotiations, and although she stresses the structuring effect of their specialized knowledge, one could also explore the specific organizational impacts of the law firms to which they belong. Insurance firms also act as coordination services firms, both with respect to clients outside the insurance industry, as with the use of environmental norms in determining insurance rates, and to other insurance firms, as in the role of reinsurers in determining the classes of risks that are accepted by the insurance industry more generally.

Mytelka and Delapierre's knowledge-based networked oligopolies fit most closely with the category that we have labeled "production alliances." With respect to private authority, a distinctive characteristic of these oligopolies is their ability to structure the technological trajectories of the industries in which they are involved. Distinguishing between these contemporary production alliances and traditional cartels, such as those analyzed by Porter, can be difficult. The former are generally considered to be legitimate because they increase the range of new products available rather than seeking, as do cartels, to restrict technological innovation in order to control prices or market shares. The chapters by Mytelka and Delapierre and Porter suggest that the close interdependence of those involved in contemporary production alliances, particularly since collaboration involves planning the shape of future markets, may involve more restrictive business practices than is generally recognized.

The chapters by Sell and by Salter provide clear examples of the contemporary international role of business associations. Interestingly, Sell indicates that the Intellectual Property Committee chose to bypass more traditional business associations in its campaign to get intellectual property regulations in the Uruguay Round. This appears to have been because of the greater flexibility and focus provided by the IPC's character as a small association of the very largest and most concerned firms. The IPC's activities were restricted to the first function of business associations that we specified in the introduction: lobbying and interest representation. By contrast, the private standards organizations discussed by Salter, while engaging in interest representation in negotiations involving states, also carry out a self-regulatory function. When associations such as the International Standards Organization sell assessments of compliance with standards, they begin to resemble coordination services firms such as debt-rating agencies. Cutler and Porter indicate that business associations have a history of structuring international markets as evident in the role of the International Chamber of Commerce in creating maritime trade terms and the Manchester Chamber of Commerce in bringing about free trade.

Because regimes may rely on informal norms, and because there is no objective criterion that can establish a required threshold at which private institutions are comprehensive enough to be considered regimes, their existence is often difficult to establish irrefutably. Furthermore, we should note that regimes are not actually the most institutionalized of our categories of interfirm cooperation, since they can be informal and somewhat amorphous. They are, however, the most comprehensive of forms of interfirm cooperation. Moreover, they may involve the integration of other forms of cooperative activity, such as that internal to large firms, which are relatively institutionalized. Four of our contributors have identified regimes that are either almost entirely private or heavily rely on the authoritative initiatives of private firms. The former "private regimes" include the insurance regime analyzed by Haufler, the emerging regime for organizing the Internet analyzed by Spar, and certain periods in which private interfirm arrangements for organizing mineral markets emerged, as analyzed by Webb. A regime in which public and private sectors work together is the international standards regime analyzed by Salter.

Further development of criteria for identifying regimes, such as the measures of institutionalization discussed below, is a topic that, while going beyond the scope of the present volume, merits more work and would be useful in establishing agreement on the presence and absence of private regimes. Other issue areas and industries discussed in this book such as certain periods in the evolution of maritime law, the early cotton industry, debt rating, and cartelized industries in the interwar period may qualify as private regimes since the private formal organizations and informal industry practices involved have had an identifiable and impressive structuring presence. By contrast, the institutions involved in the case of the oil industry in Ecuador, of the IPC, and knowledge-based oligopolies are more narrowly focused, the first on a particular country and the second two on particular projects, than one would normally associate with the regime label. It is important to note that a decision to use the regime label in any particular case in the present book, as in the analysis of international affairs more generally, is dependent not only on the characteristics of the case in question but also on the conceptual preferences of the analyst.

As noted in the introduction, these six categories can be seen as varying from least institutionalized (informal practices) to most institutionalized or most comprehensive (full-fledged regimes, though with the caveat noted above). As Keohane has argued, institutionalization can be measured along three dimensions: *commonality*, the degree to which understandings are shared; *specificity*, the degree to which expectations are specified in rules; and *autonomy*, the ability of an institution to alter its own rules.[42] The persistence of an institution over time and its capacity to enforce compliance are also useful indicators of institutionalization. Informal practices are diverse, lack autonomy, and cannot sustain highly detailed sets of rules. Coordination services firms can draw on highly specialized bodies of knowledge, filled with specific rules, but they experience limits individually in altering those rules or ensuring that firms comply with them. Business associations, including self-regulatory organizations, and private regimes may have the capacity to foster the negotiation and research that can autonomously produce common and specific new sets of rules. Assessing with confidence the degree of institutionalization associated with any particular type of private authority is difficult, however, in part because of the difficulty in making comparisons across the three dimensions, and in part because of the difficulties of establishing the boundaries of an institution. For instance, the impact of debt-rating agencies and of the Intellectual Property Committee have been much greater than one would expect given the lack of institutionalization of any individual agency or the IPC itself, an effect that is due to the relationship of the particular institution to a larger field of well-defined practices or to other more institutionalized arrangements, such as the larger state-led trade regime.

Scope and Domain in the Reach of Private Authority

It has become well recognized that an important step in analyzing the operation of power is to specify who is affected and the range of ways in which they are affected. These two attributes of power have come to be called domain and scope respectively.[43] It is useful in assessing the international operation and significance of private authority to employ a similar distinction.

Our cases of private authority vary noticeably in their domain. Three points on a continuum can be distinguished. On one end of a continuum those exercising private authority and those subject to it are the same firms to a large degree. Mytelka and Delapierre's knowledge-based networked oligopolies provide a clear example. The firms involved seek indirectly to influence the behavior of actors, if in no other way than to convince them to buy the products resulting from the network arrangements, but the primary behavior needing to be structured is that of the member firms.

In the middle of the continuum a second category can be discerned: cases where coordination involves parties who are not stable members of a coordinating institution but who are integrated in some form into well-established industry practices. The securities markets that debt-rating agencies contribute to structuring are exemplary: corporate finance departments, government finance ministries, and most investors, while not as interdependent as the participants in knowledge-based networks, consider themselves as participating in an industry—the securities industry—in which behavior is shaped by well-recognized financial practices.

At the other end of the continuum a third category can be discerned: one in which the structuring effect of private authority must reach beyond its architects and its industry in order to operate effectively. Cutler's case of maritime trade law is illustrative: a wide range of actors who can ship goods by sea must be subject to the authority of this trade law for it to work, but these actors are only peripherally integrated into the shipping industry. Similarly rules on intellectual property had to be extended to a wide range of firms to achieve the effect desired by the Intellectual Property Committee.

It is useful to note that the inward exercise of private authority, over its architects, and the outward exercise of private authority, over other industries and citizens, can be mutually reinforcing. The interwar cartels analyzed by Porter required an internal discipline in order to exercise control over new entrants and others potentially threatening to the architects' control of the market. Similarly with mineral markets, strong acceptance of an agreed direction by study groups facilitated a joint response to new challenges from Russian firms. Successful outward exercise of authority increases the incentive for the architects of authority to continue to support and produce it.

There appears to be some correlation between the domain of private authority and the six types of institutional arrangements discussed above. As we have noted, those six types were ordered by degree of institutionalization, from informal practices through business associations to regimes. Not surprisingly the capacity of private authority to broaden its reach seems to be accompanied to some degree by increased institutionalization. The knowledge-based networked oligopolies primarily involve informal and mutual practices; securities markets involve coordination services firms; and for standards there is a more complex regime. It is useful to note as well that the state can play an important role where the reach of private authority is extended beyond its architects. This is evident in the involvement of states in the standards regime, the intellectual property rights regime, and the maritime law regime. State involvement does not, however, appear to be necessary in all cases where the domain of private authority extends beyond its architects: this is particularly evident for the Internet, but as Cutler indicates, both maritime law and commercial law more generally have, in previous times, effectively extended their reach with little assistance from states. Clearly, as well, one should not underestimate the indirect effects on other industries and firms of private authority that is primarily directed toward its architects or their industry.

Considerable variation in the scope of private authority is also evident from our case studies, although this is highly interdependent with questions of domain: in general the scope of authority diminishes as one proceeds out through its domain (the scope of the private authority to which those at its periphery are subject is likely to be less than is the case for those closer to its center). Two types of variation in scope are evident. The first concerns the number of issue areas or industries that are affected. Since there is an extensive division of labor in the international economy, this dimension of scope tends to correspond to variations in domain; extensions of private authority across issue areas involve the extension of authority to new actors. Additionally, the scope of private authority may be both narrow with regard to its architects and wide with regard to others, as in the case of insurance, a well-defined industry that can shape the activities of all firms that are insured. Despite these complications it is clear that some forms of private authority are focused more narrowly on a particular industry or issue area, such as the organizations involved in organizing the early cotton trade, while others, such as the standards regime, have a broader focus.

The second type of variation in scope relates to the degree to which private authority obligates its recipients to alter their conduct and organization. Some forms of private authority mainly govern routine maintenance of ongoing transactions, while others involve firms in strategic planning processes that have profound effects on their whole organization. Examples of the first are the ongoing activities of bond-rating agencies, insurance companies, and cartels in mature markets, while examples of the latter include the knowledge-based networked oligopolies and the standards regime, to the extent that both set technological trajectories in conditions of interdependence, and the Intellectual Property Committee, which brought about a major alteration in rules governing knowledge-intensive transactions. This distinction should not be overdrawn, however. For instance, as Sinclair makes clear, bond rating is not simply about the application of generalized rules to particular borrowers, since it also involves the creation of those rules, which operate to establish the parameters of acceptable economic activity, a process that in important respects is more strategic, and requires more profound alterations in behavior, than more explicitly strategic activities such as devising new standards.

The relationship between these variations in scope and the six types of private authority is less clear than for domain. One can expect that strategic planning, which deals with contingencies and often is difficult to accomplish in large groups, cannot be too institutionalized, but this would not mean that less institutionalized sites for strategic planning could not be embedded within more institutionalized arrangements. Thus both the knowledge-based oligopolies and the standards regime rely heavily on informal mutual practices, but the former is more standalone, while the latter supports smaller specialized groups within a larger regime.

Enforcement and Private Authority

Authority, by definition, operates through a sense of obligation rather than coercion, one of its distinctive features that makes it particularly suited to the analysis of international affairs where enforcement capacity is weak. Despite the absence of coercive capacity there are certain institutional features of our cases that help explain how compliance with authority is fostered. These can be separated into three distinct categories. The first of these involves informal arrangements in which continued commitment is reinforced by an ongoing practical interdependence. The clearest such case is the knowledge-based networked oligopolies analyzed by Mytelka and Delapierre. Participants are tied to the arrangement by large sunk costs, by heavy investments that must be fully implemented if returns are to be realized, and by a configuration of their current organizational resources in anticipation of future interdependence. Interests cannot be safeguarded by a threat to exit momentarily or by a careful legal specification of the distribution of future benefits (as these are unclear)—instead the relationship needs to generate a degree of trust. This relationship, however, is not simply based on equality or reciprocity; in Mytelka and Delapierre's examples some firms matter more than others. We have, therefore a relationship that can be regarded as involving a type of authority.

The second variant relies more heavily on a private organization that has a degree of autonomy, perhaps a distinct legal identity, that separates it from those it influences. The two main types of such organizations are coordination services firms and industry associations. As coordination services firms the debt-rating agencies exercise authority over both investors and borrowers for whom the type of ongoing interdependence characteristic of the first category analyzed in the previous paragraph does not exist. The threat of exit is a much more common and viable way of safeguarding interests in securities markets than in the production of new technologies. The existence of rating agencies indicates that such threats are not sufficient, however: volatility, opportunism, and information-gathering costs would escalate in securities markets that relied solely on threats to exit. Trade associations are discussed in the nineteenth-century cotton industry by Porter. Here too firms needed to cooperate, but on matters, such as supply or access to markets or technologies, for which they were not integrated on a day-to-day basis.

The third variant involves the reinforcing presence of the state. The state may be important in initiating the institutional arrangements that sustain private authority, as in the case of mineral study groups, the standards regime, or the current effort to codify maritime trade law, or it may be important in implementing and enforcing policies initiated through the exercise of private authority, as in Sell's case of the role of the private Intellectual Property Committee in bringing about the intellectual property rights agreement between states in the Uruguay Round, or in the way in which states moved into areas declared uninsurable by private actors in the insurance regime.

No case can fall exclusively into one of these three categories. For instance, even for the knowledge-based networked oligopolies the state plays some role in providing the legal identities of participating firms. In some cases, such as the standards regime, all three types of arrangements are present. Nevertheless the differences between the categories are clear enough to make the distinctions meaningful.

It should be noted that compliance can be enhanced as well by the structuring effects of information, which were discussed as part of power-based explanations for the emergence of private authority above. A firm may rule out noncompliant behavior not because it has ascertained through measurement that the cost of such behavior is too high, but rather because conventional wisdom deems that behavior to be outdated, inefficient, or improper, or simply because lack of knowledge about alternatives make them inconceivable. Such structuring effects, based on trust in an authority's expertise, as previously noted, are central to the production and deployment of authority more generally.

The Operation of Private Authority

It is evident from our discussion in this section that there are a great many types of private authority in international affairs. The institutions associated with private authority range from very decentralized and informal practices to formal hierarchical organizations. Private authority may vary in its reach—in its domain and scope: its effects may be limited to a select number of firms in a particular industry or it may be exercised over many industries and issue areas. It may as well be exercised over many types of actors, including states, firms, and citizens in general. Finally, private authority may vary in the way in which compliance with it is ensured. Compliance may be reinforced by the interdependence of the architects of private authority and those subject to it. Third parties, including coordination services firms and industry associations, may enhance compliance where such interdependence is weaker. The enforcement capacity of states may be used to encourage compliance with private authority.

Highlighting this variety is useful in offsetting the tendency to underestimate the presence of private authority in international affairs. It also invites us not to miss important lessons that can be drawn from comparative analysis of market institutions, lessons that may be missed if one focuses excessively on larger systemic changes such as globalization. Variation in the operation of private authority can help explain variation in state policies and in the strength and character of state-led regimes, a point that we explore more fully in our concluding section below.

As well as highlighting the variety of ways in which private authority operates, this section has also suggested that there is some correlation between the degree of institutionalization of private authority, its domain and scope, and the degree to which it draws on organizations such as coordination services firms, business associations, or states to encourage compliance: in general, the greater the reach of private authority, the more formally organized are the institutions that are associated with it.

WHAT IS THE CONCEPTUAL CONTEXT AND SIGNIFICANCE OF PRIVATE AUTHORITY?

In this section we consider how private authority might be conceptualized and explained theoretically. In attempting to explain what vests private action with authority we identify significant obstacles to theorizing about private authority. However, we argue that these obstacles stem from a more general problem of theorizing about international governance and do not derive from the concept of private authority as such. Indeed, we argue that a clear understanding of these obstacles provides a fertile analytical foundation for the concept of private authority. Moreover, the concept of private authority provides a powerful corrective to limitations inherent in conventional modes of theorizing about international governance. Consideration will begin with the distinction made in chapter 1 between cooperation and authority and will then turn to the obstacles that make it difficult to conceive of private authority. The section will then address the analytical vigor of the concept of private authority.

Cooperation and Authority

We opened this volume with a simple definition of authority that rests on a distinction between cooperation and authority. We suggested that authority consists of decision-making power over an issue area that is generally regarded as legitimate by participants. We also stipulated that authority need not be associated with government institutions, but can be associated with firms. The legitimacy of firm or corporate authority, in turn, derives from the deference of participants flowing from their shared perceptions of corporate expertise, historical practices that legitimate corporate authority, or from an explicit or implied grant of authority by states. Furthermore, we assumed that such authority is somehow different from interfirm cooperation and we posited that cooperative relations can be transformed into authoritative relations when they become infused with an obligatory quality. Cooperation, to cite Keohane, "requires that the actions of separate individuals or organizations—which are not in pre-existing harmony—be brought into conformity with one another through policy coordination."[44] It involves changes in behavior that are contingent upon changes in the behavior of others, and may be explained by rationalist or reflectivist theories.[45] The former account for policy coordination on the basis of the rational calculations of interests and preferences, while the latter stresses the significance of intersubjective understandings and historic-sociological practices and conditions that give rise to cooperation. In addition, cooperation may be institutionalized to varying degrees: it may be formal or informal and take the form of rules or practices that shape expectations and structure the behavior of the participants.[46] Keohane draws on definitions provided by Douglass North, James March and Johan Olson, and John Rawls to develop a composite and broad definition of institutions as "persistent and connected sets of rules that prescribe behavioral roles, constrain activity, and shape expectations."[47] In our view, institutionalized cooperation takes on the mantle of authority when the participants regard the operative rules and practices to be obligatory.

We identified six institutional variants in chapter 1, including informal industry norms and practices, coordination service firms, production alliances, subcontract relationships and complementary activities, cartels, business associations, and finally private regimes. These represent different degrees of institutionalized cooperation (though we noted that regimes vary in their degree of institutionalization and may be weakly institutionalized compared to other forms of cooperation). Moreover, while we noted that there is no necessary linear movement from lower to higher degrees of institutionalization, we argued that the hierarchical integration of these different institutional patterns can be an important source of private authority. Such hierarchical arrangement may indeed be a crucial factor in the transformation of cooperative relations into authoritative relations, but it need not be, as is evident in the extent to which informal industry norms and practices are widely regarded as legitimate and obligatory.

The important point here is that cooperative relations become authoritative when they are considered to be binding. While important, this finding is not necessarily novel. Political theorists have also fixed upon generally held perceptions of obligation as a crucial precondition for political authority. Some stress the essence of political authority as the "right to rule." Joseph Raz identifies political authority with "a right to make laws and regulations, to judge and to punish for failing to conform to certain standards, or to order some redress for the victims of such violations, as well as the right to command."[48] The right to rule, in turn, is rooted in general perceptions of legitimacy and of right. As Raz notes "neither brute force by itself nor any amount of influence or power are sufficient to constitute any person or body as an authority . . . legitimate authorities are there by right. They have the right to act as authorities."[49] This right may be linked to more formal and constitutional arrangements that give rise to the recognition of one "in authority" as a commander or a political leader. Alternatively, the right may derive from a more informal trust in and recognition of "an authority" as an expert, scholar, or specialist, or one whose knowledge and opinion are considered reliable.[50] Moreover, this right to rule derives from neither coercion nor persuasion. As noted elsewhere in this volume, authority is located between relations of force and influence because:

> Both of these exist as capacities or potentialities implicit within authority, but are actualized only when those who claim authority sense that they have begun to lose the trust of those over whom they seek to exercise it. . . . [O]nce actualized and rendered explicit they signal—indeed, they are, at least temporarily—[authority's] negation.[51]

The idea that there is an obligatory element of authority that is captured by neither relations of force and duress nor relations of persuasion and consent is repeated in the work of international regime theorists and international lawyers. Indeed, it has been observed that "the central problem" for both regime theorists and international lawyers "is to establish that laws and norms exercise a compliance pull of their own, at least partially independent of the power and interests which underpinned them and which were often responsible for their creation."[52] Moreover, if "their political impact is to be significant, international norms cannot be the automatic and immediate reflection of self-interest. There has to be some notion of being bound by a particular rule despite countervailing self-interest."[53] While rationalist approaches to regime theory stress the role of power and interests in the construction of international regimes and authoritative norms,[54] more reflectivist variants stress the importance of shared expectations and perceptions of legitimacy. Indeed, as noted in the introduction, the widely adopted definition of international regimes from the Krasner volume builds into the definition a reference to convergent expectations about legitimate authority. Thus, theorists like John Ruggie and Friedrich Kratochwil emphasize the shared nature of perceptions of authority and their historical and sociological contingency.[55] Hedley Bull, emphasizes the subjective nature of the conciousness of common interests and values that unite international society, suggesting that authority is very much a product of subjective perceptions.[56]

International lawyers also focus on the obligatory element of authority in the attempt to identify the binding source of international law. The source of legal obligation is traced to a variety of sources.[57] For example, "command" theories of law stress that to be binding law must emanate from a sovereign and be backed by a system of sanctions.[58] Other theories focus on the extent to which authority is accepted by the participants, differentiating the "acceptance model" from the "hierarchical-enforcement" or command model of authority.[59] According to the acceptance model, authority "is the structure of expectation concerning who, with what qualifications and mode of selection, is competent to make which decisions by what criteria and what procedures."[60] Thomas Franck clarifies the nature of legitimacy in stating that it depends more broadly upon perceptions of the legitimacy of rules and rule-making institutions, which in turn depend upon the determinacy and clarity of rules; their authenticity as determined by their pedigree, symbols, and rituals; the coherence of rules with more general principles; and the adherence of rules and institutions to proper procedures.[61] Authority derives from a "conjunction of common expectations with a high degree of corroboration in actual operation."[62] The idea that authority exists at the meeting point of shared expectations concerning legitimate conduct and actual compliance suggests that the obligatory element of authority is comprised of both subjective and objective elements. The subjective elements relate to shared perceptions and recognition of authority as legitimate, while the objective elements refer to actual compliance.

What unites these diverse views about authority is the perceived need to reconcile interstate cooperation in authoritative arrangements with the structural limitations posed by formal anarchy. At root they are all attempting to deal with obstacles stemming from the more general problem of theorizing about international governance in the absence of government. Those that focus on the role of sovereign command and sanctions have a problem with locating authority and finding the obligatory nature of international law in an international sphere that lacks a sovereign and centralized system of sanctions. Others who reject the command model in favor of an acceptance model find authority and legal obligation in a decentralized self-enforcement system. Still others who root authority in state power and control have a problem in accounting for norms of universal scope. Significantly though, most political and legal theorists focus on the actions and obligatory status of *public* authority. The obligatory character of *private* authority raises rather different considerations that pose obstacles to conceptualizing private action as authoritative.

Obstacles to Conceptualizing Private International Authority

There are at least two obstacles to theorizing about private international authority. The first obstacle relates to the problem just discussed of conceptualizing *international* authority in the absence of a government capable of identifying, articulating, and enforcing rules of conduct. The second obstacle concerns conceptualizing *private* action as authoritative and stems from the general tendency to associate governance with governments and states. We submit, however, that neither poses a significant obstacle and that the concept of private authority can provide a powerful analytical tool for overcoming the theoretical limitations that stem from the dominant approaches.

The first obstacle derives from the more general problem of theorizing international authority with which political and legal theorists have been concerned for some time. The debate between those who believe it is fruitful to draw analogies with domestic structures of authority in attempting to understand international relations and others who reject the domestic analogy and posit the international arena to be a unique domain that does not submit easily to political theorizing is central to international relations and law. This debate has separated thinkers such as Saint-Pierre, Kant, Saint-Simon, Oppenheim, and Lauterpacht from thinkers such as Hobbes, Spinoza, Pufendorf, Wolff, and Vattel[63] and continues to separate structural realists from neoliberal institutionalists[64] and to problematize the issue of international governance in general.[65] It has led some, such as Thomas Franck, Hedley Bull, Terry Nardin, and Oran Young, to argue that theorizing about international society is distinctly different from theorizing about domestic society and that we should not expect too much of international society. It has led others, like neoliberal institutionalists, to narrowly circumscribe international authority to cooperative efforts at cost-savings and the reduction of market failures. It has led still others, like theorists of hegemonic stability, to reject the concept of international authority in general as anything more than state power. The problem of international authority thus derives from a more general problem with theorizing about governance in the absence of government institutions. However, if one turns to consider the second obstacle, one sees that the first obstacle is transformed into a window of opportunity for conceptualizing governance without government. If states have been unable to provide convincing structures of international governance, contemporary trends are enhancing the opportunities for private actors to step in and do so.

While the first obstacle is premised upon associations of governance with the domestic sphere, the second is premised upon the association of governance with *public* authority. The association of political authority with the public sphere has a rich history involving the emergence of states as the dominant political authorities of the European states system and the location of sovereignty in initially absolutist and later in secular and republican governments. Notions of public governance evoke the concept of being "in authority" as a political leader or a commander and are tailored to definitions of authority premised upon the "right to rule" and command models of political obligation. Such models depend upon vertical and hierarchical depictions of authority relations, with the governors ranking above the governed. The governors, in turn, acquire their authority through various practices, procedures, and conventions that guarantee the appropriate constitution of representative, responsible, and accountable government. Political authority is, thus, public by definition. This is because only public judgment is regarded as legitimate and authoritative in the sense of being "entitled to prescribe behavior."[66] Only public judgment is accountable through political institutions.

Private judgment, in contrast, is "a nonauthoritative judgment" because it is not entitled to prescribe behavior; it is not accountable under republican and democratic institutions and practices. The legitimacy of political authority is inescapably linked to its public nature and is inconsistent with notions of decentralized, horizontal, and self-governance arrangements. It is also inconsistent with notions of private governance and the legitimacy of one recognized as "an authority" in the sense of holding the expertise of a scholar or an expert or specialist. This authority is simply not captured in public definitions of authority and provides the central most convincing obstacle to conceptualizing private authority.

This obstacle is only convincing, however, if one accepts that the normative statement that private power "ought" not be regarded as legitimate and binding establishes the *a priori* validity of the empirical statement that private power "is" in fact not regarded as legitimate and binding. The public dimension of authority is only an obstacle if one accepts that private power does not *in fact* operate in an obligatory way. Moreover, it is only an obstacle if one limits ones definition of "rules" to those consistent with commands and directives. Now, clearly, private actors such as corporations and business associations lack the authority to prescribe and enforce domestic laws of general application, unless such powers are delegated to or conferred on them by their governments. Moreover, under international law they lack the legal personality to engage in law creation and enforcement. However, this volume presents a complex and rich array of mechanisms by which firms, their associations, and a number of corporate entities do *in fact* govern themselves and others, both domestically and internationally.

Often the sort of rules most relevant to private activity are informal or "soft law" and commitment rules whose authority is not traceable to the command of a sovereign or, necessarily, to the sanction of the state. Soft law includes statements of principles, guidelines, understandings, model laws and codes, and declarations that as Akehurst notes are "neither strictly binding norms of law, nor completely irrelevant political maxims, and operate in a grey zone between law and politics."[67] Kratochwil observes that the normative content of "soft law" comes from "the consensual nature of the instruments and/or the reliance or consideration they create."[68] They operate on the basis of mutual trust and reciprocity. Commitment rules relate to decentralized rule that "is the basis of contract, credit, and thus the entire apparatus of capitalism."[69] They create binding obligations out of contractual promises and form the foundation for the protection and enforcement of private property rights. Commitment rules are analogous to Max Weber's notion of "the law of cooperation," which governs the private sphere, and is distinguished from the law of "subordination" that governs the public sphere.[70]

We see then that there are different attributes of authority relations depending upon the nature of the relationship one is studying. These different attributes are generally presented in terms of a distinction between public and private domains. As noted earlier, there is a tendency to equate the public domain with authority relations and the private domain with nonauthoritative individual action. Thus, the public domain represents those "in authority" and captures hierarchical, command theories of obigation and rule, which purport to exhaust the range of authoritative relations. However, there is no reason why private relations cannot also be analyzed in terms of authority relations. Private authority is often associated with more decentralized, horizontal, and often self-governing arrangements. However, private authority can take on hierarchical elements, duplicating state enforcement. Moreover, the concept of private authority is uniquely positioned to analytically capture contemporary governance arrangements that do not submit easily to analysis under hierarchical and command theories of obligation, or that reflect a hybrid of both public and private authority relations or a shifting balance between the two realms.

A number of our chapters document what appears to be a trend toward the increased private regulation of international economic relations, in some cases giving rise to a hybrid of public and private authority relations. Salter identifies a shift from public to private reguatory authority over standards, noting the hybrid nature of the contemporary regime and the "symbiotic relationship" between public and private sectors. Cutler and Porter too note the historically shifting balance between public and private authority, while Sell stresses the porous nature of the boundary between public and private by noting the ability of private actors to define their interests in intellectual property as the "public" interest of the United States. Burke highlights the "quasi-public" role of oil MNCs, while Spar illustrates how private actors function on the

Internet to provide the services generally associated with governments and the public sphere. These cases demonstrate that a variety of governance arrangements exist and suggest the fluid, porous, and historically specific nature of the boundary between public and private authority.

Political Implications of the Emergence of Private Authority in International Affairs

We return now to a number of questions posed earlier concerning the significance of private authority for state policy and autonomy, for democracy, and for the distribution of economic resources in the world. We have seen that in terms of more general historical forces, the globalization of the world economy and consequent rise of decentralized networked organizations may provide an advantage to nonstate actors that the traditional state cannot match.[71] While there are a variety of nonstate actors operating today, we highlight here the increasing relevance of the private sector as a major player in organizing the international system and increasingly in establishing the rules of the game. These rules concern who gets to play, what are the limits on play, and often who wins. This means that we should be concerned about the increase in private international authority on a number of counts. First, what does this mean for the continued functioning and existence of the state itself? Second, who gets to participate in making decisions given that corporations are not democracies? Third, are the rules the private sector establishes fair and equitable, incorporating mechanisms for access and accountability?

The rules established by the private sector, as we noted, may favor some participants over others. They may also favor industry insiders over those in other industries or over consumers more generally. Furthermore, they may advantage firms in some countries and not others, for instance, excluding full participation by developing-country firms. The asymmetrical operation of private authority is evident in the standards regime, where, as Salter notes, the contributions of developing countries and nonexperts are openly discounted. The exclusionary nature of epistemic authority is also evident in the activities of bond-rating agencies, the insurance industry, the regulation of maritime transport law, and the negotiation of intellectual property rights.

More importantly, they are rules established by decision-makers who are not accountable to any citizens, but are accountable only to the market itself. If the decisions being made were merely technical matters of concern to those making them then this would not be problematic. Our cases have shown, however, that private authority can have structuring effects that are quite comparable to those of public authority in terms of their significance for citizens more generally. When certain firms benefit, or certain technologies gain advantage, those outside of the industry have no source of redress, although these effects may be the result of the type of organized activity that, in a public policy context, may be considered properly the subject of democratic deliberation and constraint, and not simply the outcome of competitive market forces. This is especially the case in a decentralized system of overlapping institutions governing separate and numerous issue areas. There are, however, exceptions to the limited social accountability of private authority, as evident in Burke's analysis of the socially constructive activities of oil MNCs in Ecuador and Haufler's discussion of the potential for the emergence of corporate eco-norms. These are, however, exceptions. In the majority of cases examined, private authority operates in a manner that is responsive and accountable only to a private corporate, industry, or business constituency. Moreover, there are significant legal and political obstacles to extending notions of political accountability to the private sector. As Cutler suggests, to impute accountability to private activity "would be to turn representative democracy on its head."

Devoting greater attention to private authority is of particular importance to increase our understanding of international governance in our contemporary world. International relations scholars have, in recent years, made important advances in understanding the contribution of informal or decentralized arrangements, including regimes, for producing order and cooperation among states and in markets. Generally, however, these efforts have overlooked the role of private authority and focused primarily on governance provided by states. This volume demonstrates that in many cases governance can be almost completely provided by private firms, as in the regime for regulating the Internet, or by states relying very heavily on the social institutions constructed by firms, as in mineral markets or the standards regime. Thus, this volume points to the potential for a diminution of state capacity, limitation in participation and accountability, and the possible reinforcement of inequitable arrangements.

We started out this volume by asking, "Do corporations rule the world?" We end by returning to that theme. We argue that yes, corporations increasingly do establish institutions that "govern" in the absence of or in coordination with governance arrangements involving states at the international level.

NOTES

1. Oran Young, *International Cooperation* (Ithaca and London: Cornell University Press, 1989), p. 32.
2. See, for instance, the discussion of rationalistic approaches in Robert O. Keohane, "International Institutions: Two Approaches," *International Stud-*

ies Quarterly 32 (December 1988): 384–85, and Robert Keohane, *After Hegemony* (Princeton: Princeton University Press, 1984).

3. These literatures are large. For a constructivist approach, see for instance Alexander Wendt, "Anarchy Is What States Make of It," *International Organization* 46.2 (Spring 1992): 391–425. World systems theory and Gramscian international relations theory offer examples of structuralist and historicist approaches respectively. The term "reflectivist" is dicussed in Robert O. Keohane, "International Institutions: Two Approaches," pp. 384–85.

4. On the new institutional economics, see Eirik G. Furuboth and Rudolf Richter, eds., *The New Institutional Economics* (College Station: Texas A&M University Press, 1991); Thráinn Eggerston, *Economic Behavior and Institutions* (Cambridge: Cambridge University Press, 1990); Douglass C. North, *Institutions, Institutional Change and Economic Performance* (Cambridge: Cambridge University Press, 1990), and the literature cited in notes 6, 7, and 17 of our introduction.

5. While each of the literatures to which this paragraph refers have tended to focus primarily either on efficiency or power considerations, there are many scholars who have sought to bring both factors into their analysis. North, *Institutions*, p. 7, for instance, notes of his own trajectory: "I abandoned the efficiency view of institutions. Rulers devised property rights in their own interests and transaction costs resulted in typically inefficient property rights prevailing."

6. This point, consistent with the new institutional economics, is also consistent with Gramscian Marxist analyses of hegemony, in which a ruling class builds a successful hegemonic bloc (coalition of classes) through a program that is portrayed ideologically, and is in practice, not just in its own particular interest, but in the interest of society as a whole.

7. Keohane, *After Hegemony*, pp. 88–96. Keohane's three categories are "legal liability," "transactions costs," and "information and uncertainty." We've substituted "enforcement" for "legal liability" as it captures more accurately the "quasi-agreements" and "contracts" that, as Keohane notes, often substitute for law at the international level, and because it is a common category in the wider literature on transactions costs. See for instance North, *Institutions*. We've substituted "negotiations costs" for "transactions costs" because in the literature more generally "transactions costs" is used to refer to all three categories, and because Keohane's discussion under this category primarily focuses on negotiations. It can be noted that uncertainty and enforcement are interdependent—when enforcement is established the need for information may be reduced and vice versa. Similar points could be made about negotiations costs and the other two categories.

8. At the international level states often find it difficult to deploy their capacity in these areas because of the anarchy of interstate competition, but firms too face problems organizing internationally, including their lack of legal status in international law, and the heightened transactions costs that come with geographic, cultural, and other types of distance.

9. The difficulty experienced by states in exercising authority and providing regulatory capacity at the international level due to the anarchic state system is a central theme in the discipline of international relations. See, for instance,

David A. Baldwin, ed., *Neorealism and Neoliberalism: The Contemporary Debate* (New York: Columbia University Press, 1993); Robert O. Keohane, *After Hegemony*; Stephen D. Krasner, ed., *International Regimes* (Ithaca and London, Cornell University Press, 1983).

10. This does not mean that debt-rating agencies are always efficient processors of information, a point reinforced by their inadequate performance with respect to the East Asian currency crises of 1997 and 1998.

11. Smith quote from *Wealth of Nations*, bk. 1, ch. VIII, cited in Arthur Redford, *Manchester Merchants and Foreign Trade, 1794–1858* (Manchester, England: Manchester University Press, 1934), p. 1 and in the chapter by Porter in this volume.

12. Meindert Fennema and Kees van der Pijl, "International Bank Capital and the New Liberalism," in Mark S. Mizruchi and Michael Scwhartz, eds., *Intercorporate Relations* (New York: Cambridge University Press, 1987), pp. 298–317.

13. Stephen Gill, *American Hegemony and the Trilateral Commission* (Cambridge: Cambridge University Press, 1990).

14. George Stigler, *The Citizen and the State: Essays on Regulation* (Chicago and London: University of Chicago Press, 1975).

15. Klauss Stegemann, "Policy Rivalry among Industrial States: What Can We Learn from Models of Strategic Trade Policy?" *International Organization* 43.1 (Winter 1989): 73–100.

16. Grant Jordan and Klaus Schubert, eds., "Special Issue: Policy Networks," *European Journal of Political Research* 21.1–2 (February 1992).

17. Mytelka and Delapierre comment, "as traditional oligopolies come under pressure, one might expect that contestability would open markets further to competition. Instead, knowledge-based networked industrial structures by setting industry standards, rules and competitive practices, enable participating firms to control the evolution of technology, reduce the shocks of radical change, and maintain their position within these shifting hierarchies."

18. This point was made by William D. Coleman in commenting on this chapter.

19. The work of Douglass North provides a major exception to this criticism.

20. Robert O. Keohane, *International Institutions and State Power: Essays in International Relations Theory* (Boulder, Colo.: Westview Press, 1989), p. 160.

21. Ibid., p. 169.

22. *A History of Civilizations* (New York: Penguin Books, 1987), pp. 34–35.

23. The weakness of many approaches to international relations in addressing the matter of change is fairly well acknowledged in the field, as is evident in the following works: Barry Buzan and R. J. Barry Jones, eds., *Change and the Study of International Relations: The Evaded Dimension* (New York: St. Martin's Press, 1981); Friedrich Kratochwil, "The Embarrassment of Changes: Neo-realism as the Science of Realpolitik without Politics," *Review of International Studies* 19 (1993): 63–80; and Richard Ned Lebow, "The Long Peace, the End of the Cold War, and the Failures of Realism," *International Organization* 48.2 (Spring 1994): 249–77.

24. *Governing Global Networks*, p. 18.

25. Kenneth Waltz, *Theory of International Politics* (Reading, Mass.: Addison-Wesley, 1979), p. 66.

26. Stephen Krasner, "Westphalia and All That," in Judith Goldstein and Robert Keohane, eds., *Ideas and Foreign Policy* (Ithaca: Cornell University Press, 1993).

27. Susan Strange is exemplary in this regard. See *Retreat of the State* (Cambridge: Cambridge University Press, 1996); "The Defective State," *Daedalus* 124.2 (1995): 55–74; and "Political Economy and International Relations," in Ken Smith and Steve Smith, eds., *International Relations Theory Today* (University Park: Pennsylvania State University Press, 1995).

28. "Territoriality and Beyond: Problematizing Modernity in International Relations," *International Organization* 47.1 (Winter 1993): 139–74.

29. "Continuity and Transformation in the World Polity: Toward a Neorealist Synthesis," in Keohane, *Neorealism and Its Critics*.

30. "Territoriality and Beyond."

31. *The Great Transformation: The Political and Economic Origins of Our Time* (Boston: Beacon Press, 1944).

32. John Ruggie, "At Home Abroad, Abroad at Home: International Liberalisation and Domestic Stability in the New World Economy," *Millennium: Journal of International Studies* 24.3 (1995): 507–26.

33. Fredric Jameson, *Postmodernism or, the Cultural Logic of Late Capitalism* (Durham: Duke University Press, 1994); Stephen Gill, "Theorizing the Interregnum: The Double Movement and Global Politics in the 1990s," and Robert Cox, "Critical Political Economy," both in in Björn Hettne, ed., *International Political Economy: Understanding Global Disorder* (Halifax, Nova Scotia: Fernwood Books, 1995).

34. Jessica Matthews, "Power Shift," *Foreign Affairs* 76.1 (1997): 50.

35. Philip Cerny, "Paradoxes of the Competition State: The Dynamics of Political Globalization," *Government and Opposition* 32.2 (1997): 251–74.

36. As David Harvey in *The Condition of Postmodernity* (Oxford; Basil Blackwell, 1989), p. 201, suggests about our inability to perceive postmodern "hyperspace."

37. The literature on globalization is vast, however, the following provide fairly good overviews of the main analytical issues and debates concerning globalization: Paul Hirst and Graehme Thompson, *Globalization in Question: The International Political Economy and the Possibilities of Governance* (Cambridge: Polity Press, 1995); Robert Boyer and Daniel Drache, eds., *States against Markets: The Limits of Globalization* (London: Routledge, 1996); and Philip Cerny, "Globalization and Other Stories: The Search for a New Paradigm for International Relations," *International Journal* 51.4 (Autumn 1996): 616–37.

38. See Cerny, "Paradoxes of the Competition State," p. 254.

39. James N. Rosenau, *Turbulence in World Politics* (Hemel Hempstead, England: Harvester/Wheatsheaf, 1990).

40. Scott Lash, "Reflexivity and Its Doubles: Structure, Aesthetics, Community," in Ulrich Beck, Anthony Giddens, and Scott Lash, *Reflexive Modernization: Politics, Tradition and Aesthetics in the Modern Social Order* (Stanford:

Stanford University Press, 1994), pp. 110–73, quote is on p. 111; emphasis in the original.

41. See Janice E. Thomson and Stephen D. Krasner, "Global Transactions and the Consolidation of Sovereignty," in Ernst-Otto Czempiel and James N. Rosenau, eds., *Global Changes and Theoretical Challenges* (Lexington: Lexington Books, 1989), pp. 195–219; and Hirst and Thompson, *Globalization in Question*, chapter 2.

42. Keohane, *International Institutions*, pp. 4–5.

43. David A. Baldwin, "Neoliberalism, Neorealism, and World Politics," in Baldwin, *Neorealism and Neoliberalism*, p. 16.

44. Keohane, *After Hegemony*, p. 51.

45. Keohane, "International Institutions."

46. Ibid.

47. Ibid.

48. "Introduction," *Authority*, p. 2.

49. Ibid., p. 3.

50. As noted elsewhere in this volume the Latin term authority stems from *auctoritas*, which is a surety in a transaction, the testimony of a witness, or other means of verifying a fact, such as a document. Friedman, "On the Concept of Authority in Political Philosphy," p. 74, shows how this meaning of authority is related to another Latin term *auctor*, which comes from the verb *augere* or "to augment, increase, enrich, tell about" and relates to the authority of an author or an actor who provides the beginnings or source of a decision or opinion. The idea is that one may have authority by virtue of one's special knowledge and experience or one's authoritative interpretation and yet not be "in authority" as a legitimate leader or commander.

51. Bruce Lincoln, *Authority*, p. 2.

52. Andrew Hurrell, "International Society and the Study of Regimes: A Reflective Approach," in Volker Rittberger, ed., *Regime Theory and International Relations* (Oxford: Clarendon Press, 1995), pp. 49–72.

53. Ibid.

54. This is particularly so for hegemony stability theories that directly link power and regime formation and for transaction cost analysis that focuses on the mutualities of interests in cooperating in international regimes.

55. John G. Ruggie, "Continuity and Transformation in the World Polity: Toward a Neorealist Synthesis," in Robert O Keohane, ed., *Neorealism and its Critics* (New York: Columbia University Press, 1986) and Friedrich Kratochwil, "Rules, Norms, and Decisions: On the Conditions of Practical and Legal Reasoning," in *International Relations and Domestic Affairs* (Cambridge: Cambridge University Press, 1989).

56. Hurrell, " International Society and the Study of Regimes," makes this point about Hedley Bull, Martin Wight, and others influenced by modern theorists of international society.

57. For a somewhat dated but excellent review of the different attempts that international lawyers have made to account for the binding nature of international law, see Oscar Schachter, "Towards a Theory of International Obligation," *Virginia Journal of International Law* 8.2 (1968): 300–322. Schachter identifies the

following sources and some of the representative theorists: state consent (P. Corbet, Tunkin); customary practice (H. Kelsen); a sense of rightness or juridical conscience (Krabbe); natural law or reason (H. Wheaton); social necessity (G. Schelle); the will or consensus of the international community (C. Jenks, H. Lauterpacht); direct intuition (Stone); common purposes of participants (C. de Visscher, S. Hoffman); effectiveness (J. Brierly, W. Friedmann); sanctions (J. Austin); systemic goals (M. Kaplan and N. Katzenbach); shared expectations as to authority (M. McDougal); rules of recognition (H. Hart). One might extend and update this list in the following way: agreement over procedures (T. Nardin, T. Franck); patriarchy (H. Charlseworth, C. Chinkin, S. Wright); zones of aggreement and cooperation (A. Slaughter); common moral awareness (A. Hurrell); epistemic communities (Haas); international regimes (R. O. Keohane, Mark W. Zacher); the structure of legal discourse and ideology (David Kennedy, M. Koskenniemi).

58. This view is generally associated with John Austin and informs the legal positivist view that international law is only valid or binding if it derives from the consent of states. See generally, Beck et al., *International Rules*, chapter 3.

59. Gidon Gottlieb, "The Nature of International Law: Toward a Second Concept of Law," in R. Falk, F. Kratochwil, and Saul Mendolvitz, eds., *International Law: A Contemporary Perspective* (Boulder, Colo.: Westview Press, 1985), pp. 187–204.

60. McDougal and Lasswell, "The Identification and Appraisal of Diverse Systems of Public Order."

61. This is discussed more fully in the Cutler chapter.

62. McDougal and Lasswell, "The Identification and Appraisal of Diverse Systems of Public Order." See also the chapter in Beck et al., *International Rules*, on the New Haven approach to international law.

63. See Hidemi Suganami, *The Domestic Analogy and World Order Proposals* (Cambridge: Cambridge University Press, 1989).

64. See Joseph Grieco, "Anarchy and the Limits of Cooperation: A Realist Critique of the Newest Liberal Institutionalism," *International Organization* 42 (1988), and see Baldwin, ed., *Neorealism and Neoliberalism*.

65. For a very powerful analysis of this problem of political theory, see R. B. J. Walker, *Inside/Outside: International Relations as Political Theory* (Cambridge: Cambridge University Press, 1993).

66. Friedman, "On the Concept of Authority in Political Philosophy," pp. 78–79.

67. *Modern Introduction to International Law*, p. 54.

68. *Rules, Norms, and Decisions*, p. 201.

69. Nicholas Greenwood Onuf, *World of Our Making: Rules and Rule in Social Theory and International Relations* (Columbia: University of South Carolina Press, 1989), pp. 208, 215. Commitment-rules are associated with decentralized relations of authority common in the commercial world. They are differentiated from directive-rules, which are associated with asymmetrical and hierarchical power relations and command theories of law. However, Onuf notes how Weber failed to recognize that commitment-rules too reflect asymmetries in power and he attributes this failure to the obscurity of the power-basis of private commercial activity stemming from the liberal assumptions that contracting par-

ties are autonomous and of equal bargaining power. He identifies a different form of rule, "heteronomous rule," which is characterized by a "paradox": "Rules positing autonomy in relations ensure the asymmetry of those relations."

70. See Onuf with Frank K. Klink, *World of Our Making*, chapter 6.

71. As Jessica Mathews, "Power Shift," recently pointed out.

CONTRIBUTORS

PAMELA L. BURKE is a Ph.D. candidate, University of Maryland, College Park. She is currently finishing her doctoral dissertation entitled "The Globalization of Contentious Politics: Amazonian Indigenous Peoples and Oil MNCs in the Amazon."

A. CLAIRE CUTLER is Assistant Professor of International Relations and International Law in the Political Science Department, University of Victoria, Victoria, Canada. She is editor (with Mark W. Zacher) of *Canadian Foreign Policy and International Economic Regimes* (Vancouver: University of British Columbia Press, 1992).

MICHEL DELAPIERRE is a Charge de Recherche in the CNRS and Director of the Centre de Recherche sur les Entreprises Multinationales, Université de Paris–X, Nanterre. He is the author of numerous books and articles on the electronics industry and the strategy of multinational corporations.

VIRGINIA HAUFLER is Senior Associate at the Carnegie Endowment for International Peace, and Associate Professor in the Department of Government and Politics at the University of Maryland, College Park. She directs a project at the Carnegie Endowment on the role of the private sector in international affairs. She is author of *Dangerous Commerce: Insurance and the Management of International Risk* (Ithaca: Cornell University Press, 1997).

LYNN KRIEGER MYTELKA is current Director of the Division on Investment, Technology and Enterprise Development at the United Nations Conference on Trade and Development (UNCTAD) in Geneva. She is on leave from her positions as Professor in the Institute of Political Economy at Carleton University, Ottawa, Canada, and Director of Research, at the Centre d'Études et de Recherches sur les Entreprises Multinationales (Forum-CEREM), Université de Paris-X, Nanterre, France. Recent publications include: *Technological Capabilities and Export Success: Case Studies from Asia*, edited with Dieter Ernst and Tom Ganiatsos (London: Routledge, 1998); *Competition, Innovation and Competi-*

tiveness in Developing Countries, edited (Paris: OECD Development Centre, 1997), *Strategic Partnerships: States, Firms and International Competition,* edited with two authored chapters (London: Pinter Publishers, 1991).

TONY PORTER is Associate Professor of Political Science, McMaster University, Hamilton, Canada. He is author of *States, Markets and Regimes in Global Finance* (Basingstoke, England: Macmillan, 1993).

LIORA SALTER is Professor of Law at Osgoode Law School, York University, Canada, and Fellow of the Royal Society of Canada. Her publications include, *Outside the Lines: Issues and Problems in Interdisciplinary Research,* with Alison Hearn (Montreal/Kingston: McGill-Queen's University Press, 1996); *Mechanisms and Practices for the Assessment of the Social and Cultural Implications of Science and Technology* (Ottawa: Industry Canada, 1994); *The Mandates and Workplans of Seven Designated Canadian Standards Organizations* (Ottawa: Department of Communication [now Industry Canada], 1992); *Mandated Science: Science and Scientists in the Making of Standards* (Dordrecht/Boston, Kluwer, 1988); *Managing Technology: Social Sciences Perspectives,* edited with David Wolfe (Toronto: Garamond, 1990); *Communications Studies in Canada,* edited (Toronto: Butterworth, 1981); and *Culture, Communications and Dependency: The Tradition of H. A. Innis,* edited with William H. Melody (Norwood, N.J.: Ablex, 1981).

SUSAN K. SELL is Associate Professor of Political Science and International Affairs at George Washington University. She is the author of *Power and Ideas: North-South Politics of Intellectual Property and Antitrust* (Albany: State University of New York Press, 1997).

TIMOTHY J. SINCLAIR is a member of the Department of Politics and International Studies, University of Warwick, and is an external research associate at the Center for International and Security Studies, York University, Toronto. His publications include *Approaches to World Order,* with Robert W. Cox (Cambridge University Press, 1996); *Approaches to Global Governance Theory,* edited with Martin Hewson (Albany: State University of New York Press, 1999); and *Structure and Agency in International Capital Mobility,* edited with Kenneth P. Thomas (Macmillan/St. Martin's Press, 1999).

DEBORA SPAR is Associate Professor at Harvard Business School, where she teaches in the Business, Government and Competition area. Her publications include *The Cooperative Edge: The Internal Politics of*

International Cartels (Ithaca: Cornell University Press, 1994); *Beyond Globalization: Remaking American Foreign Economic Policy*, co-authored with Raymond Vernon (New York: Free Press, 1989); *Iron Triangles and Revolving Doors: Cases in US Foreign Policymaking*, co-authored with Raymond Vernon and Glenn Tobin (New York: Praeger, 1991).

MICHAEL C. WEBB is Associate Professor of Political Science at the University of Victoria, Victoria, Canada. He has published *The Political Economy of Policy Coordination* (Ithaca and London: Cornell University Press, 1995).

INDEX